WOMEN
and MADNESS

Phyllis Chesler

Lawrence Hill Books
Chicago

ALSO BY PHYLLIS CHESLER

Letters to a Young Feminist
Mothers on Trial: The Battle for Children and Custody
A Politically Incorrect Feminist
With Child: A Diary of Motherhood
Woman's Inhumanity to Woman

———

Copyright © 2005 by Phyllis Chesler
Published by arrangement with the author

All rights reserved
This edition published in 2018 by Lawrence Hill Books
An imprint of Chicago Review Press Incorporated
814 North Franklin Street
Chicago, Illinois 60610
ISBN 978-1-64160-036-1

Cover design: Lindsey Cleworth Schauer
Interior design: planettheo.com

Printed in the United States of America

Some of the material from Chapters Two, Three, and Four has appeared in different form in:

"Women and Psychotherapy," *The Radical Therapist*, September 1970.

"Patient and Patriarch: Women in the Psychotherapeutic Relationship," *Woman in Sexist Society: Studies in Power and Powerlessness*, edited by Vivian Gornick and Barbara K. Moran, New York: Basic Books, 1971.

"Stimulus/Response: Men Drive Women Crazy," *Psychology Today*, July 1971.

"Women as Psychotherapeutic Patients," *Women's Studies*, Summer 1972.

Grateful acknowledgments are made to the following for permission to include copyrighted selections:

Excerpts from "Double Jeopardy: To Be Black and Female" by Frances Beale from *The Black Woman: An Anthology* edited by Toni Cade. Published by the New American Library, reprinted by permission of the author.

Excerpts from *Mothers and Amazons* by Helen Diner. Copyright © 1965 by Helen Diner. Reprinted by permission of Julian Press.

Excerpts from *Margaret Fuller: American Romantic* edited by Perry Miller. Copyright © 1963 by Perry Miller. Used by permission of Cornell University Press.

Excerpts from *Anarchism and Other Essays* by Emma Goldman published in 1917. Reprinted in 1970 by Dover Publications, Inc.

Excerpts from *Black Rage* by William H. Grier and Price M. Cobbs, New York: Basic Books, Inc., 1968.

Excerpts from "On Sexism and Racism" by Nancy Henley, resource paper published as part of the Report of the Subcommittee on Women of the Committee on Equal Opportunity in Psychology of the American Psychological Association, February 1971.

Excerpts from *Notes from the Third Year* by Anne Koedt. Copyright © 1971 by Anne Koedt. Reprinted by permission of the author.

Excerpts from *The Politics of Experience* by R. D. Laing. Copyright © 1967 by R. D. Laing. Reprinted by permission of Penguin Books, Ltd.

Excerpts from an article by Toni Morrison from the New York *Times Magazine*, 8/22/70. Copyright © 1970 by the New York *Times*. Reprinted by permission.

Excerpts from "Newlywed Swings In" from the New York *Post*, February 19, 1970.

Copyright © 1970 by New York Post Corporation. Reprinted by permission of the New York Post.

"Medusa" copyright © 1965 by Ted Hughes and "Lady Lazareth" copyright © 1963 by Ted Hughes from the book *Ariel* by Sylvia Plath. Excerpts from *The Bell Jar* by Sylvia Plath copyright © 1971 by Harper & Row, Inc., published by Faber & Faber, copyright © 1966 by Ted Hughes. Reprinted by permission of Harper & Row, Inc., and Olwyn Hughes.

Excerpts from *Wilheim Reich: A Personal Biography* by Ilse O. Reich. Reprinted by permission of St. Martin's Press, Inc., Macmillan & Co., Ltd.

Portion of "Snapshots of a Daughter-in-law," from *Snapshots of a Daughter-law: Poems 1954-1962*, by Adrienne Rich. By permission of W. W. Norton & Company, Inc. Copyright © 1956, 1957,1958, 1959,1960,1961, 1962, 1963, 1967 by Adrienne Rich Conrad. Excerpts from "The Flight from Womanhood" from the article as it appears in *Feminine Psychology* edited by Harold Kelman. Copyright © 1967 by W. W. Norton & Company, Inc., originally published by the International Journal of Psychoanalysis.

Excerpts from *Candy* by Terry Southern. Copyright © 1958, 1959, 1962, 1964 by Terry Southern. Reprinted by permission of Coward-McCann & Geoghegan, Inc.

Excerpts from *The Myth of Mental Illness* by Thomas S. Szasz. Reprinted by permission of Harper & Row, Inc.

Excerpts from *The Persecution and Assassination of Jean-Paul Marat As Performed by the Inmates of the Asylum of Charenton Under the Direction of the Marquis De Sade* by Peter Weiss. English version by Geoffrey Skelton. Verse adaptation by Adrian Mitchell. Copyright © 1965 by John Calder Ltd. Originally published in German. Copyright © 1964 by Suhrkamp Verlag. Reprinted by permission of Atheneum Publishers.

Excerpts from *Les Guerilleres* by Monique Wittig, translated by David Le Vay, English translation Copyright © 1971 by Peter Owen. Reprinted by permission of the Viking Press, Inc.

Excerpts from *Love Between Women* by Dr. Charlotte Wolff, reprinted by permission of St. Martin's Press, Inc., Macmillan & Co., Ltd., and Gerald Duckworth & Co., Ltd.

Credits for illustrative material appear on page 414.

They all looked half drugged or half asleep, dull, as if the creatures had been hypnotized or poisoned, for these people walked in their fouled and disgusting streets full of ordure and bits of refuse and paper as if they were not conscious of their existence here, were somewhere else: and they were somewhere else . . . each was occupied in imagining how it, he, she, was triumphing in an altercation with the landlord or the grocer or a colleague, or how it was making love. . . . It was painful in a way she had never known pain, an affliction of shameful grief, to walk here today, among her own kind, looking at them as they were, seeing them, us, the human race, as visitors, from a space ship might see them. . . .

But the most frightening thing about them was this: that they walked and moved and went about their lives in a condition of sleepwalking: they were not aware of themselves, of other people, of what went on around them . . . they were essentially isolated, shut-in, enclosed inside their hideously defective bodies, behind their dreaming drugged eyes, above all, inside a net of wants and needs that made it impossible for them to think of anything else.

Doris Lessing
The Four-Gated City

CONTENTS

MADNESS

WOMEN

2005 Acknowledgments

Without my editor Airié Stuart's ardent desire to have this work out in an updated form, it would not exist as such. I am in her service. I am also grateful to Melissa Nosal, my assistant Robin Eldridge, and researcher-writer Courtney Martin for their exceedingly thoughtful and efficient research and to the entire team at Palgrave Macmillan. My agent Joelle Delbourgo effortlessly made this happen. As always, I am indebted to my family, and to all those health care givers and support staff who keep me in good writing shape.

I also now stand on the shoulders of many Foredaughters and Foresons whose continued work in the areas which I first pioneered in *Women and Madness* you will find in the updated bibliography. I am indebted to them for that work.

1972 Acknowledgments

I thank Lillian, my mother, for giving birth to me, and for taking care of me long before I could write such a book—and for whatever dreams, whatever wisdom she and Leon, my father whispered or sang to me while I slept.

I thank my friends for their love and support, and for certain evenings, weekends, and conversations: especially, Vivian Gornick, Ruth Jody, Judy Kuppersmith, and Marjorie Portnow.

I thank the women I "interviewed" for surviving—and for sharing their experiences with me.

I thank the members of the Association for Women in Psychology, especially those in the Chicago collective, and those feminists without whose existence, encouragement, and examples this book may not have been written just now.

I thank Natalie Bravermen, Louise Brown, Lillian Chesler, Catherine Clowery, Bici Forbes, Mary Shartle, Martha Hicks, and Angie Waltermath for their secretarial assistance.

I thank my students for their interest and for their help in various phases of the data-collection and statistical analysis: Elizabeth Friedman, Doris Fielding, Delsinea Jamison, George Sideris, Marina Rivas, and Roland Watts. I especially thank my colleagues in the Department of Psychology at Richmond College, and George Fischer and Larry Mitchell for their loyalty and support during the winter of 1971.

I thank Betty Prashker and Diane Matthews Reverand of Doubleday for their invaluable help in seeing this book through to its hardcover publication in 1972.

Much appreciation is due the MacDowell Colony for housing and feeding me during most of the summer of 1971; to Shirley Willner of the Biometrics Branch of the National Institute of Mental Health for answering all my questions promptly and sympathetically, and for sending me all the necessary data; to Laura Murra of the Women's History Research Library in Berkeley, California, for sharing the files with me; to Sylvia Price of the New School for Social Research for getting me many of the books I needed—and for her help when I needed them still longer; to Stuart Kahan of the Downstate Medical Center in Brooklyn for his review of the statistical analyses; and to Sara Whitworth of the Whitney Museum for her suggestions about Amazons and goddesses in Greek art.

2005 INTRODUCTION

MUCH OF WHAT WE TAKE FOR GRANTED TODAY was not even whispered about fifty or sixty years ago. During the 1950s and 1960s, clinicians were still being taught that women suffer from penis envy, are morally inferior to men, and are innately masochistic, dependent, passive, heterosexual, and monogamous. We also learned that it was mothers—not fathers, genetic predisposition, accidents, and/or poverty—who caused neurosis and psychosis.

None of my professors ever said that women (or men) were oppressed, or that oppression is traumatizing—especially when those who suffer are blamed for their own misery and diagnostically pathologized. No one ever taught me how to administer a test for mental health—only for mental illness.

I still think of this as psychiatric imperialism.

In graduate school, in my clinical internship, and in the psychoanalytic institute where I was trained in the 1960s and early 1970s, I was taught that it was both helpful and even scientific to diagnostically pathologize what might be a totally normal human response to trauma.

For example, we were taught to view the normal female (and human) response to sexual violence, including incest, as a psychiatric illness. We were taught to blame the victim for what had happened to her. Relying on a superficial understanding of psychoanalytic theory, we blamed the woman as "seductive" or "sick." We believed that women cried "incest" or "rape" in order to get sympathetic attention or revenge.

In my time, we were taught to view women as somehow naturally mentally ill. Women were hysterics (*hysteros*, the womb), malingerers, child-like, manipulative, either cold or smothering as mothers, and driven to excess by their hormones.

We assumed that men were mentally healthy. We were not taught to pathologize or criminalize male drug addicts or alcoholics, men who physically battered, raped, or even murdered women or other men. We did not have diagnostic categories for male sexual predators or pedophiles. The psychiatric literature actually blamed the mothers, not the fathers, of such men, for having sent them over the edge. But mainly, we were trained to understand and forgive such super-manly men ("boys will be boys").

In other words, our so-called professional training merely repeated and falsely professionalized our previous cultural education.

I knew that what I was being taught was neither useful nor true. At this point, I'd been attending feminist meetings almost nonstop for two years, surrounded by other women who were equally passionate, confident, vocal, and educated. In the spirit of that time, I became—and have remained—a liberation psychologist and a legal activist. I was a multi-disciplinary researcher who loved both myths and footnotes. I refused to write in an obfuscated, Mandarin language. I was psycho-analytically and spiritually oriented but I was also steadfastly political.

In 1969, I co-founded the Association for Women in Psychology (AWP). In those days, women founded new organizations every month—sometimes, every day. Emboldened by feminism, we created our own organizations where we and our ideas would be welcome and in which we could teach ourselves and each other what we needed to know. We hadn't learned it elsewhere.

For example, I had a brand-new Ph.D., had completed a hospital internship, and was still enrolled in a psycho-analytic training institute—but I knew almost nothing about how to help another woman (or a man) understand her own life.

No matter, I was secretly studying what women really wanted from psychotherapy. I planned to present my findings at the annual convention of the American Psychological Association (APA) in 1970. I went to the convention, but I did not deliver this paper. Instead, on behalf of AWP, I asked APA members for one million dollars in reparations on behalf of women who had never been helped by the mental health professions but

who had, in fact, been further abused: punitively labeled, overly tranquilized, sexually seduced while in treatment, hospitalized against their wills,
given shock therapy, lobotomized, and above all, unnecessarily described
as too aggressive, promiscuous, depressed, ugly, old, angry, fat, or
incurable. "Maybe AWP could set up an alternative to a mental hospital
with the money," I said, "or a shelter for runaway wives."

The audience of more than two thousand (mostly male members)
laughed at me. Loudly. Nervously. Some looked embarrassed, others
relieved. Obviously, I was crazy. Afterwards, colleagues told me that jokes
had been made about my "penis envy."

I started writing *Women and Madness* on the plane back to New York.
I immersed myself in the psycho-analytic literature, located biographies
and autobiographies of women who'd been psychiatrically treated or
hospitalized—women who refused to eat or who refused to marry, women
who were unable to leave home, or to lead lives outside the family. I read
novels and poems about sad, mad, bad women and devoured mythology
and anthropology, especially about goddesses, matriarchies, and Amazon
warrior women.

It is no accident that I wrote about goddesses in *Women and Madness*:
great Earth Mothers like Demeter, who rescued her daughter Persephone
from kidnapping, rape, and incest; Amazon figures like Diana, who
protected women in childbirth and who literally ran with the wild beasts.
Such goddess images are our collective human role models; we repress
them at our own peril. Both women and men are strengthened by
examples of women who embody all the human (not merely the feminine
or biologically maternal) possibilities.

It is also no accident that I did not fully examine the "dark" side of
Demeter and Persephone's relationship or other primal relationship
myths such as that of Queen Clytemnestra and her matricidal daughter
Electra. I did so embryonically in *Women and Madness* but I also did so
in more major ways over time and will discuss this later in this new
Introduction.

Back in 1970, I also began analyzing mental illness statistics and read
all the relevant academic studies. In addition, I read historical accounts of

women's lives. I located the stories of European women who'd been condemned as witches (including Joan of Arc) and, from the sixteenth century on, psychiatrically imprisoned. In the nineteenth and twentieth centuries in both Europe and North America, a man had the legal right to lock his perfectly sane wife or daughter away in a mental asylum. And some did. Authoritarian, violent, drunken, and/or insane husbands had their wives psychiatrically imprisoned, sometimes forever, as a way of punishing them for being too uppity—and in order to marry other women.

Some American women wrote lucid, brilliant, heartbreaking accounts of their confinements. Incredibly, these heroic women were not broken or silenced by their lengthy sojourns in Hell. They bore witness to what was done to them—and to those less fortunate than themselves, who did not survive the brutal beatings, near-drownings, and force-feedings, the body-restraints, the long periods in their own filth and in solitary confinement, the absence of kindness or reason—which passed for "treatment." These historical accounts brought tears to my eyes.

I found an extraordinary first-person account by Elizabeth Packard, whose only crime was that of daring to think for herself against her husband's wishes. She insisted on teaching her Sunday school class that people are born good, not evil. Packard's punishment was three years in a state mental hospital. Afterwards, she became a crusader for the rights of mental patients and married women. In her writings, she bore witness to what was done to women in asylums.

Years after I had written *Women and Madness*, Drs. Jeffrey L. Geller and Maxine Harris asked me to introduce a very important volume titled *Women of the Asylum: Voices From Behind the Walls, 1840-1945* (1994). I had read and written about some of these accounts—but even I had no idea that so many superb eyewitness accounts really existed.

For example, Elizabeth T. Stone (1842), of Massachusetts, described the mental asylum as "a system that is worse than slavery"; Adriana Brinckle (1857), of Pennsylvania, described the asylum as a "living death," filled with "shackles," "darkness," "handcuffs, straight-jackets, balls and chains, iron rings and . . . other such relics of barbarism"; Tirzah

Shedd (1862), wrote: "This is a wholesale slaughter house . . . more a place of punishment than a place of cure"; Clarissa Caldwell Lathrop (1880), of New York, wrote: "We could not read the invisible inscription over the entrance, written in the heart's blood of the unfortunate inmates, 'Who enters here must leave all hope behind.'"

According to these American autobiographical accounts, female patients were routinely beaten, deprived of sleep, food, exercise, sunlight, and all contact with the outside world, and were sometimes even murdered. Their resistance to physical (and mental) illness was often shattered. Sometimes, the women tried to kill themselves as a way of ending their torture.

It is now clear that whether the nineteenth- or early-twentieth-century female patient was entirely sane, or whether she had experienced post-partum or other depression, heard voices, or was "hysterically" paralyzed; whether she was well-educated and well-to-do, or an illiterate member of the working poor; whether she had led a relatively privileged life or had been repeatedly beaten, raped, or abused in other ways; whether she accepted or could no longer cope with her narrow social role; whether she had been idle for too long or had worked too hard for too long and was fatigued beyond measure—she was rarely treated with kindness or medical expertise.

I had also discovered that some rather accomplished women—the sculptor Camille Claudel, the writers Zelda Fitzgerald, Virginia Woolf, Lara Jefferson, and Sylvia Plath, the actress Frances Farmer, and the fictionally named Ellen West—had done "hard time," psychiatrically speaking. Despite their beauty, genius, and class/skin privilege, none were helped, and all were deeply hurt by institutional psychiatry, patriarchal therapists, and by highly abusive families.

In an allegedly post-feminist era, young women began writing accounts of their psychiatric hospitalizations and their descents into "madness." The literature almost qualifies as a new genre.

For example, the feminists Jill Johnston in *Paper Daughter* (1985), Kate Millett in *The Loony Bin Trip* (1990), and Shulie Firestone in *Airless Spaces* (1998), and the psychiatrist Kay Redfield Jamison in *An Unquiet*

Mind: A Memoir of Moods and Madness (1995), all wrote about psychiatric symptoms, medication, and institutionalization. Some insisted that although they heard voices, wanted to die, tried to kill themselves, were highly anxious, and could not function, they were not and never had been "mentally ill." Some were humbled by what had happened and acknowledged that something had gone terribly wrong. Some refused psychiatric medication. Others claimed that medication had saved their lives.

Millett, Johnston, Firestone, and Jamison all grew up in a pre-feminist era. Interestingly, by the 1990s, and continuing on through the twenty-first century, a large number of younger women, who were mainly born after 1970, began publishing accounts of their experiences with "mental illness" such as schizophrenia, depression, anxiety, and a general malaise. Here, Mari Nana-Ama Danquah, in *Willow Weep for Me: A Black Woman's Journey Through Depression* (1999); Carol Hebald's *The Heart Too Long Suppressed* (2001); Ruth Kline's *It Coulda Been Worse: Surviving a Lifetime of Abuse and Mental Illness* (2003); psychiatrist Carol North's *Welcome, Silence: My Triumph Over Schizophrenia* (1987); Julie Gregory's *Sickened: The Memoir of a Munchausen by Proxy Childhood* (2003); Rachel Reiland's *Get Me Out of Here: My Recovery from Borderline Personality Disorder* (2004) all come to mind.

But there are many more accounts by young women about suicide attempts, alcoholism, drug addiction, and self-mutilation. I am especially thinking of the following works: Susannah Kaysen's *Girl, Interrupted* (1993); Marilee Strong's *A Bright Red Scream: Self-Mutilation and the Language of Pain* (1998); Carolyn Kettlewell's *Skin Game. A Memoir* (2000); and Elizabeth Wurtzel's *Prozac Nation* (1994) and *More, Now, Again: A Memoir of Addiction* (2001).

Accounts of postfeminist eating disorders may currently comprise a new literary genre as well. Of course, Suzy Orbach wrote *Fat is a Feminist Issue* (1978) in a feminist voice and in a feminist era, as did Kim Chernin in *The Obsession: Reflections on the Tyranny of Slenderness* (1982) and *The Hungry Self: Women, Eating, and Identity* (1986), which I reviewed for the *New York Times Book Review*. *The Hungry Self* is an inspired psychoanlytic meditation on eating disorders. Both Orbach and Chernin primarily described battles with anorexia. However, Orbach's and Chernin's voices were relatively isolated ones.

The subject really gathered steam in the 1990s. For example, in 1991, Naomi Wolf published the bestselling *The Beauty Myth: How Images of Female Beauty are Used against Women*. She was also concerned with anorexia and the culturally induced need among girls and women to be too thin.

In 1995, Dr. Mary Pipher published *Reviving Ophelia: Saving the Selves of Adolescent Girls*. Pipher's work was about adolescent girls and their obsessive focus on weight gain and loss. Pipher views our culture as a "girl poisoning" culture that places impossible and contradictory demands on young women; they respond by becoming "female impersonators," and by obsessing over their weight.

As we entered the twenty-first century, college-aged Sara Shandler published *Ophelia's Daughters Speak*, a collection of teenage responses to Pipher's work. In addition, Marya Hornbacher published *Wasted: A Memoir of Anorexia and Bulimia* (1999); Carolyn Knapp published *Appetites* (2003); and Kathryn Harrison published *The Mother Knot* (2004).

Caroline Knapp writes about her own experience of anorexia, but she broadens her discussion to include many other kinds of displaced hungers and compulsions to have sex, steal, and gamble. Knapp tries to explain why young women who have grown up in a postfeminist era might still be paralyzed. In reality, they also still live in a patriarchal era, and have not yet been carefully schooled to resist the self-demeaning and contradictory choices they face. Young women are also confounded by having too many choices. Knapp suggests that they acquaint themselves with their "hungers." She writes:

A woman's relationship with hunger and satisfaction acts like a mirror, reflecting her sense of self and place in the wider world. How hungry, in all senses of the word, does a woman allow herself to be? How filled? How free does she really feel, or how held back? . . . It's about the collision between self and culture, female desire unleashed in a world that's still deeply ambivalent about female power and that manages to

whet appetite and shame in equal measure. . . . Women get psychically
larger and they are told to grow physically smaller.

Some mental health experts believe that girls and women who refuse
to eat (or who binge-eat and throw up) are engaging in a self-destructive
protest against the contradictory cultural demands that they look boy-
ishly thin, like high-fashion models—and, at the same time, look sexy and
seductive. Some say that controlling one's weight is an attempt to gain
control when one's life seems otherwise out of control.

In 2004, in the second edition of *Feminist Theories and Feminist
Psychotherapies: Origins, Themes, and Diversity*, Dr. Carolyn Zerbe Ennes
reviews some of the literature that suggests that "eating disorders may be
survival skills for dealing with anxieties about achievement. Achieving the
perfect body may be a way to avoid negative stereotypes of high-achieving
women as lonely, ruthless, unfeminine, or unattractive." Some theorists
also suggest that focusing on the "physical self" may be an attempt to
"compensate for having an underdeveloped psychological self."

Mental health experts also believe that when girls and women are
more obsessed with losing a few inches from their bodies than with
changing history by a few inches, that they are living in a nonpolitical
(postfeminist) era, and that, as isolated individuals, they do not have the
ego-strength to resist being culturally diminished and pornographically
sexualized.

I agree with all of these theoretical views. What may work, therapeutically, for a given individual, is an entirely separate matter.

But, let's return to what I did in order to create *Women and Madness*.
First, I interviewed the real experts: women who had been psychiatric and
psychotherapy patients. I interviewed white women and women of color,
heterosexual women and lesbians, middle-class women and women on
welfare, women who ranged in age from seventeen to seventy, women
whose experiences in mental asylums and therapy spanned a quarter-
century, coast to coast.

And so I began to document how patriarchal culture and consciousness had shaped human psychology for thousands of years. I was charting

the psychology of women who, as a caste, did not control the means of production or reproduction and who were, in addition, routinely shamed: sexually and in other ways. I was trying to understand what a struggle for freedom might entail, psychologically, when the colonized group was female.

Women and Madness was first published in October of 1972. It was instantly embraced by other feminists and by women in general. It received hundreds of positive reviews, including one on the front page of the *New York Times Book Review* by Adrienne Rich. Over the years, it would sell almost three million copies and be translated into many languages including Japanese and Hebrew. I was interviewed everywhere, and deluged with letters and requests.

While this book was embraced by other feminists and by many women in general, my analysis of how diagnostic labels were used to stigmatize women and of why more women than men were involved in "careers" as psychiatric patients, was either ignored, treated merely as a sensation, or sharply criticized, by those in positions of power within the professions.

My statistics and theories were "wrong," I had "overstated" my case regarding the institutions of marriage and psychiatry, I'd overly "romanticized" archetypes, especially of the Goddess and Amazon variety. Like so many feminists before me, I became a "dancing dog" on the "one night stand" feminist academic and professional circuit. Luckily, I was just about to gain tenure at a university; luckily, no father, brother, or husband wanted to psychiatrically imprison me because my ideas offended them.

It is inconceivable, outrageous, but that is *all* Elizabeth T. Stone (1842), of Massachusetts, and Elizabeth Packard (1860), of Illinois did: express views that angered their brothers or husbands. Phebe B. Davis' (1865) crime was daring to think for herself in the state of New York. Davis wrote: "It is now 21 years since people found out that I was crazy, and all because I could not fall in with every vulgar belief that was fashionable. I could never be led by everything and everybody." Adeline T. P. Lunt, (1871), of Massachusetts, noted that within the asylum, "the female patient must cease thinking or uttering any 'original expression'." She must "study the art of doffing (her) true character . . . until you cut yourself to (institutional) pattern, abandon hope." Spirited protest, or disobedience of any kind, would only result in more grievous punishment.

In her work on behalf of both mental patients and married women, Elizabeth Packard proposed, as her first reform, that: "No person shall be regarded or treated as an Insane person, or a Monomaniac, simply for the expression of opinions, no matter how absurd these opinions may appear to others." Packard was actually trying to enforce the First Amendment on behalf of women! Packard also noted that: "It is a crime against human progress to allow Reformers to be treated as Monomaniacs . . . if the Pioneers of truth are thus liable to lose their personal liberty . . . who will dare to be true to the inspirations of the divinity within them?" Phebe B. Davis (1865) was more realistic. She wrote that "real high souled people are but little appreciated in this world—they are never respected until they have been dead two or three hundred years."

Thus, more than a century after Packard lived, wrote, and crusaded, those in positions of institutional power either ignored the challenge my book posed or said that, by definition, any feminist work was biased, neurotic, and hysterical. (Yes, our critics psychiatrically pathologized an entire movement and the work it inspired—just as individual women were pathologized.) Some said my feminist views were "strident" (how they loved that word), "man-hating," and too "angry"—a real no-no.

Piffle.

Over the years, I have received more than 10,000 letters about *Women and Madness*, mainly from women. I have them still. Most confirm what I've written. (My admiration to you, dear readers, for having survived your ordeals and my thanks for all your trust.)

What has really changed since I wrote this book? The answer is too little—and quite a lot.

Despite—or because—a visionary feminist movement was alive in the world, misogyny or misogyny-under-siege continued, unabated. The so-called backlash was upon us from the very moment we drew our first,

Second Wave feminist breath. Yes, among mental health professionals too.

THE MID-1970S

Psychologist Paula Caplan, author of *The Myth of Female Masochism*, and a host of other wonderful books, including *They Say You're Crazy: How the World's Most Powerful Psychiatrists Decide Who's Normal* and *Bias in Psychiatric Diagnosis*, was a graduate student at Duke University. She "mildly critiqued Freud" in one of her term papers. Caplan writes, "My professor returned the paper to me. He had scrawled on the front, 'How many times in this century is Freud to be attacked for his views on women?'" Shortly thereafter, Caplan was "kicked out of the clinical doctoral program."

Psychotherapist Miriam Greenspan, author of *A New Approach to Women and Therapy* (1983) and the extraordinary *Healing Through the Dark Emotions: The Wisdom of Grief, Fear, and Despair* (2003), was told by her supervisors that "professionals (if they are female) must wear brassieres, that excessive anger in a woman was a sign of a character disorder, that an inordinate preoccupation with spiritual matters is a symptom of schizophrenia, that too much empathy is a serious lapse in professionalism, that too much compassion is an impediment to one's expertise as a psychotherapist."

At Harvard, psychologist Carol Gilligan began to "connect her work and her life" in the research that would lead to *In a Different Voice* (1982). Gilligan writes that, "Initially, Lawrence Kohlberg was very dismissive of my research with women and basically ridiculed my abortion decision study, getting his class to vote that abortion was not a moral problem and telling my research seminar that I had confused gossip with research. I knew the research which Kohlberg was defending had included no women. [A]s long as they (Kohlberg and Erik Erickson) could incorporate my work into their theories or regard it, as Larry used to say, as a kind of interesting cross-cultural research—a study of this other culture, called women—then everything was fine. But when listening implied changing their theories, then there was a problem."

THE 1980S

Psychiatrist Nanette Gartrell completed her three-year psychiatric residency at Harvard in 1979. She then served on the American Psychiatric Association task force to develop a curriculum on the psychology of women for psychiatric residency programs. Gartrell writes,

> When we submitted our detailed 200-page proposal two years later (1980-81), APA officials were incensed over a single sentence written by me: "Homosexuality is a normal variation in sexual expression." The magnitude of the backlash surprised me. Never mind that homosexuality had been eliminated from the DSM [Diagnostic and Statistical Manual] six years previously. Prominent female psychiatrists pressured me to delete the sentence, warning that my professional career could be ruined if I did not comply. I was also subjected to a long-term smear campaign. Despite these tactics, I refused to capitulate. I resigned from the task force, withdrew my contributions to the curriculum, and removed my name from authorship. Many colleagues followed suit. Sadly for women psychiatrists, the curriculum was never published. I became completely disillusioned about the possibility of making any changes within organized psychiatry without [encountering] major resistance.

Psychiatrist Jean Shinoda Bolen, author of *Goddesses in Everywoman: A New Psychology of Women* (1984) and the founder of the Committee of Asian-American Psychiatrists, led the fight against the American Psychiatric Association's decision to oppose the Equal Rights Amendment. She writes, "At the time, the APA was 89 percent male and two-thirds of our patients were female. Inequality, discrimination, and stereotyping affect self-esteem and limit opportunities for women; that psychiatrists who treat women did not support the ERA was appalling."

Psychiatrist Teresa Bernardez encountered trouble in her own medical school Department of Psychiatry at Michigan State University. A new chairman maintained she wasn't a "mainstream psychiatrist" because, she writes, "I did not treat depressed women with drugs and because I was against involuntary hospitalization. I had to defend my position through a grievance, which I won. My position in protecting patients who had been victims of therapists' abuse had already (resulted in) a series of disputes with a few faculty members." Bernardez left the Department of Psychiatry "with their arcane views and biological reductionism," which was "toxic to me."

Surprised? We were too.

THE 1990S

Clinical psychologist Helen Bolderston writes: "In two years of post-graduate study, I had been given just two hours of teaching on gender issues and there was no teaching on the effects on women of having been sexually abused as children. The clinical psychology training program had failed to prepare me for the nature of much of the clinical work I would be doing with women."

Psychologist Jane Ussher, author of *Women's Madness: Misogyny or Mental Illness*, writes, "In Britain, women are still more likely than men to be diagnosed and treated as mad. Sexual abuse of women still abounds—both inside and outside psychiatric institutions. There may now be more women working as clinical psychologists but the professional discourse (still) reifies psychiatric taxonomies through diagnosis and categorization of female 'symptoms.'"

In 1993-94, a student at a well-known East Coast college led a campus campaign against the male head of Psychological Services, who eventually resigned rather than face a college-ordered review. The student writes that, specifically, he "either ignored eating disorders or encouraged dieting in normal weight or anorexic students. He blamed female students when their boyfriends hit them; he sometimes encouraged them to remain in violent partnerships. He involuntarily withdrew students in crisis from the school based on his reading of the college's legal liability." In one case, he vigorously attempted to involuntarily withdraw an incest victim who was experiencing flashbacks, which nearly forced her to return to the incestuous home.

Although he was not an MD, he asserted strong, sometimes incorrect, positions on medication. Although he disapproved of psychiatric medication, he encouraged the use of birth control pills by depressed female students. In addition, he failed to properly diagnose major psychiatric disorders and failed to properly assist students who required emergency psychiatric hospitalizations.

The early studies I cited in *Women and Madness* on therapist bias have, sadly, been confirmed many times over. For example, in 1993, Drs. Kenneth Pope and Barbara Tabachnik published their findings that therapists are far from "neutral." Eighty-seven percent of 285 randomly selected clinical psychologists admitted they were "sexually attracted to a client," and 58 percent admitted feeling "sexually aroused while in the presence of a client." Between 64 and 78 percent admitted they were "angry" at their patients for a variety of reasons; nearly a third reported "hating" a client, and 46 percent said they had been so angry that they had done something to the patient they later regretted.

Few therapists are taught to expect intense emotions toward their clients, or how to deal with such emotions.

THE TWENTY-FIRST CENTURY

In 2005, Drs. Paula J. Caplan and Lisa Cosgrove published an excellent anthology titled *Bias in Psychiatric Diagnosis*. It confirms that many of the bias areas I first raised in *Women and Madness*, including sexism, racism, classism, and homophobia still exist. However, the volume extends the biases to include those against the aged, the mentally retarded, the learning disabled, and against those who suffer from eating disorders; it also challenges several legally as well as clinically relevant diagnostic categories such as "posttraumatic stress disorder," "false memory syndrome," and "parental alienation syndrome." It is masterful in its discussion of the Diagnostic and Statistical Manual of Mental Disorders.

In an article in this same volume, Drs. Jeffrey Poland and Paula J. Caplan present how bias continues in psychiatric diagnosis. They discuss real-life biases such as having to pathologize or diagnose a patient in order to receive insurance reimbursement. In addition, when clinicians are overworked and have limited time in which to see and diagnose a patient, they may literally jump to [false] conclusions. Clinicians may "tend to seek out and record information that confirms previously held beliefs and expectations and ignore or minimize information that fails to fit in . . . [clinicians also] tend to assign a higher priority to initial information received rather than to subsequently collected information."

In 2005, in the same volume, Autumn Wiley reviewed ten widely used undergraduate textbooks in abnormal psychology. Shockingly, she found that none included the feminist critique of institutional psychiatry and diagnostic practices; seven of the ten texts included no mention of sex or gender bias; and none of fourteen major feminist critics is cited in any of the books. Such feminist critics include Laura Brown, Paula J. Caplan, myself, Beverly Greene, Rachel Hare-Mustin, Hannah Lerman, Lynn Rosewater, and Lenore Walker.

Wiley concludes that "decades of feminist criticism have had little impact on the way that authors of abnormal psychology textbooks present the DSM. The absence of that criticism from the textbooks is not because it is not available or of the highest quality."

Thus, although there has been enormous progress—a sea change even—the clinical biases that I first wrote about in 1972 still exist today. Many clinical judgments remain clouded by classism, racism, anti-Semitism, homophobia, ageism, sexism, and by cultural and anti-immigrant biases as well. I have reviewed hundreds, possibly thousands, of psychiatric and psychological assessments in matrimonial, criminal, and civil lawsuits. The clinical distrust of mothers, simply because they are women, the eagerness to bend over backwards to like fathers, simply because they are men is mind-numbing. Mother-blaming and woman-hatred sizzle on each clinical page. Mothers are often psychiatrically accused of alienating a child from the child's father if that child does not resent or hate the mother, or prefer the father.

Unbelievable—yes?

Even those clinicians who are less likely to gender-stereotype still exhibit an (often unconscious) preference for men over women. Their sexism may be sophisticated, subtle. Sometimes, female clinicians are much harder on women than are male clinicians. They may feel they have to be—as a way of distancing themselves from a despised group.

For example, one 1990 study confirmed that there was less gender-stereotyping among psychiatrists in 1990 than in 1970. However, more of the female psychiatrists rated masculine traits as optimal for female patients while more male psychiatrists chose more undifferentiated, androgynous traits as optimal for both male and female patients.

Thus, women mental health professionals are not necessarily more objective or neutral about other women than their male counterparts are. Like men, women hold sexist views. Perhaps this is psychologically similar to people of color who prefer light skins and who have internalized racist views. The refusal to acknowledge such views makes it impossible to resist them.

In general, women psychologically and socially matter to each other so much that they tend to expect too much from each other. The smallest error, the most minor disappointment between women is often magnified and resented. A woman can go from being a Fairy Godmother to being an Evil Stepmother in a flash. Also, women are afraid to blame men but are not afraid to blame other women.

For example, many women report that they are far angrier at their mothers than at the fathers who raped them, far angrier at the women who refused to believe that they were raped than at their rapists. Precisely because female-female intimacy and sympathy are so important to women, it is quite painful when female intimates are not "there" for a rape or incest survivor.

According to psychoanalysts Judith Lewis Herman and her mother, the late Helen Block Lewis, daughters in (incestuous) families feel "deeply betrayed" by their mothers. Such daughters feel that they have been "offered as a sacrifice in order to propitiate a powerful male, and they despise their mothers." They also learn to expect no help from other women. Some daughters fight back or exact revenge—but mainly against their mothers.

Thus, continuing clinical bias affects patients in at least five important areas: (1) Women—and to a lesser extent, men—with medical illnesses are often, and wrongfully, psychiatrically diagnosed and medicated; (2) Women who allege rape, incest, battery, sex discrimination, or harassment are being ordered into therapy and/or diagnostically pathologized at trial; (3) Women (and men) who have no money and no insurance cannot afford therapy nor are they always respected or understood by therapists who are mainly middle-class in orientation; (4) Women—and to a lesser exent, men—of color, immigrants, Semites, including Jews, still face an extra level of clinical fear and hostility; (5) Psychotherapist-patient sexual abuse still exists.

WRONGFUL PSYCHIATRIC DIAGNOSES OF MEDICAL ILLNESSES

When I first explored sexist bias among mental health professionals in 1972, I did not realize that when western medicine does not understand and/or cannot cure an illness, it often first denies that the illness is real by saying it is merely a psychiatric disorder. As if mental illness isn't real.

Increasingly, women with disabling medical illnesses are being psychiatrically diagnosed and sedated rather than tested or treated for a non-psychiatric illness. Just as asthma and arthritis were once viewed as psycho-somatic, today lupus, multiple sclerosis, Lyme's disease, chemical and food allergies, Gulf War Syndrome, Chronic Fatigue Immune Dysfunction Syndrome, and certain neurological and endochronological diseases are still being dismissed as primarily psychiatric in nature.

Patients—usually women—are told, both by psychologists and psychiatrists, that they are probably imagining their pain, that their illness is all
in their heads. Often it is not.

While I also believe that psyche and soma are one, I know that
viruses, parasites, bacteria, fungi, sexually transmitted diseases, and toxic
chemicals are real and can cause neurological and cognitive dysfunction.
Depression is real too, and has a neurochemical basis; however, depression can also be a secondary symptom of chronic pain.

Many psychiatric inpatients are still not believed when they complain
of physical pain. Non-psychiatric medical care is often withheld until a
patient collapses—or is discovered to have a terminal illness, long past
treating.

THE DIAGNOSTIC PATHOLOGIZING OF WOMEN WHO REPORT RAPE, HARASSMENT, DISCRIMINATION, BATTERY, AND OTHER ABUSES

I must repeat: I had an excellent education. Only, I was not taught that
women or people were oppressed and that oppression and discrimination
traumatizes people.

It took a women's liberation movement to teach me that. It took
listening to and talking to women—not as inferior patients but as sisters
in a struggle for social justice—to understand that most women did not
receive equal pay for equal work and that this had definite psychological
and medical consequences; did suffer physically as well as psychologically
when they menstruated or went through menopause; were sexually
harassed on the job; and were victims of violence at home.

It took years for the women's liberation movement to understand that
the most common forms of rape were among intimates, not strangers; that
rape was rarely reported and even more rarely prosecuted; that rape is no

longer a spoil of war but has increasingly been used as a weapon of war—for example, in Algeria, Bosnia, Rwanda, and the Sudan.

However, despite all that we have learned, today, when women allege sexual harassment or sex discrimination they are sometimes disbelieved or blamed; have often been punitively diagnosed for having a normal human reaction to trauma. Sometimes, when women charge rape or sexual harassment, some truly strange things can happen.

For example, in 2005, Jessica Brakey, an Air Force Academy cadet, was one of two women who charged an Air Force officer with sexual assault. Brakey's mental health counselor, Jennifer Bier, was ordered to turn over her session notes. So far, Bier has refused to do so. In other words, if a rape victim appropriately seeks counseling, what she says can and will be used against her in a court of law. What this usually means is that the rape victim will be portrayed as "crazy" or as a "slut."

Here's another example. In the early 1990s, Lieutenant Darlene Simmons, a Navy *lawyer*, was ordered to take a psychiatric exam after she accused her commander of sexual harassment. A psychiatric exam? How absurd. How familiar.

And, in the late 1980s, Dr. Margaret Jensvold, herself a psychiatrist and the winner of a prestigious fellowship at the National Institute of Mental Health (NIH), complained that her supervisor, Dr. David Rubinow, repeatedly denied her opportunities that her male counterparts enjoyed to conduct scientific research and publish her findings. Jensvold also accused Rubinow of making sexist comments, thereby creating a hostile work environment. Jensvold was "advised" to see a psychotherapist if she wished to stay at NIH. The psychiatrist she was referred to was also an NIH employee and could not guarantee confidentiality. Ultimately, Jensvold was fired. She sued.

Jensvold is at least the second woman researcher at NIH who filed discrimination and harassment charges. Psychiatrist Jean Hamilton, who settled an EEOC complaint in 1986 against the same supervisor, testified on Jensvold's behalf that women researchers were routinely called names like witch, wicked bitch, booby lady, and, more benignly, sugar.

CLASS BIASES

According to psychotherapist Marcia Hill, "Class and classism is in the position that gender and sexism was thirty years ago: denied, surrounded with myth, silenced." Women may constitute a caste but, if every woman is, indeed, one man away from welfare or homelessness, to what class do women themselves belong? If educated and accomplished women earn far less than their male counterparts, and remain as vulnerable to male violence as other women are, in what sense are they middle class? If a working-class woman is the (only) head of household, and is treated with the respect usually reserved for men only, in what sense is she working-class? According to psychotherapist Bonnie Chalifoux, "Working-class women live on a fault-line, as Lillian Rubin has described it. They are only one crisis away from falling into poverty, and they walk the line without a safety net."

We don't have the answers to these questions, but myths about class still abound among both psychiatrists and psychotherapists, (e.g. a wealthy woman is spoiled and is probably only faking neurosis in order to get attention). A poor woman can't afford neurosis—she has to keep going, no matter what. When the workload, stress, heartbreak, and tragedies mount up, and she cracks up—as most human beings would under similar circumstances—many psychiatrists may think: Nothing to do but diagnose, medicate, and ship her off to an institution. She can't afford private therapy anyway.

Actually, these days, very few people can.

Most early feminist theories about women were really about white, heterosexual, middle-class, educated women. By definition, such theories rendered both poor and wealthy women "other."

In my time, psychotherapists were trained to "analyze" late fee payments as resistance to therapy. However, in 1996, Marcia Hill wrote, "Those with few economic resources sometimes avoid both paying and talking about the problem. The avoidance is, in my experience, more likely to symbolize feeling helpless about money (and perhaps resentful about the cost of therapy) than to signify feelings about therapy per se. On the other hand, many people from working class or poor backgrounds are particularly conscientious about paying me, because they know the importance of getting paid for one's work and feel pride in their ability to pay their bills. People with less money can find it very hard to take what they perceive as 'charity,' and I have sometimes found myself in the odd position of talking someone into paying me less."

RACE BIASES

I do not assume that the more a woman is oppressed that the "stronger" she is. This is neither fair nor true. In fact, in *Women and Madness,* I wrote, "The problems of being both black and female in a racist and sexist society are staggering, the permutations of violence, self-destructiveness and paranoia endless. . . . Racism in psychiatric diagnosis and treatment is usually further confused by class and sex biases."

Just because I—and many others—have continued to challenge the diagnostic pathologizing of poor people, people of color, immigrants, and gay people does not mean that such practices have disappeared. Double and triple diagnostic and treatment standards still exist. Native-, African-, Hispanic-, and Asian American women have good reason to—and do—mistrust the mental health care system. They know they are often seen as inferior when they are at their psychological and moral best, and as commendably self-sufficient when they are about to expire of grief.

Accordingly, many women of color are deeply suspicious of psychiatric medication and psychotherapy. Although they are more likely to be raped than white women, they may be less likely to report it to the police or to their families and, with dire consequences, less likely to seek help. If a woman is poor, or speaks no English, her chances of getting the psychological help she may need are often minimal. If she is also a lesbian, and angry—or actually freaking out—she'll probably be diagnosed as more seriously ill than her white heterosexual counterpart.

Many Latina Catholics and Asian women may feel too ashamed to report rape; they may not even think of it as "rape" but as "sex" (which is culturally forbidden to them outside of marriage, but not to men). If and when such women break down, emotionally, they may not even connect it to their having been raped. If their attackers are also members of their own race, or family, they may not want to sacrifice their attackers to a racist criminal justice system.

Most women are trained to put their own needs second, the needs of any man—including a violent man—first.

It is also important to remember that women of color are more at risk than their white counterparts. For example, according to one study, 78 percent of the women who were killed in New York City were killed at home by their husbands and boyfriends, or by someone they knew. Contrary to myth, this phenomenon was even more true of African American women who live in poverty.

SEX BETWEEN PATIENT AND THERAPIST

When I first wrote about sex between patient and therapist I was virtually alone; few others ever had written on the subject. Now, there are hundreds of studies, and many books, documenting this abuse of power. It hasn't gone away, but at least it is being documented, as well as challenged. Patients are suing for damages; I and many other professionals are testifying on their behalf.

It is unethical to engage in sex with one's patients. Prevailing wisdom suggests that once a patient—always a patient; once a therapist—always a therapist. Nevertheless, in the 1950s and 1960s, a number of leading psychoanalysts married their most beautiful, troubled, brilliant, and adoring patients. Some marriages worked out; others didn't. At the time, no one thought there was anything wrong with this. Today, a feminist analysis of sex and power suggests that such a boundary violation is analogous to psychological incest.

A minority of therapists, both male and female, gay and straight, are psychopaths. They form cults around themselves, isolate cult members from their friends and family, teach that "sexual encounters" with the leader are both an honor and an occasion for spiritual enlightenment. These are criminal and psychotic enterprises that good therapists often whisper about but, for many reasons, are unable to expose or abolish. Often, such psychopathic therapists have no advanced degrees and/or do not belong to any professional associations; even when they do, our ability to stop them is limited.

I am not saying that a therapist is forbidden from falling in love with a patient, or even from acting on it. There are once-in-a-lifetime exceptions to this rule and ethical ways of handling such a situation should it arise. This includes referring one's patient elsewhere, entering therapy oneself, ending all contact with one's patient for at least a year, and then— once a suitable separation has been established—proceeding very slowly, and with extreme caution.

Freud and Company had, of course, insisted that both "transference" (what a patient may project onto her therapist) and "countertransference" (what the analyst may project onto a patient) be carefully analyzed. Freud was very clear: "kisses" were to be avoided at all costs. But back in Vienna, analyses were sometimes concluded in months and/or within a year, analysands socialized and worked with their analysts, and boundaries blurred. Freud himself analyzed his own daughter, Anna, and, not surprisingly, denied that incestuous dynamics existed in the family: in his, or in anyone else's.

In my view, Freud was a genius. He was right about many important things: Unconscious motivation does exist, both symptoms and dreams can be interpreted, the "talking cure" can work. (The talking and listening cure was really suggested by one of Freud's patients, Anna O., aka Bertha Pappenheim, a wealthy Orthodox Jewish girl who went on to become a feminist and anti-Nazi crusader).

Freud was wrong about women's masochism and penis envy. He was also wrong about fathers and sons: it was fathers, in Judaeo-Christian and Muslim cultures, who physically and psychologically "kill" their sons, not sons who wish for their fathers' deaths. Freud did not understand the mother-daughter relationship as well as he did that between mother and son. We now understand that Freud-as-genius did not transcend the patriarchy of his time. Did anyone?

I do not want to underestimate the importance of Freud's discoveries or his popularization of concepts such as the unconscious, denial, repression, projection, dream analysis, etc. However, Freud's theories may, in fact, have become as popular as they did—and when they did—for a wide variety of reasons. What was done in Freud's name—whether Freud intended it this way or not—sometimes supported the most backward of institutional psychiatrists. While some analytic patients, both male and female, learned treasured things about themselves, more often Freudian-inspired psychoanalytic therapy in America was used to reinforce church teachings and to curtail potential feminist political fervor in each woman, one by one. As social worker and scholar Dr. Nzinga Shaka Zula writes, "Therapists are often the soft police of the dominant culture."

Even if a psychoanalytic understanding of one's life is potentially liberating—and I think it may be—psychoanalytic therapy, by itself, cannot overcome trauma, or human nature. Nor can psychological healing take place in isolation.

While society has changed—it also remains the same. For some, family life has changed radically in the last thirty-five years; more than half of all marriages end in divorce; many mothers (and some fathers) are raising children alone, both with and without extended family support; many mothers are daring to leave men who abuse them and their children; lesbians and homosexuals are creating alternative families and raising children.

Nevertheless, most girls and boys continue to experience childhood in father-dominated, father-absent, and/or mother-blaming families. Sex-role stereotyping still exists in most homes, as does maternal and paternal child abuse. Incest and family violence remain epidemic but have, increasingly, been de-politicized: first, by women who believe that appearing on television is a form of "treatment"; second, by the media, which happily capitalizes on the entertainment value of such public accusations and confessions; third, by the understandable but misguided belief in the power of individual therapeutic solutions as opposed to collective legal or social justice solutions.

I am not opposed to television confessions or discussions of trauma. On the contrary. Such programs often educate women who are otherwise totally misinformed and isolated. In a sense, daytime TV programs are the heirs of early feminist consciousness-raising groups—but without a political perspective. This missing dimension should not be underestimated.

The cumulative effect of being forced to lead circumscribed lives is toxic. The psychic toll is measured in anxiety, depression, phobias, suicide attempts, eating disorders, and such stress-related illnesses as addictions, alcoholism, high blood pressure, and heart disease. Understanding and overcoming all this is a process; no instant "exorcism" is equal to the task.

It is not surprising that many women—whether they are educated and have careers or not—still behave as if they've been "colonized." Let's not forget that in many countries the colonization is physical as well as psychological.

The image of women as colonized is a useful one. It explains why some women cling to their colonizers the way a child or a hostage clings to an abusive parent or captor; why many women blame themselves (or other women) when they are brutalized (she really wanted it, she freely chose it); and why most women defend their colonizers' right to possess them (God or loyalty to one's family demands it).

"Colonization" exists when the colonized has valuable natural resources that are used to enrich the colonizer, but not the colonized: when the colonized does the colonizer's work, but earns little of the colonizer's money; when the colonized try to imitate or please the colonizer, and truly believe that the colonizer is, by nature, superior/inferior, and that the colonized cannot exist without her colonizer.

Many women still believe that men are superior to women and that a woman is worthless without a man.

Like others who are colonized, women are often harder on themselves. Women expect a lot from each other—but rarely forgive another woman when she fails, even slightly. Women are emotionally intimate with each other but often tend to take that intimacy for granted.

Psychologically, seemingly contradictory things can be true. (Thank you Herr Doktor Freud). Women mainly compete against other women *and* women mainly rely upon other women; women envy and sabotage each other through slander, gossip, and shunning *and* women also want other women's respect and support.

In *Women and Madness*, I described asylums as dangerous patriarchal institutions. This means that both male and female staff tormented female inmates. Tragically, such snakepits still exist in America today, in which patients are wrongfully medicated, utterly neglected, and psychologically and sexually abused.

On June 23, 1997, in *Kansas v. Hendricks*, the Supreme Court upheld the 1994 Kansas Sexually Violent Predator Act that allows the state to commit a sex offender to a mental asylum—perhaps indefinitely—until he can show "that he is no longer dangerous" nor subject to "irresistible impulses." The decision stresses that such civil commitment is meant to provide "treatment, not punishment" and that "the conditions surrounding confinement do not suggest a punitive purpose . . . such restraint of the dangerously mentally ill has been historically regarded as a legitimate non-punitive objective."

If pedophiles and rapists are judicially deemed too dangerous to roam society's streets, what does the Court believe such men might do to other inmates in state custody? Especially to male or female inmates who are child-like in size or mental abilities, and may in addition be sedated, strait-jacketed, physically disabled, deaf, blind, wheelchair-bound, or lobotomized?

Patients raped in psychiatric institutions have civilly sued for damages in many states, including California, Louisiana, Michigan, New York, Ohio, and Oregon.

In 1997, a case was certified as a class-action suit in the Nebraska Federal District Court. There were four named plaintiffs, ranging in age from nineteen to sixty-two, who had been variously diagnosed as mentally ill and/or developmentally disabled. They sued the highest-ranking officials of the state's Department of Public Institutions. From July 1991 through July 1994, each of the four plaintiffs was raped, repeatedly, by the same three male patients at the Hastings Regional Center (HRC) in Nebraska. They each reported the rapes and beatings. The women asked for monetary damages and demanded structural changes in the way HRC operates.

Women who have been repeatedly raped in childhood—often by authority figures in their own families—are traumatized human beings; as such, they are often diagnosed as borderline personalities. If they are institutionalized, they are rarely treated as the torture victims they really are. On the contrary. In state custody, women are more, not less, likely to be raped again (and each time it is more, not less, traumatic). Instead of being trained to understand this, most institutional staff—psychiatrists, psychologists, nurses, and attendants alike—do not believe the rape victims, nor do they think of rape as a life-long trauma.

There is no excuse for subjecting twenty-first-century institutional inmates to the same awful conditions that existed in the nineteenth century. By this, I am referring to solitary confinement, restraints, unending physical and psychological cruelty, criminality unrestrained among the inmates by overworked or punitive staff.

Institutional psychiatry may fail us but madness still exists. I said so in 1972—but I also said that most women were not mad, merely seen as such. My own and other historical accounts of asylums strongly suggest that most women in asylums were not insane; that help was not to be found in doctor-headed, attendant-staffed and state-run institutions; that what we call madness can also be caused or exacerbated by injustice and cruelty within the family and society; and that freedom, radical legal reform, political struggle, and kindness are crucial to psychological and moral mental health.

Certain groups—who often disagree with each other—agree that institutional abuse does exist. Some antipsychiatry groups maintain that mental illness either does not exist or is not a medical illness; psychiatrists are not physicians in the same way that neurologists or cardiologists are; psychiatric medication is usually harmful, not helpful; psychiatrists continue to administer shock therapy and perform psychosurgery—even when it is harmful or ineffective; people are still institutionalized against their will or without informed consent.

Dr. David Cohen, associate professor and editor of *Mind and Behavior*, cites studies that suggest that despite de-institutionalization, involuntary commitments are as high now as they once were. He says, "Many persons are informally but effectively coerced, coerced by threats, are not aware of their legal status." In Cohen's view, the attempt to re-institutionalize the homeless as mentally ill "is similar to calls of a century ago by prominent figures to segregate America's growing dangerous classes, or of twenty-five years ago to incarcerate heroin addicts in work camps and force metha-done on them. Such reforms made things worse for the least powerful actors in the system."

According to a survivor of institutional abuse, "I survived not only childhood abuse that initiated my involvement in the mental health system, but also the re-traumatization that occurred as a patient in five hospitals. I survived solitary confinement for two weeks, without cloth-ing, and with only a rubber mattress and blanket. I survived four-point restraints, again without clothing, and the forced administration of devastating drugs."

Similarly, another survivor says, "I survived forced electroshock, along with weeks of solitary confinement and restraint. High dosages of forced neuroleptic drugs gave me seizures. I was locked up for many months."

According to Dr. Keith Hoeller, editor of the *Review of Existential Psychology and Psychiatry*, "The most dangerous political movement in America is the mental health movement. Family members pose as advocates for the so-called mentally ill, and are funded in part by the drug companies [one million dollars in 1995 alone]. The National Alliance for the Mentally Ill has succeeded in [their] desire to expand several state laws so that innocent American citizens can be incarcerated for reasons other than dangerousness to self and others."

On the other hand, the family members and friends of people who suffer from schizophrenia or depression know that something is seriously "wrong" with a relative who can no longer eat or sleep, hears voices, can't work, is afraid to leave the house, has become suicidal, verbally and physically aggressive, or homocidal. They see their family member suffer, and learn that they cannot help or even continue to live with them. Families of the mentally ill often see major improvements with psychiatric medication and psychotherapy and are, in fact, concerned about the right to treatment.

All these groups are important. Consumer education and legal action remain crucial in the struggle to humanize both institutional and noninstitutional life.

Often those who condemn institutional psychiatry, psychiatric medication, shock therapy—any kind of therapy-for-hire—do not feel responsible for the female casualties of patriarchy. Such critics, even if well intentioned, may be confusing the fact that quality mental health care is not available to all who want it with the question of whether or not quality mental health care exists at all.

So what did I mean when I said that quite a lot has changed in the last twenty-five years? For one thing, we've learned more about the genetic and chemical bases of mental illness. We've learned that those suffering from manic depression, panic and bipolar disorders, or schizophrenia often respond to the right drug at the right dosage level; that all drugs have negative side effects; that we shouldn't prescribe the same drug for everyone especially without continually monitoring the side effects; and that verbal or other supportive therapies are often impossible without such medication.

Despite the progress in biological psychiatry, both women and men are still wrongfully or overly medicated—or denied proper medication—by harried low-fee/high-fee psychiatrists and psychopharmacologists. Psychiatric inpatients are often overly medicated for the convenience of staff, who do not always treat the to-be-expected side effects with compassion or expertise.

As bad as many institutions are, turning the mentally ill loose, into the streets, is not the solution; it is merely another unacceptable alternative. People do have a right to treatment, if that treatment exists. I realize this statement is almost laughable today, given how insurance and drug companies, managed care and government spending cuts have made quality psychotherapy totally out of reach for most people. This means that just when we know what to do for the victims of trauma, there are very few teaching hospitals and clinics that treat poor women in feminist ways.

Medication by itself is never enough. Women who are clinically depressed or anxious also need access to feminist information and support.

What does a feminist therapist do that's different? A feminist therapist tries to believe what women say. Given the history of psychiatry and psychoanalysis, this alone is a radical act. When a woman begins to remember being sexually molested as a child, a feminist does not conclude that the woman's flashbacks or hysteria prove that she's lying or crazy.

A feminist therapist believes that a woman needs to be told that she's not crazy; that it's normal to feel sad or angry about being overworked, underpaid, underloved; that it's healthy to harbor fantasies of running away when the needs of others (aging parents, needy husbands, demanding children) threaten to overwhelm her.

A feminist therapist believes that women need to hear that men "don't love enough" before they're told that women "love too much"; that fathers are equally responsible for their children's problems; that no one—not even self-appointed feminist saviors—can rescue a woman but herself; that self-love is the basis for love of others; that it's hard to break free of patriarchy; that the struggle to do so is both miraculous and life-long; that very few of us know how to support women in flight from—or at war with—internalized self-hatred.

A feminist therapist tries to listen to women respectfully, rather than in a superior or contemptuous way. A feminist therapist does not minimize the extent to which a woman has been wounded. Nevertheless, a feminist therapist remains resolutely optimistic. No woman, no matter how wounded she may be, is beyond the reach of human community and compassion.

A feminist therapist does not label a woman as mentally ill because she expresses strong emotions or is at odds with her feminine role. Feminists do not view women as mentally ill when they engage in sexual, reproductive, economic, or intellectual activities outside of marriage. They do not pathologize women who have full-time careers, are lesbians, refuse to marry, commit adultery, want divorces, choose to be celibate, have abortions, use birth control, choose to have a child out of wedlock, choose to breast-feed against expert advice, or expect men to be responsible for 50 percent of the child care and housework. Women have lost custody of their children for these very reasons—pronounced unfit by courtroom psychiatrists, psychologists, or social workers.

Some feminist theorists and therapists have been moved by the radical liberation psychology in *Women and Madness*. They agree that women's control of our bodies is as important as sexual pleasure, and that we must be able to defend "our bodies, ourselves" against violent or unwanted invasions—like rape, battery, unwanted pregnancy, or unwanted sterilization.

As feminist clinician Janet Surrey says, "The work of feminist healers is to integrate our minds and our bodies, ourselves and others, human community and the life of the planet. I question our profession's fear of feminism. I refuse to do psychology without a feminist liberation theology."

In *Trauma and Recovery*, psychiatrist Judith Lewis Herman models a new vision of therapy and of human relationships, one in which we are called upon to "bear witness to a crime" and to "affirm a position of solidarity with the victim." Herman's ideal therapist cannot be morally neutral but must make a collaborative commitment, and enter into an "existential engagement" with the traumatized. Such a therapist must listen, really listen, solemnly and without haste, to the factual and emotional details of atrocities, without flight or denial, without blaming the victim, identifying with the aggressor, or becoming a detective who "diagnoses" ritual or Satanic abuse after a single session, and without "using her power over the patient to gratify her personal needs."

While the love and understanding of relatives, friends, and political movements are necessary, they are not substitutes for the hard psychological work that victims must also undertake with the assistance of trained professionals; in fact, even enlightened professionals like Herman cannot themselves undertake this work without a strong support system of their own.

The work of psychotherapist Miriam Greenspan is another good example of a feminist spiritual-political approach to human suffering. Greenspan's book *Healing Through the Dark Emotions: The Wisdom of Grief, Fear, and Despair* (2003) models a healer's shamanic journey. Greenspan describes enormous grief and terror—her own, that of the world's—and explains what it means to surrender to fear, to face straight into it, to "let it be" as the royal road to sanity, rightful action and rightful nonaction, and to exuberance and freedom.

Greenspan beholds that which is tragic about the human condition but embraces it in a daringly therapeutic and consoling way. Her values are Jewish, Buddhist, feminist, and humanist. She employs humor as well. Greenspan provides an excellent discussion of the "alchemy of fear," and of the Buddhist concept of "toglen": nonaction, action, surrender.

Now, imagine both Judith Lewis Herman and Miriam Greenspan at work in Israel, among both Arabs and Jews who have emigrated there from every continent on earth; imagine them both at work in Australia, Ireland, Italy, Japan, Mexico, the United States, and the former Yugoslavia—and you have an idea of the ground covered by Claire Low Rabin in her 2005 anthology *Understanding Gender and Culture in the Helping Process: Practitioners' Narratives From Global Perspectives.*

While Herman and Greenspan may not be thinking about how their ideas and techniques may "translate" into different cultures—Rabin, et al. are. Thus, in addition to gender violence per se, Rabin and her contributors also look at how women of different cultures respond to such violence.

Rabin suggests that culture is as important as gender and that mental health professionals must factor it in if they wish to help anyone, certainly anyone who has grown up in a nonwestern or rural culture. She and her associates are absolutely right. In their view, gender, class, race, birthplace, one's generation, clan, tribe, religion, status as an immigrant, must all be factored into understanding any living being, especially one in trouble and in pain.

Western psychoanalysis/psychotherapy tends to view the individual as the source of her own problems; in my view, this is not entirely wrong. Rabin et al. reject a medical model that focuses primarily on pathology, not on strengths, and that does not necessarily focus on the powers of elders or of the community to help one of their own. This volume proposes a different understanding of "boundaries" and of "active involvements."

The suggestions to rely upon nonwestern traditional elders as mediators and conflict-resolvers, and on holistic and indigenous healing methods are both exciting and practical. However, I doubt whether misogynist elders in Third World countries or among religious fundamentalists on every continent will uphold a woman's right to individual freedom.

Working with traditional, nonwestern peoples may require nontraditional (and old-fashioned social work) approaches. For example, helpers may need to meet in their clients' homes, not in offices, wake clients up for job interviews and accompany them too. Helpers may need to talk to women at home, while the women are cooking or caring for children.

The contributors to the Rabin volume understand that by the very act of helping, the helper can also engage in "social protest." Allowing a survivor of violence to testify—creating the "listening" conditions that makes testimony possible—is also a way of taking a moral stand against human rights atrocities. "Social injustice" may also be confronted through "understanding." Listening carefully allows the "silenced" a voice.

Make no mistake: Feminists have learned what works, what must be done. We have made extraordinary discoveries. Nevertheless, the most important feminist work has been "disappeared" (or never made its way) into the graduate and medical school canon. This is truly astounding—given that contemporary mental health professionals did not learn about incest, rape, sexual harassment, wife-beating, or child abuse from graduate or medical school textbooks but from feminist consciousness-raising and research—and from grassroots activism. We all learned from the victims themselves, who had been empowered to speak not by psychoanalysis but by feminist liberation.

As psychotherapist Sandra Butler, the author of *Conspiracy of Silence: The Trauma of Incest*, writes, "Nothing that sexually victimized women needed existed, so we had to create it. And we did."

In 1970, when I first began writing *Women and Madness*, there were few feminist theories of psychology and virtually no feminist therapists. Now we are everywhere. Feminists have established journals, referral networks, conferences, and workshops—programs that are both psychoanalytic and antipsychoanalytic in orientation. We have served incest and rape survivors, battered women, batterers, mentally ill and homeless women, refugees, alcoholics, drug addicts, the disabled, the elderly—and each other. Feminists have also published many extraordinary books and articles.

They constitute, in psychotherapist Rachel Josefowitz Siegel's words, "bibliotherapy."

Today, there are feminist psychopharmacologists, forensic experts, lesbian therapists, sex therapists, family therapists, experts on recovered memories, race, ethnicities—and, perhaps the truest sign of having arrived: feminist critics of feminist therapy!

Our influence is international. There are feminist therapy and crisis counseling centers in South America, Europe, the Middle East, Africa, and Asia. Most recently, North American and European feminist therapists and lawyers worked with their counterparts in Bosnia on behalf of the raped women and other victims of torture and genocide. Had the United Nations Tribunal in the matter of Bosnia proceeded, I (and other North American and European feminists) might have been privileged to testify about Rape Trauma Syndrome.

Over the years, I have lectured and worked with my colleagues in Canada, Europe, the Middle East—especially Israel—Australia, and Asia. In 1990, I was invited to lecture in Tokyo in celebration of the tenth anniversary of the first feminist therapy clinic, founded by my colleague, Kiyomi Kawano. There was no language barrier, we all spoke "feminist." The visit was an exhilarating one.

Despite such progress, most feminists in mental health remain frustrated. It is a sign of our ambitiousness: we understand how much remains to be done. But we have come a long way.

We now understand that women and men are not "crazy" or "defective" when, in response to trauma, they develop post-traumatic symptoms, including insomnia, flashbacks, phobias, panic attacks, anxiety, depression, dissociation, a numbed toughness, amnesia, shame, guilt, self-loathing, self-mutilation, and social withdrawal. Trauma victims may attempt to mask these symptoms with alcohol, drugs, overeating, or extreme forms of dieting.

We now understand more about what trauma is, and what it does. We understand that chronic, hidden family/domestic violence is actually more, not less, traumatic than sudden violence at the hands of a stranger, or of an enemy during war. We understand that after even a single act of abuse, physical violence is only infrequently needed to keep one's victim in a constant state of terror, dependent on her captor and tormentor.

We understand that rape is not about love or even lust, but about humiliating another human being through forced or coerced sex and sexual shame. The intended effect of rape is always the same: to break the spirit of the rape victim, to drive her (or him) out of her body and quite often out of her mind, to render her incapable of resistance. The effects of terror on men at war and in enemy captivity are similar to the trauma suffered by women at home in violent "domestic captivity."

Rape has been systematically used by men of every class and race to destroy both their own women and the women of enemy men. This terrorist tactic, coupled with childhood sexual abuse and shaming, works. Most women do not resist, escape, or kill their rapists in self-defense. When women do try to resist, or simply report the rape, they are often killed by their rapists, jailed for long periods of time, or executed—especially in the Islamic world—either by the state or by the family in what is known as an "honor killing."

Those who have interviewed and tried to help the raped women of Bosnia have found the women distraught, intimidated, withdrawn, emotional, afflicted with nightmares, insomnia, depression, panic disorders, and/or suicidal. According to Alexandra Stiglymayer, "The rape victims are broken, not thinking about revenge, for the horror of their rape and expulsion has also taken away whatever power of resistance they might have had." In addition to these typical peacetime Rape Trauma Syndrome symptoms, Zagreb psychiatrist Vera Folnegovic-Smalc also noted "anxiety, inner agitation, apathy, loss of self-confidence, an aversion to sexuality. Rape is one of the gravest abuses, with consequences that can last a lifetime."

Some feminists say that women have so little power that, even if they *do* hold sexist views, such views are not as consequential as male sexist views. I disagree. For example, consider how important it is for a female rape victim to have access to a sympathetic—or at least objective—woman police officer, mental health professional, physician, and emergency room nurse. (I do not mean to minimize the importance of sympathetic or objective men, but a minority of good or nonsexist men cannot hold up the sky alone.)

As feminists, we have also learned that women and men can survive many things—if they are believed, if others are outraged on their behalf, if others denounce and attempt to stop the abuse. Thus, the victims of rape and other forms of torture are more upset by what good people fail to do than by the crimes actually committed. As eloquently articulated by Jacobo Timerman, the Argentinian political "prisoner without a name" and torture victim, "The Holocaust will be understood not so much for the number of victims as for the magnitude of the silence. And what obsesses me most is the repetition of silence."

Sins of omission are usually psychologically experienced as greater than sins of commission. The mother who stood by and did nothing as her daughter or son was being incestuously abused is hated even more than the abuser himself.

What do the victims of violence need to ensure their survival and to maintain their dignity?

Bearing witness is important; being supported instead of punished for doing so, especially by other women, is also important. Putting one's suffering to use, through educating and supporting other victims is important; drafting, passing, and enforcing laws is important. However, as Judith Herman has written, "The systematic study of psychological trauma depends on the support of a political movement. In the absence of strong political movements for human rights, the active process of bearing witness inevitably gives way to the active process of forgetting."

In my view, in addition to therapy and political movement, we also need self-esteem, anti-pornography, anti-bullying, and rape prevention education for young girls. This might include self-defense and/or military training. We also need swift, effective prosecution of rapists; and successful civil suits for monetary remuneration in addition to criminal prosecution. Perhaps most important, we need to support women who have fought back against their batterers and rapists and are wasting away in jail for daring to save their own lives. They are political prisoners and should be honored as such—not seen as pathological masochists who "chose" to stay until they "chose" to kill.

Unlike many Mental Patient Liberation Project members, who have their own worthy agenda, I also believe that what we call "madness" does exist; that it may sometimes be caused or exacerbated by violence and by certain social and environmental conditions; that people in its grip suffer terribly; that it doesn't always last forever—although the culturally imposed stigma and shame seem to; and that the "helping" professions have been both helpful—and far from helpful.

I cannot agree with blanket political opposition to psychiatric medication and hospitalization. Sometimes, psychiatric medication helps, sometimes it harms, sometimes it makes no difference. Sometimes, the talking cure, including "feminist" therapy, helps, harms, or has no effect whatsoever. Sometimes, political and legal struggle (and whole revolutions) help, harm, or make no difference.

However, despite my own early critique of private patriarchal therapy geared primarily to high-income clients, I have come to believe that women can and do benefit from *good* therapy. Some feminists (antifeminists too) have questioned whether any therapy, including feminist therapy, is desirable. They have noted, correctly, that "therapism" may indeed siphon off activist energies. They are right—but severely traumatized women cannot always rise to the occasion of political action.

For example, an incest survivor with insomnia or panic attacks often cannot sit in a room long enough to have her consciousness raised; an anorexic or obese woman who is obsessed with losing weight may not be able to notice others long enough to engage in fundraising; a woman on a window ledge or in an alcoholic daze may not have the peace of mind to analyze her fate in feminist terms.

Being traumatized does not necessarily make one a noble or productive person. Some women rise above it; others don't. Some victims of patriarchal violence want feminist support and advice; others don't. Some women want to be saved; others are too damaged to participate in their own redemption.

As feminist author bell hooks wrote, "It had become more than evident that individual black females suffering psychologically were not prepared to go out and lead the feminist revolution. Working with women, especially black women, I have found that many of us are willing to acknowledge the evils of sexism, the way it wounds and hurts everyone, but are reluctant to make that conversion to feminist thinking that would require substantive changes in habits of being." This applies to women of all colors.

As feminist clinician E. Kitch Childs said, "We have a moral responsibility to take care of ourselves. Women of color are not 'minorities.' We are, world-wide, in the majority. Black women in America are not taking care of ourselves. We need a whole new level of consciousness-raising groups and networks. We must learn to speak our bitterness about each other to each other. It will liberate our energies to keep on working together."

Often, those who condemn institutional psychiatry, Freudian psychoanalysis, grassroots feminist shelters and feminist therapies—all in the same breath—do not feel personally, professionally, or politically responsible for the female casualties of patriarchy and do not know how to listen to others—especially to women. Such critics, even if well intentioned, do not comprehend how healing it is to be listened to in a loving and skillful "holding" environment; or how psychologically wounded women, men, or politically active people also are.

Such critics may also be confusing the fact that quality mental health care is not available to all who want it with the question of whether or not quality mental health care exists at all.

We need Feminist Institutes of Mental Health that are both local and global; learning communities that last beyond our lifetimes; clinical training programs that are not patriarchal; health and spiritual retreats with intellectual, political, and legal agendas; places where feminists can come together to learn and teach in ways that are inspired, rigorous, humane, and healing.

I wanted to create such an Institute from the moment *Women and Madness* was on the way. In the early 1970s, Jeanette Rankin herself (!) actually offered me a physical structure in Athens, Georgia, to begin this work. Sadly, I did not accept her generous offer. I had too many other books to write and campaigns to organize. But others began to do this work.

For example, the Cambridge Hospital Victims of Violence (VOV) Program was cofounded in Massachusetts in 1984 by Drs. Mary Harvey and Judith Herman. It offers crisis intervention, supportive therapy, and group support to "survivors of rape, incest and childhood sexual abuse, domestic violence, and physical abuse/assault." A multidisciplinary staff develops programs, presents workshops, and conducts in-service trainings. VOV offers groups in Trauma Information, Parenting for Mothers with Trauma Histories, Time-Limited Rape Survivors Groups, Male Survivors of Childhood Trauma, etc.

We need such programs in every city, every community, worldwide.

The ideas in *Women and Madness* announced and anticipated many of the next steps in feminist theory and practice, including many of the themes I myself would subsequently explore.

For example, *Women and Madness* may have been the first Second Wave feminist work to discuss the mother-daughter relationship; the psychology of both incest and rape; the importance of female role models; the nature of female heroism; and the enduring role that mother and warrior goddesses play in the collective female unconscious. (They're role models—which was precisely the subject of my Ph.D. dissertation, "The Maternal Influence in Learning by Observation in Cats and Kittens," which I published in *Science* magazine, in 1969. The unconscious always moves in rather obvious ways.)

In addition to analyzing the mistreatment of madness and the sexism of mental health care, I wrote about what it means for women to be psychologically mothered—or maternally deprived. I also analyzed the essentially incestuous model of most male-female relations, i.e., most such pairings arc with ever-younger dauughter-like women and older father-like figures.

My major themes, first sounded in *Women and Madness*, unfolded in each of my fifteen subsequent books, and in countless lectures, articles, press conferences, congressional press hearings, lawsuits, and educational, political, and legal campaigns.

In 1976, in *Women, Money, and Power*, I analyzed women's psychological relationship to money and power. Despite enormous gains, this psychological relationship still remains constant. I also wrote about the "psycho-economics of female beauty." I addressed, early on, the danger of women's obsession with being thin, young, and beautiful, but I also attributed this to the growing power of advertising and pornography. In the same volume, my coauthor addressed economic realities from a legal point of view.

Many views attributed to me are based primarily on my work in *Women and Madness*. It remains a landmark work and I stand by it—but I have also moved on theoretically. I have changed my focus or my emphasis and I have also changed my mind. For example, I developed a more serious appreciation for and understanding of motherhood and the important role it plays in female psychology. My younger Amazon self rejected biological motherhood under patriarchal conditions as too difficult for an intellectual warrior. As I got older, I chose to become pregnant, and to have and to mother a child. Clearly, my views were changing.

And then, I wrote about motherhood in at least five of my subsequent books. For example, in 1978, in *About Men*, I wrote about male uterus envy in all its manifestations: psychological, economic, religious, and technological. At the time, I also wanted to understand men. For example, if they were, as a gender-caste, more powerful than women, how can we explain their dreadful conformity and obedience to other men and their utter dependence on women, whom they also needed to despise?

To correct the mother-blaming literature, I also discussed how fathers "kill" sons—psychologically, symbolically, and sometimes literally; and how male rage and anguish about not being loved and protected by other men is displaced onto women and children. I explored brotherhood, fratricide, and the mother-son bond. I ultimately related many of these themes to the patriarchal worship of death.

In 1979, in *With Child: A Diary of Motherhood*, I chose a literary approach to sound the great existential themes of pregnancy, childbirth, and newborn motherhood. I suggested that a psychological hero can also be a woman in labor, laboring; or a child being born; or a mid-wife assisting the process. Years later, when he was twenty-one, my beloved son Ariel wrote a wonderful new introduction to the volume.

In 1986, I published *Mothers on Trial: The Battle for Children and Custody*, and in 1987, I published *Sacred Bond: The Legacy of Baby M*.

Under patriarchy, mothers have no rights, only obligations. Mothers are women and as such, have never had custodial rights to their children in any country on earth. This slowly began to change in America at the turn of the twentieth century—but not by much. When fathers contested custody, even of infants, "good enough" mothers would consistently lose children due to (false) allegations of mental illness or sexual promiscuity.

Most people, including many second wave feminists, (who had enormous psychological ambivalence toward biological pregnancy and patriarchal motherhood), wrongfully assumed that mothers would somehow win their freedom by unjustly losing custody of their children to fathers who had never been primary child caretakers. Many feminists also assumed that paternal custody of children (even when the fathers were violent or neglectful) was still a sign of feminist progress.

In my opinion, the custody issue is, in a sense, the abortion controversy—but after birth. Thus, *Mothers on Trial* examines the history and importance of mothers losing custody of children when it was contested either by fathers or by the state. I also studied how mothers under custodial siege fight. They try to do so in heroically nonviolent ways. In *Sacred Bond* I looked at the psychiatric literature concerning adoption as well as surrogacy.

In 1985, the incomparable feminist historian and theorist Dale Spender, in an essay about *Women and Madness*, noted my concern with an absence of sisterhood among feminists and among women in general. Although no one noticed this (even I did not stress it), she was right, the information was already there. In 2002, after working on it on and off for nearly twenty years, I published *Woman's Inhumanity to Woman*, in which I spend three chapters discussing the mother-daughter relationship.

The egg, the origin, of this book was contained in *Women and Madness*. Here, in *Woman's Inhumanity to Woman*, I looked at the "darker" side of the Demeter-Persephone relationship, which is prefigured in the Clytemnestra-Electra relationship.

Psychologically, we are all *also* Electra (the Greek daughter who conspired in her mother's murder); certainly, we are all Electra's daughters. We too have conspired in psychological matricide and are therefore also mistrustful of our own daughters.

This material was quite explosive. When I first presented these ideas at a conference of feminist therapists in 1990, the place went wild. Therapists stood up to deny their own matricidal impulses; they also hotly denied that feminists had internalized any sexist beliefs or were competitive or aggressive toward each other.

And these were the *feminist therapists*.

My latest works also continue themes I first raised in *Women and Madness*. For example, I put together a "dream team" of experts to testify in the case of the so-called first female serial killer who was eventually executed in Florida. I wanted to expand the battered woman's defense to include prostituted women. I published several law review articles on the case and am still working on an unpublished manuscript.

In *Women of the Wall: Claiming Sacred Ground at Judaism's Holy Site* (2002), I discuss the ways in which women's full and public participation in religious rituals may also enhance women's self-esteem and authority. In *The New Antisemitism: The Current Crisis and What Must be Done About It*, I continue my anti-racism work, which, in this instance, concerns Jew-hatred among Islamists and among western intellectuals, including feminists.

Finally, in my newest book, *The Death of Feminism: What's Next in the Struggle for Women's Freedom*, I begin to outline Muslim, Middle Eastern, and Arab female and male psychology. I also analyze the dangers of Islamic gender Apartheid and implore westerners, especially feminists, to take a stand against it, both in principle and in practice. Once understandable, politically correct multicultural approaches have ultimately failed our founding feminist principles of espousing one universal standard of human rights for every woman. In the shadow of the attacks on 9/11 (New York City), 3/11 (Madrid), and 7/7 (London), we can no longer minimize or appease the dangers of Islamist terrorism, which includes misogyny.

The women who were institutionalized in the nineteenth century wrote with courage and integrity. They were moral, philosophical, often religious. Their frame of reference, and their use of language was romantic—Christian and Victorian. They wrote like abolitionists, transcendentalists, suffragists. The twentieth-century women were keen observers of human nature and asylum abuse—but they had no universal frame of reference. They faced "madness" and institutional abuse alone, without God, ideology, or sisterhood. What or who helped these women? Friends, neighbors, and sons sometimes rescued them; changes in the law did too.

But what else proved invaluable?

Phebe B. Davis (1865) wrote that "Kindness has been my only medicine"; Kate Lee (1902) of Illinois proposed that "Houses of Peace" be created, where women could learn a trade and save their money, after which they could "both be allowed and required to leave." Kate Lee suggested that such "Houses of Peace" "operate as a home-finder and employment bureau . . . thus giving each inmate a new start in life [which] in many cases [will] entirely remove the symptoms of insanity." Margaret Isabel Wilson (1931) wrote that "Nature was her doctor." *Leaving* the asylum helped Wilson. She wrote:

It took me months to get over the effects of my incarceration . . .
Through companionship, my appetite came back; I could sleep in peace,
and there was nobody to annoy me. There were no maniacal shrieks to

make me shudder; no attendants to yell out orders; no nurses to give me arsenic and physics; no doctors to terrify me . . . the things [I] sorely missed while institutionalized: (1) liberty; (2) my vote; (3) privacy; (4) normal companionship; (5) personal letters and uncensored answers; (6) useful occupation; (7) play; (8) contacts with intelligent minds; (9) pictures, scenery, books, good conversation; (10) appetizing food.

I agree with them all.

Thus, freedom and justice does wonders for one's mental health. So, in response to my esteemed brother Sigmund Freud's infamous query, what do women want? For starters, and in no particular order: freedom, food, nature, shelter, leisure, freedom from violence, justice, music, poetry, supportive families and communities, poetry, compassionate support during chronic or life-threatening illness and at the time of death, independence, books, physical/sexual pleasure, education, solitude, the ability to defend ourselves, love, ethical friendships, the arts, health, dignified and useful employment, political friendships.

MADNESS

Demeter and Clytemnestra Revisited

In the beginning, if there ever was such a time, Demeter, the goddess of life, gave birth to four daughters, whom she named Persephone, Psyche, Athena and Artemis. The world's first children were unremarkably happy. To amuse their mother—with whom they were all passionately in love—they invented language, music, laughter, and many more useful and boisterous activities.

One morning Persephone menstruated. That afternoon, Demeter's daughters gathered flowers to celebrate the loveliness of the event. A chariot thundered, then clattered into their midst. It was Hades, the middle-aged god of death, come to rape Persephone, come to carry her off to be his queen, to sit beside him in the realm of non-being below the earth, come to commit the first act of violence earth's children had ever known.

Afterwards, the three sisters agreed that he was old enough to be Persephone's father. Perhaps he was: who else could he be? There were no known male parents . . . and thus they each discovered that in shame and sorrow childhood ends, and that nothing remains the same.

Persephone's sisters came home without her. Demeter raged and wept. Her bones seemed to shrink, her cheeks became wrinkled. She bound up her hair and turned wanderer, but could not find her eldest daughter anywhere on earth. Finally the sun spoke and told Demeter what had happened, that her daughter was married and a queen. He counseled her:

"Why mourn the natural fate of daughters—to leave their mothers' home, to lose their virginity, to marry, and to give birth to children?"

Demeter was grieved beyond and before reasoning. Remembering an oracle's prophecy of a splitting, a scattering, and an exile, she said to the sun:

"Yea, if that be the natural fate of daughters, let all mankind perish. Let there be no crops, no grain, no corn, if this maiden is not returned to me."

Because Demeter was a powerful goddess, her wishes were commands and Persephone returned. Persephone still had to visit her husband once each year (in winter, when no crops could grow), but her union with him remained a barren one. Persephone was childless. Neither husband nor child—no stranger would ever claim her as his own. Persephone belonged to her mother. That was Demeter's gift to herself. (In those days, goddesses were still able to perform the miracle of "not choosing." They were both virgins and mothers, mortal and immortal, forever the same and forever changing.)

But "oh" and "oh" and "oh" sighed Persephone's sisters after they had seen everything: the maiden's helplessness and rape, the young bride's childlessness, the mother's suffering—the terrifying simplicity and repetition of it all.

"Yes," they said of the maiden and the mother, "yes, she rules both beneath and above the earth, but she cannot keep us here any longer."

Psyche was the first to speak. "I am beautiful some say more beautiful than all my sisters, and still no man claims me as his wife." (Actually, Psyche and Persephone looked quite alike: you could not tell them apart.) "Sisters! I am longing for love. I am lonely and frightened in our mother's house. I wish a husband—with strong and handsome eyes—and I wish to have a child."

Athena spoke next: "I am not beautiful—and care not for such things. (She was in fact exceedingly beautiful, but was very tall—even for the daughter of a goddess.) "Sisters! My childhood is over and must be relived. I wish to be born again—and of man. I wish to plot the clash of heroes from afar, dressed in the finest armor, moved by the finest wisdom. I wish for my own wholeness and not for children or a husband."

Artemis spoke last. (She too was tall, and of a darker complexion than her sisters.) "Sisters! Perhaps I wish for the impossible and will have to wander even farther than our mother did in search of it. I, too, want heroic clashes and great deeds. But I also want love and children. My head aches with visions of swords and altars, dazzling cities, and beautiful maidens. There is a music in my ears strange to our mother's house."

Well, as this conversation is common knowledge among schoolgirls, we know what each sister arranged for herself.

Psyche went home to plead for a husband. Demeter and Persephone were astounded by such a strange desire, yet they knew it must be satisfied. In secrecy, for such a thing had never before happened, Psyche was married to Eros—to Love himself, to Cupid, Aphrodite's son. Psyche lived alone with her husband, in a splendid palace, set high on a nameless mountain. Silent, invisible servants brought her whatever she wished. At night, and only at night, Love came to visit: Psyche's husband—but she didn't know who he was or what he looked like. Love had warned her never to look at him, but to love him in darkness. One midnight, after he had fallen asleep, Psyche lit a small oil lamp for a single, guilty look— and woke Love, who fled the palace. Miserable and frightened, Psyche set out to find him. After many near perilous failures, Love finally rescued his unhappy wife. He brought her to Heaven to live in an even more splendid palace. There, surrounded by the immortals, Psyche, Love, and their daughter, Pleasure, lived happily forever after—the first heavenly Holy Family.

Athena never returned to her mother's house. Instead, she went straight to Zeus, the god of gods, and proposed a bargain much to his vain and clever liking: to be re-born of him. She asked him to become her mother. And so Athena became twice-born, the second time of man. She emerged fully grown from Zeus's head, wearing the armor she so desired. Like Persephone, Athena remained childless and fiercely loyal to her one parent. Unlike Persephone, Athena was never raped, abducted, or made a king's unwilling queen. She needed no rescuing. If there was rescuing to do, Athena herself would do it. Indeed, she rescued many a male hero, helped him slay hideous monsters, capture unobtainable prizes, win great wars, and destroy ancient cities. This stately daughter of Demeter seemed to have no memory of her earthly and female origins. She never understood why certain men still insisted on sacrificing to her before planting and after harvesting. She smiled to herself. Didn't they know it was a strange tribute to one who had chosen her own parent—and, in so doing, had stopped turning on the wheel of repetition?

Artemis, the youngest of Demeter's daughters, returned to her mother's house. First she had Demeter consecrate her to the moon, so that no matter how far she'd have to wander, she would never forget, never betray her origins. That done, Artemis quickly perfected the arts of hunting and riding and warfare, of plant healing and midwifery. Then, with the moon for guide, she left to found a city—no, it was a tribe—no, it was a culture, the likes of which the world had never known. Every woman in it was a soldier and a mother, tears were as common as physical bravery, marriage was scorned, rape unthinkable, and the love of young girls praised in poems written by even the most hardened war veterans. Artemis herself had many female lovers, and many daughters, each of whom founded other Amazon cities in Africa, in South America, and elsewhere in Asia.

Goddesses never die. They slip in and out of the world's cities, in and out of our dreams, century after century, answering to different names, dressed differently, perhaps even disguised, perhaps idle and unemployed, their official altars abandoned, their temples feared or simply forgotten. What of Demeter and her four daughters?

Demeter, the goddess of life, and Persephone, her ghostly, embryonic maiden-daughter, were for a long time celebrated in elaborate secret ceremonies by the most sophisticated of the ancients, and more openly by everyone else. But somehow—no one really knows why—such celebrations of mothers and daughters certainly ceased. That which had gone before could no longer be worshiped. Fierce prophets proclaimed martial law against the past. Even fiercer prophets proclaimed martial law against the present. Monotheism changed the fate of mortals and immortals alike.

Still, not everything changed. Mother worship shifted, ever so subtly, ever so keenly, from Demeter to her daughter Psyche. Gentle Psyche, in love with Love, in love with marriage, was soon enshrined as the gentle Virgin Mother Mary, her daughter, Pleasure, became a son named Jesus. And it happened as quickly as this. Demeter was stripped of her powers, torn from her maidenhood, and exiled into history as a wretched, fearful wanderer. No longer was she a mother-goddess. Now Demeter appeared only as a stepmother, often a cruel one, or as a witch, often an evil one, come to haunt children in their fairy tales and nightmares. Children cried at the sight of her. Their fathers tortured and burned her many times at the stake.

And what of Persephone and Psyche and the Virgin Mary? Why, they became Cinderella, Snow White, the Sleeping Beauty, struck dumbly domestic by a Demeter turned stepmother. They all turned to princes and white knights to rescue them from this rather incomprehensible turn of events.

In our time, Psyche has three children but is very depressed. Lately, she never gets up before noon. The Virgin Mary is an alcoholic, hiding behind drawn shades. Persephone is frigid—and worries about it. Cinderella is anxious, paces back and forth a great deal, and has twice tried to kill herself.

In our time, the stepmother wander still—exiles, with no memory of what has gone before. Demeter has been known to curse at passing airplanes, to dress in shapeless mourning costumes, to talk to herself, to talk nonsense. . . . Often these days, when Demeter gives birth to a child, she abandons her then and there, turning her own face to the hospital wall. Sometimes, as in a trance, Demeter tries to keep her daughter at home with her again forever.

What of Artemis and Athena? Some say that Artemis and her daughters drowned in a flood—or, like angels, left earth in sorrow, before their work was done. Others say that after losing some very great battle, they killed themselves. Still others claim to have heard them decide to retreat, break up, and wait for better times. Even Athena, that most exceptional woman, had eventually to put away her shield and helmet, and take up books, rosaries, knitting needles, and gossip—and occasionally a royal crown or a university post.

Today both Artemis and Athena have increasingly been caught at violence—at crimes of passion, greed, even of honor. Most often, they do whatever is required of them, these proud and lonely two, do their jobs well, too well. Sometimes Athena, sometimes Artemis, is well known for some accomplishment—envied, admired, misunderstood—until she turns on the gas, poisons herself, drowns—and is done with it once more.

Demeter is only one face of the many-faced Great Mother archetype. And, Persephone is not always willing to compliantly merge with her mother, to repeat her mother's life. Many women may want but may also fear a relationship with a powerful, (over)protecting mother. The reunion of Demeter and Persephone requires a transformation in both mother and daughter: Demeter must overcome her rage and grief; Persephone must return—different, but still the same.

According to classical scholar Erich Neumann, "The Eternal Feminine" never lets anything go—in his words, it "tends to hold fast to everything that springs from it and to surround it like an eternal substance." Thus, the union and reunion of mother and daughter are fraught with peril and require enormous psychological generosity in each woman.

Nevertheless, most daughters long for their mothers' love, approval, support, wisdom, and protection. Maternal absence is suffered far more than maternal abuse. According to British psychoanalyst Nini Herman, a mother remains the object of her daughter's "deepest passion." Nini Herman believes that a "secure" and "fulfilled" mother can let her daughter grow, both intellectually and sexually. But, if she envies this "young competitor," her daughter may

> linger at the stage where she has a need to please, in order to obtain reassurance that her destructive phantasies and her hostile impulses have not caused lasting harm [to her mother.] Then she may turn out to be excessively preoccupied with making herself beautiful, because a beautiful body is felt to serve as evidence that all is well inside too.

The repetition of the maternal destiny is what terrifies many contemporary women who also want to enact paternal-heroic destinies. A daughter needs to differentiate herself from her mother, but the smallest difference is often experienced by both mother and daughter as a profound betrayal. Mother-daughter differences are maddening, but so are the similarities.

Some Demetrian mothers refuse to let their daughters go. They bind them with maternal envy, disapproval, anger, insecurity, depression; they remain merged together in embattled relationships.

It is important not to demonize mothers, but it is equally important not to deny the realities of maternal-daughter abuse. To escape the danger of being incorporated or destroyed by her mother, a daughter might have to "kill" her. This is precisely what the mythic Queen Clytemnestra's daughter, Electra, does.

According to Greek myth and drama, Queen Clytemnestra is the mother of three children: Iphigenia, Electra, and Orestes. She is also the wife of Agamemnon and the sister of Helen of Troy, who is married to Agamemnon's brother, Menelaus. Helen runs off with Paris, a prince of Troy. The two brothers mount an expedition, ostensibly to win Helen back, but also to win the riches of Troy. For more than a decade, the warrior-brothers lay siege to Troy, which some say was an earlier, matriarchal civilization.

Agamemnon tricks Clytemnestra into sending their daughter Iphigenia to visit him, presumably to betroth her to a great prince. Instead, her father ritually sacrifices her in full view of his troops as an offering to the gods. Agamemnon captures and destroys Troy, kills and enslaves its people, and sets sail for home. He brings his slave mistress, the Trojan visionary and princess Cassandra, back with him. His abandoned queen, Clytemnestra, has taken a lover, Aegisthus. Electra is wild with rage and grief. In her view, her mother has cheated her of everything: a father, a royal marriage, respectability. Clytemnestra insists, cruelly, on remaining the only sexual woman; Electra feels doomed to chastity and childlessness.

Clytemnestra refuses to yield to her daughter's inevitable sexual ascent. Electra is one of our earliest, patriarchal heroines. She is a daughter who does not identify with her mother; she hates her mother. Electra is a quintessential "Daddy's Girl." Like mother, like daughter. In different ways, both women prefer men, not women. This is precisely what they most hold against each other.

But, Electra is not merely competing with her mother for the same man: her father; she is also competing with her father/brother/sisters/mother's male lover, for the same woman: her mother.

Clytemnestra's daughter, Electra, conspires to kill her mother for having murdered Agamemnon. Electra plans her mother's murder; Orestes commits the matricide. Electra kills her mother "indirectly"; technically, her hands remain clean. Orestes is haunted and pursued by the (female) Furies. The tormented Orestes demands and receives a divine jury. The Gods are deadlocked. Athena, a male-identified goddess, casts the deciding vote in Orestes' favor. Henceforth, husband-murder is viewed as a more serious crime than matricide. The Furies do not pursue Electra. Her postmatricidal torment, if any, remains unknown to us.

To escape being swallowed alive by one's mother, many women psychologically enact the mythic Electra role: they psychologically murder their mother in order to replace her, to become her, to stand in her place. These primal psychological dramas take place in the theater of the unconscious. Just as women are all Persephone, merged, they are also all Electra, defiant and murderous; certainly, women are all Persephone/Electra's daughters. Like Electra, women are not necessarily haunted by the Furies afterward. What is amiss between Electra and Clytemnestra is what they already symbolize: The Fall, the end of (childhood's) mother-rule.

I have turned to these myths here and in other books because they embody tabooed, unconscious, psychological processes that are, nevertheless, normal, and because I need to find a way to pierce the amnesia that accompanies many female conversations about the "shadow side" of relationships between mothers and daughters and between women in general.

Nini Herman believes that the unresolved issues "which are active at the core of the mother-daughter dyad" are, to some extent, what psychologically holds women back and accounts for women's unconscious collusion with patriarchal edicts. I agree. Herman believes that the unexamined mother-daughter relationship is precisely where women are "obstinately marking time" rather than moving toward freedom.

This is a book about female psychology—or, if you will, about the many faces of Demeter and her four daughters. It is also about Clytemnestra, her daughter Electra, and about what has happened to them in the twentieth and twenty-first centuries, and how it has been viewed and treated in psychiatric settings. Certain myths reveal a great deal about the origins and models of contemporary female personality. I draw upon them often, as I describe the relationship between the female condition and what we call madness—that divinely menacing behavior from whose eloquence and exhausting demands society protects itself through "reason" and force.

This is a book about the dramatically increasing numbers of American girls and women of all classes and races, who are seen, or who see themselves, as "neurotic" or "psychotic," and who seek psychotherapeutic help and/or are psychiatrically hospitalized. This is a book about the many "whys" of such help-seeking behavior; about "what" is experienced and viewed as in need of help; and about "how" these women are or aren't—helped.

Chapters One and Ten discuss the basic psychological dimensions of female personality in our culture. Chapter One presents the lives and psychiatric histories of women, based on autobiographical, biographical, and case history material. These, and modern women in general, are viewed in terms of what growing up female in the family means. The mother-daughter relationship is analyzed, as is the role played by mythological or historical heroines, such as the Virgin Mary or Joan of Arc, in female experiences of "normality" and "abnormality." Chapter One describes how female reproductive biology, patriarchal culture, and the modern parent-daughter relationship have so combined as to insure such characteristically female behaviors—and ideals as self-sacrifice, masochism, reproductive narcissism, compassionate "maternality," dependency, sexual timidity, sexual frigidity and sexual promiscuity, father-worship— and the overwhelming dislike and devaluation of women.

Chapters Two and Three view both the mental asylum and private therapy as recapitulations or mirrors of the female experience in the family. Clinicians all too often treat their patients, most of whom are women, as "wives" and "daughters," rather than as people: treat them as if female misery, by biological definition, exists outside the realm of what is considered human or adult. A double standard of mental health—and humanity—one for women, another for men, seems to good-naturedly and unscientifically dominate most theories—and treatments—of women and men. Traditional and contemporary clinical theories and practices are reviewed in Chapter Three. A new definition or, rather, a different way of understanding female "psychiatric" symptoms (such as depression or frigidity), male "psychiatric" symptoms (such as alcohol and drug addiction, or sociopathic personality), and what we call madness (or schizophrenia) is presented in Chapter Two. The types of behaviors that are hospitalized in America are also related to caste (sex and race), age, class, and marital status.

Chapter Four presents an analysis of our nation's "mental illness" statistics. These chapters document the extent to which women, more than men, and in greater numbers than their existence in the general population would predict, are involved in "careers" as psychiatric patients: women who are depressed, anxious, agoraphobic, and who are having "nervous breakdowns," crying fits, temper tantrums, paranoid delusions; women who attempt suicide, who under- or overeat and who take unknown quantities of drugs to smother their anxieties, their hostilities, their ambitions, their panics, their sexual unhappiness—and their visions.

Chapters Four through Nine describe the patient "careers" of women whom I interviewed about their experiences in psychiatric hospitals and private or clinic outpatient therapy. The women I spoke with were of European, Latin-American, and African descent. Their ages ranged from seventeen to seventy. Their sexual, marital, maternal, and political involvements were as far-ranging. Only a minority of these women experienced what I would call genuine states of madness. Most were simply unhappy and self-destructive in typically (and approved) female ways. Their experiences made it very clear to me that help-seeking or help-needing behavior is not particularly valued or understood in our culture. Help-seekers are pitied, mistrusted, tranquilized, physically beaten, given shock therapy, lied to, yelled at, and ultimately neglected— and all "for their own good." Many women in American state mental asylums participated in sex-role-typed slave labor, i.e., they worked as domestics for no or token payment. Many were also medically abused— or neglected; sexually repressed—or exploited; ridiculed and abandoned—by family and professional establishments alike; and given very little "therapy," verbal or otherwise. Many women who were lucky or rich enough to buy the best verbal treatment therapists could offer were not always or often understood or helped.

It has never been my intention to romanticize madness, or to confuse it with political or cultural revolution: certainly because of the pain our mistreatment of it insures, certainly because of the pain that it may intrinsically involve. (Such pain is to be understood and respected—but never romanticized.) Most weeping, depressed women, most anxious and terrified women are neither about to seize the means of production and reproduction, nor are they any more creatively involved with problems of powerlessness, evil, and love than is the rest of the human race.

I speak in many voices throughout this book: as a psychological researcher, theoretician, and clinician—and as a literary and philosophical person, a lover of poetry and myths.

In bringing you this book, I feel like a time-traveler turned messenger, a bearer of bad news. I wonder how you will receive it, I wonder what will you do?

I first wrote about Demeter and Persephone in 1972. (I did not write about Clytemnestra and Electra until the mid-80s). I was indeed treated as a "bearer of bad news" by many, but as a visionary and truth-healer by many more. Women and some men responded to this work in many ways. Some quit their psychiatric residencies on the spot; I know, they told me. Others signed themselves out of mental asylums, left psychotherapy treatment, sued oppressive employers, and exited abusive marriages; some entered "feminist"-oriented therapies.

Many women joined feminist groups and began to understand that many of their personal problems were due to collective political realities. Some women discovered that they were lesbians, or celibate, or that they truly loved the husbands they already had. Some readers left feminist groups due to female-female hostility and bullying that some of us wrote about and called "trashing."

Most of my readers went on to become physicians, lawyers, judges, clergywomen, and mental health professionals. They did research and presented and published their findings. They saved and enhanced the quality of many lives. Many continue to battle entrenched patriarchal biases in their fields.

As I re-read this volume for the first time in many years, I was struck by how relevant it still is. I so much enjoyed visiting with my interviewees whose words remain as fresh and as haunting as when I first heard them. As you will see, I have, to some extent, expanded and updated each chapter. Now, I stand on the shoulders of all of those who came after me and who have continued the work, as I have also done.

I wonder how much more I will have to say for the fiftieth anniversary edition of this book?

CHAPTER ONE

WHY MADNESS?

ATHENA:

For I did not have a mother who bore me.

No, all my heart praises the male.

Aeschylus, *The Oresteia*

Sigh no more, ladies

Time is male

and in his cups dr inks to the fair.

Bemused by gallantry, we hear

our mediocrities over-praised,

indolence read as abnegation,

slattern thought styled intuition,

every lapse forgiven, our crime

only to cast too bold a shadow

or smash the mould straight off.

For that, solitary confinement,

tear gas, attrition shelling.

Few applicants for that honor.

Adrienne Rich[1]

CHARLOTTE CORDAY:

Now I know what it is

like when the head is

cut off the body. . . .

In my room in Caen on

the table under the

open window lies open

the Book of Judith.

Dressed in her legendary beauty

she entered the tent of the enemy

and with a single blow,

slew him.

Peter Weiss[2]

"The first time a boy hurt me" said Lillian to Djuna "it was in school. I don't remember what he did. But I wept. And he laughed at me. Do you know what I did? I went home and dressed in my brother's suit. I tried to feel as the boy felt. Naturally as I put on the suit I felt I was putting on a costume of strength. . . . I thought that to be a boy meant one did not suffer. That it was being a girl that was responsible for the suffering. . . . Then there was another thing. . . . I discovered one relief, and that was action. . . . I felt if only I could join the war, participate, I wouldn't feel the anguish and the fear . . . if only they would let me be Joan of Arc. Joan of Arc wore a suit of armor, she sat on a horse, she fought side by side with the men. She must have gained their strength."

Anais Nin[3]

The surprising thing about the myths of Demeter . . . is her restless search for her [raped and abducted] daughter [Persephone] . . . a great Goddess could . . . in a single figure which was at once Mother and Daughter . . . represent the motifs that recur in *all* mothers and daughters.

C. Kerenyi[4]

Perhaps the angry and weeping women in mental asylums are Amazons returned to earth these many centuries later, each conducting a private and half-remembered search for her Motherland—a search we call madness. Or perhaps they are failed Goddess-Mothers, Demeters, eternally and miserably unable to find their daughters or their powers. . . .

> (A romantic thought of my own)

There is nothing wrong with me—except I was born at least two thousand years too late. Ladies of Amazonian proportions and Berserker propensities have passed quite out of vogue and have no place in this too damned civilized world . . . here I sit—mad as the hatter—with nothing to do but either become madder and madder or else recover enough of my sanity to be allowed to go back to the life which drove me mad.

> Lara Jefferson[5]

WOMEN IN ASYLUMS: FOUR LIVES

Mrs. Elizabeth Packard (1816-c. 1890)
Mrs. Ellen West (c.1890-c. 1926)
Mrs. Zelda Fitzgerald (1900-1948)
Mrs. Sylvia Plath Hughes (1932-1963)

HOW DID AMERICAN WOMEN GET INTO ASYLUMS IN THE PAST? The answer is: against their will and without prior notice. Here is what happened. Suddenly, unexpectedly, a perfectly sane woman might find herself being arrested by a sheriff; removed from her bed at dawn, or "legally kidnapped" on the streets, in broad daylight. Or: her father or husband might ask her to accompany him to see a friend to help him with a legal matter. Unsuspecting, the woman might find herself before a judge or a physician, who certified her "insane" on her husband's say-so. Why did this happen?

Battering, drunken husbands had their wives psychiatrically imprisoned as a way of continuing to batter them; husbands also had their wives
imprisoned in order to live or marry with other women.

Ada Metcalf (1876), of Illinois, wrote: "It is a very fashionable and easy
thing now to make a person out to be insane. If a man tires of his wife, and
if befooled after some other woman, it is not a very difficult matter to get
her in an institution of this kind. Belladonna and chloroform will give her
the appearance of being crazy enough, and after the asylum doors have
closed upon her, adieu to the beautiful world and all home associations."

At thirty-two, the unmarried Adriana Brinckle (1857), of Pennsylvania, conducted an economic transaction of her own: she sold some
furniture. Charges were brought against her for selling furniture for which
she had not fully paid. For the crime of embarrassing her physician
father's sense of "family honor," Brinckle's father and his judge-friend
sentenced Brinkle to twenty-eight years in a psychiatric hospital.

In 1861, Susan B. Anthony and Elizabeth Cady Stanton wrote: "Could
the dark secrets of those insane asylums be brought to light . . . we would
be shocked to know the countless number of rebellious wives, sisters and
daughters that are thus annually sacrificed to false customs and conven-
tionalisms, and barbarous laws made by men for women."

Most women in asylums were not insane. According to Adeline T.P.
Lunt (1871), "A close, careful study and intimacy with these patients
(finds no) irregularity, eccentricity, or idiosyncracy, either in language,
deportment, or manner, than might be met with in any society of women
thrown together, endeavoring to make the most of life under the most
adverse and opposing circumstances."

However, psychiatrically hospitalized women feared, correctly, that
they might be driven mad by the brutality of the asylum itself, and by their
lack of legal rights as women, and as prisoners. As Adriana Brinckle,
wrote: "An insane asylum. A place where insanity is made." Sophie Olsen
(1862) wrote: "O, I was so weary, weary; I longed for some Asylum from
'Lunatic Asylums!'"

During the nineteenth and twentieth centuries these four women—
Elizabeth Packard, Ellen West, Zelda Fitzgerald and Sylvia Plath—were

hospitalized for various psychiatric "symptoms." All were uncommonly stubborn, talented, and aggressive. Some became socially withdrawn: they no longer cared how they "looked," they refused to eat, they became sexually disinterested in their husbands. One woman "heard" things. Two others repeatedly attempted to kill themselves. Ellen West and Sylvia Plath finally committed suicide when they were in their early thirties. Zelda Fitzgerald burned to death in a mental asylum fire. Elizabeth Packard managed to escape after three years in an Illinois asylum. She published an account of her hospital experience and fought for the legal rights of mental patients and married women.

These women share a rather fatal allegiance to their own uniqueness. For years they denied themselves—or were denied—the privileges and rewards of talent. Like many women, they buried their own destinies in romantically extravagant marriages, in motherhood, and in approved female pleasure. However, their repressed energies eventually struggled free, demanding long overdue and therefore heavier prices: marital and maternal "disloyalty," social ostracism, imprisonment, madness, and death.

There is at least one important difference between Elizabeth Packard and the other women. Packard was a devout believer in both Christianity and motherhood. Romantic passion, doubt, creative egoism, and anguish were either flawlessly subdued or never part of her grandly practical sensibility. Her sins of individuality concerned religious freedom. Packard's husband literally forbade her to express her own opinions on theological matters. Her conscience did not allow her to obey him. Unlike Packard, Fitzgerald, West, and Plath were not churchgoers. They were impractical and romantic. And unlike Packard, these three women were as dangerously wedded to Eros—to love—as was his first and mythological wife Psyche.

According to myth, Psyche remains unmarried despite (or because) of her great physical beauty. Finally, in desperation, her parents consult an oracle. They are advised to abandon their daughter on a mountain crag. Symbolically speaking, they abandon her to the inevitable Virgin's death (in marriage), and to an unknown, possibly bestial husband. But Psyche's husband is none other than Eros (Amor), Aphrodite's son. Psyche is ecstatically happy: she is also very lonely. Her husband visits her only at night, under cover of darkness, and she is warned against "seeing" him. When Psyche finally violates this wifely taboo, Eros flees. Psyche must then perform a series of "Hero's" tasks in order to be reunited with Eros, bear their child, and constitute a Holy Family in heaven.[6]

Like Psyche's, the Packard, Fitzgerald, West, and Plath marriages were consecrated in darkness. Unlike Psyche, however, they failed—or refused—to complete the maiden's pilgrimage toward divine marriage and motherhood. Esther Greenwood, Plath's heroine in her autobiographical novel *The Bell Jar*, says:

> . . . one of the reasons I never wanted to get married [was that] the last thing I wanted was intimate security and to be the place an arrow shoots off from. I wanted change and excitement and to shoot off in all directions myself . . . the trouble was, I hated the idea of serving men in any way. I wanted to dictate my own thrilling letters . . . maybe [marriage and children] was like being brainwashed and afterwards you went about numb as a slave in some private totalitarian state. . . .[7]

Ellen West was a wealthy, sensitive, and suicidal young married woman whose fear of eating was so great that she eventually refused to eat at all. (This symptom was psychiatrically interpreted as a fear of becoming pregnant. Ludwig Binswanger, her "anthropological case historian," recorded her life and psychiatric history.[8]) West is presented to us as having preferred "trousers" and "lively, boyish games" until she was sixteen. Her childhood motto was "Either Caesar or nothing." In a poem written when she was seventeen, she expressed the desire "to be a soldier, fear no foe, and die joyously, sword in hand." She became an ardent horsewoman, diarist, and poet. After feverishly and competently performing a variety of approved female activities (doing volunteer work with children, taking non-matriculated university courses, engaging in serious love affairs), she grew suicidal and stopped eating. She said:

. . . something in me rebels against becoming fat. Rebels against becoming healthy, getting plump red cheeks, becoming a simple, robust woman, as corresponds to my true nature. . . . For what purpose did nature give me health and ambition? . . . It is really sad that I must translate all this force and urge to action into unheard words [in her diary], instead of powerful deeds. . . . I am twenty-one years old and am supposed to be silent and grin like a puppet. I am no puppet. I am a human being with red blood and a woman with quivering heart. . . . Oh, what shall I do, how shall I manage it? . . . I am not thinking of the liberation of the soul; I mean the real, tangible liberation of people from the chains of their oppressors. . . . I want a revolution, a great uprising to spread over the entire world and overthrow the whole social order. I should like to forsake home and parents like a Russian nihilist, to live among the poorest of the poor and make propaganda for the great cause. Not for the love of adventure! No, no! Call it the unsatisfied urge to action. . . .[9]

Zelda Fitzgerald's husband was a famous writer who was (therefore) incapable of understanding or nurturing his wife's talents. Scott Fitzgerald experienced Zelda's dancing lessons as pathetic and foolish. Nancy Milford, in her excellent biography of Zelda Fitzgerald,[10] quotes Scott's letter to Dr. Forel, one of Zelda's psychiatrists, in which Scott complains that for the last six months, Zelda had taken no interest in their child.[*] Dr. Forel pointed out that before Zelda had become "devoted" to the ballet, she had devoted herself to her tasks as a wife and mother. He described her increasing absorption with dancing, dancers, and with *herself* as distressingly egoistic and boring. Scott explains his own alcoholism in terms of Zelda's growing individuality and "madness." He told the doctor that he had to fortify himself with wine in order to put up with a woman whose tastes were different or "diverging" from his own. Although he describes her behavior—or its effects on him—as embarrassing and "maddening" he still

---

[*](I was unable to obtain permission to quote directly from Scott and Zelda Fitzgerald's letters and conversations with each other and with Zelda's various psychiatrists. However, the material is completely available in Nancy Milford's book.)

recognized a certain boldness and honesty in Zelda's actions. In describing her, Scott's tone ranges from self-pity and impatience with Zelda's stubborn childishness to a sense of real loss and concern for her.

Scott was extremely jealous and threatened by Zelda's considerable literary talent. He reacted with fury when Zelda completed an autobiographical novel before Scott had finished his own novel—a "story" of Zelda's life and psychiatric confinement. In a letter to Dr. Meyer, another of Zelda's many male psychiatrists, Scott admitted that perhaps Zelda could have developed into a genius if they had never met. But the fact was that they did meet and marry, and her insistence on a career as an author was hurting Scott and their daughter. Zelda was being entranced, practically "possessed," by dreams of success and recognition dangerously like his own. Zelda's "genius," an adolescent and demonic inconvenience, really, was hurting him and their marriage. Certainly, Zelda experienced and was broken by this very conflict. Milford quotes from the stenographic transcription of a conversation between Zelda, Scott, and Dr. Rennie, Zelda's psychiatrist in 1933. Scott accuses Zelda, rather hysterically, of being a "writer of limited talent" and reminds her of his worldwide literary reputation. Milford notes that "Scott had some very fixed ideas of what a woman's place should be in a marriage." He thought of himself as being in charge—something like a pilot charting the course. He was firm in his resolve that Zelda halt her efforts to write fiction. (When monkeys and serving wenches begin to write, can the Eumenides be far behind?) Zelda says she does not want to be "dependent" on Scott, either financially or psychologically. She wants to be a "creative artist": she wants "work." Only if she does "good work" can she defend herself against Scott's slighting comments. She says she is tired of being forced into accepting Scott's opinions and decisions about everything. In fact, she would not do so, she would rather be hospitalized. She feels that their marriage has been nothing but a struggle from the beginning. Scott's reply to this was that as a couple they were envied by the world. She suggested that they had put on a very good show.

In her paper entitled, "The Paradox of the Happy Marriage," Jessie Bernard has shown that men, in general, have different (more positive) opinions about their marriages than their wives do. Many husbands expect less from marriage than their wives and gain more in terms of domestic and sexual convenience and in emotional support.[11]

In 1860, Elizabeth Packard's husband psychiatrically imprisoned her because she dared to engage in "free religious inquiry."[12] She insisted on teaching her Bible class that human beings are born "good" and "not evil."

Packard's husband, a clergyman, kidnapped her against her will (although he was within his legal rights to do so) and removed her to an asylum at Jacksonville, Illinois. He forbade her children, whose ages ranged from eighteen months to eighteen years, to communicate with or talk about her. He kept her own (inherited) income from her. He deprived her of her clothes, books, and personal papers and misrepresented her situation to her parents. Dr. MacFarland, the psychiatrist-director of the asylum, remaindered her outgoing mail and seized her few books and smuggled-in writing paper. Despite these events, Mrs. Packard never lost her "wits." She always referred to the asylum as a "prison"—and never as a "hospital." She began a secret diary of asylum events and ministered to the other inmates, most of whom she regarded as sister-victims of the patriarchy. However, she still believed in marriage and in male chivalry; she never wanted a divorce. She was thoroughly devoted to her children, and to a (male) Godhead. She "forgave" Dr. MacFarland his "sins"—until, in a moment of fury, he nearly strangled her normally docile roommate, Bridget. (Bridget had refused to do some domestic dirty work for him, and the doctor became enraged.) After this, Mrs. Packard was

> . . . converted from the theological error of vicarious suffering. I have never since asked my Father to let me bear the punishment of any other brother or sister, due them for their own sins; neither have I asked any other intelligence to bear punishment due me for my own sins.

Her account of asylum abuses is lucid and at times brilliant. She describes many female asylum suicides as due to constant harassment, loneliness, and despair. She condemns the "torture" of women who *she* felt were really "witless." It is Elizabeth Packard who first made the analogy of Institutional Psychiatry and the Inquisition.

In Christian times, women have also been murdered, not only as "witches" but as "religious heretics" who espoused more sexual and compassionate creeds than their male counterparts. For example, in the sixteenth century, during the reign of England's Henry VIII (the royal Bluebeard), Anne Askew was accused of heresy and sentenced to death. She reminded the Lord Chancellor that, according to the Scriptures, neither Christ nor his disciples had ever put anyone to death. She argued religious doctrine for two hours after being submitted to the rack, and was burned to death later that year. In America, in the seventeenth century, Anne Hutchinson was excommunicated from the Church and exiled from Boston for being a powerful "preacher woman." Interestingly enough, she too emphasized more love, gentleness, mercy, and peace—within this lifetime—than did the male Puritan authorities. Mrs. Anne Yale, Lady Deborah Moody, Mrs. King, and Mrs. Tilton were all excommunicated in New Haven for publicly opposing the "baptism of infants" (male churchly maternity). Mary Dyer was exiled from Boston and eventually hanged there for Quakerism; she had supported Anne Hutchinson.[13]

Some psychiatrically institutionalized women believed that something really was wrong with them. The talented and well-connected Catharine Beecher (1855), and the feminist writer Charlotte Perkins Gilman (1886), wanted "help" for their overwhelming fatigue and depression. Beecher, after years of domestic drudgery, and Gilman, after giving birth, found themselves domestically disabled. Gilman couldn't care for her infant daughter; Beecher could no longer sew, mend, fold, cook, clean, serve, or entertain. Beecher wrote:

"What (my sex) had been trained to imagine the highest earthly felicity (domestic life), was but the beginning of (heartaches) care, disappointment, and sorrow, and often led to the extremity of mental and physical suffering . . . there was a terrible decay of female health all over the land."

Nevertheless, both women blamed themselves; neither viewed their symptoms as possibly the only way they could (unconsciously) resist or protest their traditional "feminine" work—or overwork. Beecher and Gilman described how they weren't helped or, how their various psychiatric cures damaged them even further. In Gilman's words, Dr. S. Mitchell Weir ordered her to

> live as domestic a life as possible. Have your child with you all the time. (Be it remarked that if I did but dress the baby it left me shaking and crying—certainly far from a healthy companionship for her, to say nothing of the effect on me.) Lie down an hour after each meal. Have but two hours' intellectual life a day. And never touch pen, brush or pencil as long as you live.

This regime only made things worse. A desperate Gilman decided to leave her husband and infant to spend the winter with friends. Ironically, she wrote, "from the moment the wheels began to turn, the train move, I felt better."

Sylvia Plath's life is known to us through her own writing, through various biographical materials, and, increasingly, through new facts and writings her recent "death-cult" popularity has made available. Many of Plath's contemporary admirers are, of course, women. Their admiration is rooted in their recognition of her fine poetry and, especially, in how finely it speaks to the female condition. Plath is also an excellent Christ-figure: and women, like men, have never had any trouble worshiping a victim "they" have destroyed or, more particularly, in "forgiving" a talented woman her talent—after her death.

Plath grew up in Massachusetts and began writing poems and stories when she was very young. Her poems and her autobiographical novel, *The Bell Jar*, describe her battle as an *artist* with the female condition—a battle she did not necessarily see in feminist terms. Before she was thirty, Plath attempted suicide, was psychiatrically hospitalized, finished college, published her work, got married, moved to England, and became the mother of two children. A. Alvarez, in a memoir of Plath, says that

> . . . in those [English] days, Sylvia seemed effaced: the poet taking a back

seat to the young mother and housewife. . . . Considering the conditions in which she worked, her productivity was phenomenal. She was a full-time mother with a two-year-old daughter, a baby of ten months, and a house to look after. By the time the children were in bed at night she was too tired for anything more strenuous than "music and brandy and water." So she got up very early each morning and worked until the children woke. . . . In those dead hours between night and day, she was able to gather herself into herself in silence and isolation, almost as though she were reclaiming some past innocence and freedom before life got a grip on her. Then she could write. For the rest of the day she was shared among the children, the housework, the shopping, efficient, bustling, harassed, like every other housewife.[14]

Of course, "housework" and "motherhood" are not necessarily more time-consuming or degrading than a fifteen-hour day in an office, factory, or coal mine. But then, most male poets do not work in coal mines, and for such long hours. Somehow, once recognized, they gain some sort of acceptance, however seedy, however limited, by the male literary brother-hood. Not so for Plath. Alvarez notes that he was at first shocked that Sylvia *Plath* was Mrs. Sylvia *Hughes*. He reacted to her as to a "bright young housewife." Although he came to respect her work enormously, he became Ted's and not Sylvia's drinking mate and occasional friend. With great honesty, he retells his early reactions to such strongly feminist poems as *Daddy* and *Lady Lazarus*: he was "appalled . . . at first hearing, the things [poems] seemed to be not so much poetry as assault and battery." Many later critics, including female critics, have felt the same way. Plath was lonely and isolated. Her genius did not earn for her certain reprieves and comforts tendered the male artist. No one, and especially men of culture, felt "responsible" for her plight or felt responsible to honor the poet by "saving" the woman. After separating from her husband, Plath continued to write and keep house for her children. On the night of February 10, or the morning of February 11, 1963, she killed herself.

Those of us who love Plath's poetry and who have read what Plath has written about her relationship to her mother and about her psychiatric hospitalization tend to view Plath sympathetically. Many have viewed her as a feminist martyr, trapped in the 1950s, cruelly abandoned by a philandering husband. There is, however, another side to Plath. Biographer Anne Stevenson, in *Bitter Fame: A Life of Sylvia Plath*, described Plath as

> first the bright and smiling mask that she presented to everyone, and then, through that, the determined, insistent, obsessive, impatient person who snapped if things did not go her way, and (who) flew into sudden rages. Plath wrote that "if anyone ever disarranged my things I'd feel as if I had been raped intellectually." Indeed, when a friend penciled some passages in a book she had borrowed from Plath, "she brought down the wrath of the avenging angel."

According to Dr. Christine Anne Lawson in *Understanding the Border-line Mother*, Plath—and other "borderline hermit mothers"—might view suicide as an "accomplishment," a "last act of free will." Lawson, quoting from the Stevenson, Hughes, and McCullough biographies of Plath, suggests that Plath was cold, secretive, asocial, "guarded her lesson plans as though they contained classified information," and was "intensely jealous." According to Lawson, long before her husband, the poet Ted Hughes, had been unfaithful to her, Plath assumed that he had. Once, while Hughes was at a business meeting, Plath ". . . became hysterical and destroyed his manuscripts, as well as his favorite book, The Complete Works of Shakespeare, in a vicious display of unbridled rage, irrational jealousy, and paranoia. Hughes later confided in a friend that the incident was a turning point in their marriage."

Few feminist supporters—myself included—ever paused to acknowledge that Plath, the victim, could also be Plath, the victimizer. Indeed, this is precisely how intergenerational patterns of pathology tend to work. In Plath's view, her own mother, Aurelia, had dominated her children through martyrdom. Plath wrote:

> The Children were her salvation. She put them First. Herself bound to the track naked and the train called Life coming with a frown and a

choo-choo around the bend. The burden upon Redeeming children is
too great, unfair. What to do with her, with the hostility, undying, which
I feel for her? . . . She's a killer. Watch out. She's deadly.

These four women were treated and/or imprisoned by male psychiatrists—most of whom were, quite literally, agents for their husbands'
"will." Packard's psychiatrist-jailer offered to testify for her husband at her
insanity hearing. Dr. MacFarland knew that Elizabeth Packard was not
"mentally ill." After sexually approaching her and being rebuffed, he
abandoned her to the brutality and anonymity of the "back wards." She
clearly saw that Dr. MacFarland's "cure" was the "subjection of the wife to
the husband's will." Her "therapy" consisted of imprisonment and domestic servitude to the other women. She washed them, prayed with them,
comforted them, and tried to shield them from beatings. She also freely
"chose" to participate in slave labor.

By sewing for the State, as its imprisoned slave, I can buy the
privilege of exchanging the putrid, loathsome air of the ward, for the
more wholesome purer atmosphere of the sewing room for half a day.
[The male inmates could choose to work on Dr. MacFarland's private
farm.]

Such slave labor still exists in rural American state mental asylums:
the jobs are neatly parceled out along sex-role lines.

According to her biographer, Barbara Sapinsley, Elizabeth Packard
"herself was locked in the screen room [solitary confinement], for trying
to help a patient who was being straightjacketed for screaming with pain
from an injury acquired during an earlier punishment. The nurse in
charge was eventually dismissed for abusing patients and six months later
reappeared as a patient herself." Undaunted, Elizabeth "took charge" of
the Eighth Ward. She ministered to her sisters in bondage. She washed
(both them and their rooms, daily), comforted, and prayed with them.
She tried to shield them from beatings and from suicide. Against all odds,
Elizabeth never lost her "wits."

Theophilus, her husband, forbade their children, whose ages ranged from eighteen months to eighteen years, to communicate with or talk about her. He kept her inherited income from her, deprived her of her clothes, books, and personal papers and misrepresented her situation to her father and brothers. Dr. Andrew McFarland, the psychiatrist-director of the asylum, remaindered her outgoing mail and seized her few books and smuggled-in writing paper.

For three and a half years, Elizabeth was not allowed to see her minor children. Elizabeth finally convinced the asylum trustees that she was God-fearing and sane. After forty-two months, Elizabeth was released to her oldest son who had just turned twenty-one—*but against her will*. Fiercely logical, Elizabeth did not want to return to Theophilus' custody since he had the power to commit her again somewhere else. (And would soon try to do exactly that).

Theophilus was unemployed and at home, full-time. The house was dirty, the children disheveled. Theophilus forbid the children to speak to their mother. He also intercepted Elizabeth's mail, forbid her to leave the house, and then locked her in the bedroom. After six weeks of being a prisoner in her own home, Elizabeth smuggled out a note. Friends took the note to a judge who issued a writ of habeas corpus. Before Theophilus could act on his plan to psychiatrically imprison her again, this time in Massachusetts, Theophilus first had to prove to a jury in Kankakee, Illinois, that Elizabeth was, in fact, "insane." The trial was a sensation. The local ladies turned out in full force in support of Elizabeth. In 1864, a jury of twelve men "acquitted" Elizabeth of insanity. She returned home, triumphant, only to discover that Theophilus had mortgaged her dowry-bought house and fled to Massachusetts with their underage children. Elizabeth was homeless and penniless.

Thus, she began selling a printed version of her *Asylum* writings to passersby for ten cents apiece. From 1864 on, Elizabeth supported herself by selling copies of her autobiography entitled *Modern Persecution: Insane Asylums Unveiled* (Vol. 1) and *Married Women's Liabilities* (Vol. 2). She drafted bills on behalf of the rights of married women to retain their own wages, and to be heard by a jury, or a judge, before being committed to an asylum. She championed the rights of mental patients to send and receive mail.

In 1865, the Illinois State Legislature passed what became known as "Mrs. Packard's Personal Liberty Bill." Elizabeth was maligned as "insane," a follower of "spiritualism" and "Goddess worship," a "strumpet," and "immoral." Elizabeth understood that to obtain justice for herself meant obtaining it for others in her situation. Utterly canny, clear-sighted, *Elizabeth* wanted to be sure that Theophilus had no legal right to hospitalize her again; no way of seizing her earnings or real property; no right to deny her any visitation or to retain custody of their minor children. She miraculously prevailed.

Zelda Fitzgerald's psychiatrists, in Nancy Milford's words, tried to "re-educate her in terms of her role as wife to Scott." When Zelda said she wanted to be an artist, her male psychiatrist asked her whether being a famous writer would be more important to her than her life with Scott. Holding up the specter of old age and lovelessness, he asked her whether that would be enough for her when she was over sixty. All of Zelda's psychiatrists consulted with Scott about his wife's "condition" and about what was "good" for her. In 1931, when Zelda was released after a year and three months of treatment, her "case" was summarized as an inferiority complex—particularly toward Scott. The psychiatrists declared her ambitions to be forms of self-deceptions, which had deeply troubled their marriage. Over the years, despite Zelda's pitiful requests for freedom, her obedient confessions of self-blame, and her promises of "good behavior," the men decided if and when she could spend "vacations" outside the asylum.

Zelda tells Scott that she is so unhappy she would rather be in an asylum. His response is cold and defensive: he doesn't care to hear such things. Zelda, in heroically and tragically self-destructive fashion, sees that there is no difference between being hospitalized and being married. She would rather be open about it; she would rather stop the social lie. Let her dependency, helplessness, abandonment, and unhappiness be seen for what it was. Of course, Zelda remains a financial and psychological burden to Scott—one that he bears—as long as she is willing to isolate herself and view herself as "sick" or "bad." However, neither "madness" nor mental asylums offered her "asylum" or "freedom."

Plath's autobiographical heroine, Esther Greenwood, remains unmarried but is sent to a male psychiatrist named Dr. Gordon. He sits, happily enthroned at his polished desk, surrounded by books and family photographs. Esther wonders:

> How could this Dr. Gordon help me anyway, with a beautiful wife and beautiful children and a beautiful dog haloing him like the angels on a Christmas card?

He intones the standard "suppose you try and tell me what you think is wrong" and Esther

> . . . turned the words over suspiciously like round, sea-polished pebbles that might suddenly put out a claw and change into something else. What did I think was wrong? I only thought it was wrong.

Dr. Gordon recommends shock therapy for her. Plath's description of this treatment of choice for "manic-depressives," most of whom are women, is as follows:

> Doctor Gordon was fitting two metal plates on either side of my head. He buckled them into place with a strap that dented my forehead, and gave me a wire to bite.
>
> I shut my eyes.
>
> There was a brief silence, like an indrawn breath. Then something bent down and took hold of me and shook me like the end of the world. Whee-ee-ee-ee, it shrilled, through an air crackling with blue light and with each flash a great jolt struck me till I thought my bones would break and the sap fly out of me like a split plant.
>
> I wondered what terrible thing it was that I had done.

One of Ellen West's psychiatrists, thought she was getting better because

> . . . whereas during the summer she was repulsively ugly, since then she
> has grown more and more feminine and almost pretty.

During one of her asylum periods she, like Esther Greenwood, developed a "homo-erotic" attachment—which, of course, was certainly not encouraged. West's last letter before fatally poisoning herself was written to this woman.

Fitzgerald, Plath, and West were desperately and defiantly at odds with the female role. They attempted to escape its half-life by "going crazy." Plath describes the asylum inmates as "blank and stopped as a dead baby." There, as "helpless" and "self-destructive" children, they were superficially freed from their female roles as wives and mothers. Plath correctly saw that there was nothing very different about

> . . . us in Belsize and the girls playing Bridge and gossiping in the college
> to which I would return. Those girls, too, sat under bell jars of a sort.

Uncannily, Ellen West also referred to her condition as being in a "glass ball."

> I feel myself excluded from all real life. I am quite isolated. I sit in a
> glass ball. I see people through a glass wall, their voices come to me
> muffled. . . . I stretch out my arms toward them; but my hands merely
> beat against the walls of my glass ball.

All four women existed under a "bell jar"—both inside and outside the asylum. For them, madness and confinement were both an expression of female powerlessness and an unsuccessful attempt to reject and overcome this state. Madness and asylums generally function as mirror images of the female experience, and as penalties for *being* "female," as well as for desiring or daring *not* to be. If the dare is enacted deeply or dramatically enough, death (through slow or fast suicide) ensues. I. J. Singer portrays this in "The Dead Fiddler," a story about a young girl's possession by a dybbuk or demon.[15] The girl, Liebe Yentl, is reared in an orthodox Jewish household in which her father "paid little attention to her (and) prayed to God to send her the right husband." Despite this, she spends most of her time alone, reading. She "complained that the girls of the town were common and backward: as soon as they were married they became careless and slovenly." A marriage is arranged, but the groom dies before the wedding. A second betrothal is arranged, but unconsummated, as Liebe Yentl is "invaded" by a dybbuk—with a male voice. The dybbuk is a boisterous adventurer—a fiddler—who demands liquor, laughingly insults the townspeople, both quotes and mocks the Torah—and all in singsong rhyme. Soon the fiddler has the village dancing in Liebe Yentl's bedroom, as he-she

> . . . told each one exactly what he was: a miser or a swindler, a sycophant
> or a beggar, a slattern or a snob . . . most of the time he heaped mud and
> ashes upon the respected leaders of the community and their wives . . .
> his jests provoked both astonishment and laughter.

Suddenly, Liebe Yentl is invaded by a second, and female, dybbuk, who is a barmaid and whore. Beyle Tslove, for that is her name, sings "ribald songs and soldiers' ditties." She calls Liebe Yentl's father a "short Friday—nothing but bone and beard."

Liebe Yentl is able to avoid an unwanted husband through her "madness"—it is the only way she can. Only in "madness" can she also tyrannize her parents, inspire fear and respect, "name" reality as she sees it, criticize the community's hypocrisy, and engage in some very "unfeminine" behavior: drinking, boasting, and dirty-joke telling. It is important to note that she doesn't become a rabbi or a highway-woman; she remains in a feminine reclining position. After the two dybbuks depart her body, Liebe Yentl still refuses to marry her parents' bridegroom choice. Isolation, poverty, neglect, and death are her fate. She is discovered dead, one day

. . . among piles of garbage, in a long shift, barefoot, her red hair loose.
It was obvious that she had not been among the living for many days.

MOTHERS AND DAUGHTERS:
A MYTHOLOGICAL COMMENTARY ON THE LIVES

Women in modern Judeo-Christian societies are motherless children.
Painting after painting, sculpture after sculpture in the Christian world
portray Madonnas comforting and worshiping their infant sons. Catholic
mythology symbolizes the enforced splitting of Woman into either
Mother or Whore—both of whom nurture and ultimately worship a dead
man and/or a "divine" male child. The fierce bond of love, continuity, and
pride between the pagan Demeter (the Earth Mother) and her daughter
Persephone (the Kore-Maiden) does not exist between women in Catholic
mythology or culture.

Demeter is the goddess of life, corn, or grain. As we have seen, her
daughter Persephone is abducted, raped, and married by Pluto (Hades),
god of the underworld (or by Zeus or Dionysius, either of whom may have
been Persephone's own father), while she is playing in a field of poppies.
Demeter seeks her daughter and remains inconsolable at her absence.
Finally, in anger, she refuses to let any crops grow if Persephone is not
returned to her. Eventually a compromise is reached: Persephone will
remain with her mother for most of the year (spring, summer, and
autumn) and with her husband during winter (when no seed or crops can
grow). This tale, which incorporates many features of matriarchal and
early agricultural societies, also comprised the heart of the Eleusinian
mysteries—a Mother-Daughter religion in later—and patriarchal—Greek
society.[16]

In Judeo-Christian times, mothers have neither land nor money to
cede to their daughters. Their legacy is one of capitulation, dependence
or drudgery. For example, poor mothers and mothers of color in America
may be employed outside the home—but as drudges, whose labor does
not result in economic, military, or political power. Middle- and upper-

class mothers who are not employed outside the home, or whose employment is "frivolous" or non-paid, cannot provide their daughters with legacies of dignity and self. It is true that some women are more cooperative and sympathetic to each other where "male" and "female" roles are sharply and traditionally defined and segregated, as in non-Western Islamic societies, or in traditional, rural, ghetto and immigrant subcultures within the Western world. However, such cooperation is based on unindividuated uniformity, discontent, and powerlessness. Neither mother nor daughter can redeem the other from certain harsh realities that define the female as "mother" and "loser" under bio-patriarchal rule. As we shall see, this is true of Demeter and Persephone also—but in an era where maternity and biology are more highly valued than today.

Female children are quite literally starved for matrimony: not for marriage, but for physical nurturance and a legacy of power and humanity from adults of their own sex ("mothers"). Most mothers prefer sons to daughters and are more physically and domestically nurturant to them.[17] Within modern society, woman's "dependent" and "incestuous" personality probably stems from not being experienced as "divine" by their mothers (and fathers). Most women are glassed into infancy, and perhaps into some forms of madness, by an unmet need for maternal nurturance. I say "maternal" because the hourly care of infants and children in most families is entrusted to biological women and rarely shared by biological men. It can certainly be argued that infant males are emotionally scarred by being deprived of "maternal" (Dionysiac) nurturance from their fathers and "paternal" (Apollonian) nurturance from their mothers. Perhaps the male fear and hatred of women, as well as male violence and ego-greediness, stems from sex-role stereotyped families; perhaps it stems from male human nature—and the way in which culture has enhanced it.

I am using the word "nurturance" somewhat loosely. I mean the consistent and readily available gift of physical, domestic, and emotional support in childhood, together with the added gift of compassion and respect in adulthood. "Nurturance" or, mythologically speaking, "protection," "guidance," and "intervention," is depicted most often by pagan gods and goddesses helping mortal *men* on their pilgrimages to heroism: Athena helps Odysseus and Perseus to either escape from or slay female powers as embodied by Circe and Medusa. It is interesting to note that Psyche, one of the few mortal heroines in pagan culture, is helped on her pilgrimage toward an essentially "feminine" destiny only by *non-human* objects. No wise or powerful goddess or god (save her husband Eros) intervenes for her. Her "protectors" are an ant, a reed, water, an eagle, and a tower.

Female children turn to their fathers for physical affection, nurturance, or pleasurable emotional intensity—a turning that is experienced as "sexual" by the adult male, precisely because it is predicated on the female's (his daughter's) innocence, helplessness, youthfulness, and monogamous idolatry. This essentially satyric and incestuous model of sexuality is almost universal. It is reflected in marriage laws and practices, and in the rarity with which rapists, child molesters, and frequenters of prostitutes are legally prosecuted. This model of sexuality is mythologically Olympian in origin: Zeus, the father, made a habit of seducing, raping, and impregnating as many Virgin Maidens as possible. The Catholic Father apparently preferred virgins for his divine offspring also.

Daughters don't turn to their mothers for "sexual" initiation, or, as Freud would have it (but couldn't explain it), they specifically turn away from them, for a number of reasons. Mothers are conditioned not to like women and/or the female body. They are phobic about lesbianism; they are jealous of their daughters' youth—rendered so by their own increasing expendability. Also, mothers must be harsh in training their daughters to be feminine in order that they learn how to serve in order to survive. This harshness traditionally characterizes fathers' training their sons to be masculine. Any society with sex-role stereotypes implies an often crippling harshness between adults and children of the same sex. However, bio-patriarchal culture is still essentially a male homosexual one—in spirit and/ or in practice. It is neither lesbian nor bisexual in spirit or practice.

The way in which female children grow up—or learn how not to grow up—is initiated by the early withdrawal or relative absence of the female and/or nurturant body from their lives. Nurturance-deprivation, and the sexual abuse of female children are possibly the two most important factors involved in making female children receptive to "submission" conditioning—at a very early age. Female children move from a childhood dominated or peopled by members of their own sex to a foreign "grown-up'" world dominated, quite literally, by members of the opposite sex. Male children graduate from a childhood dominated or peopled by members of the opposite sex (women) to a "grown-up" world dominated by members of their own sex. Unlike women, they can safely go home again by marrying wives, who will perform the rites of maternal, domestic, and emotional nurturance, but who are usually younger, economically poorer, and physically weaker than themselves.

In patriarchal society, the basic incest taboo (between mother and son and father and daughter) is *psychologically* obeyed by men and disobeyed by women. One-quarter to one-third of female children are raped or molested by their fathers or by adult male relatives in our culture; maternal incest is a far rarer occurrence. Psychologically, women do not have initiation rites to help them break their incestuous ties. While most women do not commit incest with their biological fathers, patriarchal marriage, prostitution, and mass "romantic" love are psychologically predicated on a sexual union between daughter and father figures. Psychologically speaking, in a matriarchal or Amazonian society, the incest taboo would have another purpose entirely, and *women* would not violate it. The taboo would function as a way of keeping sons and husbands away from daughters— who would be their mothers' only heiresses. This particular distance is precisely what is breached by patriarchal mores: the breach immediately tells us which sex is dominant, i.e., which sex controls the means of production and reproduction.

What would female sexuality be like if women did not violate the incest taboo, did not willingly marry father figures, or were not seduced or raped by them? How would women know pleasure, love, and economic security? How would they reproduce themselves when and if they wished to? And how would they raise their children?

The institution of marriage makes a parasite of woman, an absolute dependent. It *incapacitates* her for life's struggle, *annihilates* her social consciousness, paralyzes her imagination, and then imposes its gracious protection, which is in reality a snare, a travesty on human character. . . . If motherhood is the highest fulfillment of woman's nature, what other protection does it need save *love* and *freedom*? Marriage but defiles, outrages, and corrupts her fulfillment. Does it not say to woman, Only when you follow me shall you bring forth life? Does it not condemn her to the block, does it not degrade and shame her if she refuses to buy her right to motherhood by selling herself? Does not marriage only sanction motherhood, even though conceived in hatred, in compulsion? Yet, if motherhood be of free choice, of love, of ecstasy, of defiant passion, does it not place a crown of thorns upon an innocent head and carve in letters of blood the hideous epithet, Bastard? Were marriage to contain all the virtues claimed for it, its crimes against motherhood would exclude it forever from the realm of love.

Emma Goldman[18]

Female biology obviously includes the capacity for sexual pleasure, physical prowess, and childbearing. Whether or not human childbearing constitutes the "greatest pleasure" for women,[19] whether or not it is a "natural" or a "learned" activity, is irrelevant.[20] What is relevant is the price modern women are forced to pay for this pleasure and the overwhelming lack of other available pleasures and privileges. Women are forced to choose between reproduction and (hetero) sexual pleasure; reproduction and physical prowess; or reproduction and worldly or spiritual power.

Today, women are still choosing maternity for traditional reasons: in order to survive economically and psychologically and because contraception and abortion are still inadequate, illegal, expensive, dangerous, and increasingly morally censured for most women. The twentieth-century phenomenon of romantic love also accounts for—or justifies—the traditionally *inevitable* female destiny of marriage and children. Contemporary women are "free" slaves: they choose their servitude for "love."[21] Women are trained to be those creatures who are supposed to get so carried away emotionally that they cannot think clearly, if at all. Pluto (Zeus, Dionysius) had to *carry* the Daughter-Maiden Persephone away from her mother Demeter; for centuries families have *arranged* this leave-taking for their daughters; today, contemporary women carry *themselves* headlong down the same path to the Underworld.

Maternity has been glorified and feared, by ancient and modern people, as *the* most eloquent and effective human response to the fact of biological death. Mothers have been eulogized—and I use the word advisedly—as more powerful than kings and soldiers who, in turn, have defended motherhood in speeches and destroyed its labors in battle. Poets, scientists, and philosophers have sighed over the time-bound vanity of male accomplishment and have continued their creative work.

Modern businessmen envy the female maternal "out"—often to the point of disease—but remain involved with the accumulation and circulation of money, an activity best done without children underfoot. Despite the numerous ways in which men have attempted to mimic or colonize the gloriousness of biological maternity (and consequently, to devalue or punish it in women), men, particularly in Judeo-Christian and Islamic culture, are not very "maternal" to their children, their wives, their mistresses, their prostitutes, their secretaries, their housekeepers—or to each other.

In patriarchal culture, Mother-Women, as deified by the Catholic Madonna, are as removed from (hetero) sexual pleasure as are Daughter-Women, as deified by the pagan Athena. Athena is the archetype of a motherless daughter: Zeus' forehead is her "mother." (Interestingly, Aphrodite, the goddess who persecutes Psyche, is also motherless. According to myth, she was "created from the severed phallus of Uranus which had fallen into the sea."[22]) It is Athena who casts the deciding vote in Orestes' favor and proclaims matricide to be of lesser importance than patricide. Orestes' mother kills her husband Agamemnon for sacrificing their daughter Iphigenia. Orestes avenges his father's death by killing his mother and is acquitted of the crime. In Aeschylus' trilogy, Athena says:

> "My task it is to render the last verdict,
> And I cast this stone for Orestes,

For I did not have a mother who bore me;

No, all my heart praises the male,

May Orestes win over your tied vote."

Athena, despite her warlike trappings, is an original "Daddy's girl": she does not get sexually involved with men—or women. Athena pays for her wisdom and power by giving up reproductive sexuality and (hetero) sexual pleasure. Mary, mother of Jesus, pays for her maternity by giving up her body, almost entirely: she foregoes both (hetero) sexual pleasure (Christ's birth is a virgin and "spiritual" birth) and physical prowess. She has no direct worldly power but, like her crucified son, is easily identified with by many people, especially women, as a powerless figure. Mary symbolizes power achieved through receptivity, compassion, and a uterus. (There is nothing intrinsically wrong with a consciously willed "receptivity" to the universe; on the contrary, it is highly desirable, and should certainly include "receptivity" to many things other than holy sperm and suffering.)

A more feminist (or rather, matriarchal) interpretation of the Catholic Virgin birth certainly exists: it symbolizes the unique and "miraculous" ability of women to conceive and bear children. Childbearing—the union of body and spirit that overcomes death—resides in the female principle. Men do not enter this realm, either socially or biologically. Thus, it is just as we all thought as children: all our mothers immaculately conceived us and we are all divine.

In many pagan and Catholic "downfall" myths, the male god is usually stripped of his full former powers by being sent "earthward," the female, by being sent "skyward." For example, Poseidon was sent to the sea; Pluto, as well as the Judeo-Christian Lucifer, were sent beneath the earth. Mythologically, one expression of power loss for men is to be returned to the earth, to the concrete. Often for women, the expression of power loss is to be removed from the earth, or from their (heterosexual) bodies. Goddesses such as Athena, Diana, or the Catholic Madonna are virgins, i.e., either unmarried or childless, (hetero) sexually uninvolved, or "innocent" of experience.

Psychologically speaking, in Amazon society, a "virgin" is not chaste, but unmarried; in Catholic mythology a "virgin" is married and chaste. The pagan Artemis (Diana), the Virgin-Huntress, is not motherless. She is raised together with her brother Apollo and, unlike Athena, is probably a lesbian goddess of Amazon origin. She requested—and received from Zeus—sixty ocean nymphs and twenty river nymphs as companions. According to one myth, she *rescues* Iphigenia from being sacrificed by her father Agamemnon. According to another myth, one of her lovers is the woman Callisto—whom Artemis' father, Zeus, seduces—*only by taking Artemis' form.*[23]

Virginity, *one* form of mind-body splitting, is the price that women are forced to pay in order to keep whatever other "fearful" powers they have: childbearing, wisdom, hunting prowess, maternal compassion. Of course, de-virginization via heterosexual *rape* is as maddening a split in female mind-body continuity.

HEROINES AND MADNESS: JOAN OF ARC AND THE VIRGIN MARY

How do mythological figures such as Athena or the Catholic Madonna, or historical heroines such as Joan of Arc, relate to what we call madness? On one level, not at all. (Mythology may be viewed as the psychology of modern history. It seems to represent the interaction of human nature with early culture, just as history represents the interaction of human nature with later culture. Myths may also refer to actual historical events or personages.) Many women who are psychiatrically labeled, privately treated, and publicly hospitalized are not mad. Like Plath, West, Fitzgerald, and Packard, they may be deeply unhappy, self-destructive, economically powerless, and sexually impotent—but as women they're supposed to be.

There are very few genuinely (or purely) mad women in our culture. Society generally banishes such experiences from understanding, respect—and from plain view. Madness is shut away from sight, shamed, brutalized, denied, feared, and drugged. Contemporary men, politics, science—the rational mode itself—does not consult or is not in touch with the irrational, i.e., with the events of the unconscious, or with the meaning of collective history.

Such madness is best understood within a mythological context. For example, some mad women in our culture experience certain transformations of self or incorporate the meaning of certain heroines such as Joan of Arc and the Catholic Madonna. Some women also experience themselves as female Christs or as Dionysus. Dionysus is essentially androgynous but is most often depicted as a man. The male Dionysus is the mirror image of Persephone's or the passive Maiden's sacrifice. Dionysus is killed by women—by women whom he has driven mad.

Phillip E. Slater, in *The Glory of Hera*, sees Dionysus as a male child, forever envied, loved, hated, and seduced by his cruelly imprisoned and crippled mother. In understanding Dionysus, he also says that: "Dionysus' characteristic attribute of boundary-violator is symbolized by the Orphic myth of his serpent birth—a myth whose great antiquity is alleged by Kerenyi (cf. also *Euripides: The Bacchae*). Demeter is said to have hidden Persephone in a cave in Sicily, guarded by two serpents. While the maiden was engaged in weaving, however, Zeus came to her in the shape of a serpent and copulated with her, Dionysus being the fruit of this union (Kerenyi, 1960). His ability to shatter cognitive boundaries is thus intrinsic, and does not depend upon any external power. He is in fact born with it—it is the child itself which drives the mother mad by its very existence. Just as the child has twice violated the physical boundaries of the mother by its conception and birth, so it drives her to raving infanticide by its having ceased to be a psychological part of her. In the child-murdering myths of Dionysus, one can easily discern some of the underlying ideation of the postpartum psychosis."[24]

Joan of Arc and the Catholic Madonna involve the sacrifice of the Maiden (Persephone-Kore) for purposes of male renewal. In the Madonna's case, the renewal is achieved through classic patriarchal rape-incest; in Joan's case, first through military victories and then through patriarchal crucifixion, and sanctification-expiation.

Joan of Arc is the only Persephone-Kore Maiden in modern history who is not raped or impregnated by her father—be it by her biological or divine father; she was probably raped by her British captors. Joan remains a "daughter" figure. As such, she is one of Christianity's prime remembrances of Amazonian cultures. Joan, like earlier mythological heroines, such as Athena, is a virgin-warrior who helps men. It is important, however, that Joan herself, at her trial of condemnation, said that she bore her banner or standard aloft "when we went forward against the enemy, I held the banner aloft to avoid killing anyone. I have killed no one."[25]

Although, like all Kore-Maidens, she serves as a source of male renewal, she does so through her military victories and her subsequent political and sexual persecution. Her identity, as such, is a crucial one for women. Although she is doomed (and women might identify with her on this ground alone), she is also physically and spiritually bold; she is a leader of men; she does not become a mother. She embodies the *avoidance* of both the Demeter-Mother fate and the Persephone-Daughter fate. As such, she begins to step completely outside the realm of patriarchal culture. For this, she is killed in her own lifetime—and sometimes re-experienced by those women who are mad enough to wish to "step outside" culture also.

It is frightening to read the account of Joan's imprisonment by Aeneas Sylvius Piccolomini (the future Pope Pius II), quoted by Regine Pernoud: "It is known that, taken in the war, the Maid was sold to the English for ten thousand gold crowns and conveyed to Rouen. In that place, she was diligently examined to discover whether she used sortileges (spells) or diabolical aid or whether she erred in any way in her religion. Nothing worthy to be censured was found in her, excepting the male attire which she wore. And that was not judged deserving of the extreme penalty. Taken back to her prison she was threatened with death if she resumed the wearing of man's clothes . . . her gaolers brought none but male attire."[26] It is as tragic as it is inevitable that female warriors in patriarchal mythology are necessarily denied that part of their sexuality that includes biological maternity. What this always signifies is grief at not having been born male—because of the nurturance-deprivation being female implies.

Phillip Slater, describing the mythological Atalanta, says:

> . . . like Artemis, she is a virgin huntress, and punishes the attentions of would-be suitors with cruel death. Furthermore, her own history reveals the origin of this attitude, for it is said (Apollodorus: iii 9.2) that her father had wished for a boy, and had exposed her on a mountain top, where she was suckled by a bear which the goddess sent to her aid. In her refusal to marry, in her competitions with men (beating them at racing and at wrestling), and in her general masculine demeanor, Atalanta both complies with this wish and expresses her resentment of it.[27]

After women psychologically, unconscoiusly, and collectively grasp the meaning—and limitations—of Joan of Arc, they seek protection and redemption—from the Catholic Mary, the compassionate and powerful mother. Unfortunately, Mary is no Demeter. Catholic mythology has not granted Mary either a daughter or Demeter's bartering power with men and gods. Nevertheless, women in madness wish to give birth to the world (and to themselves) anew. They wish to avoid Joan's crucifixion and can do so only by becoming Virgin-Mothers. They also wish to become their own much-needed mothers. The women whom I spoke with who *did* have Virgin Birth experiences all gave birth to sons. However, some experienced their *own* rebirth at the same time.

Mary avoids crucifixion, but she is condemned to asexuality and piercing sorrow.

Joan and Mary are very painful experiences for those women who psychologically incorporate their meaning. They are the modified (and tragic) Christian equivalents of the pagan Demeter and her daughter Persephone. However, Joan and Mary are separated in time and biology. Joan, unlike Persephone, is not kidnapped; Mary, unlike Demeter, gives birth to a son and not a daughter. Neither of these Christian figures gives rise to or symbolizes a Mother-Daughter religion. C. G. Jung understood the effect of this. He says:

It is immediately clear to the psychologist what cathartic and at the same time rejuvenating effects must flow from the Demeter cult into the feminine psyche, and what a lack of psychic hygiene characterizes our culture, which no longer knows the kind of wholesome experience afforded by the Eleusinian emotions.[28]

However, it is important to realize that the "Eleusinian emotions" are rooted in an acceptance of nature and biology's supremacy. Demeter's world is one in which women, despite their fecundity, do not initiate *sexual* contact with either men or women. Only heterosexual rape exists—and only for procreative purposes. Neither Demeter nor Persephone *act*. They *react*—to rape or to the loss of a daughter or virgin self. Demeter and Persephone are not Amazon figures. Their cult is essentially one of Earth-Mother-worship: mothers who produce more mothers to nurture and sustain mankind with their miraculous biological gifts of crops and daughters. The inevitable sacrifice of self that biology demands of women in most societies is at the heart of the Demetrian myth. Even so, or precisely because this is so, modern women, deprived of both maternal nurturance and dignity, would be very comforted by Eleusinian rituals: after all, we live in a culture in which science and Christianity have increasingly devalued female biology, without yet freeing women from being defined solely in biological terms.

While it is true that Demeter rescues Persephone from isolation in a male world, she also condemns her to a universally female fate: an identity no different from her mother's. As Kerenyi notes:

> To enter into the figure of Demeter means to be robbed, raped, to fail to understand, to rage and grieve, but then to get everything back and be born again. And what does all this mean, save to realize the universal principle of life, the fate of everything mortal? What, then, is left over for the figure of Persephone? Beyond question, that which constitutes the structure of the living creature *apart from* this endlessly repeated drama of coming-to-be and passing-away, namely the *uniqueness* of the individual and its *entrallment to non*-being.[29]

This "uniqueness" and "heroism" are precisely what define Persephone's male mythological counterpart—the divine male child and male adult hero.

Persephone does not wish to be raped, nor do most contemporary women necessarily wish to recapitulate their mother's identity. But the modern Persephone still has no other place to go but into marriage and motherhood. Her father (men in general) still conforms to a rape-incest model of sexuality. And her mother has not taught her to be a warrior, i.e., to take difficult roads to unknown and unique destinations—gladly. Her mother and father neither prepare her for this task nor rejoice in her success. They do not mourn or comfort her in crucifixion, be it as a warrior (as Joan of Arc) *or* as a mother (as the Virgin Mary).

> Any woman born with a great gift in the sixteenth century would certainly have gone crazed, shot herself, or ended her days in some lonely cottage outside the village, half witch, half wizard, feared and mocked at. For it needs little skill in psychology to be sure that a highly gifted girl who had tried to use her gift for poetry would have been so thwarted and hindered by other people, so tortured and pulled asunder by her own contrary instincts, that she must have lost her health and sanity to a certainty.
>
> Virginia Woolf[30]

Virginia Woolf was herself a victim of childhood sexual abuse and ultimately a suicide. Is she telling us that her own "dark spells" were due to the thwarting of her genius?

Zelda Fitzgerald, Sylvia Plath, and Ellen West, for example, want and need mother love—but not at the price of "uniqueness" or glory. They are probably as maddened by the absence of maternality in their lives as they would be by the demands it would eventually place upon their freedom. The combination of nurturance-deprivation *and* restrictions upon their uniqueness or heroism is deadly. They cannot survive as just "women," and they are not allowed to survive as human or as creative beings—*male* creativity is usually so valued that eccentricities, cruelties, emotional infantilism, alcoholism, promiscuity, even madness are usually over-looked, forgiven, or "expected."

All women who bear children are committing, literally and symboli-cally, a blood sacrifice for the perpetuation of the species. In this sense, female sacrifice in patriarchal and prescientific culture is concretely rooted in female biology. To the extent to which the interaction of human biology and culture produces myths that shape our personalities, so too will female sacrifice (and psychological self-sacrifice) continue to exist.

Women are impaled on the cross of self-sacrifice. Unlike men, they are categorically denied the experience of cultural supremacy and individuality. In different ways, some women are driven mad by this fact. Their madness is treated in such a way as to turn it into another form of self-sacrifice. Such madness is, in a sense, an intense experience of female sexual and cultural castration and a doomed search for potency. The search often involves "delusions" or displays of physical aggression, grandeur, sexuality, and emotionality—all traits which would probably be more acceptable in pro-woman or female-dominated cultures. Such traits in women are feared and punished in patriarchal mental asylums.

CHAPTER TWO

ASYLUMS

The entire existence of madness, in the world now being prepared for it, was enveloped in what we may call, in anticipation, a "parental complex." The prestige of patriarchy is revived around madness . . . henceforth . . . the discourse of unreason will be linked with . . . the dialectic of the family . . . the madman remains a minor and for a long time reason will retain for him the aspect of the father. . . . He [Tuke, a psychiatrist] isolated the social structure of the bourgeois family, reconstituted it symbolically in the [mental] asylum, and set it adrift in history.

Michel Foucault[1]

THE MENTAL ASYLUM

AS EARLY AS THE SIXTEENTH CENTURY, women were "shut up" in madhouses (as well as in royal towers) by their husbands.[2] By the seventeenth century, special wards were reserved for prostitutes, pregnant women, poor women, and young girls in France's first mental asylum, the Salpêtriére.[3]

The impoverished and prostituted women must have been the victims of extraordinary chronic violence both sexually and physically. Their eventual breakdowns were not understood as normal human responses to persecution and trauma. In fact, many of the hysterics whom Dr. Breuer hypnotized were prostitutes who had led endangered lives.

By the end of the nineteenth and throughout the twentieth centuries, the portraits of madness executed by both psychiatrists and novelists were primarily of women.

Today, more women are seeking psychiatric help that at any other time in history. We must not forget: (1) that more men are too; (2) that both the number of clinicians and therapeutic promises have also increased.

Some critics insist that "therapism"—the belief that the human condition can be "cured" by a paid healer—renders people, both women and men, increasingly passive. These critics prefer self-sufficiency and religious, moral, and cognitive-rational approaches to human problem-solving. Other critics insist that only the "talking cure" can help people understand themselves and take charge of their lives.

However, it is clear that women, more than men, do seek "help" and are comfortable talking about their feelings and problems with a sympathetic expert. An increasing number of girls and women wish to break free of abuse, find salvation.

This increase may be understood, not only in the context of the "help-seeking" nature of the female role or the objective oppression of women, but in the context of at least three recent social trends. Traditionally, most women performed both the rites of madness and childbirth more invisibly—at home—where, despite their tears and hostility, they were still needed and kept. While women live longer than ever before, and longer than men, there is less and less use, and literally no place, for them in the only place they "belong"—within the family. Many newly useless women are emerging more publicly as depressed, anxious, phobic, or as suffering from an eating disorder.

The patriarchal nature of psychiatric hospitals has been documented by M. Foucault, T. Szasz, E. Goffman, and T. Scheff.[5] Journalists, social scientists, and novelists have described, deplored, and philosophized about the prevalence of overcrowding, under-staffing, and brutality in America's public mental asylums, jails, and medical hospitals. It is obvious that *state* mental asylums were and still are the "Indian reservations" for America's non-criminally labeled poor, old, black, Latino, and female populations. It is also obvious that the state hospital, much like the poor or workhouse of old, functions as a warning specter, particularly to those women involved in earlier or more part-time phases of their "careers" as psychiatric patients.

Mental asylums rarely offer asylum. Both their calculated and their haphazard brutality mirrors the brutality of "outside" society. The "scandals" about them that periodically surface in the media are like all atrocities—only everyday events, writ large. Madness—as a label or reality—is not conceived of as divine, prophetic, or useful. It is perceived as (and often further shaped into) a shameful and menacing disease, from whose spiteful and exhausting eloquence society must be protected. At their best, mental asylums are special hotels or collegelike dormitories for white and wealthy Americans, where the temporary descent into "unreality" (or sobriety) is accorded the dignity of optimism, short internments, and a relatively earnest bedside manner. At their worst, mental asylums are families bureaucratized: the degradation and disenfranchisement of self, experienced by the biologically owned child (patient, woman), takes place in the anonymous and therefore guiltless embrace of strange fathers and mothers. In general, psychiatric wards and state hospitals, "therapy," privacy, and self-determination are all either minimal or forbidden. In such settings, I have heard legitimate and pitiful patient requests for cigarettes or spending money, or complaints about overmedication and all-too-real medical problems "interpreted" psychodynamically by student psychiatrists, psychologists, social workers, nurses, and orderlies. Experimental or traditional medication, surgery, shock, insulin coma treatment, isolation, physical and sexual violence, medical neglect, and slave labor are routinely enforced. Mental patients are somehow less "human" than either medical patients or criminals. They are, after all, "crazy"; they have been abandoned by (or have abandoned dialogue with) their "own" families. As such, they have no way—and no one—to "tell" what is happening to them.

The mental asylum closely approximates the female rather than the male experience within the family. This is probably one of the reasons why Erving Goffman, in *Asylums*, considered psychiatric hospitalization more destructive of self than criminal incarceration. Like most people, he is primarily thinking of the debilitating effect—*on men*—of being treated like a woman (as helpless, dependent, sexless, unreasonable—as "crazy"). But what about the effect of being treated like a woman when you *are* a woman? And perhaps a woman who is already ambivalent or angry about just such treatment?

Adjustment to the "feminine" role was the measure of female mental health and psychiatric progress. The American Adeline T. P. Lunt (1871) wrote that the patient must "suppress a natural characteristic flow of spirits or talk . . . [she must] sit in lady-like attire, pretty straight in a chair, with a book or work before [her], 'inveterate in virtue', and that this will result in being patted panegyrically on the head, and pronounced 'better.'" Margaret Starr (1904), of Maryland, wrote: "I am making an effort to win my dismissal. I am docile; I make efforts to be industrious."

Some women felt they were helped in the asylum, and afterward, by a private physician. For example, Lenore McCall (1937-1942) wrote that she recovered because of the insulin coma therapy. She also attributed her recovery to the presence of a nurse, who had "tremendous understanding, unflinching patience (and whose) sole concern was the good of her patient." After Jane Hillyer (1919-1923) was released from the asylum, she consulted a private doctor whom she feels rescued her from ever having to return. Hillyer wrote:

> I knew from the first second that I had made harbor. I dropped all responsibility at his feet. . . . I need not go another step alone. I perceived at once the penetrating quality of his understanding. . . . He said afterwards he felt as if he were the Woodsman in the fairy tale who finds the lost Tinker's daughter in a darkly enchanted forest. . . . I am sure the necessity of intelligent after-care cannot be sufficiently stressed. . . . My relief was indescribable. If ever one human being went down into the farthest places of desolation and brought back another soul, lost and struggling, that human being was the Woodsman.

McCall and Hillyer were in the minority. Most psychiatrically hospital-ized women who wrote documented that power was invariably abused; that fathers, brothers, husbands, judges, asylum doctors, and asylum attendants did anything that We, the people, allowed them to get away with; and that women's oppression, both within the family and within state institutions, remained constant for more than a century in the United States.

Perhaps one of the reasons women embark and re-embark on "psychiatric careers" more than men do is because they feel, quite horribly, at "home" within them. Also, to the extent to which *all* women have been poorly nurtured as female children, and are refused "mothering" by men as female adults, they might be eager for, or at least willing to settle for, periodic bouts of ersatz "mothering," which they receive as "patients." Those women who are more ambivalent about or rejecting of the female role are often eager to be punished for such dangerous boldness—in order to be saved from its ultimate consequences. Many mental asylum procedures *do* threaten, punish, or misunderstand such women into a real or wily submission. Some of these women react to such punishment (or to a dependency-producing environment) with increased and higher levels of anger and sex-role alienation. If such anger or aggressiveness persists, the women are isolated, strait-jacketed, sedated, and given shock therapy. They certainly aren't recruited by the Marines—or by an Olympic committee. One study published by four male professionals in the *Journal of Nervous and Mental Diseases* describes how they attempted to reduce the aggressive behavior of a thirty-one-year-old "schizophrenic" woman by shocking her with a cattle prod whenever she "made accusations of being persecuted and abused; made verbal threats; or committed aggressive acts."[6] They labeled their treatment a "punishment program" and noted that the "procedure was administered against the expressed will of the patient."

Celibacy is the official order of the asylum day. Patients are made to inhabit an eternal American adolescence, where sexuality and aggression are as feared, mocked, and punished as they are within the family. Traditionally, mental hospital wards are sex-segregated; homosexuality, lesbianism, and masturbation are demeaned.

However, sexual abuse of female or of vulnerable male patients by both staff and other patients is rampant—and freely chosen sexual relationships are still discouraged.

The female-"dominated" atmosphere of hospitals means a (shameful) return to childhood, for both men and women. However, the effect of sexual repression, for example, is probably different for female than for male patients. We must remember that in state hospitals approximately fifty percent of the male patients are drug addicts and alcoholics—groups which are already somewhat withdrawn from heterosexual activity, for any number of reasons (lack of money, lack of desire for family "responsibilities," passivity, anxiety, physiological incapacity, misogyny, etc.). Women have already been bitterly and totally repressed sexually; many may be reacting to or trying to escape from just such repression, and the powerlessness that it signifies, by "going mad." Many male patients may be escaping the demands of a compulsive and aggressive heterosexuality by "going mad." Its absence is *perhaps* not as psychologically or physiologically devastating as it is in the case of women.

Female patients, like female children, are closely supervised by other women (nurses, attendants) who, like mothers, are relatively powerless in terms of the hospital hierarchy and who, like mothers, don't really like their (wayward) daughters. Such supervision, however, doesn't protect the female as patient-child from rape, prostitution, pregnancy, and the blame for all three—any more than similar motherly supervision protects the female as female child in the "real" world, either within or outside the family. Over the years, there have been numerous newspaper accounts of the prostitution, rape, and impregnation of female mental patients by the professional and non-professional staff, and by male inmates. Over the years, I have testified for a number of such women.

THE FEMALE SOCIAL ROLE AND PSYCHIATRIC SYMPTOMS: DEPRESSION, FRIGIDITY, AND SUICIDE ATTEMPTS

Why are women psychiatrically "disturbed" and hospitalized? Why do they seek private therapy? What is schizophrenia or mental illness like, or about, in contemporary women?

Two researchers stated that men are really as "psychologically disturbed" as women are:

> There is no greater magnitude of social stress impinging on one or the
> other sex. Rather [each sex] tends to learn a different style with which
> it reacts to whatever fact has produced the psychological disorder.[8]

I would not so much disagree with this statement as qualify it in several
important ways. Many men *are* severely disturbed—but the form their
disturbance takes is either not seen as neurotic or is not treated by
psychiatric incarceration. Theoretically, all men, but especially white,
wealthy, and older men, can act out many disturbed (and non-disturbed)
drives more easily than women can. Men are generally allowed a greater
range of acceptable behaviors than are women. It can be argued that
psychiatric hospitalization or labeling relates to what society considers
unacceptable behavior. Thus, since women are allowed fewer total
behaviors and are more strictly confined to their role-sphere than men are,
women, more than men, will commit more behaviors that are seen as ill
or unacceptable.

The greater social tolerance for female help-seeking behavior, or
displays of emotional distress, does not mean that such conditioned
behavior is either valued or treated with kindness. On the contrary. Both
husbands and clinicians experience and judge such female behavior as
annoying, inconvenient, stubborn, childish, and tyrannical. Beyond a
certain point, such behavior is "managed," rather than rewarded: it is
treated with disbelief and pity, emotional distance, physical brutality,
economic and sexual deprivation, drugs, shock therapy, and psychiatric
diagnoses.

Given the custodial nature of asylums and the anti-female biases of
most clinicians, women who seek help or women who have symptoms are
actually being punished for their conditioned and socially approved self-
destructive behavior. Typically female and male symptomatology appear
early in life. Studies of childhood behavior problems have indicated that
boys are most often referred to child guidance clinics for aggressive,

destructive (anti-social), and competitive behavior; girls are referred (if they are referred at all) for personality problems, such as excessive fears and worries, shyness, timidity, lack of self-confidence, and feelings of inferiority. Self-destructive or "loser" behavior, from suicide attempts to a fearful narrowing of life experience, is only fully punished as the female grows older. The female child is usually praised for the maturity of her submissiveness, obedience, and unadventurousness.[9] Similar, sex-typed symptoms exist in adults also:

> . . . the symptoms of men are also much more likely to reflect a destructive hostility toward others, as well as a pathological self-indulgence. . . . Women's symptoms, on the other hand, express a harsh, self-critical, self-depriving, and often self-destructive set of attitudes.[10]

A study by E. Zigler and L. Phillips, comparing the symptoms of male and female mental hospital patients, found male patients significantly more assaultive than females and more prone to indulge their impulses in socially deviant ways like "robbery, rape, drinking, and homosexuality."[11] Female patients were often found to be "self-deprecatory, depressed, perplexed, suffering from suicidal thoughts, or making actual suicidal attempts."

This may still be true. However, an increasing number of female adolescents and adults have increasingly engaged in drinking, drug-taking, and in physically aggressive behavior toward others. But in general, most women display "female" psychiatric symptoms such as depression, frigidity, paranoia, suicide attempts, panic, anxiety, and eating disorders. Men display "male" diseases such as sex addiction, alcoholism, drug addiction, personality disorders, sociopathic personalities, and brain diseases (see Table 1). There are still fewer men hospitalized for "male" diseases than women hospitalized for "female" diseases. Typically female symptoms all share a "dread of happiness"—a phrase coined by Thomas Szasz to describe the "indirect forms of communication" that characterize "slave psychology." He writes:

In general, the open acknowledgement of satisfaction is feared only in situations of relative oppression (e.g. all-suffering wife vis-á-vis domineering husband). The experiences of satisfaction (joy, contentment) are inhibited lest they lead to an augmentation of one's burden . . . *the fear of acknowledging satisfaction is a characteristic feature of slave psychology.* The "properly exploited" slave is forced to labor until he shows signs of fatigue or exhaustion. Completion of his task does not signify that his work is finished and that he may rest. At the same time, even though his task is unfinished, he may be able to influence his master to stop driving him—and to let him rest—if he exhibits signs of imminent collapse. Such signs may be genuine or contrived. Exhibiting signs of fatigue or exhaustion—irrespective of whether they are genuine or contrived (e.g. "being on strike" against one's boss)—is likely to induce a feeling of fatigue or exhaustion in the actor. I believe that this is the mechanism responsible for the great majority of so-called chronic fatigue states. Most of these were formerly called "neurasthenia," a term rarely used nowadays. Chronic fatigue or a feeling of lifelessness and exhaustion are still frequently encountered in clinical practice.

Psychoanalytically, they are considered "character symptoms." Many of these patients are unconsciously "on strike" against persons (actual or internal) to whom they relate with subservience and against whom they wage an unending and unsuccessful covert rebellion.[12]

The analogy between "slave" and "woman" is by no means a perfect one. However, there is some theoretical justification for viewing women, or the sex-caste system, as the *prototype* for all subsequent class and race slavery.[13] Women were probably the first group of human beings to be enslaved by another group. In a sense, "woman's work," or woman's psychological identity, consists in exhibiting the signs and "symptoms" of slavery—as well as, or instead of, working around the clock in the kitchen, the nursery, the bedroom, and the factory.[14]

Depression

Women become "depressed" long before menopausal chemistry becomes the standard explanation for the disease. National statistics and research studies all document a much higher female to male ratio of depression or manic-depression at all ages.[15] Perhaps more women *do* get "depressed" as they grow older—when their already limited opportunities for sexual, emotional, and intellectual growth decrease even further. Dr. Pauline Bart studied depression in middle-aged women and found that such women had completely accepted their "feminine" role—and were "depressed" because that role was no longer possible or needed.[16]

Traditionally, depression has been conceived of as the response to—or expression of—loss, either of an ambivalently loved other, of the "ideal" self, or of "meaning" in one's life. The hostility that should or could be directed outward in response to loss is turned inwards toward the self. "Depression" rather than "aggression" is the female response to disappointment or loss. The research and clinical evidence for any or all of these views is controversial. We may note that most women have "lost"—or have never really "had"—their mothers; nor is the maternal object replaced for them by husbands or lovers. Few women ever develop strong socially approved "ideal" selves. Few women are allowed, no less encouraged, to concern themselves with life's "meaning." (While this may *also* be true for many men, it is certainly not *untrue* for most women.) Women lose their jobs as "women," rather than any existential hold on life's meaning. In a sense, women can't "lose" what they've never had. Also, as I'll discuss in Chapter Ten, women are conditioned to "lose" in order to "win."

Women are in a continual state of mourning—for what they never had—or had too briefly, and for what they can't have in the present, be it Prince Charming or direct worldly power. It is not very easy for most women to temper, idle, or philosophize away their mourning with sexual, physical, or intellectual exercises. When female depression swells to clinical proportions, it unfortunately doesn't function as a role-release or respite. Sometimes "depressed" women are even *less* verbally "hostile" and "aggressive" than nondepressed women; their "depression" may serve as a way of keeping a deadly faith with their "feminine" role.[18] "Depressed" patients were actually *less* verbally hostile than "normal" control patients—and their verbal hostility and "resentment" decreased even further as they "improved"—i.e., became less "depressed" according to clinical and self-rating. One classic study done by Dr. Alfred Friedman consisted of 534 white patients, hospitalized in Philadelphia. Seventy-one percent were women, with a median age of forty-two, who attended but did not complete high school; eighty-nine percent of the female patients were or had been married. (Depressed male patients were more verbally hostile than their female counterparts.) Dr. Friedman's interpretation of this finding is as follows: he hypothesizes that the "depressive" *usually* expresses very little verbal hostility (or other forms of) hostility, and become "depressed" only when the "usual defenses break down":

> It may be that it is their [the depressives'] inability to verbalize the hostility spontaneously to the person for whom they feel it at the time when it is appropriate [that] is part of their predisposition to become depressed. The tendency to deny the "bad" in significant others and to perceive them selectively so they do not consciously become angry or depressed may be one of the ways to ward off a disturbed or depressive reaction.

It is important to note that "depressed" women are (like women in general) only *verbally* hostile; unlike most men, they do not express their hostility physically—either directly, to the "significant others" in their lives, or indirectly, through physical and athletic prowess. It is safer for women to become "depressed" than physically violent. Physically violent women usually lose physical battles with male intimates; are abandoned by them as "crazy" as well as "unfeminine"; are frequently psychiatrically or (less frequently) criminally incarcerated. Further, physically strong and/or potentially assaultive women would gain fewer secondary rewards than "depressed" women; their families would fear, hate, and abandon them, rather than pity, sympathize, or "protect" them. Psychiatrists and asylums would behave similarly: hostile or potentially violent women (and men) who are oppressed and powerless are, understandably, hardly ever treated ethically or legally—or kindly—by others.

As I've noted previously, many new diagnostic categories (and treatments) exist today. For example, Rape Trauma Syndrome, Battered Woman's Syndrome, Post Traumatic Stress Disorder, and so on. The violence and hatred of women involved in rape, incest, or battery often lead to situational or even life-long depressions.

In 1974, I cofounded the National Women's Health Network, which remains in existence today. Our initial focus was on the dangers of medication for women, especially the birth control pill. Over time, other issues emerged, such as the medicalization of menstruation, pregnancy, and menopause. Initially, feminists did not want women's bodies or normal life-cycle realities to be further pathologized or psychiatrically diagnosed.

However, it became increasingly clear to me that "mood swings," rage, and depression did often correlate with some women's menstrual and menopausal cycles and could be alleviated with a variety of either herbal or pharmaceutical medication. In addition, postpregnancy depression was real, not imagined and could have potentially dangerous consequences, if not acknowledged and treated.

In 2003, a University of Michigan researcher, Dr. Sheila Marcus, found that 1 out of 5 expectant mothers suffer from depression that mainly goes untreated, even by psychotherapy. Many factors may be involved, including hormonal changes, economic and relationship stress, previous traumas, and a genetic pre-disposition toward depression. Some physicians are reluctant to medicate pregnant women; others have found that anti-depressants do not have a negative effect on the developing foetus.

According to the Massachusetts General Hospital's Center on Women's Mental Health, during the postpartum period, about 85 percent of women experience some type of "mood disturbance" or Postpartum Depression (PPD). Symptoms may appear within 48 to 72 hours of childbirth. This form of the "blues" is mainly short-lived and quite normal. New mothers may feel sad, guilty, exhausted, and unable to concentrate; they may experience mood swings, an eating disorder, anxiety, tearfulness, and irritability; they may also suffer from a sleep disturbance and have suicidal thoughts. This usually passes within a few weeks. Interestingly, many women who exhibit these symptoms also suffer from certain risk factors. For example, they experienced depression in the past, either during a previous pregnancy or in general; they recently were very stressed; or they are suffering from marital discord and an absence of social support.

Ten to 15 percent of women develop more "significant symptoms of depression or anxiety," which last longer. About 1 to 2 per 1,000 women suffer from postpartum psychosis in which they suffer from delusions such as hearing voices that tell them to kill themselves or their infants. Short-term therapy may help with postpartum depression but not with postpartum psychosis. The right medication may be needed in both instances.

Frigidity

A hoarder of secret sexual grievances, a wife.

Joan Didion[19]

A great deal of information has now been circulated regarding the political basis of female frigidity; women are sexually repressed by patriarchal institutions which enforce fear, dislike, and confusion about female sexual and reproductive anatomy in both men and women. Phallus-worship is well represented in myth, painting, sculpture, and modern bedroom practices: clitoris-worship and/or non-reproductive vagina-worship is not. I do not wish to repeat or even review this information here, except as briefly as possible.

Clinical case histories, psychological and sociological surveys and studies—and our own lives—have documented the extent to which most pre-feminist twentieth-century women were not having orgasms; or not having the "right" kind of orgasms; or not having *any* kind of orgasms very frequently or very easily; or having orgasms only under conditions of romantic monogamy, legal prostitution, or self-degradation; or only after much purposeful "learning."[20] One psychoanalyst, Marie Robinson, has characterized the proper female orgasm as one in which the woman may be rendered unconscious for up to three minutes. Women have been seen as sexually "insatiable" by witch-hunters and modern scientists; they have also been seen as not really "needing" orgasms as much as they need love, maternity, and fine silverware.[21] Nevertheless, the psychoanalytic tradition (combined with a growing addiction to instant pleasure) has viewed "neurosis" and even "psychosis" as stemming from sexual repression. Consequently, most clinicians have tried hard to help their female patients "achieve" heterosexual orgasms—usually by counseling a joyous and/or philosophical acceptance of the female role as envisioned and enforced by men: as Madonna-housewife and mother, or as Magdalene Earth Goddess. Even sexual liberationist pioneers, such as Wilhelm Reich, have posited the primacy of vaginal eroticism, and viewed bisexuality and lesbianism as "regressive" or "infantile."

Most clinicians have not thought deeply about the sociopolitical— or the psychological—conditions that are necessary for female sexual self-definition or agency. Women can never be sexually actualized as long as men control the means of production and reproduction. Women have had to barter their sexuality (or their capacity for sexual pleasure) for economic survival and maternity. Female frigidity as we know it will cease only when such bartering ceases. Most women cannot be "sexual" as long as prostitution, rape, and patriarchal marriage exist, with such attendant concepts and practices as "illegitimate" pregnancies, enforced maternity, "non-maternal" paternity, and the sexual deprivation of "aging" women. From a psychological point of view, female frigidity will cease when female children are surrounded by and can observe non-frigid female adults.

In the years since I first wrote this, some things have changed. Many more divorces are initiated by women who want freedom from violence for themselves and their children, and companionate intimacy, including sexual intimacy for themselves.

Historically, both royal and ruling-class women—and impoverished women—have engaged in extramarital or recreational sex. Today, more middle-class women do so, as well. And they better understand the importance of foreplay and the role of the clitoris in achieving orgasm. In addition, feminist- and post-feminist-era girls and women have experimented with lesbianism, bisexuality, multiple heterosexual partners, and sex with younger men or women.

At the same time, many men, including HIV positive men, have insisted on unprotected sex with ever-younger women and with children in both America and in Third World countries and have infected their female partners with the deadly AIDS virus.

Male lust and greed continue to drive an unholy worldwide trafficking in girls and women. Rape, including public and videotaped gang rape became weapons of war in the early 1970s in Bangladesh; in the 1990s in Bosnia and Algeria; and most recently in Rwanda and Sudan, where the women have previously been genitally mutilated and vaginally sewn up. This means that gang rape amounts to serious physical torture, which may also have grave medical consequences.

Christian religious communities continue to preach abstinence, celibacy, and sex within marriage only. Muslim religious communities continue to allow polygamy, concubinage, female genital mutilation, and slavery, including sexual slavery. Jewish religious communities outlawed polygamy nearly a thousand years ago, but do not punish men who routinely visit prostitutes or have girlfriends. Religious Jewish women can be divorced, lose custody of their children, and be ostracized by their communities for having an affair—or even for being accused of doing so.

Although homophobic bias certainly still exists, in the three decades since I wrote *Women and Madness,* mental health professionals decided that homosexuality, bisexuality, and lesbianism are not psychiatric illnesses and that in some instances transsexual surgery might alleviate suffering. They have a better understanding of incest, rape, and pedophilia for which there is no known cure. They also understand that many male sexual predators have themselves been physically and sexually traumatized in childhood, mainly by their fathers.

Teenage girls still have difficulties achieving orgasm, as do some women. Sexually traumatized women, especially in war zones, and horrifically persecuted women, especially in the Islamic world, routinely kill themselves.

Suicide Attempts

I have done it again.
One year in every ten
I manage it—
. . . .
Dying
Is an art, like everything else.
I do it exceptionally well.

I do it so it feels like hell.
I do it so it feels real.
I guess you could say I've a call.

It's easy enough to do it in a cell.
It's easy enough to do it and stay put
It's the theatrical

Comeback in broad day
                    Sylvia Plath[22]

In the past, men commited actions; women commited gestures. Both sexes were imprisoned by separate vocabularies. "Manfully," men kill themselves, or others—*physically*. Women *attempt* to kill themselves physically far more often than men do, and fail at it more often. Suicide is not an apolitical occurrence: the politics of caste (sex and race) shape American patterns of suicide. One study found that sixty-nine percent of attempted suicides in America are female and, conversely, that seventy

percent of completed suicides are male.[23] They also found that housewives comprised the largest single category of both "attempted and
completed suicides" and, further, that about five times as many widows
commit suicide as attempt suicide (twenty percent vs. four percent).
Twice as many widowers commit suicide as attempt suicide (six percent
vs. three percent). A government pamphlet entitled *Suicide Among Youth*
documented that attempted suicide is far more frequent among student-
age females than males but that student-age males complete more
suicides.[24] Nonwhite males between fifteen and twenty-five have the
highest suicide commitment rate.

Physical action—even the exquisitely private act of taking one's own
life—is very difficult for women. Conditioned female behavior is more
comfortable with, and is defined by, psychic and emotional self-
destruction. Women are conditioned to experience physicality—be it
violent, destructive, or pleasurable—more in the presence of another, or
at male hands, than alone or at (their own) female hands. Female suicide
attempts are not so much realistic "calls for help" or hostile inconvenienc-
ing of others as they are the assigned baring of the powerless throat,
signals of ritual readiness for self-sacrifice. Like female tears, female
suicide attempts constitute an essential act of resignation and helplessness—which alone can command temporary relief or secondary rewards.
As we have noted, however, women who try to kill themselves are not
necessarily treated very kindly. Suicide attempts are the grand rites of
"femininity"—i.e., ideally, women are supposed to "lose" in order to
"win." Women who succeed at suicide are, tragically, outwitting or
rejecting their "feminine" role, and at the only price possible: their death.

SCHIZOPHRENIA IN THREE STUDIES

It is important to realize that schizophrenia, or madness, is crucially
different from female symptoms such as depression or anxiety. Schizophrenia, in both women and men, always involves opposite as well as
same-sex behavior. For instance, female schizophrenics are more openly

hostile or violent, or more overtly concerned with sexual and bisexual pleasure, than are female "depressives." Both groups of women still share many "feminine" traits such as mistrusting their own perceptions, feeling inferior, helpless, and dependent. Just as schizophrenia is no entreé into power for women, neither are "female" diseases such as depression, promiscuity, paranoia, eating disorders, self-mutilation, panic attacks, and suicide attempts. Such "disorders," whether hospitalized or not, consti-tute female role rituals, enacted by most women. As we shall see, whether and what kind of "treatment" is afforded these rituals is a function of age, class, and race.

Thirty-forty years ago psychologists discussed "schizophrenia" in a very interesting way: in terms of sex-role alienation or sex-role rejection. Dr. Shirley Angrist compared female ex-mental patients who were returned to asylums with those who weren't.[25] She found that the rehospitalized women had refused to function "domestically" in terms of cleaning, cooking, child care, and shopping. The rehospitalized women were no different from the ex-mental patients in terms of their willingness to participate in "leisure" activities, such as traveling, socializing, or enjoying themselves. The rehospitalized women were, in Angrist's terms, slightly more "middle class and more frequently married than their non-returned counterparts." Further, the husbands who readmitted their wives expressed significantly lower expectations for their total human functioning. They seemed more willing to tolerate extremely childlike and dependent behavior in their wives—such as incessant complaining and incoherence—as long as the dishes were washed. These husbands also expressed great alarm and disapproval about their wives' "swearing," "cursing," and potentially violent "temper tantrums."

Dr. Angrist published a book, entitled *Women After Treatment*, in which she compared both early and late "returnees" with "normal" or housewife female controls.[26] A double standard of mental health accounts for such methodological and ideological practices as defining the "nor-mal" woman as the "unemployed" housewife. Angrist found that the original differences between returned and non-returned women in the domestic performance area had completely disappeared. All "returned" women and all female ex-mental patients performed more poorly domestically than did "normal" housewives. In a further refinement of her data, in which she controlled for educational level, age, race, and social and marital status, these differences in domestic performance were eliminated. The differences between ex-mental patients and "normal" housewives were now in the "psychological" area—at least according to Angrist's informant-observers. Ex-patients, whether they were rehospitalized or not, swore more often, attempted aggressive acts more frequently, got drunk, did not want to "see" people, and "misbehaved sexually"—behaviors considered more "masculine" than "feminine." However, the ex-patients also exhibited many "feminine" behaviors, such as fatigue, insomnia, pill-taking, and general "inactivity."

It is interesting to note that both ex-patients and housewives equally displayed certain behaviors—behaviors which are negatively viewed. Angrist notes:

> [It was surprising] that so many of the controls [the normal housewives] were reported to have evidenced similar behavior as the ex-mental patients. Forty-six percent were described as restless; fifty-nine percent as worn out; sixty percent as tense and nervous; fifty-seven percent as "grouchy."

The husbands and mothers of both groups of women described them as

> making no sense when talking; walking, sitting, or standing awkwardly; moving around restlessly; saying she hears voices; trying to hurt or kill herself; needing help in dressing; being bad tempered; not knowing what is going on around her; saying she sees people who aren't there.

Dr. Frances Cheek published a compelling study entitled "A Serendipitous Finding: Sex Role and Schizophrenia."[27] She compared male and female "schizophrenics" between the ages of fifteen and twenty-six with their "normal" counterparts, expecting to find a classic profile of schizophrenic passivity, withdrawal, and emotionally constrained behavior. Dr.

Cheek observed and rated a mainly verbal patient-parent interaction. The task behavior that Dr. Cheek rated as "dominant" or "aggressive" involved opinion-giving or clarification of the subject being discussed. She found that female schizophrenics were more dominant and aggressive with their parents than were female—or male—normals or male schizophrenics. (This information was obtained in a private communication.) The male schizophrenics presented a more "feminine" (or schizophrenic) pattern of passivity, more so than schizophrenic females and normal males.

It is important to note that the male schizophrenics were still very similar to normal males in the expression of negative social-emotional behavior, such as expression of hostility and disagreement. For example, the male ex-mental patients involved in various Mental Patients Liberation Projects are aware—and troubled by their excessive hostility and/or indifference to women. The female schizophrenics were less "negative" emotionally than were female or male normals or male schizophrenics. Nevertheless, female schizophrenics were perceived by both their parents as the "least conforming" of all the groups. Their parents remembered them as unusually "active" (for girls?) during childhood. This reference to "activeness" may not refer as much to physical or aggressive behavior as to perceptual, intellectual, or verbal behavior. Perhaps it was this rather specific rejection of one aspect of the female role that caused family conflict, and ultimately led to psychiatric labeling and incarceration.

Dr. Cheek refers to an earlier study done by Letailleur, in which he suggests that "the overactive dominating female and the underactive passive male are cultural anomalies and are therefore hospitalized."[28] The "passive" female schizophrenic is probably not hospitalized at so early an age, any more than is the "active" male schizophrenic. Letailleur thinks that the "role reversal" is a function of the disease process. I think that what Cheek calls the role "reversal" or "rejection" is what is labeled "crazy," or is, partly, what the disease is about. However, I do not think "role rejection" is the appropriate term. The male schizophrenics were similar in many ways to normal males; the female schizophrenics were similar to—or even more "female" than—the "normal" females. Sex-role alienation is probably a better term—and is the exact phrase used by Drs. David McClelland and Norman Watt in their study.[29]

McClelland and Watt compared twenty male and twenty female hospitalized schizophrenics between the ages of twenty and fifty with a number of "normal" control groups: "employed" males and females and "unemployed" housewives. The study measured conscious attitudes and preferences, attitudes to one's own body, fantasy and storytelling patterns, and preferences for abstract geometric figures. (Most of these measures had previously been standardized among "normal" populations, and clear sex differences had emerged.) The researchers found a general pattern of more "masculine" test behavior among female schizophrenics and more "feminine" test behavior among male schizophrenics.

There are many methodological criticisms to be made of this study; however, I think that the study's findings are essentially correct. For example, female schizophrenics significantly favored the "intruding" and "penetrating" abstract geometric figures, usually preferred by normal males; female schizophrenics were significantly less "nurturant" and "affiliative" than normal female controls—but, in this regard, were no different from either normal or schizophrenic males; female schizophrenics chose "male" roles in imaginary plays: they preferred being "devils" to "witches," "policemen" to "secretaries," "bulls" to "cows." Unfortunately, McClelland doesn't make much of the fact that, to a great extent, the housewife control group preferred to play opposite-sex roles in this imaginary play. When shown a picture of a bull in a bullring, female schizophrenics evidenced "normal" male reaction—i.e., they said they would kill the bull. Male schizophrenics reacted as "normal" women and said they would flee the bullring.

Perhaps this study's most significant finding concerned satisfaction or dissatisfaction with various body parts, such as lips, face, elbows, body hair, hands, etc. Female schizophrenics were significantly less sensitive to their "feminine" appearance than were either normal female or male schizophrenics. (As we shall see in Chapter Three, this lack of concern has dire consequences for female mental patients in terms of releasing them from asylums.) In fact, sixty-nine percent of the female schizophrenics compared with fifty percent of the male normals were "satisfied" with their male or "strength" body parts. This should be compared with Cheek's finding that female schizophrenics were more "dominant" (verbally) than male normals. McClelland and Watt do not always compare female schizophrenic performance to male normal performance. It is therefore difficult to evaluate how much female schizophrenics are "threatening" because they have not only deserted certain posts of the "feminine" role but have adopted certain "masculine" posts even more boldly than normal men. It is important to note that male schizophrenics were as "satisfied" with their male body parts as were male normals: they were simply more "satisfied" with their feminine or appearance body parts than normal males were. Female schizophrenics were relating to their bodies—at least verbally, in fantasy, or during a test—in a more recognizably "male" fashion. McClelland and Watt feel that concern with the body is a "primary and unconscious mode of expressing identity" and predates more second-ary sex-role reversal behaviors, such as female wage-labor "employment" or "intellectual assertiveness."

The researchers are confused by the greater schizophrenic female than male "indifference" to all parts of their bodies.

> By itself such indifference might be attributable to long hospitalization but this explanation would not account for the differential results for the schizophrenic males. It seems plausible to conclude that some parts of the schizophrenic woman's unconscious self-image is insensitive and more masculine, whereas some part of the schizophrenic man's self-image is sensitive and more feminine. Whether this difference predates their entry to mental hospitals is a question for further research.

Most women, while morbidly concerned with their "appearance," are actually quite removed from their bodies in terms of either "satisfaction," "confidence," or "activity." It is not surprising to find a continuation of this among female schizophrenics—who are, after all, "females." More important, however, is the fact that the essentially female nature of psychiatric confinement is, in a certain sense, more enraging to women—

who have already been through it and been driven "mad" by it—than to men. If asylums are where you go for being alienated from your sex role, then you might as well act out that alienation as much as possible; there is nowhere else to do so. It is not surprising, therefore, that female psychiatric wards have been characterized as generally "noisier" than male wards[30]; as more "excitable" than the "apathetic" male wards[31]; as dominated by more mood swings, more belligerent, bossy, and interpersonally disruptive behavior[32]; and as more potentially "violent" than male wards.[33] What we must remember, however, is that such "masculine protests" are both ineffective and effectively punished, and are ultimately self-destructive. Patients on female wards have also been characterized as generally unable to make effective decisions, or to reason abstractly, and have been characterized by a marked lack of "ego strength."[34] Such traits often characterize long-term psychiatric patients and may, indeed, also be a function of hospitalization.

Today, many schizophrenics are ambulatory, homeless, or living at home. Drugs (if taken) can often control the "voices," nightmares, insomnia, super-aggressiveness, suicidal and homicidal ideation. Often, the drugs have extremely unpleasant and humiliating side-effects. Frequently, patients stop their medication—and the descent into schizophrenia or bi-polar disorders begins again.

In my opinion, short-term hospitalizations, if they are not abusive, are often necessary to adjust or change medication, or for detoxification purposes.

A THEORETICAL PROPOSAL

Neither genuinely mad women, nor women who are hospitalized for conditioned female behavior, are powerful revolutionaries. Their insights and behavior are as debilitating (for social reasons) as they are profound. Such women act alone, according to rules that make no "sense" and are contrary to those of our culture. Their behavior is "mad" because it represents a socially powerless individual's attempt to unite body and feeling. For example, Valerie Solanas, the author of *The Scum Manifesto* and the woman who shot Andy Warhol, the filmmaker, was considered both "crazy" and a "criminal" for acting on what many people are content simply to "name" and verbally criticize: the existence of misogyny in patriarchal culture and, in her case, the exploitation of female talent.

Perhaps what we consider "madness," whether it appears in women or in men, is either the acting out of the devalued female role or the total or partial rejection of one's sex-role stereotype. Women who fully act out the conditioned female role are clinically viewed as "neurotic" or "psychotic." When and if they are hospitalized, it is for predominantly female behaviors such as "depression," "suicide attempts," "anxiety neuroses," "paranoia," eating disorders, self mutilation, or "promiscuity." Women who reject or are ambivalent about the female role frighten both themselves and society so much so that their ostracism and self-destructiveness probably begin very early. Such women are also assured of a psychiatric label and, if they are hospitalized, it is for less "female" behaviors, such as "schizophrenia," "lesbianism," or "promiscuity." "Promiscuity," like "frigidity," is both a "female" and a "non-female" trait: either can mean a flight into or a flight from "femininity."

Men who act out the female role and who, for example, are "dependent," "passive," sexually and physically "fearful," or "inactive," or who, like women, choose men as sexual partners, are seen as "neurotic" or "psychotic." If they are hospitalized they are usually labeled as "schizophrenic" or homosexual. It is important to note, however, that men in general are still able to reject more of their sex-role stereotype without viewing themselves as "sick," and without being psychiatrically diagnosed or hospitalized, than are women. Women are so conditioned to need and/or to service a man that they are more willing to take care of a man who is "passive," "dependent," or "unemployed"—than men are willing to relate to, no less take care of, a "dominant," "independent," or "employed" woman. What this means is that clinically "depressed" or "suicidal" females who do not serve men (or husbands) are as often rejected by them, and thereby subjected to relative poverty, or illegal and life-threatening prostitution, as are clinically "schizophrenic" or "hostile" females. Married men seek psychiatric help less frequently and remain in asylums for shorter time periods than do married women or single men.[35] Homosexuals, although psychiatrically "labeled" and legally persecuted, seek help less frequently than lesbians do and, like male schizophrenics, still exhibit fewer (devalued) female traits than do lesbians or female schizophrenics.[36]

Men who act out the male role—but who are too young, too poor, or non-white—are usually incarcerated as "criminals" or as "sociopaths," rather than as "schizophrenics" or "neurotics." In order to be "men," less powerful men in our society have to "steal" what more powerful men can "buy." (And they are punished for doing so.) The kinds of behaviors that are considered "criminal" and "mentally ill" are sex-typed. They are also typed by race and class, and each sex is conditioned accordingly. Psychiatric categories themselves are sex-typed. Many more women than men manifest, seek help, and are hospitalized for what we categorize as a "psychiatric disease." It is important to know what type of clinical treatment these psychiatric patients receive; how many clinicians there are, the theories on which the clinicians draw, and how these psychiatrists and psychologists view their patients.

CHAPTER THREE

THE CLINICIANS

I met Wilhelm Reich in October 1939 shortly after his arrival in the States. I became his wife, secretary, laboratory assistant, bookkeeper, housekeeper, and general factotum, soon thereafter, the mother of his son in 1944. . . . I had to continue my work, which at that time and place consisted mainly of typing Reich's manuscripts. I also had to take care of the baby. I remember well typing away at a manuscript while pushing the carriage back and forth with one foot to keep the baby quiet because Daddy could not bear to hear him cry. Or Reich, very graciously telling me in the late afternoon to take off for a while and go fishing out on the lake while he would look after the baby, then after half an hour, his waving to me frantically because the baby needed to be changed, an ordeal which he could not face.

Ilse Ollendorf Reich[1]

At home [Freud's] family revolved around him and his work. . . . "I am afraid I do have a tendency toward tyranny" he admitted more than once. . . . Unlike his success with adopted [intellectual] daughters, Freud had trouble with all his "sons" in psychoanalysis. Especially for men, working for such a genius could be very frustrating: it was bound to offend a man's sense of autonomy. . . . [Helene Deutsch's] career seems to contradict the Freudian theories of femininity which she expounds in her book. Far from being clinging and dependent, as a psychiatrist she was both active and independent, yet toward Freud and his concepts, which she did so much to make popular, Helene remained passive and receptive. . . .

[Freud psychoanalyzed Deutsch's] "Oedipal situation" [and told her to continue her "identification" with her father—and with himself].

Paul Roazan[2]

Freud was merely a diagnostician for what feminism purports to cure ... a thorough restatement of Freud in feminist terms would make a valuable book.

Shulamith Firestone[3]

The Women's Liberation Movement cannot afford to indulge the bad poetry about women, when we have a science we can use, explore, criticize, amend. For psychoanalysis, like all sciences, is open, not closed.

Juliet Mitchell[4]

By an irony nearly tragic, the discoveries of a great pioneer [Freud], whose theories of the unconscious and of infant sexuality were major contributions to human understanding, were in time invoked to sponsor a point of view essentially conservative . . . the effect of Freud's work, that of his followers, and still more that of his popularizers was to rationalize the invidious relationship between the sexes, to ratify traditional roles, and to validate temperamental differences. . . . Although the most unfortunate effects of vulgar Freudianism far exceeded the intentions of Freud himself, its anti-feminism was not without foundation in Freud's own work.

Kate Millett[5]

PSYCHIATRISTS AND PSYCHOLOGISTS are no more misogynist than politicians, soldiers, poets, physicists, or bartenders are. However, they are no less so—despite their rather special concern with and power over individual women. We owe our familiarity with feminine "hysteria," as well as our ambivalence about whether such behavior is universal and "normal," or universal and "abnormal," to such scientific fathers and mothers. I do not think that any one social or professional group is "responsible" for or can change the entire fabric of social reality, although at a given moment, each group or individual threads its way rather unalterably through it. I do believe that individual exceptions exist, and are valuable, as well as limited to those individuals involved. Individual exceptions are also irrelevant to any understanding of the rules or forces to which they take exception.

In this chapter, I would like to present some general facts about clinicians:

(1) The extent to which the professions of psychiatry and psychology in America are numerically dominated by men.

(2) The extent to which most *contemporary* female and male clinicians, whether they are disciples of a particular psychoanalytic or psychological theory or not, currently share and act upon traditional myths about "abnormality," sex-role stereotypes, and female inferiority.

(3) The extent to which most traditional psychoanalytic and therapeutic theories and practices perpetrate certain misogynistic views of women and of sex-role stereotypes as "scientific" or "curative."

(4) The extent to which both modern and traditional ideologies are played out within the *institution* of private therapy, which is, like that of the mental asylum, a mirror of the female experience in patriarchal culture.

HOW MANY CLINICIANS ARE THERE IN AMERICA?

Clinicians, like ghetto schoolteachers, do not study themselves or publicize their own motives, personalities, and values as easily or frequently as they do those of their neurotic patients or "culturally deprived" pupils. Most clinicians are too busy, too unwilling, or too "important" to fill out questionnaires or be experimental subjects. The response of psychiatrists and psychologists to questionnaire inquiries is generally rather low; they are not willing subjects and they are often too busy to do so.[6] Nevertheless, the major professional organizations do publish membership lists; government research bureaus do publish estimates of psychiatric hospital staffing patterns; psychologists and psychiatrists have published studies about their profession's attitudes, behaviors, and "personal" lifestyles; psychoanalytic theorists and clinicians have published their case histories and theories; their disciples have often published their biographies.

In the past, the membership of the American Psychiatric Association totaled 11,083, of whom 10,100 were men and 983 were women. Over time, their membership increased to 17,298, of whom 14,267 were men and 1,691 were women. (The sex of 1,340 names on the membership list is unclear.) Thus, ninety percent of all psychiatrists during the 1960s and 1970s were men. It is important to remember that psychiatry is the most powerful of the mental illness professions, in terms of prestige, money, and *ultimate* control over psychiatric policies, both in private practice and in mental hospitals. Psychiatrists, both medically and legally, decide *who* is insane and *why*; *what* should be done to or for such people; and *when* and *if* they should be released from treatment. (As we shall see, both their medical training and their legal responsibility predispose most psychiatrists to diagnose "'pathology" everywhere—even, or especially, where non-experts are blind to it.)

I italicized the word "ultimate" above because, powerful as psychiatrists are, there are far too few of them to carry out their opinions in all psychiatric wards at every moment. For example, years ago, the National Institute of Mental Health conducted a survey of staffing patterns in transitional mental health facilities.[7] Based on a sample, they documented that psychiatrists comprise no more than five percent of the staff—and that the majority of them are employed on a part-time basis. Sixty-eight percent of the full-time and thirty-seven percent of the part-time staff in these facilities are "non-professionals." Social workers constitute ten percent of the full- and part-time staff; psychologists comprise about two percent of the staff. In community mental health facilities, psychiatrists were seen as constituting fourteen percent of the staff involved in consultation and education.[8]

Within mental asylums, most psychiatrists function as well-paid administrators whose minimal and prima donna presence lends a paternal air of scientific and legal efficiency. Their will *will* be done—even in their absence. The non-professional staff is influenced by their "expert" views which, after all, are not very different from the supposedly less enlightened views and practices of social workers, nurses, dieticians, and orderlies. (Also, since the less prestigious hospital professionals are mainly women, there is a conditioned and much reinforced tendency to serve, please, and second-guess the male psychiatrist before he even makes his judgment known.)

In the past, the American Psychological Association totaled 18,215 members. This increased to 30,839 members. This Association does not publish an accurate sex-ratio count of their members but, in a personal communication, estimated that twenty-five percent are women. (Personal communication from Ms. Jane Hildreth, American Psychological Association Membership Office.) This would mean that approximately 4,580 women in the 1960s and 7,500 women in the 1970s were psychologist-members at all levels of "expertise." We must remember that not all psychologists are clinicians. Many teach and/or do research—exclusively. (Most psychiatrists combine their research or teaching with clinical responsibilities in both hospital and private settings.) In any event, however many *clinical* psychologists there are, they occupy positions subordinate to psychiatrists, especially within the hospital hierarchy. I would estimate that women have comprised fifteen percent of all clinical psychologists and that they, together with female psychiatrists, comprise no more than twelve percent of America's two most powerful clinical professions.

Today, as I've noted in the 2005 introduction, more women have joined the ranks of psychiatry and psychology; many are feminists, many are not. As I've also noted in the new introduction, like male mental health professionals, women have also internalized sexist views and are not always mindful about it.

Feminist thought has influenced many clinicians but an even greater number have remained immune to it or are phobic about feminism.

Of course, there are more clinicians in America, both male and female, than are listed as members of the American Psychiatric and Psychological Associations. The number of lower-"ranking" clinicians has increased tremendously during the last decades, and include degreed and non-degreed social workers, lay analysts, behavior therapists, traditional and anti-traditional and/or encounter group specialists, marriage and family counselors, school and vocational counselors, and "trained" and "untrained" paraprofessionals involved in community mental health and drug addiction projects. All such clinicians are subordinate to and take their cues from psychiatrists and psychologists. The male-female ratio is probably more equal in some of these professions—and to less avail. Predictably enough, these women are disproportionately involved in "women's work" within the profession: they see preadolescent children and women. "Troubled" male adolescents are usually referred to male therapists for fatherly role-modeling; and adult males—as well as females—prefer male therapists.[9]

Today, whether there are more female or feminist-oriented clinicians is not as important as whether insurance will or will not cover treatment, including psychotherapy, medication, and hospitalization for indigent or working poor patients. Hospital wards are overcrowded, there are never enough beds, people in need are either not admitted or are quickly discharged. While on the ward, few patients get high quality or any expert attention.

Some time ago, Dr. William Schofield sent basic information questionnaires to randomly selected practitioner members of the American Psychiatric and Psychological Associations, and to the National Association of Social Workers.[10] Complete returns were obtained from 140 psychiatrists, 149 psychiatric social workers, and 88 clinical psychologists. He found that clinical psychologists were predominantly male, in a ratio of two to one; that ninety percent of the psychiatrists were male; and that social workers (the least prestigious and well-paying of the three professional groups) were predominantly female, in a ratio of two to one. He also found that the psychiatrists and psychologists were about the same age (an average of forty-four), and were married. (Two percent of the psychiatrists and ten percent of the psychologists were divorced.) Both the psychiatrists and psychologists had backgrounds that Schofield characterized as containing "pressure toward upward social mobility." Also, of those psychiatrists and psychologists who expressed a preferred sex in their "ideal" patient, the majority "preferred" a young, attractive female patient—with no more than a B. A. degree. Perhaps this preference makes good sense. A male therapist (whose "masculinity" is already somewhat compromised by his involvement in a "soft" and "helping" profession) may receive a real psychological "service" from his female patient: namely, the experience of controlling and feeling superior to a female being upon whom he has projected many of his own forbidden longings for dependency, emotionality, and subjectivity, and from whom, as a superior expert, as a doctor, he is protected as he cannot be from his mother, wife, or girl friend. There are other reasons for this preference which I will discuss later.

It is obvious that a predominantly female psychiatric population in America (see Chapters Two and Four) has been diagnosed, psychoana-lyzed, researched, and hospitalized by a predominantly male professional population. Despite individual differences among clinicians, most have been steeped, professionally and culturally, in both contemporary and traditional patriarchal ideologies—ideologies which they put into some sort of practice within a patriarchal *institution*, such as private therapy or the mental asylum.

Before reviewing some traditional psychological and psychoanalytic theories and practices regarding sex roles and women, I'd like to review some studies about what clinicians classically believed and practiced— regardless of what kind of traditional ideologies they may have been taught.

CONTEMPORARY CLINICAL IDEOLOGY

Most contemporary professionals (like most non-professionals) unthinkingly consider what happens to men as somehow more important than what happens to women. Although men are less diagnosed than women are, *male* psychiatric illness or "impairment" is viewed as more "disabling" than female illness. The ghost of female expendability and "outsiderness" haunts almost every page of psychiatric and psychological journals—even when the subject of the article is female illness. Fewer (male) "virtues" are expected of women: it is not catastrophic or even surprising when they don't manifest any—even though their absence is both socially devalued and psychiatrically diagnosed as neurosis or psychosis.

In the 1960s and 1970s, women as subjects remained quite literally "outside" of many psychological experiments, particularly in learning or achievement-motivation: female performance proved too variable or too "minimal" to yield up the manly and publishable phenomena being sought.[11] Women—even the college sophomore subject—constituted a troublesome "error" or "noise" factor which must be excluded. Unfortunately, the results of just such experiments were accepted as the standards for normal learning or "performance," standards which, by definition, women could not achieve.

Let me remind us that some of this has changed. (See the new 2005 introduction.) As I said, more studies about female psychology have been done in the last thirty to thirty-five years. And, as we have seen, such studies have not always made it into the undergraduate, graduate, medical, law, and divinity school curricula. An academic and cultural phobia about feminist approaches to mental health have prevailed—especially at the most elite universities.

Thus, the struggle to disseminate sophisticated, relevant, and often life-saving or life-enhancing feminist research and clinical practices still continues.

The classical clinical research literature documents, challenges, and is guilty of certain biases shared by most practicing clinicians. I would like to discuss five major biases—all of which I have been "taught" either directly or indirectly, in my training as a psychologist.

(1) Everyone Is "Sick"

In general, most clinician-theorists are trained to find "pathology" everywhere: in women, in children, in men, in nations, in entire historical epochs. This is dangerous because, in doing this, we banish the concepts of good and evil from the arena of human responsibility. This bias has been more easily attacked than avoided, and I will not dwell on it at length. Dr. Maurice K. Temerlin described an experiment that took place in Oklahoma, which demonstrated the extent to which psychiatrists and psychologists are predisposed to diagnose "pathology"—wherever they look—significantly more so than non-professionals; and the extent to which the prestige of authority accounts for the kind of diagnoses made in hospital settings.[12] Temerlin asked a group of psychiatrists, clinical psychologists, and graduate students in clinical psychology to watch a taped, televised interview, on the basis of which they would make diagnoses of "psychotic," "neurotic," or "healthy." (The interviewee was a male actor who had memorized a script that was prepared in accordance with consensus judgments of what is "normal" and "healthy.") Before watching him each of the three professional groups were told by a "high-prestige" person within their own field that the man was "very interesting because he looked neurotic but actually was quite psychotic." Sixty percent of the psychiatrists, twenty-eight percent of the clinical psychologists, and eleven percent of the graduate students diagnosed "psychosis." Control (or comparison) groups, composed of professionals who did not hear any prestige suggestion, never diagnosed psychosis. Most important, perhaps, is the fact that a control group composed of non-professional people, who were randomly selected from a jury wheel and asked to watch the tape at a county courthouse, unanimously considered the man "sane." (They were told that the court was experimenting with new sanity-hearing procedures.) Temerlin interprets these findings in terms of the medical training that predisposes judgments of "illness"—especially when in doubt—combined with the tendency toward diagnostic conformity which prestige figures enforce and reward. After one of the subject-psychiatrists was "debriefed," he still defended his diagnosis as follows:

"Of course he looked healthy, but hell, most people are a little neurotic, and who can accept appearances at face value anyway?"

(2) Only Men Can Be Mentally Healthy

Thus, many clinicians think their patients are "crazy" (dysfunctional, self-destructuve, unstable) but they think their female patients are "crazier" yet. Many double standards of mental health and treatment exist: one for people of color, another for whites, one for the poor, another for the wealthy, one for natives, one for immigrants, and, of course, one for women and another for men. A study done by Dr. Inge K. Broverman et al. demonstrates the extent to which contemporary clinicians still view their female patients as Freud viewed his—and still hold to a double standard of mental health.[13] (Although this study was done 35 years agto, the results, in my opinion, are still relevant.) Seventy-nine clinicians (forty-six male and thirty-three female psychiatrists, psychologists, and social workers) completed a sex-role stereotype questionnaire. The questionnaire consisted of 122 bipolar items, each of which described a particular behavior or trait. For example:

very subjective   very objective

not at all aggressive   very aggressive

The clinicians were instructed to check off those traits that represent healthy male, healthy female, or healthy adult (sex unspecified) behavior. The results were as follows:

(1) There was high agreement among clinicians as to the attributes characterizing healthy adult men, healthy adult women, and healthy adults, sex unspecified.

(2) There were no differences among men and women clinicians.

(3) Clinicians had different standards of health for men and women. Their concepts of healthy mature men did not differ significantly from their

concepts of healthy mature adults, but their concepts of healthy mature women did differ significantly from those for men and for adults. Clinicians were likely to suggest that women differ from healthy men by being more submissive, less independent, less adventurous, more easily influenced, less aggressive, less competitive, more excitable in minor crises, more easily hurt, more emotional, more conceited about their appearances, less objective, and less interested in math and science.

It is clear that for a woman to be healthy she must "adjust" to and accept the behavioral norms for her sex even though these kinds of behavior are generally regarded as less socially desirable. As the authors themselves remark, "This constellation seems a most unusual way of describing any mature, healthy individual." The ethic of mental health is masculine in our culture. This double standard of sexual mental health, which exists side by side with a single and masculine standard of *human* mental health, is enforced by both society and clinicians. Although the limited "ego resources," and unlimited "dependence," and fearfulness of most women is pitied, disliked, and "diagnosed," by society and its agent-clinicians, any other kind of behavior is unacceptable in women! The disquieting "submissiveness," "shyness," and "pettiness" of female children is never treated as a problem: it is viewed as evidence that girls "grow up" (into their eternal childhoods) more quickly than boys do. The only reason that the "aggressive" behaviors of male children are treated as a problem is because patriarchy wants male youth to wait until it grows older before being given its license to practice "masculinity."

It is important to note that gender stereotyping traditionally protected girls and women from being accurately observed. Thus, girl-on-girl cruelty (bullying, taunting, ostracizing, slandering) was rarely "seen" by school teachers, social workers, or psychologists.

Similarly, female-on-female aggression and competition was rarely discussed—partly because female-on-female violence is far less dramatic and lethal than male violence and partly because no one much cared what women did to each other; people, including mental health professionals, cared about female aggression toward boys and men.

Still, female adolescents and adults run serious risks when they persist in "male" activities. The reverse is often true too, of course. Their parents and husbands will ostracize and psychiatrically commit them for this—and the psychiatrists will keep them in hospitals until they assert their "femininity."

Less educated and more "attractive" women are probably released sooner and more easily from state hospitals and from private treatment; they are probably also sexually propositioned more often within the hospital (a blessing or a curse, depending on your viewpoint).[14] Certainly, "feminine" domestic tasks—as opposed to "man's work"—is the slave labor of choice for women in state asylums.

In a study by Dr. Nathan Rickel, entitled "The Angry Woman Syndrome," those husbands who "put up" with their middle-aged wives' "angry" and male-like behavior are described as suffering from a "Job complex."[15] The author notes that while the reverse is often seen, namely, "where men are the angry protagonists and women the passive recipients . . . our society is so geared that it more readily accepts this as only an exaggeration of the expected masculine-feminine roles." Rickel's "angry" women are all highly successful professionally and are "neurotic" because they exhibit "male" behaviors such as

> an inability to brook criticism or competition; bursts of uncontrollable temper; the use of foul language; possessiveness or jealousy; the use of alcohol or drugs; and consorting with spouses who accept such behaviour.

Like Angrist's and McClelland's female schizophrenics (Chapter Two), they also exhibit much female behavior such as suicide threats and attempts and a "very good memory for minor slights." If such "male" behavior is "neurotic" or "self-destructive," then it should be seen as such for both sexes. (Of course, when women do the very same things as men, it always has a completely different meaning and set of consequences:

even here, it is the *wives* who are seeking treatment—the husbands, for all their "female"-like suffering, are not.)

Looking back, I find it amazing that Rickel and so many other researchers did not focus on male domestic violence at all. Obviously, both research, clinical practice, and laws and prosecution have changed in this area. True, there are still not enough beds in shelters for battered women, nor are there enough funded programs for battered women in terms of education, employment, housing, and health care, including mental health care, but it is still a different world.

And in terms of mental health care, battered women are still often blamed for choosing their batterers—or for refusing to leave them; and for leaving them "knowing" that their batterers would become even more dangerous when abandoned. Being battered does not make a woman likeable. Think of her as a hyper-vigilant war veteran with insomnia, flashbacks, a drinking problem, panic attacks, and a bad temper.

In the past, whenever sex-role stereotype lines are crossed, clinicians enforced the double standard of mental health. For example, a report tells how a male psychiatrist, Dr. Herbert Modlin, "managed" a group of "paranoid" women back to "feminine" health: he helped them re-establish their relationships with their husbands.[16] The author's therapeutic technique was as reprehensible as his goal. He decided that his "paranoid" patients needed "strong" male control, both within their marriages and within the hospital.* Modlin notes that many of these women's husbands were too "passive and compliant." He therefore "demonstrated to the man his wife's need of him [and helped] him assume a stronger position for her sake." Within the hospital, the psychiatrists were instructed to be firm and authoritarian, to disbelieve and be wary of the women's "inclinations to interpret, react to, and manipulate [their] environment on the basis of their distorted perceptions."

---

* I wonder whether he would have treated white middle-class men this way. Certainly, many psychiatrists in city hospitals serving the poor treat drug addicts and blacks, Latinos, and/or female patients similarly: their professional competence or *machismo* is measured by their contempt for and distance from their "sneakily manipulative" patients.

In another study by Dr. Franklin Klaf, the majority of female paranoid patients reported that *men* were "persecuting" them. Of course, their perceptions may not be distorted at all: they may represent an appropriately panicked reaction to reality. For example, Modlin notes that the "precipitating factor" in all the "paranoid" cases was "an actual alteration in the husband-wife relationship" which often led to a decrease or cessation of sexual intercourse. Many of the husbands were involved in work that was more important to them than their marriages, and were not only happily absent from home for long periods but sexually ungiving when present. These women were not only sexually deprived—they were nearly out of jobs. Their "paranoia" was both a way of fulfilling and avoiding the consequences they feared and saw approaching: psychological and financial unemployment.

Dr. Modlin may have listened to his patients but he did not hear what they were saying. He neatly glides over the meaning of such "delusions" as "conversations with the Devil," reported by one of his "paranoid," sexually deprived, and probably monogamous patients. The "Devil" is persuading her to become a "prostitute"—i.e., the only image of a sexually *involved* woman in our culture is that of a prostitute, and she (the patient) wished to be sexually involved. Accusations of "infidelity" are also considered as "delusionary" as is one of Dr. Modlin's female patient's complaints that twenty-one "previous shock treatments" had "ruined her brain." (They might have done so.) Rickel also somewhat underestimates (but does not overlook) the fact that one of his patients, like Freud's patient Dora, was in treatment as a "captive." He says:

> . . . she constantly expressed the fear with some basis, that her mother
> and older brother would like to see her put away. In fact, the brother
> called me with that thought in mind.

Another psychologist, in a study of female psychology, glosses over the perceptiveness of those female college students who explained their "frigidity" in terms of what the author calls "unconscious prostitution fears."[17] There is nothing very unconscious—or distorted—about such fears. For thousands of years, patriarchal society and, more recently, psychiatric and psychological journals have allowed men to separate love and sex and to condemn, prohibit, and punish female lust and agency.

Traditional patriarchal themes, like bad dreams, have reappeared in a number of published accounts of female psychology and sexuality, like Mary Jane Sherfey's conclusions at the end of her classic monograph on female sexuality, i.e., that "civilization" at its best would be undermined by female sexual liberation.[18] Dr. Judith Bardwick wrote the first academic book about female psychology after the second feminist movement occurred in America.[19] Bardwick presents a reasonable, thoughtful, and comprehensive review of various studies, accompanied by deceptive protestations of objectivity and political neutrality. Despite her clear understanding that American females never develop "selves" or "independence," she is still a Dutiful patriarchal Daughter, in the best Helene Deutsch-Esther Harding tradition. She apparently accepts a double standard of mental health, lauding the "female virtues" for women but not for men. Although she criticizes Freud's views of women, she joins him in the comfort of an "anatomy is destiny" bias. Like Horney, her version of it is "my vagina is bigger than your penis." Many of her "professional" opinions sound remarkably similar to conventional opinions. She proclaims that female children develop sexuality later than male children; that, because the clitoris is so anatomically small, female children do not masturbate or "suffer" sexual frustration, nor do they experience prepubertal vaginal sensations; that male children suffer a harsher socialization than female children; that sex for women is much more tied up with love than it is for men; that the most basic pleasure for women is that of maternity; that the vaginal orgasm exists "psychologically" and "involves fusion with a loved man."

I do not question that women report and/or experience different intensities of orgasm. What I do question is whether this picture of female sexuality is indeed biologically predetermined or whether it is culturally and economically predetermined. However, she makes an intersting point: that women are more dependent on men than on other women because of the "indifferent (or hostile) relationships they've had with their mothers and girlfriends." Horney does not interpret this in feminist terms at all. These are all familiar and "unprovable" views which, however, are more rewarded than an opposite and equally "unprovable" set of views would be.

(3) "Real" Women All Are Mothers—but Once You're A Mother, Anything That Goes Wrong Is Your Fault

Clinician-theorists still share the belief that women need to be mothers and that children need intensive and exclusive female mothering in order for both to be mentally "healthy." The absoluteness of this conviction is only equaled by the conviction that mothers are generally "unhappy" and inefficient, and are also the cause of neurosis, psychosis, and criminality in their children. Child-development textbooks are filled with these views, as is the research literature on the "schizophrenogenic" mother; the mother who produces "promiscuous" daughters, "homosexual" sons, and "criminal" or "neurotic" children.

Joseph Rheingold, in his *The Mother, Anxiety and Death*, claims that he has "been struck by the number of women who almost indifferently admit the desire to abuse, rape, mutilate, or kill a child, any child.[20] I have never known a man with this cold-blooded animosity for children."

While maternal abuse of children does exist and is exacerbated by poverty, drug addiction, unemployment, and overburdened single motherhood, most mothers do not sexually or physically abuse, neglect, abandon, or kill their children. Most women are "good enough" mothers. Some studies confirm that many fathers or live-in boyfriends have less patience with infants and children than women do and more routinely compete with, batter, abandon, or even kill children.

On the other hand, in the last 30-35 years, more western men have gotten involved in joint and hands-on parenting both during marriage and after divorce or the death of a spouse. Homosexual couples and single men have also adopted children and have fought for the right to create intergenerational families. Nonviolent fathers have also battled for and won sole custody.

Fathers do not often parent the same way mothers do—but, for the most part, they do parent.

(4) Lesbianism And Homosexuality Are Diseases

Most clinicians once viewed lesbianism and homosexuality as "pathological" or, at best, as "second best." Heterosexuality, rather than bisexuality, was the norm. Few clinicians differentiated between (male) homosexuals and (female) lesbians.

As I've noted, homosexuality and lesbianism are no longer considered to be psychiatric illnesses. Some researchers suggest that sexual preference is genetically predetermined.

However, homophobia still exists as a clinical and patriarchal cultural bias. Pre-adolescents and adolescents are taken to therapists by fundamentalist parents who view "feminine" boys and "masculine" girls as unnatural and unacceptable. Adolescents are sometimes sent to punitive military academies or to cult-like "reprogramming" centers to de-program their homosexual, bi-sexual, or lesbian inclinations.

(5) Certain Pregnancies Are Illegitimate; Certain Women Are Promiscuous

Clinician-theorists once accepted patriarchal notions of "illegitimate" pregnancies; female "promiscuity"; female "seductiveness"; and, paradoxically, female "sexlessness."[21] They acted on such views in rather powerful ways: by convincing women that they were true, or by psychiatrically incarcerating women, especially adolescents and wives, for "promiscuity." In a personal communication, a practicing psychiatrist told me about a middle-aged American woman who was psychiatrically committed by her husband and psychiatrist in the 1950s for having taken a lover; she died ten years later in the asylum.

A lawyer told me the following story: a woman in her thirties was privately hospitalized by her husband. In 1969, she began a sexual-emotional relationship in the asylum with a man younger than herself. Both seemed much happier. The asylum authorities forcibly separated them; both suffered "relapses" and, to her (the lawyer's) knowledge, both remained hospitalized. Female children whose fathers raped them were seen as "seductive"—or the mothers were blamed for not preventing the rape-incest, or for secretly "wanting" it.[22] In any event, the tone was one of "no great harm has been done anyway." The few cases of maternal seduction and incest reported are all seen as the cause of the male child's ultimate "schizophrenia."[23] Professional prostitution has been clinically viewed as female "revenge" and "aggression"—and not as female victimization.[24]

While there are exceptions, we now understand that the majority of prostitutes are blue-collar wage earners who grow old quickly and die young. Most have fled incestuous and abusive families; they turn to alcohol and drugs in order to endure working lives in which they are repeatedly the victims of profound psychological, physical, and sexual violence.

In addition, the male demand for sex with children has grown into billion-dollar industries, which include sex tourism, the sale of one's own children into indentured servitude in brothels, and the kidnapping and luring of female children under false pretenses into the sex industry.

Only a few shelters or programs exist, worldwide, that are devoted to the needs of prostituted women who wish to escape their slavery.

These five major clinical viewpoints or biases may or may not be derived from having read the works of traditional theorists and/or from having been professionally trained. In any event, these and other similar biases certainly reflect many themes in the traditional clinical literature.

TRADITIONAL CLINICAL IDEOLOGY

Although the ethic and referent of mental health in our society is a masculine one, most psychoanalytic theoreticians have written primarily about women.

Whether this choice simply reflects the greater abundance or cooperativeness of female patients, as well as the male desire to "save" and mold them, is unclear. I think something deeper has tempted and excited male psychiatrists for the last century to write about the Eternal Feminine gone "mad." I think it was both safe and "therapeutic" for them to do this. In women, they could study madness without dread. They would not be turned into stone or pigs—Valerie Solanas (the woman who shot Andy Warhol) was no Medusa; Zelda Fitzgerald was no Circe; mad women had no power.

I am not saying that Medusa or Circe were mad. On the contrary. Precisely because such women had power, they have become images that are despised and feared. Also, while many "mad" women are hostile and unpredictable, they are still women, and not as physically dangerous as their male counterparts. (Although certainly some are—and are feared as such.) More important, men of science (and art) cannot, except momentarily and romantically, and therefore safely, identify strongly with their female subjects. Their own sanity can remain firmly moored between their legs.

The subject of women has traditionally elicited the most sentimental yet authoritative pronouncements in the psychoanalytic literature, all of which imply, accept, and desire a double standard of mental health or normality.

Sigmund Freud:

[Women] refuse to accept the fact of being castrated and have the hope of someday obtaining a penis in spite of everything. . . . I cannot escape the notion (though I hesitate to give it expression) that for woman the level of what is ethically normal is different from what it is in man. We must not allow ourselves to be deflected from such conclusions by the denials of the feminists who are anxious to force us to regard the two sexes as completely equal in position and worth.[25]

We say also of women that their social interests are weaker than those of men and that their capacity for the sublimation of their interests is less . . . the difficult development which leads to femininity [seems to] exhaust all the possibilities of the individual.[26]

Erik Erikson:

For the student of development and practitioner of psychoanalysis, the stage of life crucial for the understanding of womanhood is the step from youth to maturity, the state when the young woman relinquishes the care received from the parental family and the extended care of institutions of education, in order to commit herself to the love of a stranger and to the care to be given to his or her offspring . . . young women often ask, whether they can "have an identity" before they know whom they will marry and for whom they will make a home. Granted that something in the young woman's identity must keep itself open for the peculiarities of the man to be joined and of the children to be brought up, I think that much of a young woman's identity is already defined in her kind of attractiveness and in the selectivity of her search for the man (or men) by whom she wishes to be sought.[27]

Bruno Bettelheim:

. . . as much as women want to be good scientists and engineers, they want, first and foremost, to be womanly companions of men and to be mothers.[28]

Joseph Rheingold:

. . . woman is nurturance . . . anatomy decrees the life of a woman. . . . When women grow up without dread of their biological functions and without subversion by feminist doctrines and therefore enter upon motherhood with a sense of fulfillment and altruistic sentiment we shall attain the goal of a good life and a secure world in which to live.[29*]

Carl G. Jung:

But no one can evade the fact, that in taking up a masculine calling, studying, and working in a man's way, woman is doing something not

---

* Anatomy, like the bubonic plague, is history, not destiny. Of course, there are bio-anatomical differences between the sexes. The question now is whether these differences—or the cultural conclusions drawn from them—are either necessary or desirable.

wholly in agreement with, if not directly injurious to, her feminine nature. . . . [Female] psychology is founded on the principle of Eros, the great binder and deliverer; while age-old wisdom has ascribed Logos to man as his ruling principle.[30]

M. Esther Harding:
A personal motive will carry a woman through an almost unlimited amount of monotonous work, without risk of losing her soul. For instance, she can make an infinite number of stitches if the embroidery is for a special place in her house; or she can knit sweaters and socks indefinitely for her husband and boys. . . . [Woman's real goal is the] creation of the possibility of psychic, or psychological, relation to man. . . . It is a significant turning point in [the successful woman's] relation to a man, when she finds that she can no longer look him frankly in the eyes, for it means that her real feeling which may not be shown openly has begun to stir . . . one of the factors accounting for an older woman's interest in a man much younger than herself, lies in her own emotional immaturity. Such a woman has put all her energies and attention into developing her individual and professional qualities but little into developing her feminine values . . . so long as her own emotional nature is immature, she will continue to seek her fulfillment by making someone else dependent on her, her own inner childishness being projected, or reflected, in the man to whom she is attracted.[31]

These are all familiar, prescribed, and therefore extremely seductive views of women. Their affirmation by experts has indirectly strengthened such views among men and more directly tyrannized women: events such as childbirth and marriage which, in others centuries, was unavoidable, common, and unromanticized, are here being touted by experts as spiritual luxuries, which women must *strive for*. The unchosen necessities of the past (perhaps no different from poverty, disease, or early death) were revived as salvation myths for twentieth-century women by the major psychoanalytic theorists. American middle-class women were also "seduced and abandoned" by the institution of psychotherapy and the tyranny of published "expert" opinion which stressed the mother's importance (and sole responsibility) for healthy child development. Most child development research, like most birth control research, has centered around women, not men: for this is "woman's work," for which she is totally responsible, which is "never done," and for which, in a wage-labor economy, she is never directly paid. She does it for love and is amply rewarded—in the writings of Freud et al.

Freud's views and self-professed confusion about women have been embraced, often romantically and devotedly, by female theoreticians, such as Freud's analysand and disciple Helene Deutsch, and by Marie Bonaparte, Marie Robinson, and Marynia Farnham, and by male theoreticians such as Frederick Lundberg, Erik Erikson, Bruno Bettelheim, and Joseph Rheingold. Freud's views have been more subtly supported by C. G. Jung and his disciple, Esther Harding, whose approach to human psychology is more "spiritual" and anthropological than Freud's; however, their female ideal is essentially a maternal-feminine one.

Women are biologically and therefore psychologically different from men and *vive la difference*! Woman's real problems stem from a resistance to her very unique and glorious capacity for a life of love, feeling, and maternity. Of course, modern society devalues such a life, but then, more's the pity. Women, preferably well-educated and wealthy, like Jung's female disciples, should, as individuals, transcend such devaluing.

The "Freudian" vision beholds women as essentially "breeders and bearers," as potentially warmhearted creatures, but more often as cranky children with uteruses, forever mourning the loss of male organs and male identity. The headaches, fatigue, chronic depression, frigidity, paranoia, and overwhelming sense of inferiority that Freud recorded so accurately about his many female patients was rarely *interpreted* in remotely accurate terms. Female "symptoms" were certainly not viewed by Freud as the indirect communications characteristic of slave psychologies. Instead, such symptoms were viewed as "hysterical" and neurotic productions, as underhanded domestic tyrannies manufactured by spiteful, self-pitying, and generally unpleasant women whose *inability to be happy as women* stems from unresolved penis envy, unresolved Electra (or female Oedipal) complexes, or from general, intractable, and mysterious female stubborn-ness.

In rereading some of Freud's early case histories of female "hyster-ics," particularly his "Case of Dora," what is remarkable is not his brilliance or his relative sympathy for the female "hysterics"; rather, it is his tone: cold, intellectual, detective-like, controlling, and sexually Victorian.[32] He really does not like his "intelligent" eighteen-year-old patient. For example, he says:

> For several days on end she identified herself with her mother by means of slight symptoms and peculiarities of manner, which gave her an opportunity for some really remarkable achievements in the direction of intolerable behaviour.

The mother has been diagnosed, unseen, by Freud, as having "house-wife's psychosis."

Dr. Leonard Simon reviews the plight of Dora, whose father brought her for therapeutic treatment for a variety of Victorian "symptoms."[33] He notes that Freud's case study

> could still stand as an exemplary effort were it not for a single, but major, problem having to do with the realities of Dora's life. For throughout his therapeutic examination of Dora's unconscious Freud also knew that she was the bait in a monstrous sexual bargain her father had concocted. This man, who during an earlier period in his life had contracted syphilis and apparently infected his wife . . . was now involved in an affair with the wife of Mr. K. There is clear evidence that her father was using Dora to appease Mr. K., and that Freud was fully aware of this. . . . At one point Freud states: "Her father was himself partly responsible for her present danger for he had handed her over to this strange man in the interests of his own love-affair." But despite this reality, despite his full knowledge of her father's predilections, Freud insisted on examining Dora's difficulties from a strictly intrapsychic point of view, ignoring the manner in which her father was using her,

and denying that her accurate perception of the situation was germane. . . . Freud appears to accept fully the willingness of these men to sexually exploit the women around them.

Although Freud eventually conceded (but not to Dora) that her insights into her family situation were correct, he still concluded that these insights would not make her "happy." Freud's own insights—based on self-reproach, rather than on Dora's reproaching of those around her—would hopefully help her to adjust to, or at least to accept, her only alternative in life: housewife's psychosis. If Dora had not left treatment (which Freud views as an act of revenge), her cure presumably would have involved her regaining (through desperation and self-hypnosis) a grateful respect for her patriarch-father; loving and perhaps serving him for years to come; or getting married and performing these functions for a husband or surrogate patriarch.

Freud was not the only one who disliked Dora. Twenty-four years later, as a forty-two-year-old married woman, Dora was referred to another psychiatrist, Felix Deutsch, for "hysterical" symptoms. Let me quote his description of her:

> The patient then started a tirade about her husband's indifference toward her offerings and how unfortunate her marital life had been . . . this led her to talk about her own frustrated love life and her frigidity . . . resentfully she expressed her conviction that her husband had been unfaithful to her . . . tearfully she denounced men in general as selfish, demanding, and ungiving. . . . [She recalled that] her father had been unfaithful to her mother, [spoke] of her unhappy childhood because of her mother's exaggerated cleanliness . . . and her lack of affection for her . . . she finally spoke with pride about her *brother's* career, but she had little hope that her son would follow in his footsteps . . . more than thirty years have elapsed since my visit at Dora's sickbed . . . from [an] informant I learned the additional pertinent facts about the fate of Dora . . . she clung to [her son] with the same reproachful demands she made on her husband, who had died of a disease—slighted and tortured by her almost

paranoid behaviour, strangely enough, he had preferred to die . . . rather than divorce her. Without question, only a man of this type could have been chosen by Dora for a husband. At the time of her analytic treatment she had stated unequivocally "men are all so detestable that I would rather not marry. This is my revenge!" Thus her marriage had served only to cover up her distaste of men.[34]

Thomas Szasz comments on the "hysterical" symptoms of another of Breuer and Freud's female patients, Anna O., who fell "ill" while nursing her father.[35]

Anna O. thus started to play the hysterical game from a position of distasteful submission: she functioned as an oppressed, unpaid, sick-nurse . . . young middle-class women in Freud's day considered it their duty to take care of their sick fathers. . . . Notice how similar this is to the dilemma in which many contemporary women find themselves, not, however, in relation to their fathers, but rather in relation to their young children. Today, married women are generally expected to take care of their children; they are not supposed to delegate this task to others.

To Breuer and Freud, however, it was to Anna's "great sorrow" that she was no longer "allowed to continue nursing the patient." Anna O.'s identity was first revealed by Ernest Jones in 1953. She was Bertha Pappenheim, an Orthodox Jewish feminist who fought for the rights of unwed mothers, illegitimate children, and prostitutes.

In my opinion, Bertha Pappenheim did suffer a genuine bona fide breakdown and had to be hospitalized on and off for years. She saw and heard things that weren't there and spoke nonsense and spoke in tongues. She was also catatonic for long periods of time.

However, she was the patient who created the "talking cure" and she went on to accomplish great deeds. Melinda Given Guttmann wrote the first full-length biography of this remarkable woman: *The Enigma of Anna O.: A Biography of Bertha Pappenheim*. The biography is also quite wonderful.

All or some of Freud's views about women have been extensively reviewed, criticized, and rejected by many female theoreticians: by Karen Horney, Clara Thompson, Margaret Mead, and more recently Simone de Beauvoir, Betty Friedan, Kate Millett, Shulamith Firestone, Eva Figes, and Germaine Greer. Male theoreticians such as Bronislaw Malinowski, Alfred Adler, Harry S. Sullivan, Wilhelm Reich, Ronald Laing, David Cooper, and Thomas Szasz have refuted him also but not necessarily or primarily because of his views of women.

In her 1926 essay entitled "The Flight from Womanhood," Karen Horney says:

> The present analytical picture of feminine development (whether that picture be correct or not) differs in no case by a hair's breadth from the typical ideas that the boy has of the girl.
>
> We are familiar with the ideas that the boy entertains. I will therefore only sketch them in a few succinct phrases, and for the sake of comparison will place in a parallel column our ideas of the development of women.

> THE BOY'S IDEAS
> Naive assumption that girls as well as boys possess a penis
> Realization of the absence of the penis
> Idea that the girl is a castrated, mutilated boy
> Belief that the girl has suffered punishment that also threatens him
> The girl is regarded as inferior
> The boy is unable to imagine how the girl can ever get over
> this loss or envy
> The boy dreads her envy

> OUR PSYCHOANALYTIC IDEA OF FEMININE DEVELOPMENT
> For both sexes it is only the male genital which plays any part
> Sad discovery of the absence of the penis
> Belief of the girl that she once possessed a penis and lost it by castration

Castration is conceived of as the infliction of punishment
The girl regards herself as inferior
Penis envy
The girl never gets over the sense of deficiency and inferiority
 and has constantly to master afresh her desire to be a man
The girl desires throughout life to avenge herself on the
 man for possessing something which she lacks[36]

Freud's indirect rejoinder, made in his 1931 essay entitled "Female Sexuality," is as follows:

> It is to be anticipated that male analysts with feminist sympathies, and our women analysts also, will hardly fail to object that such notions have their origin in the man's "masculinity complex," and are meant to justify theoretically his innate propensity to disparage and suppress women. But this sort of psychoanalytic argument reminds us here, as it so often does, of Dostoevsky's famous "knife that cuts both ways." The opponents of those who reason thus will for their part think it quite comprehensible that members of the female sex should refuse to accept a notion that appears to gainsay their eagerly coveted equality with men. The use of analysis as a weapon of controversy leads to no decision.[37]

At this point I would like to discuss the views of four of Freud's critics who are regarded as "revolutionary" theorists, or as profoundly innovative clinicians. Earlier theoreticians such as Karen Horney, Melanie Klein, and Clara Thompson certainly criticized Freud specifically in terms of his views of women. However, they are not popularly considered as "radical" theoreticians or clinicians—and in a certain broad sense they are not. They were not political or social visionaries, nor did they develop single standards of mental health for both women and men. I suppose that a closer reading of these theoreticians—and of others such as Melanie Klein, Anna Freud, Edith Jacobson, etc., might surprise even me with the extent of their "radicalness." I am not yet familiar enough with their work to competently review them here.[*]

I am concerned with whether a theoretician's frame of reference for what is "human" is female. I feel that any clinical theory or practice which does not have, or is opposed to, this concern, is philosophically limited and socially oppressive to both women and men.

The theorists are all male psychiatrists: Wilhelm Reich, Ronald Laing, David Cooper, and Thomas Szasz. Frantz Fanon will be discussed in Chapter Eight, "Third World Women." All four theorists are concerned with normality as well as abnormality, and with society as well as personality. All are "important": Reich for his vision of sexual and political freedom; Laing for his descriptions of schizophrenia and for his clinical call to arms; Cooper for his attempt to exorcise the demons of the family and for his feminist sympathies; Szasz for charting the psychology of power relationships, and for his moral and legal sensitivity. I will not weigh, sum up, or compare them on the basis of *all* their work. I will share my thoughts with you about each theorist in terms of only *some* of their writing.

Wilhelm Reich

Of course I knew about his jealousy, but I found at that time a moralistic attitude in him such as he usually attacked in others. The double standard of sexual behavior was quite apparent in his attack. I was not allowed to question his faithfulness to me during that period, but I was quite certain that he did not apply to himself the same standards that he expected of me. In fact, I knew that he had had an affair although he didn't tell me so.

In Oslo, I talked at length to Grethe, the woman who shared Reich's life during this period. Many of the agonies that I had experienced during my last three years with Reich were repeated in her experiences. Accusa-

---

[*]   I am now more familiar with their work. I admire Klein's understanding of the early maternal-infant bond and its ramifications, especially for mother-daughter and female-female relationships.

tions of infidelity during the last month of their life together when the relationship had deteriorated—interestingly enough with some of the same men that had figured in his accusation of me—demands of confessions, often heavy drinking, and frightening moments. . . .

Dr. Havrevold . . . once tried to refer a very worthy professional man to Reich for training, but when Reich heard that the person was a homosexual he not only refused to accept him, but said, "*Ich will mit solchen Schweinereien nichts zu tun haben.*" [I don't want to deal with such filth.]

Ilse Ollendorf Reich[38]

As a theoretician, Wilhelm Reich was a feminist.[39] He consistently condemned the patriarchal family as the primary institution of sexual and political repression in general, and of female enslavement in particular. He was fiercely opposed to prostitution, "compulsive marriage," and alienated labor. He sought a single (pan-sexual) standard of mental health for women and men. And, although he attaches a clinician's sense of importance to his own patient's individual "breakthrough" into sexual-mental health, he nevertheless remained convinced that mental health could never exist without the elimination of poverty and the oppression of women. Ideal mental health, like freedom, exists for one person only if it exists for all people. He stressed the importance of "preventive social measures" in order to rid people of the "psychic plague." He conducted free sex education clinics and stressed the importance of therapy for the poor at a time when his colleagues were trying to become respectable in order to attract a middle-class clientele. He rarely romanticized the psychology of oppression:

The well-to-do citizen carries his neurosis with dignity or he lives it out in one way or another; in working-class people, it shows itself as the grotesque tragedy it really is.

He was as sensitive to the often early, traumatic, and brutal introduction of poor women to sex as he was to the middle-class woman's lifelong non-introduction to it.

Reich's ideas about the nature and importance of "orgastic potency" (or "healthy" orgasms) can easily be, and have been, misinterpreted as "proof" that "good sex will make you free." Reich's repetitive expositions about orgasm, and about what constitute a "healthy" one, does assume the proportion of a staunch and hysterical religious doctrine, an idée fixe, that often bizarrely and shrilly invades his analyses of fascism, poverty, the family, and madness. Freud's ideas about infantile sexuality, repression, and death, and Skinner's about conditioned learning are like this also.

Reich's definition of "orgastic potency" is

> the capacity for surrender to the flow of biological energy without any inhibition, a complete discharge of all dammed up sexual excitation through involuntary pleasurable contractions of the body.

Reich certainly understood why feminists, "bluestockings," the majority of women, and male "moralists" were—and are—intolerant of male-originated notions of "free sex" or sexual liberation. He describes (with a little too much naiveté) how, in his clinical practice, he discovered that sex is experienced by the average man as a debased and degraded activity, in which power and mastery (his) must be expressed. Reich describes the universality of his male patient's pornographic and sadistic masturbation and other sexual fantasies, and his female patient's masochistic and passive fantasies. Male fantasies, then as now, involved the penis as a "murderous weapon"; as a means of "proving" potency; as a compulsively Don Juan-like "ejaculation followed by a reaction of disgust." Reich considered such sexuality as "perverse"—no matter how many orgasms are achieved.

> This sexuality is a pathological caricature of natural love. The usual evaluation of sexuality refers to its caricatures and its condemnation is justified. Thus, any controversy in the sense of fighting for or against sexuality is senseless and leads nowhere. In such a controversy the moralists would and should win. The caricature of sexuality should not be tolerated. The sexuality exercised in brothels is disgusting.

Reich claimed that once his male patients became "orgastically potent" they were

> no longer able to go to prostitutes . . . wives, once they were orgastically
> potent, could no longer submit to husbands they didn't love or submit
> when they were unaroused.

Unlike Freud, he does not suggest that we "sublimate" our sexuality for the sake of "civilization": quite the contrary. Reich claims that, once healthy genitality was asserted in his patients, they tried to find more meaningful relationships in work and in love. He claims (with no less and no more proof than Freud's) to have found a "decent nature" in every patient—if he (Reich) was able to penetrate deeply enough. "Sex-economy regulation" always led to a natural morality that was superior to a compulsive morality.

Reich, like all those who wish to understand and "champion" the insane, is caught in a dilemma: on the one hand, he says that "the profundity of some mental patients makes them more valuable from the human point of view than the Babbitts with their nationalistic ideals"; yet he also sees the insane as people who "act out," often grotesquely and suicidally, and with a great deal of suffering, both what is "wrong" and what is "repressed" in all of us. The insane are both heroines and victims, courageous and doomed. Doomed, certainly, in no small part, because of the way they are treated by sane people.

For Reich, the schizophrenic *is* schizophrenic because she is over-whelmed by anxiety (as she has been conditioned to be), when pleasurable genital and body sensations "break through"—sensations which she has *not* been conditioned to feel, and which, therefore, break through rather mysteriously. Reich is absolutely correct in stressing the importance of the body in madness. I think, in fact, that a person is considered mad, both by herself and by others, when she *acts out* her thoughts and feelings with her body. When a person does this *alone*, without any group support or consensus, she is considered "mad." As I noted elsewhere, Valerie Solanas was "crazy" (as well as "criminal") because she *acted on* what many people are content to just think about or criticize in print: namely, gross male misogeny as embodied by a particular man. Traditionally, misogyny, or woman-hating, has been so widespread that it is almost invisible; and, when highly visible, has been deemed understandable and acceptable.

Like Freud, Reich found sexual repression at the heart of every neurosis and psychosis. Its purpose was the ultimate and total submission of the individual to the family, to the state, and to work. It is sexual repression, beginning with the repression of infantile sexuality, that leads to the "fixation" on the family (to the necessity of re-creating family-like relationships for the rest of one's life). It is never quite clear whether Reich is seriously recommending that we break the incest taboo and, if so, in what manner; i.e., women in a patriarchal society are already, and to their detriment, encouraged to break the incest taboo. Reich is also unclear about the type and stages of infantile sexuality and in what way it is repressed in the infant. The prohibition against adolescent sexuality makes the now twice-repressed child "submissive" and capable of "compulsive marriage."

Reich sees sexual energy at work in the whole body, not just in the genitals. He is careful to distinguish between perverted and healthy sexuality, and between sexuality and reproduction. He views, without contempt or superficiality, the results of total and lifelong sexual unhappiness in women. He is seriously concerned with the role of the body, and with our difficulty in uniting body and mind. He views an element of "involuntary surrender" as essential for both men and women in "healthy" heterosexual intercourse.

However, in a patriarchal culture it is destructively romantic to talk too much about female "surrender" in heterosexual intercourse and, for that matter, to talk too much about the importance of female sexual happiness, without talking about the importance of female *power*. The use of sex, like drugs, can become a compulsive pacification-opiate, especially for those without the power to define themselves.

In his zeal to create a pan-sexual, normal psychology (and in his sympathy for men), Reich fails to emphasize the *enormous* male-female differences that exist in the quality and quantity of "submissiveness" and "sexual monogamy" in women and men. The family *does* repress both male and female children—but female children more so. We may also have to consider the possibility that what Reich calls a "caricature" of sexuality is actually *male* sexuality. As such, men may not be as sexually unsatisfied as women—or as open to making certain changes in the interest of sexual happiness. (Men may not really be that interested in a female-dictated definition of sexual happiness.)

Reich proclaims the existence of a primary vaginal eroticism in female children, which he feels is "socialized" out of them. This, together with the fact that he is far too silent on the importance of the clitoris in female sexuality, is disturbing; but for a pioneer of sexual liberation to *also* proclaim that all bi- and homosexuality is "unhealthy" and "regressed" is positively alarming. (Of course, he doesn't clearly differentiate homosexuality from lesbianism.)

Reich is dangerous or certainly limited when he or his devotees romanticize human sexuality to the exclusion of other human activities—or when they assume, rather naively, that ego, self, peace, and love will, like children, simply and "naturally" follow the Pied Piper of orgasm. The right to "sexual happiness" may exist in the most advanced technological-fascist state.

Ronald D. Laing

Here he is, in his own words:

> What we call "normal" is a product of repression, denial, splitting, projection, introjection, and other forms of destructive action on experience . . . it is radically estranged from the structure of being . . . if our experience is destroyed, our behavior will be destructive.
>
> Jack may act upon Jill in many ways. He may make her feel guilty for keeping on "bringing it up." He may invalidate her experience. This can be done more or less radically. He can indicate merely that it is unimportant or trivial, whereas it is important and significant to her. Going further, he can shift the modality of her experience from memory to imagination: "It's

all in your imagination." Further still, he can invalidate the content: "It never happened that way." Finally, he can invalidate not only the significance, modality, and content, but her very capacity to remember at all, and make her feel guilty for doing so in the bargain.

This is not unusual. People are doing such things to each other all the time. In order for such transpersonal invalidation to work, however, it is advisable to overlay it with a thick patina of mystification. For instance, by denying that this is what one is doing, and further invalidating any perception that it is being done by ascriptions such as "How can you think such a thing?" "You must be paranoid." And so on.

There are sudden, apparently inexplicable suicides that must be understood as the dawn of a hope so horrible and harrowing that it is unendurable.

In our "normal" alienation from being, the person who has a perilous awareness of the non-being of what we take to be being (the pseudo-wants, pseudo-values, pseudo-realities of the endemic delusions of what are taken to be life and death and so on) gives us in our present epoch the acts of creation that we despise and crave.

From the moment of birth, when the Stone Age baby confronts the twentieth-century mother, the baby is subjected to these forces of violence, called love, as its mother and father, and their parents and their parents before them, have been. These forces are mainly concerned with destroying most of its potentialities, and on the whole this enterprise is successful.

We are effectively destroying ourselves by violence masquerading as love.

Ronald D. Laing

In the book entitled *Sanity, Madness and the Family,* Laing, like Freud before him, chose women as his subjects.[40] Like Freud, he is "sympathetic" to his English female "schizophrenic" subjects. His clinical and journalistic method of interviewing is highly successful. Like Freud, however, Laing is describing the phenomena correctly, but without fully understanding their significance. Throughout the book, he remains unaware of the universal and objective oppression of women and of its particular relation to madness in women.

Most of the "schizophrenogenic" families that Laing describes are not atypical in their treatment of their daughters. All the families are involved in: (1) the sexual and intellectual repression of their daughters; (2) covert and overt patterns of paternal tyranny and incest; (3) the deep division between mother and daughter, which is characterized, on the mother's part, by an obsessive "policing" coupled with a lack of physical affection for her daughter, and on both mother's and daughter's parts, by a preference for the father-husband, and a sacrificing of each other for family stability or for temporary feelings of well-being.

(1) This repression occurs in all eleven families that Laing depth-interviewed. One of the women, Ruby Eden, became pregnant when she was seventeen. Her mother and aunts called her "slut," blamed her for the "mess" and "disgrace" she got herself into, and subjected her to all the well-known home ordeals to induce an abortion—so much for the reification of maternity in male-dominated society. We should really be asking, How do women cope with such brutal rejection of their bodies? Another of the women, Lucie Blair, is *sterilized* after giving birth to a baby girl. Both her family and the psychiatrists have viewed her as "sexually wanton." Her father says he wanted her to be a pure, virginal, "spinster gentlewoman." Maya Abbott's family is obsessed with "cleanliness and neatness" for her; Hazel King's mother is completely—and typically—sexually uninformed. According to Laing, Mrs. King

> doesn't know whether she has an orgasm, whether she has intercourse "properly" with her husband or not, whether or not he uses a contraceptive, or whether he ejaculates inside or outside of her.

This same Mrs. King has "hardly ever been outside the house unaccompanied by her own mother and father"—*since her marriage.*

The intellectual and artistic repression of daughters (and wives) is fairly total in these eleven families. Only one of the daughters interviewed (Ruth Gold) even *wants* to be an artist—and, unlike her brother, she is discouraged and punished for it. The fact that she even attempts such a task is what makes her family think she is "mentally ill." Most of these families act as if their daughters won't ever have to work at *menial* employment in the outside world—let alone at higher forms of self-development. Lucie Blair says:

> My father doesn't believe in the emancipation of women. He doesn't
> believe women should support themselves.

She further tells the interviewer that she "gets no support in anything she wants." Ruth Gold, the would-be artist, answers Laing's question, "Do you feel you have to agree with what most of the people around you believe?" with "Well, if I don't, I usually land up in a hospital." Women are often psychiatrically incarcerated for rejecting their "femininity" as defined by those close to them—and are released or are considered as "improved" when they regain it.

(2) Lucie Blair's father is typically maniacal in his (sexual) possessiveness of his daughter. He constantly told her that she would be "raped or murdered" if she went out alone. Lucie's "illegitimate" child (illegitimate because her father had not conceived it) could never be mentioned in the house. Another of the daughters, Agnes Lawson, sat on her father's (not her mother's) lap every evening while he read stories to her until she was fourteen.

(3) All of Laing's subjects had mothers of the extreme "feminine" variety: psychologically insecure, sexually repressed, poorly educated, and economically dependent—prisoners and guards of The Home, in an era when The Home is devalued. From whom could their daughters learn to be both female and human? Mrs. Blair, according to Laing, "sees herself as the subject of a forty-year-long

persecution by her husband." She says she hasn't left him because the world outside is just as persecutory, if not more so . . . the only solution is to accept one's helplessness in the persecuted position; there is nothing to be done.

While the presence of so deformed a spirit as Mrs. Blair's tempts us (and Laing) to consider *her* as "mentally ill" also, let us pause for a moment: Mrs. Blair's analysis of things is essentially correct. She has chosen the evil of persecution within the family, rather than the evil of persecution in a mental asylum, or in the "outside" world. Finally, despite paternal tyranny, most of the daughters typically preferred their fathers—at least at some time—to their mothers. The only act of near violence reported, in fact, took place when one of the daughters, Maya Abbott, took a knife to her mother.

If most of Laing's subject-families are typical in their treatment of women, the question still remains: Why are *these* eleven daughters hospitalized and/or "schizophrenic"? It may be argued that what exists in most families exists in an *extreme* form in the schizophrenogenic one. Perhaps madness is just "more of the same." It may also be argued that perhaps the mothers are as "hospitalized" within their marriages as their daughters are within the asylums. It may also be argued that sooner or later most women become, are perceived as, or think they are mad. If Laing had used "normal" (non-hospitalized) control groups he would find the same patterns. If he *followed* his "normal" control groups over time, he might even have found that the "normal" control "daughters" eventually embarked on careers as psychiatric patients.

In general, Laing is correct in placing the schizophrenic process within its social setting; correct in "making sense" out of what our society has stubbornly insisted is the essence of senselessness. Ideally, this is what *all* psychiatrists are supposed to do. However, his standards of "mental health" are as obscure or absent as were Freud's; his occasional and increasing equation of madness with mass political revolution or art forms is confused and inaccurate.

While madness and art may both be protests against and escapes from forms of oppression, and while both experiences involve pain *and* being discriminated against, I suppose I still "discriminate" between the totally *personal* and *invisible* modes of madness and the potentially *public* and *tangible* modes of art.

Laing is his own best critic. In his most recent introduction to *Sanity, Madness and the Family*, he says that the concept of "family pathology" is a "confused" one.

> It extends the unintelligibility of individual behaviour to the unintelligi-bility of the group. It is the biological analogy applied now, not just to one person, but to a multiplicity of persons . . . [it is a form of] "pan-clinicism" . . . in which all of society is seen in need of psychological "curing."

The danger of such pan-clinicism is its fearful optimism. Thomas Szasz calls this "psychiatric imperialism." While society may indeed be in need of "curing," the traditional psychoanalytic method, with or without insight, and based on the illusion of individual freedom, cannot do such "curing"; especially if the major social institutions remain "uncured"; and if the "patient" has had to suffer their socializations for many, many years.

David Cooper

> [paranoia is a] poetic protest against the invasion by one's family and by others . . . the poetry is unappreciated by society and gets treated by psychiatry if spoken too loud . . . (paranoia) is not a resolvable fantasy . . . we must use and not resolve our persecution anxieties.
>
> David Cooper

David Cooper, in his book, *The Death of the Family*, presents a poetic summary of much of Reich's and Laing's condemnation of the nuclear family, sexual repression, and society's misunderstanding and brutalization of madness.[41] He makes some good statements about female socialization such as

> A little girl, before she can be her own baby is plied with object-babies [the more "perfect" dolls being the most expensive], so that she can learn to forget her experiences of birth and childhood and become not her own child but childlike; so that if later in life, she wants to return to this area, she can become childish, [regressed, hysterical, etc.] . . . she was educated to be a mother like her mother, like all other mothers who are educated not to be themselves but to be "like mothers."

However with even this much of a feminist consciousness, Cooper still systematically refers to his idealized "non-leader" leaders and therapist-prophets as "he" rather than "she." He begins using the pronoun "she" as often as "he" only when he refers to patients or children. He is still more linguistically and therefore psychologically advanced than other theoreticians, to be sure. Also, while he doesn't *blame* mothers for the evils of family-influences, he talks more about the mother-child relationship than the father-child relationship—which, to me, connotes his acceptance or romanticization of the female as the *exclusive* maternal agent in civilization.

Cooper often writes as if he were the Pied Piper of psychiatry: he is a sleight-of-phrase clown, a self-proclaimed Holy Idiot, a prophet for the sexual and cultural indulgences of (white) men. Telling men to withdraw from deep or monogamous commitments is not very revolutionary: few men are committed to the ethic of love or sexual monogamy. The majority of women cannot "withdraw" from these ethics and practices as long as marriage and prostitution remains their primary mode of psychological and economic survival, and as long as they do not control the means of reproduction. Telling white men to "ready" themselves *culturally* for the *structural* revolution that the brown, black, and yellow people of the world will accomplish *for* them (with their blood and bodies) is hardly "revolutionary." Cooper also contradicts himself here: he admires the tyrants and mass murderers Mao and Castro as "embodiments" of the "leadership principle"—but these are two men who put their bodies where their principles were and, unlike mad people and Holy Idiots, "won" their battles—in their lifetime and in the flesh.

The problem is that Cooper is unable to come to terms with biology, with the body. He certainly is not alone in this failing. For example, he (incorrectly) analogizes the spiritual hunger of the "First World" with the physical hunger of the "Third World": he emphasizes the desirability of same-sex relationships but, like Reich, rather nervously and glibly insists that it is "immaterial" whether or not we make love—sexually—with members of our own sex. He displays his most dangerous misunderstanding of the body's role, especially in relation to female oppression—and just where he is trying to be most sympathetic. Let me give two examples.

First: Cooper has a typically male voracious longing for the incorporation of experience in general, and for colonizing or, in his case, "embodying" the "female principle" in particular. Women are conditioned to shun "experience" or adventure as destructive to their non-self selves; men are conditioned to accumulate it in order to develop their non-self selves. He is, from a liberal point of view, *commendably* interested in "being" (which is "female") as well as in "doing" (which is "male"). He proclaims that men must live out the reality of the "woman," the "child," and the "wise old woman-man." However, men simply *cannot* live out the reality of women—who, by definition, cannot *choose* to live the female reality but are condemned to do so.

In order to live out the female principle, Cooper would have to give up the privileges and psychology of the male principle—which is impossible. Perhaps Cooper is *able* to desire or experiment with "femaleness" only because he already has "maleness" under his belt (literally). It is no accident that Cooper shies away from male homosexuality. Despite the fact that in one sense it is an extreme expression of misogyny, it is also the closest that some men come to experiencing the "female reality" in our culture, i.e., other men despise and brutalize them.

Cooper is interested in what he conceives to be the "spiritual" aspects of being female—more than in its reality. How different is what he is implying from what the countless myths of male maternity (Zeus as Athena's mother, Adam as Eve's mother, the Church as the mother of us all) have implied, namely, the devaluation or distortion of that very same activity in women?

Men can only *be* when women can *do*: perhaps both sexes can both *be* and *do* only after the way in which culture discriminates on the basis of *biological* differences between them is modified or eliminated. Further, the cultural revolution's dictum that *being* is better than *doing* places women in a rather familiar (and disadvantaged) position: now, they are barefoot, pregnant, psychologically dependent, and abandoned on communes rather than in suburbs. As for the "wise old woman-man" principle: only when female biological aging is as valued and rewarded (by sexual and political power) as is *some* or (ideal) male aging, then, and only then, will what Cooper suggests here be meaningful.

When Cooper suggests that "we must learn to play with pain" and that "irony is the most revolutionary sentiment of all," I am reminded of Chekov's Dr. Ragin, in the story "Ward Six." Dr. Ragin philosophizes about the "pain" involved in being a mental patient—until he becomes one himself. Then, behind bars, he is seized with terror, despair, rising anger, and complete impotence. After being beaten, he goes "mad" with very unphilosophical anger, and is dead by the next day.

Another example of how crucially Cooper misunderstands the role of the body in female oppression is his comparison of the traditional therapist (whom "one pays by the hour" to be "all things for anyone") with the female prostitute. There is a very obvious and important difference between female prostitutes and male therapists. Prostitutes are degraded and punished by society; it is their *humiliation* through their *bodies*—as much as their *bodies*—which is being purchased. It is true that in a wage-labor and advanced capitalist society, people are encouraged or forced to "sell" most things, their time, skills, physical labor, etc. However, female prostitution may exist in a somewhat separate category from these other "sales" of self.

Psychotherapists are (at least in some circles) the priests of our society. Their patients do not pay for their humiliation. And even when therapists do have sexual relations with their female patients, the psychological dynamics never involve a reversal of sex-roles.

Cooper espouses many of Reich's and what were the "counterculture's" myths or, more realistically, hopes: (1) that, contrary to Freud's pessimistic and, therefore, bourgeois concepts, we have unlimited energy at our disposal; (2) that we can "love" many people; (3) that spontaneous "groupings" of people are sufficiently better and different from the nuclear monogamous family, and that unlike every other social institution, they would not mirror it, or would not impose a family or state-like tyranny over individual liberty (4) that charismatic anti-leader leaders are *not* leaders, or conversely, that "leadership" is intrinsically evil; (5) that "madness" is somehow "revolutionary"—when in fact, in our culture, it is a cry of powerlessness and an illness which is mercilessly punished.

Thomas Szasz: Witches And Madness

Here he is, in his own words:

> The fundamental conflicts in human life are not between competing ideas—one of which is true and the other false, but rather, between those that hold power and use it to oppress others, and those who are oppressed by power and seek to free themselves of it.
>
> Witches and mentally ill patients are actually created through the social interaction of oppressors and oppressed. If the observer sympathizes with the oppressor, then the witches are "mad." If the observer sympathizes with the victim, then the oppressor is "mad." Both explanations bypass, conceal, excuse, and explain away the terrifyingly simple but all important fact of man's inhumanity to man [and I add: to woman] . . . the image of the knight in armor, the symbol of mobility, and of the black witch as a symbol of depravity embodies the sexocidal hatred of women . . . [for the] knight is always male [and the] witch is always female in all the fairy tales and mythologies of (medieval and modern) times.

There can be no abuses in institutional psychiatry because institutional psychiatry, by definition, is an abuse.

Social oppression in any form, and its manifestations are varied, among them being . . . poverty . . . racial, religious, or sexual discrimination . . . must therefore be regarded as prime determinants of direct communication of all kinds (e.g. hysteria).

Thomas Szasz

Thomas Szasz has been concerned with the extent to which "politics" produces medical and ethical consequences which are psychiatrically "incurable." In *The Myth of Mental Illness,* he analyzes the psychology of (female) "hysteria" as a "slave state," and criticizes Freud's patriarchal and authoritarian theories and practices. In *Law, Liberty and Psychiatry,* he condemns the violation of the legal and constitutional rights of the "mentally ill"; the cruel irony of the humanely intended insanity defense; and the pervasive correlation between poverty and psychiatric incarceration. In *The Manufacture of Madness,* he develops Elizabeth Packard's analogy between institutional psychiatry and the Inquisition: he labels the persecution of witches as "sexocidal," and compares their treatment to that of mental patients.[42]

Our knowledge of witches is at best conjectural. Their case histories were kept by their more socially powerful male persecutors—just as hospital records are kept by psychiatrists and psychologists, and not by the mental patients themselves. Were witches really cultural and political revolutionaries, matriarchs, and Amazons come back to do battle with the Church? Were they wealthy and powerful women whose property was coveted? Were they beautiful women whose sexuality was both feared and desired? Perhaps all of these things—perhaps none. Jules Michelet in *Satanism and Witchcraft: A Study in Medieval Superstition,*[43] suggests that many witches were midwives and healers, whose knowledge of painkillers, abortion, and herbal or "faith healing" threatened the Church's anti-scientific, anti-sexual, and anti-female doctrines.* Szasz suggests that, "by aiding the weak, the white witch tended to undermine the established hierarchy of dominance—of priest over penitent, lord over peasant, man over woman—and herein lay the principal threat of the witch and [is] why the Church set out to crush her." The designation of witches as (good) "white" or (bad) "black" witches once more denotes Christian cultures' deep racism—predating both slavery in America and industrialization.

Una Stannard, in an article entitled "The Male Maternal Instinct," describes the Church's successful attempt to both usurp the female power of childbirth (the Church, through baptism, really gives "birth" to children) and devalue this same function in women (Christ's was a Virgin birth).[44] Male "spirits" can enter "receptacle" women to plant their holy or devilish seeds. Thus, women could indeed be "possessed"—or, worse still, through contraception, could control whether and by whom they would be "possessed." *

John Putnam Demos, Carol F. Karlsen, and others have suggested that witches were also women who lived alone and had property or wealth that was not under any man's control and that the church coveted. Some historians have suggested that some accused witches were actually battered women.

Michelet also suggests that the combination of feudal poverty and Catholicism so brutalized women that some turned "strange": they lived alone, or with each other, and were not subject to husbands. He suggests, further, that witches were persecuted for their presumed (or actual) ritualization of sexuality, including incest, lesbianism, homosexuality, and pagan group sex. In celebrating what the Church prohibited—and which occurred anyway—the witch cults constituted a strong opposition, or complementary religion. Szasz notes that

---

*   I am suspicious of women romantically identifying with witches, who, after all, were tortured and martyred. Whoever they "really" were, witches were defeated; whatever their psychological and religious truths, they attained too little material power. Further, they (supposedly) still worshiped a *male* Devil and had ritual intercourse with phallus substitutes.

*   The Malleus, a kind of religious handbook of male superiority, claimed that "among women midwives (who often could perform abortions), surpass others in wickedness . . . all witchery comes from carnal lust [which in women] is insatiable." On either count, they were dangerous to and therefore persecuted by the male Church.

. . . the witch, like the involuntary mental patient, is cast into a degraded and deviant role against her will; is subjected to certain diagnostic procedures to establish whether or not she is a witch; finally is deprived of liberty and often of life, ostensibly for her own benefit.

Of course, many witches—and some female mental patients—no longer wish to suffer or lead lives as pariahs. Szasz quotes an English witch, who, when led to the stake, tells the crowd not to blame her judges:

I want to die. My family shunned me. My husband repudiated me. If I live I could only be a disgrace to my friends. I longed for death and I lied to gain my end.

The role of the witch—or the mental patient—is often, like suicide, the only resolution (the "cure") for having been born female. Psychiatrists and inquisitors share certain views of women-witches: because they aren't men, they are mysterious and therefore dangerous; they are really inferior beings—but with hidden powers; they are responsible for male sexual aggression because of their "sinfully" seductive natures. Women have "power" not because they are Satan's agents but because the psychiatrist's mother was a woman—and she had (and still has) "power" over him. Witch-hunters often considered masturbation as proof of "witchcraft"; nineteenth-century psychiatrists thought it caused "insanity" and some-times cured it by performing clitoridectomies.

Szasz describes the inquisitors' insatiable and psychiatric-like curios-ity about their victims' sexual fantasies and activities. Isolation, social ostracism, hydrotherapy, physical beatings, shock therapy—all psychiat-ric techniques—were first practiced by witch-hunters. Although the straitjacket, solitary confinement, brain surgery, and systematic physical violence were traditionally psychiatric "treatments," they are now being replaced by tranquilizers, anti-depressants, and shock therapy. The Inqui-sition's more *obviously* violent methods are no longer needed to attain a female's submission and belief in her inferiority and sinfulness; however, we shouldn't write off as non-violent the often serious negative effect involved in the long-term administration of standard psychiatric drugs.

Twentieth-century mental patients are not burned at the stake or subjected to the "water ordeal"—in which a witch's "innocence" was established if she *drowned*. Many mental patients *are* sexually and physically assaulted; their earning capacity (as wives or in other capacities) is even more seriously damaged than a criminal inmate's; their property and money are handed over to their husbands or children when they are declared "insane and incompetent"; like witches, they are publicly and constantly humiliated, and made to "confess" their sexual and other wrongdoings. While all of their body hair is not shaved off in a search for the "Devil's mark," many (male) mental patients are close-shaved and both male and female patients are kept short-haired and "anonymous"-looking, in regulation hospital-prison clothing.

Szasz notes the similarity of zeal with which inquisitors and psychiatrists hunt and classify (or diagnose) witches and mental patients. (I have rarely heard of a psychologist diagnosing "normality" or "health" on the basis of projective test results; even more rarely have I heard of a psychiatrist presenting a "healthy" case history at a hospital staff meeting.) Armed with a fearful knowledge of illness and sinfulness, both the Holy Father (the Inquisitor) and the Scientific Father (the psychiatrist) are interested in saving female souls. Their methods: confession, recantation, and punishment. Of course, modern psychiatrists would not think that "helping" an "unhappy" woman accept her feminine role is at all similar to "helping" a witch return to Christ.

Szasz is a provocative and political thinker, with a strong commitment to civil liberty, and a highly developed moral sensibility. I do not agree with him that private therapy is either very "private" or that it is necessarily freed from a variety of social abuses. Nor do I believe that madness does not exist. I agree that madness can be understood in terms of oppression and conditioning, but I am not sure *our understanding* alone will be enough to change what oppression has wrought—in our lifetime. Szasz is certainly right when he concludes that our treatment of "madness" is itself unethical and oppressive. However, I think he underestimates the deeply conditioned nature of woman's *compliance* with her literal and psychological self-sacrifice. Many female mental patients view themselves as "sick" or "bad" and commit themselves, quite voluntarily, to asylums or to private psychiatrists. The fear of economic, physical, and sexual deprivation or punishment teaches women to value their own sacrifice so highly that they quite "naturally" perform it. And if their anger about this natural self-sacrifice drives them "mad," asylum practices will exact their sacrifice anyway.

The "revolutionary," contemporary, and traditional ideologies and practices I've discussed thus far all subscribe to a double standard of mental health and/or to many patriarchal myths about "femininity." As I've mentioned earlier, not every American clinician necessarily believes or acts upon *all* of these beliefs. However, he or she probably believes a good many. Further, all clinicians are involved in the *institution* of private practice—an institution which, like a mental asylum, is structurally modeled upon that of marriage and the patriarchal family.

THE INSTITUTIONAL NATURE OF PRIVATE THERAPY

A great deal has been written about the covertly or overtly patriarchal, autocratic, and coercive values and techniques of psychotherapy. Freud believed that the psychoanalyst-patient relationship must be that of "a superior and a subordinate."[45] The psychotherapist has been seen, by his critics as well as by his patients, as a surrogate parent (father or mother), savior, lover, expert, and teacher—all roles that foster "submission, dependency, and infantilism in the patient: roles that imply the therapist's omniscient and benevolent superiority and the patient's inferiority. Thomas Szasz has remarked on the dubious value of such a role for the patient and the "undeniable" value of such a role for the "helper."[46] Practicing psychotherapists have been criticized for treating unhappiness as a disease (whenever it is accompanied by an appropriately high verbal and financial output); for behaving as if the psychotherapeutic philosophy or method can cure ethical and political problems; for teaching people that their unhappiness (or neurosis) can be alleviated through individual rather than collective efforts (or can't be alleviated since the human condition is "tragic"); for encouraging and legitimizing the tendency toward moral irresponsibility and passivity; and for discouraging emotionally deprived persons from seeking "acceptance, dependence, and security in the more normal and accessible channels of friendship."[47] The *institution* of psychotherapy can also be viewed as a form of social and political control that offers those who can pay for it temporary relief, the illusion of freedom, and a self-indulgent form of self-knowledge; and as an institution that punishes those who cannot pay for such illusions by being forced to label *their* unhappiness as psychotic or dangerous, thereby helping society consign them to asylums.

The institution of private therapy is a patriarchal one—regardless of whether the individual clinician is female or male. As such, most clinicians are no more divinely inspired or in touch with their own emotions than anyone else is in our culture. Our culture's criteria for an "expert" are the same for engineers and soul-healers: objectivity, rationality, impersonality. Clinicians, with rare and feared exceptions, are not oracles, priestesses, prophets, or tribal shamans. They do not make *personal* intercessions for their patients with the unknown or with the unconscious. As scientists, they probably do not believe in the "unknown," or, if they do, wish to conquer it. Clinicians are more respected and trusted by their teachers, colleagues, and patients if they remain unavailable and impersonal. Unfortunately, some male clinicians who agree with such a critique have sometimes gotten involved in self-revelatory and "touching" or sexual behaviors with their patients. Given our culture, such behaviors are especially abusive to their female patients.

Traditionally, any analysis or comparison of private therapy with mental asylums would be a class-based one. Poor people are hospitalized; middle- and upper-class people are not; or are hospitalized privately for a shorter time; or have access to private treatment. Nevertheless, with the increase in psychiatric outpatient clinics, community mental health centers, and "therapeutically" oriented case work in social agencies and schools, poor and people of color, especially women, are experiencing more contact with some of private therapy's practices and ideas. Many more women than men are involved in private therapy, both as private and as clinic outpatients.

For most women (the middle-class-oriented), psychotherapeutic encounter is just one more instance of an unequal relationship, just one more opportunity to be rewarded for expressing distress and to be "helped" by being (expertly) guided or dominated. Both psychotherapy and white or middle-class marriage isolate women from each other; both emphasize individual rather than collective solutions to women's unhappiness; both are based on a woman's helplessness and dependence on a stronger male authority figure; both may, in fact, be viewed as re-enactments of a little girl's relation to her father in a patriarchal society; both control and oppress women similarly—yet, at the same time, are the two safest (most approved and familiar) havens for middle-class women in a society that offers them few—if any—alternatives.

Both psychotherapy and marriage enable women to express and defuse their anger by experiencing it as a form of emotional illness, by translating it into hysterical symptoms: frigidity, chronic depression, phobias, anxiety and eating disorders, panic attacks, and the like. Each woman, as patient, thinks these symptoms are unique and are her own fault: she is "neurotic." She wants from a psychotherapist what she wants—and often cannot get—from a husband: attention, understanding, merciful relief, a *personal solution*—in the arms of the right husband, on the couch of the right therapist. The institutions of therapy and marriage not only mirror each other, they support each other. This is probably not a coincidence but is rather an expression of the American economic system's need for geographic and psychological mobility—i.e., for young, upwardly mobile "couples" to "survive" and to remain more or less intact in a succession of alien and anonymous urban locations, while they carry out the function of socializing children and making money. Most therapists have a vested interest, financially and psychologically, in the supremacy of the nuclear family. Most husbands want their wives to "shape up" or at least not to interfere with male burdens, male pleasures, or male conscience.

The institution of psychotherapy may be used by many women as a way of keeping a bad marriage together or as a way of terminating it in order to form a good marriage. Some women, especially young and single women, may use psychotherapy as a way of learning how to catch a husband by practicing with a male therapist. Women probably spend more time during a therapy session talking about their husbands or boy friends—or lack of them—than they do talking about their lack of an independent identity or their relations to other women.

However, like male therapy patients, women often talk about their mothers first and for a very long time before they talk about their fathers. And, as women have entered the work force at higher income levels, they have encountered women as employers, employees, physicians, judges, lawyers, spiritual counselors, and so on, and they do increasingly talk about them in therapy sessions.

The institutions of middle-class psychotherapy and marriage both encourage women to talk—often endlessly—rather than to act (except in their socially prearranged roles as passive women or patients). In marriage, the talking is usually of an indirect and rather inarticulate nature. Open expressions of rage are too dangerous and too ineffective for the isolated and economically dependent women. Most often, such "kitchen" declarations end in tears, self-blame, and in the husband graciously agreeing with his wife that she was "not herself." Even control of a simple—but serious—conversation is usually impossible for most wives when several men, including their husbands, are present. The wife-women talk to each other, or they listen silently, while the men talk. Very rarely, if ever, do men listen silently to a group of women talking; even if there are a number of women talking and only one man present, the man will question the women, perhaps patiently, perhaps not, but always in order to ultimately control the conversation from a superior position.

In psychotherapy, the patient-woman is encouraged—in fact directed—to talk, by a therapist who is at least expected to be, or is perceived as, superior or objective. The traditional therapist may be viewed as ultimately controlling what the patient says through a subtle system of rewards (attention, interpretations, and so forth) or rewards withheld—but, ultimately, controlling, in the sense that he is attempting to bring his patient to terms with the female role, i.e., he wants her to admit, accept, and "solve" her need for love. However, such acceptance of the human need for other people, or for "love," means something very different when women are already our culture's "acceptors" and men our culture's "rejectors." Such acceptance is further confused by the economic nature of the female need for "love."

Traditionally, the psychotherapist has ignored the objective facts of female oppression. Thus, in every sense, the female patient is still not having a "real" conversation—either with her husband or with her therapist. But how is it possible to have a "real" conversation with those who directly profit from her oppression? She would be laughed at, viewed as silly or crazy and, if she persisted, removed from her job—as secretary or wife, perhaps even as private patient.

Psychotherapeutic talking is indirect in the sense that it does not immediately or even ultimately involve the woman in any reality-based confrontations with the self. It is also indirect in that words—any words—are permitted, so long as certain actions of consequence are totally avoided—such as not paying one's bills.

Private psychoanalysis or psychotherapy is still a commodity available to those women who can buy it, that is, to women whose fathers, husbands, or boy friends can help them pay for it. Like the Calvinist elect, those women who can *afford* treatment are already "saved." Even if they are never happy, never free, they will be slow to rebel against their psychological and economic dependence on men. One look at their less privileged (poor, black, older, and/or unmarried) sisters' position is enough to keep them silent and more or less gratefully in line. The less privileged women have no real or psychological silks to smooth down over, to disguise their unhappiness; they have no class to be "better than." As they sit facing the walls in factories, offices, whorehouses, ghetto apartments, and mental asylums, at least one thing they must conclude is that "happiness" is on sale in America—but not at a price they can afford. They are poor.

Given the traditional and contemporary psychological ideologies about women and/or the patriarchal nature of the *institution* in which they are practiced, in what way should women relate to either the ideologies or the institutions? In what ways can therapy "help" women? Can female therapists "help" female patients differently than male therapists do? Can feminist or "radical" therapists "help" female patients in some special or rapid way? Can a technique based on transference, or on the resolution of an Oedipal conflict—i.e., on a romanticization of a rape-incest-procreative model of sexuality—wean women away from this very sexual model? What new "curative" techniques can emerge from a feminist analysis of human psychology?

There are a number of contemporary clinicians who wish to "help" women. (Contemporary clinicians' views regarding feminism are discussed in Chapter Nine.) Many still share the profession's and our culture's bias against or genuine ambivalence and confusion about feminism. Many such clinicians are trying to develop new views that will lead to new techniques. Many clinicians are trying to return to the originally revolutionary implications of Freudian psychoanalysis. And many women, dedicated feminists and anti-feminists alike, are still seeking "help" of some sort. I would like to share several thoughts with both the patients and the clinicians.

First, contrary to what their hysterical detractors may think, these clinicians are not hot-headed nihilistic extremists. As a group, they are predominantly young, white, male, and middle-class. They have been steeped in "social reformism" and the importance of the individual. (None of which is bad.) As a group, they have little power and consequently, are often too unreflectively or impractically idealistic. They often tend to be as ideologically inflexible as establishment groups. Radical projects such as therapy communes and "freak-out" centers may be short-lived, and at best palliative, if larger social forces (over which clinicians have little control) don't change. Another paradox or danger in radical as well as in any other mass psychiatric project involves viewing basic human needs for security and communication as "therapy," rather than as normal human needs—and rights.

The role that insight plays in effecting behavioral and emotional change is, like the effect of ideas on history, a matter resolved more by faith and experience than by scientific proof. To achieve political insight about one's own oppression is no more a sure road to paradise on earth than is the achievement of personal insight a guarantor of individual happiness. Group defined and achieved insights or "alternative" working and living arrangements may not prove any more invulnerable to the pull of early conditioning or surrounding social forces than do individual solutions. Unfortunately, reality is not so easily captured, no less proclaimed away, by either tragic ideologies, for example by Freudian, Christian or liberal myths; or by optimistic ideologies, for example by Reichian or pagan myths. People and social structures change slowly if at all. More people inherit than experience revolutionary change. Very few people are transformed by myths before those myths have become the justificatory images of a new order. Most people simply obey new myths, as inevitably as they did old myths.

The ideas and alternative structures of a radical or feminist psychotherapy both excite and disturb me. However, the difficulty of translating one's ideology into therapeutic action remains a problem for clinicians and people, whether traditional or feminist. For example, what happens to us as children in families may be very difficult to "will" away psychologically, even in the best of peer-group structures, even by the most scrupulous "contracts" between a therapist and her patient, or between a group and an individual.

CHAPTER FOUR

THE FEMALE CAREER AS A PSYCHIATRIC PATIENT

> The insistence that femininity evolves from necessarily frustrated masculinity makes femininity a sort of "normal pathology."
> Judith Bardwick[1]

SINCE CLINICIANS AND RESEARCHERS, as well as their patients and subjects, adhere to a masculine standard of mental health, women, by definition, are viewed as psychiatrically impaired—whether they accept or reject the female role—simply because they are women. Given this fact, it is not surprising that many studies report greater female than male "neurosis" or "psychosis," often regardless of nationality, marital status, age, race, or social class. Psychologists and sociologists have always considered women as part of the social class their husbands and fathers belong to. This is not a valid classification, from either a psychological or an economic point of view.

In the past, women saw themselves as "troubled" or "disturbed." They were also viewed as such by relatives and by mental health professionals. Thirty to forty years ago, women in America, England, Canada, and Sweden were seen and considered themselves as more "disturbed" than their male counterparts. A study published by the U. S. Department of Health, Education, and Welfare indicated that, in both the black and white populations in America, more women than men *reported*

having suffered nervous breakdowns, having felt impending nervous
breakdowns, psychological inertia, and dizziness.[2] Both black and white
women also reported higher rates than men for the following symptoms:
nervousness, insomnia, trembling hands, nightmares, fainting, and headaches.

White women who were never married reported fewer symptoms
than white married or separated women. These findings are essentially in
agreement with an earlier study published by the Joint Commission on
Mental Health and Illness.[3] The Commission reported the following
information for non-hospitalized American adults:

(1) Greater distress and "symptoms" were reported by women than
    by men in all adjustment areas. Women reported more distur-
    bances in general adjustment, in their self-perception, and in
    their marital and parental functioning. This sex difference was
    most marked at the younger age intervals.
(2) A feeling of impending breakdown was reported more frequently
    by divorced and separated females than by any other group of
    either sex.
(3) The unmarried (whether single, separated, divorced, or widowed)
    had a greater potential for psychological distress than did the
    married. This was a very controversial issue. For instance, in a
    study of the psychiatric "health" of the Manhattan community,
    higher psychiatric "impairment" was found among single men
    when compared with married men than among single women
    when compared with married women. Among married people the
    sexes did not differ in the proportions rated psychiatrically
    "impaired."[4] The HEW report also documented the fact that
    single white women in the general population reported less
    "psychological distress" than married or separated white women.
    Hagnell, in his study of a Swedish population, found a higher
    probability of mental disorder in married than single women.
    Perhaps women who were single and employed behaved, in some
    ways, more like men than married women do: as such they were
    seen as "healthy"—but only up to a point.
(4) While the sexes did not differ in the frequency with which they

reported "unhappiness," the women reported more worry, fear of breakdown, and need for help.

Dr. Dorothy Leighton et al.,[5] in a study of English- and French-speaking Canadians, found that women had a higher risk of "psychiatric disorder" than did men, at all ages (twenty to seventy), and that "symptomatology" increased with age. Dr. Olle Hagnell found a greater incidence of "mental disorder" among Swedish women than men.[6]

In the years between 1960 and 2005, it became clear to me that men, not women, were jailed for dysfunctional, unbalanced, and anti-social behavior, but were not necessarily diagnostically pathologized for it; male criminals, including drug addicts and alcoholics, did not necessarily see themselves as "mentally ill," nor were they veiwed by others this way.

In this same period of time, more women than ever before were also jailed for drug- and aggression-related crimes, but they were often viewed as "mentally ill," not as master career criminals. Many imprisoned women have been beaten and raped in childhood and battered or prostituted as adults; they often find that jail is the first time in their lives where they can lead relatively violence-free lives. They are often very eager to join therapy groups in prison.

In 2000, Elizabeth A. Klonoff, Hope Landrine, and Robin Campbell found that women, more than men, had more "depressive, anxious, and somatic symptoms" because women "experienced a deleterious stressor that men do not: sexist treatment." In fact, those women who experienced "frequent [or violent] sexism" (rape, battery) had "significantly more symptoms" than either men did or than other women did whose experience of sexism was less. Therefore, in their opinion, "gender specific stressors" play a role in "psychiatric symptoms among women" and may also account for "well-known gender differences in those symptoms as well."

In other words, gender-violence leads to suffering and to diagnosable psychiatric symptoms. So, even though there is much to criticize about what the various versions of the DSM are actually diagnosing, it is also clear that oppression and violence in general and gender-violence in particular lead to a variety of "mental disorders," and that women are therefore truly suffering—and are also being diagnosed in various ways.

In 2000-2001, the World Health Organization (WHO) found that more women than men, worldwide, suffer from gender-violence and therefore from specific kinds of "mental illness." The WHO also relates the various female symptoms to "gender specific risk factors such as gender based roles, stressors, negative life experience . . . gender-based violence, socioeconomic disadvantage, low income and income inequality . . . and unremitting responsibility for the care of others." It also indicates that sexual violence is very high for women, worldwide, and that women suffer from a "correspondingly high rate of Traumatic Stress Disorder (PTSD)." WHO estimates that a "lifetime prevalence rate of violence against women ranges from 16%-50%" and that one in five women suffer rape or attempted rape."

In 2001, the National Institute of Mental Health (NIMH) reported that 22 percent of Americans (or 50 million people) suffer from a diagnosable mental disorder; that four of the ten leading causes of disability in the United States and other developed countries is a "mental disorder" such as depression, bi-polar disorder, obsessive-compulsive disorder, anxiety disorder, eating disorder, post-traumatic stress disorder. According to the NIMH's statistics, approximately 18.8 million Americans are depressed in a given year. Interestingly, while NIMH does note that eating disorders are primarily a female problem, it does not provide a gender breakdown of the most frequently diagnosed illnesses.

And, in 2003, a study by Dr. Badri Rickhi et al. found that more Canadian women sought "complementary therapy" for a variety of reasons than did their male counterparts.

A double standard of mental health—combined of course, with misogyny and the female help-seeking and distress-reporting role— affects women far more seriously than by presenting relatively unflattering academic studies of them. Only some of the studies mentioned above are concerned with how many of these "psychologically distressed" women are also in various kinds of psychiatric and psychological treatment.

Many factors have already been discussed that would suggest or predict a large female involvement with psychiatric facilities. For example, the real oppression of women—which leads to real distress and unhappiness; the conditioned female role of help-seeking and distress-reporting—which naturally leads to patient "careers" as well as overt or subtle punishment for such devalued behavior; the double or masculine standard of mental health used by most clinicians—which leads to perceiving the distressed (or any) female as "sick," whether she accepts or rejects crucial aspects of the female role. Men are not usually seen as "sick" if they act out the male role fully—unless, of course, they are relatively powerless contenders for "masculinity." Women are seen as "sick" when they act out the female role (are depressed, incompetent, frigid, and anxious) and when they reject the female role (are hostile, successful, and sexually active—especially with other women). Large female involvement with psychiatric facilities is also predicted by the comparatively limited social tolerance for "unacceptable" behavior among women—which leads to comparatively great social and psychiatric pressure to adjust—or be judged as neurotic or psychotic; the female need for some sort of vacation from the female role, yet one that would satisfy her needs for dependence and nurturance; and finally, the female nature of the psychotherapeutic and hospital institutions—which leads to their being accepted more easily by women than by men. Additional facts would also predict a large and increasing female psychiatric population. For example, female longevity, coupled with the relative shortening of the child-rearing years (and the emphasis on female youth), leaves many women "unemployed" at an early age; just as public employment discrimination against women and lack of job training and opportunities leave most women "unemployed" at every age—and with few alternatives to home life.

The data documents a consistently large female involvement with psychiatry and psychotherapy in America, an involvement that has been increasing rather dramatically since 1964. During the 1960s, adult women, far more than adult men, constituted the majority of private psychotherapy patients, as well as the majority of patients in general psychiatric wards, private hospitals, public outpatient clinics, and community mental health centers.[7]

A pattern of frequent and recurring hospital commitments, as well as lengthy stays, seems to characterize the female "career" as a psychiatric patient.[8] There is some evidence that women are detained longer and die sooner than men with the same psychiatric diagnosis, and that the personality characteristics of long-term hospital "stayers" are "feminine" in nature.[9] Although more men than women are admitted to state and county hospitals, women are detained for longer periods—especially women over thirty-five.

The female "career" as a psychiatric patient in America seems to follow a certain pattern as a function of age, marital status, social class, race, and most certainly, "attractiveness" (of course, this last is hard to document). It is important to remember that many more people are hospitalized for "mental illness" than for "mental retardation"—a basically genetic and biological phenomenon which, as a biological event shows a relatively stable prevalence rate over time. "Mental illness," a primarily cultural event, increases and decreases over time. Also, more people may be incarcerated or diagnosed and treated in America for "mental illness" than for criminal offenses.

Thirty to forty years ago, women were most concentrated in outpatient facilities between the ages of twenty and thirty-four. Kadushin noted that among all the private therapy patients he surveyed, "young housewives [had] the most complaints."[10] In terms of age, twenty to thirty-four are women's "prettiest" and childbearing years. Even if they are "unhappy" or functioning at low levels, their child-rearing responsibilities and/or sexually youthful appearance keep them within the "outside" patriarchal institutions such as marriage and private psychotherapy. The largest number of women in both general and private hospitals (institutions where women have predominated as psychiatric patients) were between the ages of thirty-five and forty-four. This was also true for men, but there were *still* significantly fewer men than women in this age bracket who were psychiatrically hospitalized. White and/or wealthy women in private hospitals, women of color and/or poor women in general psychiatric wards are reacting to being both overworked and, paradoxically, to the beginning signals of their sexual and maternal "expendability." Hospitals provide them with warning therapy (via pills, shock treatments, and humiliation) to make as little protest about this state of affairs as possible. If they persist in being "depressed" about this state of affairs, or reacting with "hostility," repeated or longer confinements in private and public hospitals await them. State and county asylums function as a final dumping-ground for "old" women.

The female "career" as a psychiatric patient requires a closer and more thoughtful analysis than statistics or small-sample studies can yield. Therefore, I wanted to talk to women about their patient experiences. I was curious to see to what extent the kind of psychiatric patient "career" suggested by national statistics also exists at a grassroots level. I also wanted to see how much my theoretical approach to "madness" would describe the circumstances surrounding female psychiatric hospitalization or treatment. I wanted to see how many of the clinical biases I outlined in Chapter Three would be spontaneously reported by "naive" women.

THE INTERVIEWS

As women, most of our lives with men are dramatic and theatrical affairs. We "play" at being women; we dress up like Mommy—for Daddy's sake; we're always on stage, working at being some other woman—a "beautiful" woman, a "happy" woman, a well-paid-for woman.

Our lives with women are generally less dramatic. The "play," for better or worse, ended long ago. We talk more to women. Men don't have the time, the interest, or the capacity to engage in "woman's talk"—which never seems to "go" anywhere and often makes no "sense." Thus, dialogue, words, interviews between women, reveal more about the female condition than do test scores or statistics.

I spoke with sixty women, whose ages ranged from seventeen to seventy, about their experiences in private therapy and mental asylums. Collectively, their experiences spanned a quarter century and a continent (from Rhode Island to California). Two women were in private therapy and mental asylums in England. The majority of these experiences took place in large cities in New York, New Jersey, Illinois, and California.

The interviews were very informal and were held in either of our homes, over long cups of coffee, and often more than once. They were tape-recorded—as long as and whenever it didn't interfere with spontaneity or rapport. I encouraged and answered any questions about myself and about why I was, in effect, "interviewing" them. I did have a standard questionnaire form, which usually wasn't properly filled out (by either the women or myself). We tended to "talk out" the details. I participated very actively in the conversations and, after no more than an hour's grace, expressed my own views.

I met some kindred spirits—and some not; I made and received many midnight phone calls, some of which were exhausting and depressing. Hope often united with humor: for example, when someone would exclaim, with great surprise, that she was "telling me things she would never even tell her therapist!" I was as exhilarated as an amateur detective when different women told me about the *same* therapist or hospital. Unknowingly, they duplicated and corroborated one another's experiences, and helped me re-create several years in the life of a particular therapist or hospital. I was more exhilarated when several of the women, who at first were even reluctant to talk to me privately, attended professional conferences of psychiatry and psychology some four months later in New York City where they were very vocal, angry, and thoughtful about their experiences.

More often, sorrow, anger, helplessness, and guilt marked my interviewing days. I remember arguing with someone about whether or not she was "crazy": after six years of therapy and two hospital commitments, she thought she was, I thought she wasn't. Slowly, some remembered fear silenced her. Slowly, and quite emphatically, she began agreeing with me—with *Dr.* Chesler, of course. (There is a possibility that that type of "experimenter effect" happened *throughout* the interviews—without my awareness. My report of the interviews, like any scientific or artistic report, will be as "truthful" as my sensitivity, integrity, and basic premises allow). I helped a lonely and unmarried woman avoid an unwanted psychiatric commitment. Afterward, quite understandably, she wanted to live with me "for a while." I offered her money and other temporary shelters, both of which she refused. I never saw her again. I was constantly asked to find lawyers, physicians, employers, landlords, therapists, and baby sitters. I failed these requests more often than not. I am not by temperament a "social worker." My failings and strengths are those of an intellectual and an artist rather than those of a "crisis-intervener" or an organizer. However, these requests for help were from women who were less in need of "social work" than of a station on a feminist underground railroad.

At no time did I wish to classify these already "overclassified" women. I *did*, however, originally seek them out in terms of one of five categories of experience. These women comprise a non-random sample, in that they were sought because they *had* certain kinds of experiences: women who (1) had sexual relations with their therapists (SWT women); (2) had been hospitalized in mental asylums (MA women); (3) were lesbians (The word "lesbian" is problematic: it identifies a woman as strictly in terms of her *sexual* activities as the word "woman" does. It also, unfortunately, has a historically negative valuation. However, many lesbians think it a very "respectable" word—and those who don't, think it should be used more often and positively in order to make it so); (4) were Third World women (TW women); and (5) were feminists in therapy. This categorization wasn't simple. For example, in talking to a particular lesbian about her experiences in private therapy, it sometimes became apparent that she had also been psychiatrically hospitalized and had since become a feminist. Some Third World women, feminists, and SWT women had *also* been psychiatrically hospitalized. Naturally, since they were all women, their "psychiatric careers" often turned out to be rather extensive.

Table 1 presents a comparison of these five groups in relation to some aspects of their psychiatric patient careers. Fifty-four women are presented. Of the original sixty interviewed, five women were sexually propositioned by their therapists and refused him. They are not here included. One black woman who was also a lesbian but who had no private therapy experience, is not included either. As is indicated, the averages for a particular variable within each experience-category are based on a *different* number of women. Not all the SWT women were psychiatrically hospitalized (only four were, as compared to eleven MA women); not all the women in any of the five categories ever saw a female therapist, etc. Thus, there are usually unequal and often small numbers of women being compared on a particular category average. I decided not to run any statistical tests for this reason—and for a more important reason. Those trends that are important are as visible to my eye as to your own. Trends which echo those found in the national statistics (and there are many) will be better understood by an intelligent discussion of the individual interviews than by a clean bill of statistical "health." Also, each of these fifty-four women has a universe of experience to relate—a universe that cannot be inhabited by any other woman. And what happened to this group as a whole happened absolutely. However, their experiences seem to parallel and make human sense out of the studies and statistics cited earlier.

Since racism is as deep, as complicated, and as absolutely evil a factor in American society as is sexism, I decided to view the Third World women shown in Table 1 as a separate group—regardless of any differences in their class origins, educational backgrounds, political beliefs, sexual preferences, and types of psychiatric experience. For a similar reason, I viewed all the (white) lesbians shown in Table 1 separately, regardless of any differences in class origins, political beliefs, types of psychiatric experience, etc. These two decisions, which I made beforehand, and for strictly ideological reasons, were fruitful ones.

Looking at Table 1, it is evident that these fifty-four women were experts about the "mental illness" profession. Nearly half of the women (N=26) are or were legally married at least once. Nearly a fifth of them (N=12) have children. Twelve of the forty women in the non-feminist categories expressed some feminist awareness or defined themselves as feminists (one of the SWT women; seven of the lesbians; two of the MA women, and two of the TW women). They had seen a total of 136 therapists and "averaged" (by category) between three and four therapists

Table 1: Fifty-four Women: Some Comparative Information Regarding Their Psychiatric Hospitalization and Private Psychotherapeutic Experiences: 1945-1971

	Sex with therapist N-11	Lesbians N-9	Mental asylum N-11	Third World N-9	Feminist N-14
Average age at first hospital commitment	N- 4 AV.- 25	N- 6 AV.- 21	N- 11 AV.- 29	N- 3 AV.- 26	N- 0 AV.- 0
Total average duration in hospital (in days)	N- 4 AV.-103	N- 6 AV.-320	N- 11 AV.-476	N- 3 AV.-428	
Private hospitals (in days)	N- 2 AV.-131	N- 4 AV.-245	N- 6 AV.- 60	N- 0	
General and state hospitals (in days)	N- 2 AV.- 75	N- 4 AV.-190	N- 9 AV.-550	N- 3 AV.-428	
State hospitals (in days)	N- 1 90	N- 1 730	N- 6 AV.-722	N- 2 AV.-575	
Number of therapists seen	N- 11 TOT.- 35 MODE- 3.0	N- 8 TOT.- 21 MODE- 3.0	N- 8 TOT.- 29 MODE- 4.0	N- 7 TOT.- 18 MODE- 3.0	N- 14 TOT.- 33 MODE- 2.0
Number of male therapists seen	N- 11 TOT.- 23 MODE- 2.0	N- 5 TOT.- 9 MODE- 2.0	N- 5 TOT.- 21 MODE- 3.0	N- 6 TOT.- 10 MODE- 2.0	N- 10 TOT.- 15 MODE- 2.0
Number of female therapists seen	N- 8 TOT.- 12 MODE- 2.0	N- 7 TOT.- 12 MODE- 2.0	N- 8 TOT.- 29 MODE- 4.0	N- 3 TOT.- 8 MODE- 2.0	N- 10 TOT.- 15 MODE- 2.0
Total duration in therapy (in months)	N- 11 AV.- 51	N- 9 AV.- 44	N- 8 AV.- 40	N- 7 AV.- 25	N- 14 AV.- 39
Total duration with male therapists (in months)	N- 11 AV.- 40	N- 5 AV.- 39	N- 8 AV.- 35	N- 6 AV.- 17	N- 10 AV.- 30
Total duration with female therapists (in months)	N- 8 AV.- 14	N- 7 AV.- 21	N- 5 AV.- 8	N- 3 AV.- 24	N- 10 AV.- 19

N = Number of women
Av. = Average

Mode = Number most frequently given
Tot. = Total number of therapists

apiece. By category, they had remained in private therapy from about two years to more than four years.

They were also experts about mental asylums: twenty-four of the women had been psychiatrically committed at least once, ten for suicide attempts and five for depression. They had been hospitalized from a minimum of about four months to a maximum of about sixteen months. The average duration in hospitals for all of the twenty-four hospitalized women was about a year. However, individual variation was very great. Some women had been hospitalized only once for a relatively brief period (for two- or three-month "stretches"); still others had been hospitalized a few times for very long periods (five years or more.) By category, the women had been in private hospitals (white middle- and upper-class enclaves) from a minimum of about two months to a maximum of about eight months; in both general psychiatric wards and state hospitals from a minimum of about two and a half months to a maximum of about ten months; and in state hospitals alone from a minimum of three months to a maximum of nearly two years.

In terms of private therapy, all of the women had seen about as many female as male therapists. However, with only one important exception, they had remained in treatment at least twice or three times as long with male as with female therapists. The important exception here are the Third World women, who stayed in therapy longer with female than with male therapists, and whose total duration in therapy was shorter than that of any other group. Among white women, the lesbians saw female therapists for the longest average time period (twenty-one months). The feminists remained with female therapists for an average of nineteen months. However, both the lesbians and the feminists still saw male therapists for twice as long a period as they saw female therapists.

Table 1 may be viewed in terms of my concept of a female career as a psychiatric patient—a career whose shape is influenced by the extent to which the "feminine" role is accepted or rejected, as well as by the woman's age (or "expendability"), race, class, and marital status. For example, let's look at the age at which the women were *first* committed to asylums. Lesbians were committed at the youngest age (when they were twenty-one) of any group. What is perceived (and experienced) as an extreme rejection of one's "feminine" role is the most stressful and dramatically punished of all female offenses in our society. Let's compare the "psychiatric patient careers" of the least "feminine" of the women—the lesbians—with those of the most "feminine"—the SWT women. (I am defining "femininity" mainly in terms of dependence on a man.)

The SWT women had committed a dramatic version of father-daughter incest—a sine qua non of "femininity" in patriarchal society. Nine of the eleven SWT women were legally married at least once *before* therapy while only one of the nine lesbians had ever been heterosexually married. The psychiatric careers of the SWT women reflect their "femininity" in several ways:

(1) They remained in therapy (a marriage-like institution) longer than any other group (for an average of fifty-one months, seven months longer than the lesbians did). For SWT women, going to therapy both reflected the problems they were having with their "feminine" role and provided another way of acting out that role. The fact that lesbians remained in treatment for the second longest period of time (for an average of forty-four months) underlines the extent to which therapy is a culture for both female accepters and female rejectors of the "feminine" role—and how similarly socialized both types of women are.

(2) *Fewer* of the SWT women were ever psychiatrically committed at all; four of the eleven SWT women (less than one-third) were hospitalized, as compared with six or two-thirds of the nine lesbians. It is important to note that two of the four SWT women were committed right after, and one during, their "affairs" with their therapists. Here we may remember in what ways clinical as well as societal bias rewards "femininity" in both psychiatric and social settings—up to a certain point—as long as the woman is young and/or attractive. The totally attractive "feminine" woman is not usually hospitalized. (She may still be "depressed" or "anxious" without being incarcerated for it.)

(3) Not only were the lesbians psychiatrically committed at an earlier age, but they remained in asylums for a total average of more than three

times as long as the SWT women (for an average of ten months compared with an average of three and one-half months).

Perhaps one can argue that the SWT women were simply "caught" (Table 1) at an earlier stage of their patient "careers." When they grow older their patient careers may resemble those of the MA women and may involve even greater hospitalization periods than those of the lesbians. The SWT-type woman may get so "depressed" or "anxious" that she will have to be treated for these extreme expressions of "femininity." However, I don't think this is true. For example, the ages of the SWT women at the time I interviewed them ranged from twenty-five to fifty; the MA women ranged in age from nineteen to seventy. I think we're dealing with two different kinds of women. The SWT women may be "unhappy" but they remain committed to a "feminine" ideal throughout their lives. As such, they are not as stressed or punished by the fact and meaning of psychiatric hospitalization—as the lesbians are. The lesbians, in turn, for a number of reasons, are not as trapped into a *hospitalized* psychiatric career as are the MA women. Here we may remember the various studies that found greater "mental health" among single than married women. Of course, what is usually measured as "mental health" is male characteristics— some of which economically independent women (or women indepen- dent of men) would exhibit more than economically dependent women would.

The mental asylum (MA) women in Table 1 were *first* committed at the oldest average age of any of the groups (when they were twenty-nine years old). These eleven women probably reflect the scores of women on the national level who begin filling the psychiatric wards in general, state, and private hospitals when they reach their thirties. They have already had patient careers in private or outpatient clinic treatment during their twenties. Now, no longer "young," they are both more desperate and more "expendable." By this age they are stressed either by marriage and children—or by being unmarried and childless. Four of the eleven MA women were legally married, and two had children. Of the two women who were hospitalized for the longest time period, one was a single white woman and the other a very much married Puerto Rican mother.

Psychiatric hospitalization is perceived by them as an escape from and as deserved punishment for their desperation, unhappiness, etc.

Third World women remained in private therapy for the shortest time period of any group, for an average of twenty-five months. They were also the only group who remained in treatment longer with female than with male therapists. The simplest explanation for both these facts is that of poverty. Third World women couldn't easily afford the white middle-class luxury of "feminine" father-worship. This is not to say they didn't *want* to see male therapists or didn't *want* to remain in therapy for longer periods. Six of the nine TW women interviewed saw (and *wanted* to see) male therapists; only one saw only female therapists; two saw both male and female therapists. The three women who saw female therapists saw agency or hospital social workers or pre-doctoral psychologists. It was at a price they could afford: it was free. Explanations other than "poverty" to account for the comparatively short therapy duration among TW women would include: the fact that, for better or worse, TW women are not as well "trained" for careers as psychiatric patients as are white women (although they are better "trained" than TW men); the fact that they mistrust, fear, and have no easy access to a professional world that is usually threatening, unsympathetic, and unable to "cure" them; the fact that some of their family and friendship needs are satisfied within the ghetto culture—as long as they are willing to remain within it, on its terms.

Only three of the TW women I interviewed were hospitalized—too small a number to reveal anything conclusive about the comparative effect of race and sex on the frequency or duration of hospitalization. It is possible that female psychiatric patient careers are primarily white and/or middle-class phenomena. Third World women are hospitalized, controlled, and commit suicide in many other ways: in jails; in medical experimentation mistreatment, and neglect; in doomed attempts to be treated as "white." I will discuss this more fully in Chapter Eight.

Table 1 seems to suggest that feminists are never psychiatrically hospitalized or, as Shulamith Firestone has suggested in *The Dialectics of Sex*, that feminism is the cure for all the female disorders described by Freud. Actually, six of the twenty-four feminists were hospitalized: five were lesbians who became feminists after their hospital experiences. They are not shown as feminists in Table 1. The fourteen non-hospitalized (white) feminists ranged in age from twenty to forty-five and were mainly involved in the culture of private therapy. They saw therapists for a total average of more than three years. Among white women, feminists remained in therapy with female therapists for the second longest time period—for an average of nineteen months.

There are many other inferences to be drawn from the information in Table 1. I will not draw any. Instead, I would like to discuss each of the interviews in greater depth, beginning with the most unambivalently "feminine" of the women—those who had sexual relations with their therapists.

1. "Demeter." Marble statue from the sanctuary of Demeter at Cnidos.
   Ca. 350-340 B. C.
2. "Pluto and Proserpina" by Bernini, 1621-22

Modern women are psychologically starved for nurturance and role-models, i.e., for female heroines and protective goddesses. It is significant that mothers and daughters have been minimized or totally excluded as primary figures in Judeo-Christian mythology. Demeter and Persephone were the central figures of a mother-daughter religion—the Eleusinian mysteries—in ancient Greece. Demeter is the goddess of life, corn, or grain. Her daughter Persephone (Demeter's own virgin-self) is abducted and raped by Pluto, god of the under-world (or possibly Zeus or Dionysus, either of whom, according to myth, may have been Persephone's father). In great sorrow and anger, Demeter refuses to let any crop grow until her daughter is returned to her. Finally, Persephone is allowed to remain with her mother for most of the year (spring, summer, and autumn), and with her husband during winter, when no crops can grow. While Demeter protects and "saves" her daughter, Persephone is still denied uniqueness and individuality. Both women still symbolize the sacrifices of self that biology and culture demand of women; both women represent a rape-incest-procreation model of sexuality.

3. "Joan of Arc and Judith" from the manuscript executed in Arras in 1451 by Martin leFranc—*Le Champion des Dames*

Some women, in states of madness, identify with Joan of Arc, the not-so-legendary Maid of Orleans, and with the Catholic Madonna. These two figures are the modified Christian equivalents of the pagan goddess Demeter and her daughter Persephone. Joan is the only Persephone who is not kidnapped into marriage or impregnated. She never becomes a mother. She avoids the Demeter-mother and Persephone-daughter fate. She is our only remembrance of Amazonian culture. However, Joan is still ritually sacrificed as a source of male renewal—not through pregnancy and motherhood, but through her military victories for a male sovereign, and her subsequent political persecution—and canonization. Since Joan does not live in Amazon society, she is doomed to lead a male, rather than a female, army.

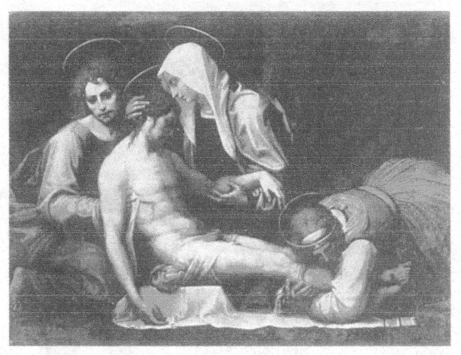

4. "The Entombment" by Fra Bartolommeo

Unlike Demeter, the Catholic Mary has no daughter. Her only contact with divinity is through her "servicing" of men: be it the Holy Father or her own son. Catholic mythology, as shown in Fra Bartolommeo's painting, symbolizes the enforced splitting of woman into either mother or whore—both of whom nurture, worship, and ultimately mourn a dead man and/or a divine male infant. Like many women, Mary foregoes sexual pleasure, physical prowess, and economic and intellectual power in order to become a mother. Sigmund Freud has said that: "A mother is only brought unlimited satisfaction by her relation to a son; that is altogether the most perfect, the most free from ambivalence of all human relationships."

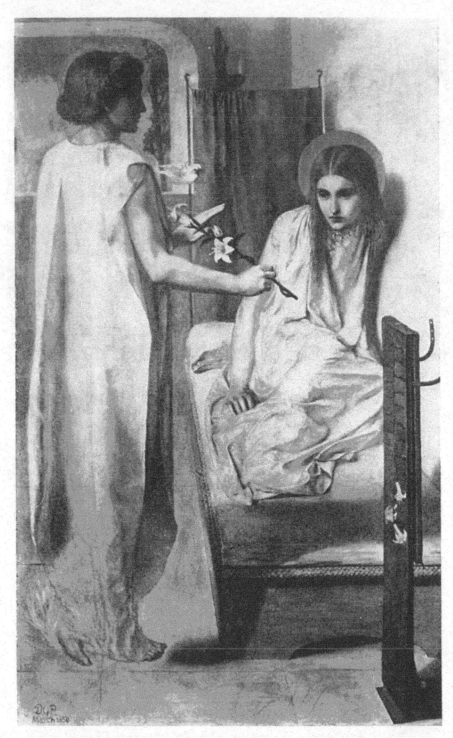

5. "The Annunciation" by D. G. Rossetti

6. "The Alba Madonna" by Raphael

Rosetti has painted a very young Mary—a somewhat terrified, trapped, and asexual girl, whose cross of sorrow, self-sacrifice, and service begins with the news of her forthcoming divine pregnancy. Unlike the pagan Demeter, Athena, or Diana, the Madonna is usually portrayed as physically undeveloped and maternally "beautiful"—as only a contented, gracious, and somewhat matronly mother can be to the male oedipal eye (as in Raphael's "The Alba Madonna"). Interestingly, the Madonna often grows younger as her son grows older until, in Michelangelo's sculpture of the Rome "Pietà," she is idealized as the eternal Virgin Mother, and looks young enough to be her son's bride. The Madonna is the primary role-model in Christian culture.

7. Insane Asylum: Crowded ward of the New York Lunatic Asylum, Blackwell's Island, 1868

Elizabeth Packard (Chapter One) was hospitalized by her husband against her will in 1860 in a private asylum that probably looked like this. Violent women, terrified women, suicidal women, women being driven mad by the hospital itself—all crowded together in a physically and psychologically humiliating setting. Women have probably always constituted the majority of patients in private hospitals. Nelly Bly, an American journalist, admitted herself to the Blackwell Island asylum in 1887, in order to write an exposé, which appeared in the New York *World*. Periodically, exposés of mental asylums and criminal prisons have appeared in American newspapers, but neither institution (like the institution of the family upon which they're patterned) has disappeared or been substantially reformed.

8. France's oldest mental asylum, the Salpetrière, reserved special wards for old and indigent women, prostitutes, pregnant women, and young girls. While the total number of female and male patients in state asylums has steadily decreased (due to drug therapy, outpatient facilities, and the increasing usage of old-age homes), the percentage of patients who are "old" women in state asylums has just as steadily increased. An "old" woman even more than an "old" man, is a useless "thing," an object of scorn, mockery, pity, and neglect.

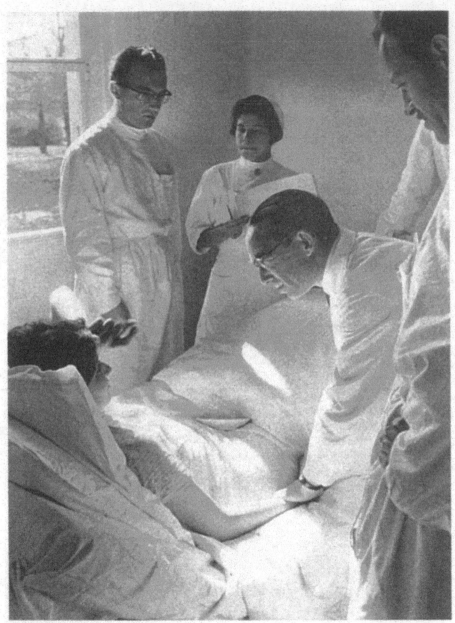

9. This photo was taken in a mental hospital. The players in the drama are as old as the witchcraft trials: distant, condescending, potentially benevolent but all-powerful male Doctor-Inquisitors; a subservient female Nurse-Handmaiden; and a female Patient-Witch "possessed" by unhappiness, powerlessness, and dependence.

10. "Artemis and Iphigenia," reconstruction by Studniczka

Artemis, or Diana, the virgin huntress, is Apollo's twin sister. Unlike Athena or Aphrodite, her "mother" is not a man, but a woman. Artemis is reportedly always attended by sixty ocean nymphs and twenty river nymphs. According to one myth, Artemis rescues Iphigenia from being sacrificed by her father Agamemnon. Artemis is a lesbian figure of Amazon origin. The only way her father, Zeus, can seduce her female lover Callisto is by assuming Artemis' form.

11. "The Conversation," sculptor unknown

These two women are strongly sensual, familiarly so, with each other, but not in a way that particularly appeals to male (or female) pornographic fantasies. They seem to be there *for each other*—and not as objects either to quell male fears of impotence or entrapment, or to excite male rape-lust.

12. In America, more non-white women of all ages develop diseases and die
    prematurely than do white women. The non-white infant mortality and adoles-
    cent suicide rate is significantly higher than comparable white rates. Many Third
    World women must raise their children alone, either with tragically inadequate
    welfare stipends, or with salaries that are significantly lower than those of
    employed black, Hispanic, and white *males*. Women's prisons in America house
    predominantly Third World women who have committed petty economic crimes
    and/or who have been battered and have killed their batterers in self-defense.

13 and 14.   In tropical Africa, although the birth rate is very high, the maternal death rate is alarming, and the infant death rate in certain regions is as high as 150-400 per 1000 live births. While most women in Africa have traditionally always worked strenuously in childbearing and rearing, in agriculture and/or commerce, they have not been political, military, or religious leaders as often as men have, nor has polyandry existed as often as polygamy. There have, however, been many female queens and warriors in Africa—as forgotten as their South American, Asian, and European counterparts. To date, most African revolutionary political leaders, militarists, judges, and priests are men, not women. The genital mutilation of women still exists in certain African countries.

Today, AIDS has a female face in Africa. Mass gang-rapes have characterized tribal and ethnic warfare, especially in Rwanda and Sudan where genocide has also ocurred.

15. Athenian Red-figured Pottery, 450 B. C.

  Most women are shocked and astounded by scenes of female warriors, who are victorious in physical battles with men or, for that matter, victorious against natural forces or political opponents. (Military or epic-romantic violence is also a metaphor for other *definitive* actions.) In Greek art, victors traditionally move from left to right (or from "feminine" to "masculine"). Here is a victorious, mounted Amazon, riding right, about to spear a fallen Greek. The helmeted Greek is about to spear another Amazon, who turns in her flight to defend herself with her ax, while her exceedingly graceful and muscular companion raises her ax in both hands to assist her. The Amazon on horseback is wearing boots with fur tops.

  All the figures are red. The full battle scene, depicted on the urn, is not shown in this photograph. It includes five other Amazons, one driving a chariot and two others watching part of the total battle between six Greeks and seven Amazons.

16. Athenian Red-figured Pottery, V-IV Century B. C.

A bearded Greek, wearing stockings, and a helmet decorated with a dolphin (a symbol of the origin, divinity, and tragedy of the male child) is attacked by two Amazons. The saber-wielding Amazon cuts a joyful, almost transcendent figure. She wears shoes, long sleeves, and trousers under a belted tunic, and an oriental cap.

Amazon weapons depicted in Greek art include axes, sabers (swords), bows and arrows (usually of the Scythian variety), shields, and spears. Animals such as panthers, lions, and dogs are shown on Amazon shields. The Amazons sometimes wear greaves, Attic or Thracian helmets, and oriental caps (with or without mantles). Footwear includes boots, shoes, sandals, ankle straps—and bare feet. In some battle and many non-battle scenes, Amazons are shown wearing short tunics and jewelry. There is evidence that Amazon societies existed in Africa, in the Mediterranean and Aegean regions, near the Black Sea, and in South America.

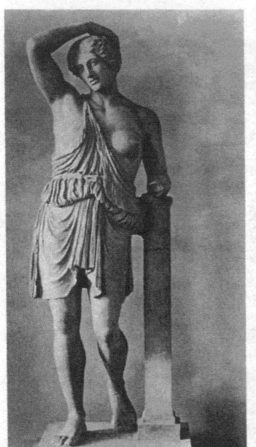 

17 and 18.   "Wounded Amazon," Roman copy of Greek statue attributed to Polykleitos or Kresilas, 440-430 B. C. This marble Roman copy of a Greek sculpture stands 6 feet 8 1/4 inches high. The Amazon is wearing a short belted chiton and an ankle strap. Her hair is short, parted, and combed back. She is said to be wounded in or above her right breast (the breast, or rather the lacteal gland, purportedly burned off in childhood in Amazon tribes). This woman is intensely beautiful, rhythmical, and serene.

WOMEN

CHAPTER FIVE

SEX BETWEEN PATIENT AND THERAPIST

To the Daddy's Girls we were—and are no longer—
I dedicate this poem and chapter.

SOMETHING BORROWED, SOMETHING BLUE
More and more lately,
there's a man
on my couch
talking about his
girl friend or his wife.

I've always loved
to borrow things
from women:
library books, perfume, cigarettes and shawls
    delicious
this dressing up for Daddy,
and as safe
as playing a part
in a play
that must end
before bedtime.

So I listen,
a gravely curious
little girl,
with eyes so clear
a woman can
drown in them
silently.

Phyllis Chesler
1970

"I am a doctor of the soul" [the Guru] said quietly. "I am certainly not interested in that silly little body of yours. . . . [Under my guidance you will learn] control of your senses, whereby you may come at will—instantaneous orgasm at my command. . . . [Regard my erection] impersonally, not as an object of love, but as a demonstration of spiritual advancement." [The Guru teaches Candy various yoga exercises, some of which] . . . in any other context would suggest the sexual and perhaps even the obscene. Candy crossly blamed herself for making the association and attributed it to her own insecure and underdeveloped spirit. [When Candy's period is overdue, the Guru] gives her a plane ticket to Tibet [where Candy meets a holy man in a Buddhist temple]. Candy began her meditation at once, concentrating all her attention on a single spot, the tip of Buddha's nose. It was wonderful for her—all her life *she* had been needed by someone else—mostly boys—and now at last she had found someone that she herself needed . . . Buddha!

[The temple is struck by lightning and, with the dung-crusted holy man seated beside her, they watch as] the huge Buddha . . . toppled forward, pitching headlong to the temple floor in a veritable explosion. Although it seemed to fall right on top of them, Candy and the holy man were miraculously unscathed, and were left bunched together. . . . In fact, she felt the holy man's taut member ease an inch or two into her tight little lamb-pit. [And pressing against her] was a section of her beloved Buddha's face—the nose! And a truly incredible thing was happening—it was slipping into Candy's marvelous derriere . . . it was then she realized . . . that wonder of wonders, the Buddha, too, needed her! She gave herself up fully to her idol, stroking his cheek, as she gradually began the esoteric Exercise

Number Four—and only realizing after a minute that this movement was having a definite effect on the situation in her honey-cloister as well, forcing the holy man's member deeply in and out as it did, and she turned to him at once, wanting to tell him that it wasn't meant the way it seemed certainly, but she was stricken dumb by what she saw—for the warm summer rain had worked its wonders there as well, washing the crust of dung and ash away as the eyes glittered terrifically while the hopeless ecstasy of his huge pent-up spasm began, and sweet Candy's melodious voice rang out through the temple in truly mixed feelings: "GOOD GRIEF—IT'S DADDY!"

> Terry Southern and Mason Hoffenberg,
>
> *Candy*

If only twenty-five percent of these specific reports [made by women about having had sexual relations with their therapists] are correct, there is still an overwhelming issue confronting professionals in this field.

> William Masters and Virginia Johnson

DRAMATIC OR EXTREME FORMS OF EXPLOITATION always signify the pervasiveness of less dramatic forms. Atrocities and scandals are often everyday events—writ large. Physical brutality in American state mental asylums and prisons signifies the dailiness of brutality in the "outside" society. Prostitution,[1] rape,[2] incest, and sexual molestation of female children by adult males are so common they are usually invisible—except when sensationalistic accounts focus them, distortedly, into view.[3]

Female prostitution and harems have existed among all races, in nearly every recorded culture, on every continent, and in all centuries: it predates Judaism, Catholicism and industrial capitalism. It *always* signifies the relatively powerless position of women and their widespread sexual repression. It *usually* also signifies their exclusion from or subordination within the economic, political, religious, and military systems.

"Sex" between private female patients and their male psychotherapists is probably no more common—or uncommon—an occurrence than is "sex" between a female secretary or housekeeper and her male employer. From a financial point of view, the therapist and not his patient is the employee. Psychologically, however, the female is as much—if not more—a dependent supplicant here as she is elsewhere.[4] Both instances generally involve an older male figure and a young female figure.[5] The male transmits "unconscious" signals of power, "love," wisdom, and protection, signals to which the female has been conditioned to respond automatically. Such a transaction between patient and therapist, euphemistically termed "seduction" or "part of the treatment process," is legally a form of rape and psychologically, a form of incest.[6] The *sine qua non* of "feminine" identity in patriarchal society is the violation of the incest taboo, i.e., the initial and continued "preference" for Daddy, followed by the approved falling in love with and/or marrying of powerful father figures.

Men may marry mother figures but only if they are safely powerless. Wives are generally younger, less mobile, and physically smaller than their husbands—and than their husbands' *childhood* mother. Men do not violate the incest taboo; they do not re-create certain crucial conditions of their childhood in marriage.

There is no real questioning of "feminine" identity in psychotherapy. More often, an adjustment to it is preached—through verbal or sexual methods.

Although there are many individual therapists and several therapist "families" in New York and California who have systematically preached and practiced "sex" with their female patients for over a decade, such intercourse is by no means a recent innovation. There are even therapists who "specialize" in treating *other* therapists' "guilt" or "conflict" about having sexual relations with their patients. Many analysts in Freud's time had love affairs or married their female patients—when the comparatively short (three- to six-month) treatment process was completed. Paul Roazen reports that Reich's first wife, Bernfeld's last wife, Rado's third wife, and one of Fenichel's wives were former patients; that Freud's disciple Tausk had a love affair with a former female patient, sixteen years his junior; and that Freud himself encouraged a prominent American analyst to marry a former patient.[7]

It is now known that Carl Jung had an affair with his patient Sabina Spielrein. Judd Marmor writes about the "tragic end of the career" of W. Bern Wolfe, a gifted psychiatrist who was forced to flee the United States in the 1930s for "impairing the morals of a girl whom he had under treatment,"[8] the late James L. McCartney, who encouraged "sex" between male therapists and their female patients (when "necessary"), claims that a number of well-known psychiatrists (Hadley, Sullivan, Alexander, and Reich) "told him, despite their writings to the contrary, that they allowed their patients physically to act out."[9] Freud is quoted by Marmor as chiding Ferenczi on his habit of kissing his patients:

> If you start with a kiss [you risk an ultimately very] lively scene . . . Ferenczi, gazing at the lively scene he has created, will perhaps say to himself, maybe I should have halted my technique of motherly affection.[10]

I do not seek a simple alliance with those Puritans who censure all forms of doctor-patient contact. I am not in favor of great and grave professional distances between people, especially between therapists and patients. (Many "schizophrenics" need and should have access to specifically physical contact.) Puritanism usually implies an acceptance of the myth of "feminine evil." For example, Leon J. Saul, in an article condemning patient-therapist sexual contact, is more sensitive to the *analyst's* than to the patient's vulnerability.[11] He says: "Let the analyst beware. In the face of sexual love needs, let him recall the Lorelei and Delilah and the many other beauties who have revealed that appearance need not be reality . . . if the analyst is tempted to follow Ferenczi in experimenting with Eros let him be certain . . . [that] no matter how obvious Eros may be, hostility is the inevitable middle link."

There are many kinds of "distance," other than sexual, to be tenderly and/or experimentally bridged between therapist and patient. However, "sexual" contact does not necessarily insure any other kind of communication: it often impedes it. Most important is the fact that most such "sexual" contacts take place between middle-aged male therapists and younger female patients.[12] It does not usually occur between female therapists and male (or female) patients of any age; or between male therapists and male patients, unless the therapist is homosexual.[13] Dahlberg reports one case of an attempted seduction by a male homosexual therapist.[14] The male patient, who was also homosexual, refused his advances. Perhaps men are more conditioned than women to refuse sexual encounters that they do not initiate, cannot control, or in which they see neither pleasure nor profit.

The fact of the matter is that sexually seductive (or assaultive) therapists are quite ordinary in their ethical failure. Despite their occasional pretenses of being radicals whom society crucifies, they are not very "radical," i.e., they do not perceive or challenge basic assumptions and social behavior.* For example, they are generally extremely anti-homosexual and anti-lesbian. McCartney, who was ousted from the American Psychiatric Association for publicly favoring "overt transference," limits it to overt heterosexual transference.[15] He recommends "transferring" his sexually aroused male patients to a female therapist— or sends them home to "practice" on their wives and girl friends. McCartney notes that "it is not so easy for a female [as for a male] analysand to find a [sexual] surrogate, so the analyst may have to remain objective and yet react appropriately, in order to lead the immature person into full [heterosexual] maturity." McCartney also seems to measure "success" in terms of the female patients' subsequent marriage and maternity. Further, McCartney treats his female patients who are in need of "overt transference" (sex) as children: he asks for their parents' or

---

* The issue of sexuality, childhood, and family life is a crucial one. The fact that we are not supposed to experience sexual pleasure with our childhood relatives, but with strangers, no doubt limits our sexuality. Nevertheless, I don't think that remedial psychotherapy for adults is the place, time, or way to solve this particular moral mystery. Further, while McCartney is correct in condemning the originally harmful distance between parent and child, and the harmful effects of sexual repression, he is shortsighted in his understanding of the differences in treatment of male and female childhood sexuality. Female children have already been (over) exposed to heterosexual sexuality with their fathers; male children, while well nurtured maternally, are forced to severely repress their heterosexual sexuality in relation to their mothers. Few men achieve mature heterosexuality—and I don't think sexual intercourse with a female therapist is the solution to this problem. Also, both male and female children are deprived of sexuality with their same-sex parent or with other nurturant same-sex adults. I doubt whether such bisexual deprivation could be remedied for adults through "acting out" in psychotherapy.

husbands' permission before sexual contact occurs. Most important, he recommends that the therapist remain as emotionally uninvolved, as removed from risk-taking, as "performance"-oriented, as a Playboy stereotype. He emphasizes the distinction between "transference love" and "romantic love," and describes the therapist's role as passive, unemotional, and "responsive" to the patient's initiative. Perhaps male therapists, like male artists in our society, are seen, or fear themselves, as more "feminine" than business executives, soldiers, or politicians. Thus, it is important to them to be able to "have" as many women as their presumably more "masculine" counterparts do. Male poets and novelists are as notorious (as they are "forgiven") for their frantic and sexually selfish and abusive treatment of women. Some psychotherapists, although less inspired, may behave similarly.

Dr. Charles Dahlberg presents the seductive therapist as a man who chose to practice psychotherapy between 1930 and 1945, and who was probably

> withdrawn and introspective, studious, passive, shy . . . [more] intellectually [than] physically adventurous . . . among other things, this adds up to being unpopular with the opposite sex. None of this stops a person from having fantasies of sexual conquest. It may well encourage sexual fantasies.[16]

Such typically "deprived" men now find themselves in a professional position where many young women may be expressing fantasies of sexual desire for them. The therapists *can't help* being "flattered" by the situation; and they *refuse* to help, exploiting the situation for their own ends.

Dahlberg, in his presentation of nine cases of patient-therapist "sexual" contact, draws a composite portrait of the "seductive" therapist as "always over forty; from ten to twenty-five years older than the patient; always a man; and with the [one] exception of the homosexual, the patient is always a young female." Most of Dahlberg's nine therapists are married; many experience premature ejaculation with their patients; some "seduce" the wives of their male patients; some terminate therapy—

or payment for therapy—once sexual contact begins; others continue both therapy and payment.

Many of these therapists are what Dahlberg terms "grandiose." He cites the example of one therapist who offered to "cure" his married female patient's "frigidity" on a two-week holiday. The patient panicked, told her husband, and together they sought legal action. The suit wasn't pursued because of the patient's "paranoid" tendencies: the lawyers feared that the woman would not be believed and would lose the case. Another therapist hypnotized his female patient and then suggested to her that sexual contact might increase her "transferential" involvement with him. When she finally refused to pay for such treatment and began seeing another therapist, the first therapist told her he would continue seeing her for "sex," and would not "charge" her for it—but wouldn't listen to her "problems" any longer. Dahlberg's paper presents only two cases where sexual contact occurred during therapy; four such contacts took place almost immediately after therapy was terminated, and three were propositions for sexual contact which never took place.

I was interested in talking with women whose sexual contact with their therapists took place during treatment. I also spoke to five women who refused their therapists' sexual propositions. Ten of the eleven women I interviewed had "sex" with their therapists during the treatment process. Five of these sexual contacts were initiated and continued in the therapist's office. For seven of the women, therapy continued after such contact. Seven women continued paying for therapy for an average of four months. The duration of these contacts ranged from one night to eighteen months.

At the time of sexual contact, the women's ages ranged from twenty-two to forty-five. Their average age was thirty-one. Four women were married, four were separated or divorced, and three were single. The husbands of the four married women were in treatment with the same therapist at the time of sexual contact. The ten therapists were, on an average, fifteen years older than their patients. Their average age was forty-seven. Seven of the therapists were married, two were separated or divorced, and one was single. Seven were psychiatrists and three were psychologists. Two of the women saw the same therapist—and did not know about each other, or about his many other female patients similarly "contacted."

Nine of the ten therapists assumed a "missionary" position during sexual intercourse for the first time and in general throughout the sexual "treatment." Seven of the women did not experience orgasm at this time; four women never did throughout the "treatment"; seven of the women eventually experienced orgasm, from within one to nine months. Four of the therapists had difficulty maintaining an erection throughout the sexual contact period. At the risk of superficiality, one might simply conclude from this information that "seductive" therapists are lousy lovers.

As a group, these women were the most reluctant to talk with me. I did, however, manage to speak to every woman I contacted. They were indecisive about meeting times, broke appointments, set time limits, and forgot about time once we started talking. Their lives were filled with clamor and crises. They received many phone calls: their children needed them, their lovers were waiting, their *lovers'* children needed them. And yet—a very quiet and despairing eye looked out at me from the center of this storm.

Those women who were over thirty-five when the sexual encounter occurred seemed more "worldly": sophistication was their body armor, compassion their shield. They were the most vocal advocates of "pity" and "understanding" for the therapists—and for all men.

MELISSA: I have tremendous sympathy, compassion for men. I think from my experience that they need much more assurance and love and affection and sympathy.

PHYLLIS: Even when they aren't capable of giving it to you?

MELISSA: Right. In fact, people are seldom capable of giving it, they're so wrapped up in pain. He [the therapist] had trouble maintaining an erection. It had to do with his being sixty, I think. He fumbled around a lot, which was a little bit surprising. I began to feel a little anxious too. I began to fall into old patterns of reassuring him as I had been reassuring men all my life, that it didn't matter [that I didn't have an orgasm], that I was so happy with him but he wasn't very skillful.

PHYLLIS: Did you tell him?

MELISSA: No, because it didn't really matter. *Now* it would matter . . . but he said that I was so lovely, that I was a beautiful thing, and he was an old man that I was not a doll or a child but a charming, fully mature woman, intelligent and delightful.

This somewhat sad and very "human" aging male therapist was married—and had also been treating Melissa's husband for several years, for marital and sexual problems.

Three of the over-thirty-five "sophisticated" women refused to reveal their therapists' names (even before I asked), for fear of "harming his reputation." They insisted that *they* were to blame; *they* were the real seducers.

MELISSA: I think that he just finally couldn't resist me any more. I think I just put too much pressure on him. I was making moves from the very beginning. . . .

DONNA: I had a fantastic tan and I was high, and I'm very attractive when I'm high. I'm irresistible. I wanted to look nice for my therapy sessions. I always took off my glasses and combed my hair before I went.

ROSLYN: Actually, in a certain way, I was seducing him all along unconsciously. I wasn't aware of it until one time he came to a party at my house. I always had to seduce every man.

MARTHA: He was really attracted to me and I was attracted to him beforehand . . . the night he gave me flowers I was hoping he'd make love to me. But I wasn't as conscious about those things then.

And yet these women described as many fantasies of love and marriage about their therapists and felt as little-girl betrayed, as the younger, less "sophisticated" women did. Ellen had been in therapy for six years before the sexual affair began.

ELLEN: I wanted him to marry me but he wouldn't. His wife and children, his reputation, and his failing health made it hard for him. I haven't been able to shake the relationship and it's been eight months and he won't see me at all now.

MARTHA: I had just left my husband after twenty years and was I depressed! I was living alone for the first time in my life and needed everything: emotional support, solace, approval, friends, a better job— everything. I guess I really wanted another husband. I was still looking to romantic love for security. Do you know, I found out much later that he was involved with at least one other woman at the same time as me.

ROSLYN: I thought, I fantasied, that he would leave his wife and marry me, that he was going to give up his other life and start a new life with me. I was so happy that my therapist loved me. Who cared about anything else? Look how worthy I am. I said to him, "You don't have to leave your wife. You don't have to do anything like that. Just see me." But he couldn't do that either he didn't want to get involved.

STEPHANIE: I finally asked him if he would marry me and he just laughed and said no. I *thought*, he's going to be really old soon and needs someone to take care of him. I thought I loved him, that he had it within his power to make me happy, that he could do it if he only will but he was more interested in my typing for him than in talking about this.

DONNA: I was enamored. I guess I would have been in love had I let myself think that at thirty an intelligent woman could fall in love with a man so fast. I left my husband. [The therapist] was a doorway to finding things out about myself. We haven't slept apart since I moved in with him.

JOYCE: I know I needed him very, very badly. It was like he was God. He was mistreating me, and I didn't want to admit that, because I needed him badly. I loved him. Then he offered me a job as his typist but he wouldn't sleep with me any more. I was so depressed and upset and I wanted some help and called up, hysterical, "Please talk to me on the phone," and he said, "I can't talk to you now, I'll call you back." And he never called back. I felt deserted and all alone and usually when I talk about this with my shrink [now] I'm just in tears.

Although many of the women described being humiliated and frustrated by their therapists' emotional and sexual coldness or ineptitude, it was the therapist, more often than the patient, who ended the "affair." And in every case the woman was further hurt by the abandonment. Women *are* conditioned to "suffer"—as long as it keeps them in a relationship to a man. The "suffering" matters less than the "relationship." After the therapist's withdrawal, one woman tried to kill herself; two others lapsed into a severe depression; a fourth woman's *husband*, who was also in treatment with the same therapist, killed himself shortly *after* if not *because* he found out about the affair. This particular therapist's rather sadistic and grandiose attempt to cure this woman's "frigidity" one night resulted in her developing a "headache" that wouldn't subside for a year. This therapist systematically had "sex" with as many of his female patients as he could. He also "employed" them as baby sitters, secretaries, cooks, errand-runners, chauffeurs, etc. His behavior was depressingly typical.

SHEILA: I got stoned on grass because I was so scared. And he never even took his clothes off. He just dropped his pants. I was up for having an affair, but this didn't feel like an affair. He told me I was blocked, that there were things I had to work out with my father and that maybe we could solve it on a non-verbal level if I would just trust him. And that I was going to have to trust him. So maybe he's bizarre and unattractive—I didn't feel too straight myself. Oh, God. Then he got up, dropped his pants, said, "Take your pants down," or something really insensitive, unsensual, and he just got on top of me. He came, I didn't come. And then I said, "I'd like to get on top of you." And then he told me that that was my problem, that I wanted to be in control.

CINDY: He'd interpret everything I said as "transference love" or sexual desire for him . . . but there was very little affection between us. We started having a drink after the session was over. Then one night he said he wanted to see what my place looked like. He got undressed all at the same time and we went to bed together—and it was a very strange thing, there was almost no tenderness or prelove play and I remember thinking afterwards when I said, "That was great," or "That was very good"—some insane comment that I made, thinking that it wasn't really. Then all of a sudden, "Excuse me, I have to make a train," because his wife was sitting out in the Bronx with this kid. I'd never slept with a married man before. It was probably the coldest affair I've had in my life.

STEPHANIE: It took ten minutes. He jumped up, washed in the bathroom, and was back at his typewriter. I thought we'd talk till four in the morning. If anyone should know what he's doing a therapist does. If I don't have an orgasm here, then it's really my fault.

JOYCE: He was always on top of me. And he said things to me, too. He'd say: "Cock. I want to put my cock in your cunt." And he wanted me to say that back to him. I couldn't handle it. It was extremely stimulating. I was being very whorey. I was depraved and he was a beast, he grunted and groaned louder than any animal I had ever heard. He asked, "Does the thought of having another couple watch stimulate you? Should I smack you on the behind?" He said he wouldn't hurt me, not in the face, but on the behind. I was beginning to get terrified.

Victims make us uncomfortable. We grow uneasy, guilty, finally annoyed by the sight of them. Our pity turns to anger. Their suffering, their mutilation, which we fear so much ourselves, must somehow be their own doing. That beggar in rags is to blame for his misfortune: pass him by without a backward glance. "Naive" women who are "taken advantage of"—how positively *Victorian* it all is: are there still shopgirls and serving-maids stupid enough to be seduced? Well, if they can't learn to protect themselves, they, like Candy-Candide, deserve whatever they get. . . . With the exception of one woman, the earning capacity and educational level of these women was never more than a fraction of that of their therapists. At the time of sexual contact, two of the women were students, two were secretaries, two were housewives, one was a waitress, one a recreational counselor, one a saleswoman, one a private secretary, and one a sociologist. Yes, these women like most women, *are* tremendously "naive": their naiveté proclaims their "helplessness," which alone may earn them a Benefactor, a Savior, a Father.

As I noted in Chapter Four, these eleven women were the most overtly or superficially unambivalent about being "feminine." They were all conventionally and frantically "attractive"; they were all economically limited and intellectually insecure; they were both sexually fearful and sexually compulsive; they were paralyzed by real and feared loneliness and self-contempt; they all blamed themselves for any "mistreatment" by men; they all confused economic and selfhood needs with romantic "love"; and they were slow to express any anger. (Anger is a painful and dangerous display for those who feel and are relatively powerless.)

At the beginning of one conversation with one of the "sophisticated" women, she described her therapist as a "really nice guy," and her experience with him as "her fault" and as "not really important." After about an hour (during which I was relatively silent), she described this period in her life as one in which she "went through the most severe pain." Surprised by this memory, she suddenly grew angry:

MARTHA: I was really very vulnerable and dependent upon him. How could he so miscalculate the situation and behave so selfishly? He was reinforcing my dependency needs without questioning them—or even satisfying them.

Very quickly though, she moved on to another topic: her intense dislike for her next therapist—who was a woman.

I was able to speak to two women who had "sex" with the same therapist, and to a number of women who were all sexually propositioned by another therapist—all but one of whom refused him. I also spoke with several other of this same therapist's non-propositioned female and male patients. On the basis of these interviews, a certain composite portrait emerged. One of these psychiatrists had an office on Central Park West, the other on the Upper East Side in New York City. The New York psychiatrists and psychologists discussed in this chapter are all highly "reputable" professionals in terms of legitimate medical or doctoral training, some sort of psychoanalytic or clinical training, well-established practices, and office locations in expensive buildings on the Upper East side, the Upper West Side, and Greenwich Village.

Both men were involved in creating primal patriarchal family-empires, consisting of one male guru (themselves) and many "wives" (female patients, legal wives, mistresses). (We may note that while Freud certainly never had "sex" with his patients—and, reportedly, not too frequently with his legal wife, he was nevertheless polygamous: according to Roazen, his wife and his wife's sister both lived with him and took care of his domestic and emotional needs; and his many female disciples served him as Dutiful Daughters.)[17] The two sexually seductive male therapists used their female patients as secretaries, typists, baby sitters, sexual partners, errand-runners, plant-dusters, therapy "assistants," and all-round cheering squad. Both men kept very odd office hours, and even odder treatment hours. "Sessions" lasted from ten minutes to four hours, and no questioning of this arbitrary "spontaneity" was brooked—even from other patients who had to wait long beyond their scheduled appointment times. Both men were married. Both described their wives as "crazy," "hopeless," "dependent," and "too old." Both men were cold and/or inadequate sexual partners and lovers; both apparently had "sex" with as many of their female patients—simultaneously—as they could, often presenting it as either necessary for the "cure" or as a unique instance of "love."

Both of these therapists prescribed drugs for everyone for anything. Both were very authoritarian in directing and ordering their patients' lives: they *told* their patients whom to sleep with and when; what jobs to leave and what jobs to take; where to live and with whom. Both thundered at sexually reluctant female patients about how "unhealthy" their sexual "repression" was and how they'd "better start fucking a lot" if they wanted to get rid of their "hangups." Both therapists insisted that only they could "help" or "save" their patients—and warned their unhappy or rebellious female patients to leave only at their own risk. Both therapists were quite cruel to protectors or deserters. For example, one woman refused to sleep with one of these therapists—and told her husband, who was also in treatment with him, about the proposition. She also decided against continuing "treatment."

SANDRA: I decided, though, that I owe it to Mark [her husband] to go up with him and confront the group we're all in together. So I go up and there's Dr. X and his two assistants sitting there and I figure, well, the cards are stacked against me. Dr. X says, "Well, well, tell us what happened." So I tell the story again and then he proceeds to tell the group how I was provocative to him, how I wore a miniskirt—which I always wear. He made it look as if I were coming up there to seduce him, not to have a session. Then he says I'm using this lie of a proposition to cop out of therapy. He reminded me that I didn't quit a job I once had just because my boss made a pass at me. Then all of a sudden we're sitting there and he's starting to say things like, "Sandra, you know how dishonest you are, how dishonest you are with Mark, there are things you haven't told him" [he was referring to a brief affair she'd had], and I started crying, "I'm getting out of here," I mean it was like a kangaroo court and when we left, Mark said to me, "What haven't you told me, what did you do?" He forgot all about what Dr. X did. Everything got twisted.

Another woman who refused her therapist's sexual advances told her group therapy mates about it. The therapist denied everything and told the group she was "crazy." This woman—and her boy friend—were also both involved in "consciousness-raising" groups. The woman's group sympathized with her outrage: the male group went together to confront the therapist and "beat him up." The woman told me this anecdote proudly and couldn't understand my crestfallen expression (the men were still engaged in protecting "their" female territory; the women were still incapable of defending themselves). When she understood, we laughed and moaned in unison.

Both of these therapists exhibited another trait, one often found among certain "seductive" men over sixty, and traditionally attributed to "schizophrenogenic" mothers: they said something—and denied they'd said it; they made sexual advances—and then, half teasingly, half testingly, but totally seriously, denied having made them. The doctors were "guilty" and afraid of being rejected.

> JOYCE: And then I had a dream about going to bed with him. And he said, "Ah, transference at last"—in his accent. The week before he'd made me put my head on his lap just like I used to do with my father when I had a bad headache, and he'd stroked my hair. It was very warm; I was a little girl and he was my father. Then his hand slipped. The next session he helped me on with my coat, turned me around to him, and kissed me quite passionately. And I was quite shocked and then I burst into tears. I'm melodramatic anyway, but I was really upset. Because I didn't know what to make of it. And I said, "Why did you do that?" It was a stupid question to ask, really, and he said, "What? Do what? What are you talking about?" And I said, "Kiss me." "I don't know what you mean," he said. He was really playing into my hangup. Because my parents would do that to me. Whenever my mother did something or said something and I said: "Why did you do that?" she'd go "What? I didn't do anything."

Clearly, none of these women were "helped" by their seductive therapists. They were neither helped into self-definition, self-esteem, or independence, nor were they tenderly indulged or protected for their conditioned helplessness. I cannot *measure* how "hurt" they were by having sexual contact with their "soul-doctors." What I can do is introduce two of the women. Both are thirty-two and are self-supporting. Joyce has a twelve-year-old daughter but receives no child support. Stephanie is a secretary; Joyce teaches in a private school. Both women speak quietly and are quietly attractive. Both are currently in therapy. Both were in therapy for the first time when the sexual contact occurred. Both fell very much "in love" with their therapist and enjoyed the sexual contact (Joyce immediately and Stephanie after nine months). Both continued paying for "therapy" for some time after the sexual contact began. Stephanie's "affair" began after ten months of treatment and lasted for nearly a year. Joyce's "affair" began after more than a year of treatment and lasted for five months. Joyce first saw her therapist for three months, when she was twenty-one, and then again when she was twenty-four. The therapist was in his late fifties at the time. Stephanie saw her therapist when she was thirty. Both women saw the same therapist.

> STEPHANIE: I've always been isolated. My older brother is an alcoholic and another brother killed himself. My sister who was so bright left school to get married and the dishes just piled up. No, I never talk to my family. I left them years ago and finished high school on my own.

> JOYCE: My parents were always threatening to lock me up in a nuthouse—when my first boy friend told me he was marrying someone else I got really hysterical and went home crying and screaming like a nut. And my parents had this thing against crying. You're not allowed to cry. So they smacked my face and they were holding me down and they told me they'd call a nuthouse ambulance if I didn't shut up. When I got rheumatic fever they said, no one's ever going to want me, I'll never get married and they went miles out of their way to buy medicine because God forbid somebody should find out.

> STEPHANIE: I started therapy because I was so depressed. I was sleeping

a lot and gained a lot of weight. Life just had no meaning. I used to see him [the therapist] for ten minutes at a time in the beginning. I thought it was peculiar but I never asked about it. He gave me lots of pills for my depression and weight, and insisted I take birth control pills even though I wasn't sleeping with anyone.

JOYCE: I went to this doctor twice. First, after my boy friend got married. I had to drop out of school and work because my parents wouldn't pay for it. Then I stopped when I became pregnant and the man I was living with said, "It's a choice between your psychiatrist or me. If you want me to take care of you and the baby, you've got to stop seeing your psychiatrist." Which I did. He never would marry me though. I went back for therapy when he left me about three years later.

STEPHANIE: I always thought I was ugly, hideous, plain, plain Jane. I thought he must be crazy to flatter me so. Sometimes he used to stand over my chair as I talked. Once he chased me into a closet. After about three months he put his arm around me and kissed me on the head and said, "I love you and want to make you happy." I was grateful for that but I didn't believe him.

JOYCE: The first time, when I was twenty-one, he said to me, "Do anything you want here in this office. It's not just speaking. If you want to do something, you can act it out. Any fantasy you can act out. Some women like to take their clothes off. Some women like to jump around. You can do anything. But I didn't feel like getting undressed and jumping around. When I went back to therapy I was working as a waitress and he [the therapist] asked me to be his secretary, but it never worked out.

STEPHANIE: He always kissed me good-bye after a session, but crudely, never affectionately. When I tried to tell him this, he got annoyed and said, "Try to pretend you like it." But I'd go home and cry. I hadn't slept with anyone for nearly three years when I started therapy. My marriage—well, he was the first man I ever slept with and it ended after six months. I was never sexually satisfied.

JOYCE: After that first passionate kiss I was really upset. I told a close friend about it who had me talk to a psychiatric resident. "Are you sure this really happened?" he said. "Yes." "Well," he said, "many times, a doctor might give you a little peck on the cheek and you can blow it up in your mind to be something other than that." And I said, "No, I didn't," and he said, "All I can tell you is, work it out with your analyst." Funny, I talked to another young psychiatrist, who was a friend, about it. He said, "As a professional all I can tell you is stop seeing him." I should have listened to him but his answer left me kind of perplexed and I suppose I didn't really want to give up the relationship. So I finally went to bed with him.

STEPHANIE: He was always after me to lay on the couch and I didn't want to. When I finally did he would lay down next to me. I didn't want to sleep with him—I was very depressed after it happened. I remember thinking: Well, if I allow this then maybe he'll be more affectionate. . . . He jumped right up afterwards and went back to his typewriter. He didn't seem to notice that I was sad. That I hadn't had an orgasm. All he said was "You don't mind if I don't take you home—I've got so much work to do."

JOYCE: We would start a session and then all of a sudden I would find him lying on the couch next to me. I was still paying for therapy and asked whether I should be, but very hesitantly. We never really resolved it.

STEPHANIE: If I didn't have an orgasm here it was my fault. He's an analyst and should know what he's doing. Besides, I wasn't in a position to comment on anyone's love-making. I'd once gone to bed with a woman, you know, but I was very frustrated and alone and couldn't talk to him. Once I screamed, a really anguished howl, and he pushed me away, got up, dressed, and said, "Don't you think you owe me an explanation?" He said: "There's nothing wrong with our relationship, it's a perfect doctor-patient relationship, a perfect working relationship, and a perfect relationship as lovers." He had me typing letters for him—the same form letter for hundreds of different people. He made at least a hundred dollars for each letter, and gave me three dollars for typing it.

JOYCE: I had orgasm after orgasm. Even though he came pretty fast. He treated me like a whore, just like my fantasies, and I guess it worked—sexually. Psychologically it was tearing me apart.

STEPHANIE: When I got very distraught, I'd call him. He'd hang up on me a lot. Once I took a fistful of sleeping pills. He said, "Oh, it's just your subconscious bothering you, don't pay attention to it" and then he left his wife and moved into bachelor digs. The first time I went there I was absolutely mortified. He had what looked like sperm on his sheets, and there was a diaphragm in his bathroom. I asked him how could he be so thoughtless—and he said, "How can you accuse me of sleeping with another woman, just because you see a woman's umbrella—even a woman's diaphragm—in my apartment?"

JOYCE: I went to his office and told him I wouldn't be a patient any more, that he'd been mean and cruel and that it's unhealthy. And he tried to talk me out of it. He said that he wasn't using me and that the psychology books I read were old-fashioned. Modern-thinking people believe the way he did. When he saw I was really going to leave, he said, "I'm warning you. Nobody will ever, ever be able to help you. I am the only doctor in the world who can help you."

STEPHANIE: I would wait for him to call, and then he wouldn't. Once I waited home all weekend and when he called on Monday morning it was only to make sure I'd type his letters. I couldn't work and I felt like I was cracking up. He started to go away for weekends in the summer, after he'd promised to take me with him. I stayed away as long as I could and then, when I went back, he said he didn't want to sleep with me any more but did want me to type a book for him.

JOYCE: The depression, the feelings, the fear got worse and worse. A fear mostly that I was losing my mind, that I was insane. . . . I was a whore because I could feel sexual. The more upset I got, the more librium he gave me. "But I'm upset about us," I'd tell him. And then he stopped making love to me. I was hurt. I didn't want him to make love to me and yet I was terribly hurt that he didn't, because I thought maybe he doesn't want me any more. He finally told me he thought it was too much for me, that I couldn't handle it.

STEPHANIE: You know, once we were alone together, naked, in his office. The door was locked. The bell started ringing and ringing and wouldn't stop. It rang for nearly twenty minutes. He didn't answer it. I was curious and I looked out the window. I saw it was a girl standing there crying. "That's me next year," I said to myself.

JOYCE: A couple of months after I left him I went away for a holiday weekend in the country. I'm so used to doing everything for everybody. People would come into our house and I'd cook and clean for fifteen people, we'd put all of Larry's friends up [her daughter's father]. This weekend again, it was "everyone else go out to play and have a good time while I do the dishes." I really didn't want to, but there I was doing them. I don't know how it was or why, but there was a safety razor above the sink. And I found myself on the floor, trying to cut my wrists. And I didn't make a mark. I was going tickle, tickle. Then I tried to cut my wrists with my father's razor and finally made it into the hospital. I called him [the therapist] and begged him to get me out of there. "I'm here maybe because of you." He said, "Yes, I'll get you into Creedmoor."

STEPHANIE: I couldn't get it out of my head. So finally, I called him and asked for my money back—for all the "therapy." He explained to me that when a surgeon makes a mistake the patient still pays. And I told him had he been a surgeon I would certainly be dead, but he wasn't, and I'm not, and I'd please like my money back.

JOYCE: I saw him [the therapist] only once again. I thought I was pregnant and went to him for a shot, to bring on my period. He accused me of talking about him. (I'd told the girl who originally sent me to him about what happened.) Then I think I said, "I want my money back," and he said, "No." I said, "I'll blackmail you, I'll sue." And he said, "You can't, you can't prove anything. You're crazy." It's been five years now. Once in a while, when I've gotten very depressed, and very angry, I've picked up the phone and called him and hysterically screamed at him "Why did you do that to me? You tried to kill me. Why? Why?"

When I first published this chapter, some academics and clinicians quarreled with me. They challenged the chapter's accuracy and/or importance. They said: "Maybe it happens a little, but it can't possibly happen a lot." Or, they questioned my motives: Did I want to tarnish the reputation of many good clinicians because a few bad apples existed? Did feminists hate men that much? One psychiatrist sued me—but he settled the suit for one dollar the day before trial.

From 1972 on, many books and articles subsequently appeared about sex between psychiatric and psychotherapy patients and their therapists. They confirmed much of what I said in this chapter, only they refined the numbers.

For example, in 1979, K. S. Pope, H. Levenson, and L. R. Schover published "Sexual intimacy in psychological training: Results and implications of a national survey" in the American Psychologist. In 1980, J. C. Holroyd and A. M. Brodsky published "Does touching patients lead to sexual intercourse?" And, in 1983, J. C. Holroyd published an article titled "Erotic contact as an instance of sex-biased therapy."

In the mid-1980s, when Dr. Nanette Gartrell attempted to further work in this area, she encountered massive hostility and resistance from the American Psychiatric Association (APA)—and she was both a psychiatrist and the Chair of their National Women's Committee.

In 1985, Gartrell independently found that while 6 percent of psychiatrists polled admitted a sexual relationship with a patient, that 65 percent of psychiatrists admitted that they had treated patients who had been sexually abused by their psychiatrists and that the abuse had devastated them. In 1986, Gartrell published these findings together with Herman, Olarte, Feldstein, and Localio. Also in 1986, R. D. Glaser and J. S. Thorpe published their article on "Unethical intimacy: A Survey of sexual contact and advances between psychology educators and female graduate students."

In 1988, the APA supported the defense of a Colorado psychiatrist, Dr. Jason Richter, who admitted that he had been sexually abusing his patient, Melissa Roberts-Henry. Defense tactics included hiring detectives to follow Roberts-Henry and, according to Gartrell, "assasinat[e] the character of the woman psychiatrist who subsequently treated Roberts-Henry." This psychiatrist was forced to close her practice and leave the state. In 1989, Gartrell quit the APA.

In 1989, C. M. Bates and A. M. Brodksy published *Sex in the Therapy Hour.* In 1990, K. S. Pope and S. Feldman-Summers published "Therapist-patient sexual involvement. A review of the research." And, in 1993, K.S. Pope, J. K. Sonne, and J. Holroyd published "Sexual Feelings in psycho-therapy: Explorations for therapists and therapists-in-waiting." The work in this area continues, alas because the problem has not gone away.

I was also asked to testify or consult in a number of cases around the country in which private therapy or institutionalized sexually abused psychiatric patients brought charges for malpractice or damages. One such patient had been impregnated on the ward by her psychiatrist; other such patients had been repeatedly raped on the ward by other patients. The staff disbelieved and punished the rape victims. They certainly did not treat them professionally as rape victims. (I write about this in the new introduction to this book.)

In the last 30-35 years, it also came to my attention that in isolated instances, female psychotherapists have also engaged in sex with their male and female patients. They apparently did so less frequently than their male counterparts. However, I did hear about a number of lesbian-feminist cults that functioned from the 1970s on, with "therapist-healers" as the leaders.

One case involved a well-known non-credentialed "healer" and feminist author, Anne Wilson Schaef, based in Boulder, Colorado. Like her male counterparts, she not only slept with her female and male "clients;" she also had some do her laundry, housekeeping, shopping, driving, and errands and functioned as secretaries. She also accepted gifts of large amounts of cash and land.

Over the years, many women, including feminist therapists, called to tell me that Schaef was still at it or that yet another of her victims had finally broken with the cult and come to see them. I had once known and worked with Schaef and I broke with her over this very issue in the mid-1970s. At the time, I advised her to cease and desist such practices. Luckily, I kept good records of our communications.

A woman patient, Vonna Moody, whom Schaef had moved into her home as a lover, finally sued Schaef for malpractice and for having subsequently institutionalized her. In 1992, I testified for Moody. Schaef settled with her the next day.

If it's wrong when men do it, it's also wrong when women do it. No sane or moral therapist seeks to "help" anyone by sleeping with them or by exploiting them in any other way.

CHAPTER SIX

PSYCHIATRICALLY INSTITUTIONALIZED WOMEN

For years I was a bookstore browser. One night in a Greenwich Village store I found myself standing next to a frizzy-haired woman, classic shopping bag in tow, talking to herself out loud. "Word salad," my professors would say. But it was wonderful to listen to: deep and golden and endless. At some point, I said something like "Amen" or "Right on," or whatever the equivalent was back then. Startled, she stared at me suspiciously. Where the hell did I get off taking her seriously when the world had already made it plain to her that her safety lay in being misunderstood and not noticed . . . and if I were a rival victim of visions, why didn't I just go back to my own flagpole and sit on it? She literally growled at me and walked off, taking up a lonely position at a bookstall at the far end of the store, where people resumed their pitying looks.

Lady-Sister: To you, wherever you are, I dedicate this chapter.

During the sixteenth and seventeenth centuries a number of "private madhouses" had begun to spring up "especially in and around London." These houses were operated for a profit and accepted only those inmates whose families could afford the relatively high prices. Before long, evidence of abuses came to light. Wealthy husbands apparently viewed confinement in these unregulated madhouses as a comparatively inexpensive way of ridding themselves of bothersome

wives. Daniel DeFoe began to call public attention to this as early as
1687. He exclaimed against the "vile practice now so much in vogue
among the better sort, as they are called, but the worst sort, in fact,
namely the sending their wives to mad-houses at every whim or
dislike, that they may be more secure and undisturb'd in their
debaucheries. . . ." DeFoe goes on to say that "This is the height of
barbarity and injustice in a Christian country, it is a clandestine
Inquisition, nay worse. How many ladies and gentlewomen are
hurried away to these houses, which ought to be suppressed, or at
least subject to daily examination, as hereafter shall be proposed?" He
further says that "If they are not mad when they go into these cursed
houses, they are soon made so by the barbarous usage they there
suffer, and any woman of spirit who has the least love for her
husband, or concern for her family, cannot sit down tamely under a
confinement and separation the most unaccountable and unreasonable. Is it not enough to make one mad to be suddenly clapp'd up,
stripp'd, whipp'd, ill fed, and worse us'd?" He further says "All
conveniences for writing are denied, no messenger to be had to carry
a letter to any relation or friend; and if this tyrannical Inquisition be
not sufficient to drive any soul stark staring mad, though before they
were never so much in their right sense, I have no more to say. . . ."

—Allan M. Dershowitz[1]

FROM THE BEGINNING TO THE END OF THE TWENTIETH CENTURY, in
America, women of color tended to be hospitalized, not simply diagnosed.
When they sought help, they were not placed in private therapy. Perhaps
their symptoms were more severe; perhaps they were the victims of racist
as well as sexist diagnostic criteria; perhaps they could not afford or did
not want private therapy.

But in general, twentieth-century female patients (and sometimes
male patients, too) were imprisoned against their will—sometimes for up
to 30-40 years; medicated against their will; lobotomized against their
will; given electro-convulsive and insulin coma shock treatments against
their will; denied medical treatment for other ailments; and were,
afterwards, stigmatized as "mentally ill" when they sought employment
and housing or pursued legal actions.

Adolescent lesbians and homosexuals were subjected, usually by fundamentalist families, to especially horrific institutionalizations. They were put in isolation, physically beaten, subjected to propaganda and verbal abuse, were bullied, and were kept incommunicado. These practices took place both in America and throughout the world.

I was involved in one such case, in America, in which a mother and her new husband incarcerated her teenaged daughter, whom the stepfather had been sexually abusing. The mother viewed the daughter's "lesbian-like" assertiveness as a grave threat. She also did not want to acknowledge that her new husband had been preying on her daughter. Luckily, but only after a year, the girl's biological father fought for and won custody of his much-traumatized daughter.

In the twentieth century, pregnant, unmarried teenagers were also psychiatrically pathologized, and separated forcibly from their newborn infants. In the early 1970s, in the UK, it was discovered that a number of women had been psychiatrically incarcerated for *fifty years* because they had borne "illegitimate" babies. It also became clear that for years, sexually active teenagers in Ireland had simply been put in nunneries, often for the rest of their lives, and were supervised by highly abusive nuns who put them to hard labor for their sexual sins.

As we have seen, many women who were psychiatrically hospitalized were not "mad." Rather than challenge the psychological vocabulary of the female condition, they adopted its tone more surely than ever. They were depressed, suicidal, frigid, anxious, paranoid, phobic, guilty, indecisive, inactive, and without hope. Only a few women were able to reject such traits entirely, or to combine them with opposite-sex traits such as physical aggressiveness and sexual potency. Only a few women actually heard or saw "things"; those who did were not helped by too much of the wrong medication, forcible imprisonment, or the untender ministrations of a woman-hating or madness-phobic staff.

I spoke to twenty-four women who had been psychiatrically hospitalized. Twelve women clearly reported exhibiting opposite-sex traits such as anger, cursing, aggressiveness, sexual love of women, increased sexuality in general, and a refusal to perform domestic and emotional-compassionate services. Four of these twelve women also experienced "visions." The other twelve women reported a predominance of female-like traits such as depressions, suicidal attempts, fearfulness, and helplessness.

The women's present ages ranged from nineteen to sixty-five. As a group they had been hospitalized seventy times or an average of three times each. Their total hospital stays ranged from one week to nearly ten years. The number of times each woman was committed ranged from one to fifteen. Five of these women were hospitalized ten times for "depression"; ten were hospitalized fourteen times for "suicide attempts." At the time of their first commitment, five women were married, two were divorced, one was widowed, and sixteen were single. Two of the women were black and one was Puerto Rican.

Each woman had been in private therapy for approximately fifty months: forty-three months with male therapists and fourteen months with female therapists. Each woman saw approximately three different therapists, both before and after hospitalization. ("Approximately" means an exact "total average" for the entire group. This group of twenty-four women includes Third World women, lesbians, and women who had sexual relationships with their therapists. In other words, this is not the *unduplicated* comparison between the groups of women presented in Chapter Four).

Two of the women never completed high school, four completed high school, six had some college, seven received B. A. degrees, and five had completed some graduate school training. Eighteen of the twenty-four women were either only or oldest children.

Some of these women committed themselves voluntarily: their lives seemed hopeless, there was no alternative, and their parents or husbands insisted it would be "better" for them if they "cooperated" from the start. More often, these women were committed wholly against their will, through brutal physical force, trickery, or in a state of coma, following unsuccessful suicide attempts.

CARMEN: I was so sad [after my daughter's birth] and so tired. I couldn't take care of the house right any more. My husband told me a maid would be better than me, that I was crazy. He took me to the hospital for what they called observation.

KATHRYN: After my husband left me and the baby, I was too depressed to do anything. I was a twenty-year-old mother, and back home dependent on my parents. I didn't go to college because my mother didn't think I was smart enough. My father was very violent to me. It was a shitty family and I escaped it by getting married. So I come back home and said, "I'm home," and my mother said, "Like hell you are. You made your bed, lie in it." So I had to threaten that I'd kill myself to get some sympathy and my mother said, "Okay, if you're crazy you belong in a hospital. If you're depressed, go get some tests to find out why." My father knew the director of this private loony bin and they all told me to sign myself in and be grateful.

RUTH: I was married about eight years when suddenly my husband seemed to be bored with me and the children. So he kept going to meetings every night. He had fun with the boys and became very popular. But I felt neglected. So I got angry. When I asked him why he couldn't stay home sometime with me and the children he just slammed the door and said I was sick and needed a doctor. Well, I believed him and went to someone he recommended. To make a long story short, this doctor didn't ask me my problem. All he did was give me a needle and put me to sleep. Then he kept giving me shock treatments. This caused me to sleep all the time. Consequently, my children missed my attention and my husband enjoyed his freedom and had no guilt. This shock treatment went on for about six years. I was very subdued all the time and never objected to anything.

SOPHIE: My husband was a very difficult man, always losing his jobs because he fought with the boss. I had to leave one good job after another and follow him to his next job. Then my husband found a girl friend—I didn't complain, marriage is not a bed of roses—and my multiple sclerosis symptoms started. My husband told me to get shock therapy, that my symptoms were in my head. Lucky we couldn't afford it privately . . . but he [my husband] brought a psychiatrist home and they both threatened me. If I didn't commit myself, they'd commit me and that would be worse for me. So I went into the hospital.

BARBARA: My mother had me put away when I was thirteen. She couldn't control me. My father had left us, she was drinking and crying all the time. I kept running away from bad foster homes, and so she finally committed me to an institution.

Washington (AP): An associate of consumer advocate Ralph Nader says doctors are receiving inadequate warnings that a potent "chemical strait jacket" for mental patients can cause symptoms of Parkinson's disease. . . . A Food and Drug Administration official agreed the drug (stellazine) is overused, particularly for the treatment of mild anxiety and primarily trivial complaints.

New York Post

The drug industry openly acknowledges the enslavement of women, as shown in an ad with a woman behind bars made up of brooms and mops. The caption reads: "You can't set her free but you can make her feel less anxious." Another one pictures a woman who, we are told, has an M.A. degree, but who now must be content with the PTA and housework. This, we are advised, contributes to her gynecological complaints, which should be treated with drugs.

Robert Seidenberg, M. D.

All of the women received massive drug dosages (such as thorazine, chlorpromazine, stellazine, mellaril, and librium), and many received shock therapy and/or insulin coma therapy routinely, and often *before* they were psychiatrically "interviewed."

LAURA: The first thing they did was give everyone shock treatment. It didn't matter who you were. You walked in and they gave you shock three times a week. Before they decided what ward they were going to put you in, they shocked you completely. I was scared to death. I thought I was going to die. The only person who came to see me, and this is going to make you laugh a little bit, came to give me an I. Q. test.

Many of the women were physically beaten. Their requests for contact with the outside world were denied. Their letters were censored or not mailed. One woman's diary was partially destroyed. Legitimate medical complaints generally went untreated: they were condemned or brushed aside as forms of "attention getting" or "revenge." It is ironic that a *mental* patient can successfully sue an asylum for physical injuries sustained during her incarceration, but not for *mental* injuries. Nor can she successfully sue for poor or non-existent medical attention.

BARBARA: I got beat up lots of times. Then I learned the ropes and they put me in charge of beating up the younger children if they got out of line. They were beating up five- and six-year-olds. If I complained about it they'd do the same to me.

SOPHIE: I knew something was *physically* wrong with me. I was having trouble walking but they didn't believe me. I was limping and falling down and they were laughing at me. They [the attendants] kicked me, only because I asked for some good medication. Once they kicked me and threw me in a room, no bigger than a closet, to spend the night on the floor, without my clothes.

Those women remanded to state asylums were involved in sex-typed forced labor. They worked as unpaid domestics, laundresses, ward aides, cooks, and commissary saleswomen. If they refused these jobs they were considered "crazy" and "uncooperative" and punished with more drugs, shock treatments, beatings, mockery, and longer hospital stays. If they accepted these jobs, and performed them *well*, the hospital staff was often reluctant to let them go.

SUSAN: I refused to peel potatoes in the kitchen. So they threw me in solitary for a few days.

CARMEN: I was proud to be the private housekeeper for Dr. X. I cleaned and cooked, baby-sat, shopped and even tutored her son in Spanish. What I didn't like was having to wash their underwear. That I didn't like.

PRISCILLA: When I refused to mop up the ward and put the chronics' shit in the little coffee cans for them, they [the attendants] ganged up on me. They put a sheet over me, threw me down to the floor, and began punching and kicking me.

Many patients were received and discharged, while I was there, who never had five minutes' conversation with the doctors while in the asylum. Often the new arrival would . . . inquire "When am I to have an examination?" I would reply "You never have an examination after you get here, for the doctor receives you on the representation of those who want you should stay here."

> Elizabeth P. Ware Packard
> *Modern Persecution* (1873)

Only a few of these women received any psychotherapeutic attention. Therapy groups (and therapists) either interpreted their requests for information or release psychodynamically or counseled them to become more "feminine" and "cooperative."

LAURA: Fix yourself up, they told me. So every morning I got the hot sweats [insulin therapy] and every afternoon I spent in the beauty parlor with the other women. Of course, you had to pay for it. You have to hide your feelings, pretend everything is wonderful, if you want to get out.

JOYCE: I had a doctor who kept interviewing me. He'd go over the same story over and over again. I remember I was looking terrible, my hair wasn't combed, I had no make-up. He said, "Why don't you fix yourself up? A nice girl like you!" And I said, "I never want another man to look at me again."

LAVERNE: I finally figured it out. You weren't supposed to be angry. Oh no. They lock you up, throw away the key, and you're supposed to smile at them, compliment the nurses, shuffle baby—so that's what I did to get out.

CAROLE: I really was aggressive. I knew my legal rights and I was fighting mad. There I was in a human toilet bowl, a concentration camp, and I couldn't get out. They didn't like me and my college education.

Many of these women were sexually propositioned or molested while in mental asylums. However, freely chosen heterosexual and especially lesbian intercourse was discouraged and prohibited.

BARBARA: There was a girl who was raped by an attendant but the nurse went to speak to him and it was hushed up. A doctor tried to rape me during a gynecological examination and I was afraid to complain, afraid they'd say I was lying or crazy and give me shock treatments.

MARSHA: I was falling in love with a woman at the hospital—but that was considered "sick." They have these Saturday night dances you're supposed to go to, and you're not supposed to dance with another woman but only with a man. But you're not supposed to go to bed with him either.

After the story of Miss Doris Anderson, the black welfare lady from Baltimore, was printed . . . the phones began to ring and mail began to come in. The callers told of other sane, healthy people who fell afoul of bureaucratic psychiatry and were packed off to asylums against their will. Many of the callers stressed that this was not something which only happened to black women on welfare. They told of white middle-class women having the same thing done to them. No case of this happening to a man was reported—they were all women, and in no instance did any of the victims file suit against their jailers. Some remained silent because they didn't know exactly how to fight back. Either they didn't have a lawyer and weren't quite sure of how to get one or they were intimidated, as though being taken away to the funny farm had caused them to doubt their own sanity.

Nicholas von Hoffman

Washington *Post*

It was for others' interest I plead—it was of others' wrongs and woes I complained. It was for them and their sakes I deliberately laid down my position as the asylum favorite, and became henceforth the asylum prisoner. From this time, for two years and eight months, was I made a close prisoner, and never after, with but one exception, allowed to step my foot outside the asylum walls, and I fully believe it was the doctor's purpose to make a maniac of me, by the skillful use of the asylum tortures.

Elizabeth P. Ware Packard

Modern Persecution (1873)

Only two of the women had any awareness of their legal rights, and of course both were defeated in court battles and "punished" by further psychiatric incarceration. Only one of the twenty-four women considered her experience of "madness" as a positive event. Only one of the women did not consider herself as "crazy." Most of the women were humiliated, confused, fatalistic, or naive about their hospitalization and about the reasons for it. Most dealt with the brutality by (verbally) minimizing it and by blaming themselves. They were "sick"—weren't they?

LAURA: In the beginning, I wasn't shrewd at all. I was just so hurt. (Laughter.) I didn't know that they would punish me three times as much if I tried to escape. They put me in a strait jacket and this was rather cruel and kept me alone in this room for twenty-four hours. I could hardly move and I was completely stiff. They wouldn't even let me go to the bathroom. They put a bedpan under me and things like that. *But you have to understand that I was sick. I can't fake it and say I wasn't, you have to realize I was really ill.* [My italics.]

JOYCE: I remember there was this huge room. The day room. And all these people. Hundreds of people. Some of them were leaping around the room and doing all kinds of weird things. I was so terrified that I really began to cry. And my thoughts were, Oh, my God, this is it, I really am crazy now. Now I know I'm crazy because I'm here. Then I said, "I'm schizophrenic, aren't I?" And he [the psychiatrist] said, "No, you're not schizophrenic, you're hysterical and neurotic!" And I wouldn't believe him. *I insisted that [schizophrenia] was my diagnosis.* [My italics.]

LUCY: Whenever I'd question something they'd done, criticize them, especially about how they treated some of the other patients, they'd yell at me and lock me in solitude. I'd get emotional and excited, *I'm sick like that* [my italics]. They're not explicit about what's expected, but you find yourself locked up if you say too many things too loud that they don't like. *I was sick, no question about it.*

Are these women "sick"? Are they more "sick and tired" than medically "sick"? Why do they think they're "sick"? Does their sickness really consist in accepting the sick role—a female prerogative in our culture? Are these women being punished for rejecting their sex-role stereotype—or for embracing it in too deadly a manner? Are they being punished for being ambivalent about their sex roles? Are their psychiatric hospitalizations merely accidental? In any event, how should they be "treated"?

Can any of these questions be answered to everyone's satisfaction? Would any of the answers be true for all the women? Many women described ambivalence toward their sex role during and/or preceding their hospitalization. Laura may speak for them. Throughout these selected parts of the interview I have italicized some examples of typical "masculine" and "feminine" feelings or behaviors that exist very actively, side by side, in Laura. There are few places in our culture where women are actively *supported* for manifesting psychosexually androgynous or "male"-like behavior.

Fearfully, bravely, curiously, Laura came to talk with me one Sunday afternoon. "My mother told me to be careful," she said, "but Lois [a mutual friend] said it would be all right." At thirty-five, Laura "rents a room" from her mother, doesn't "go out" any more, reads voraciously, writes poetry, and sees a male psychiatrist three times a week. Although she has an M. A. degree, she works as a secretary. She is not a feminist. Laura was twice psychiatrically hospitalized and once married. She insists that she was "mentally ill."

LAURA: I can't get around it. I was really sick. I began to hallucinate, I really imagined that people were against me.

PHYLLIS: Were they?

LAURA: *No.*

PHYLLIS: How did you feel when your mother called the police?

LAURA: At the time, at the beginning, I felt she was against me and it was brutal. It *was* sort of brutal, what she did. You see, I didn't have enough money to make ends meet. I had finished graduate school and couldn't get a job, and I was writing. I asked my mother for some money and she refused me because I was supposed to be grown up and supporting myself and, if I couldn't, I should get married. We had a terrible fight over this and she called the police. I didn't realize they'd lock me up, I thought my mother was bluffing. She called them *because of my terrible temper*—she's intelligent enough to sense that something was wrong. The police handcuffed me and took me to Kings County. They took everything away from me, my clothes, a ring, and gave me a sedative.

PHYLLIS: Did you see a psychiatrist?

LAURA: Yes—my bad luck. He must have gotten the idea I was much worse than I really was *because I started crying, bawling*: everything was so horrible. This was the wrong thing to do. He took it as a sign of grave mental disturbance because I couldn't control myself. *I was a trouble-maker. I tried to escape.* I didn't want to be locked up any more. But they caught me and sent me to Central Islip where they immediately gave me shock treatment three times a week. I thought I was going to die. Nobody interviewed me for a month. Only one person came to see me during the treatments—to give me an I. Q. test. I must have done very well because they transferred me to a "better building" for "special attention"—insulin therapy on top of the shock. Mornings were taken up with insulin and by the time you got through you were dead. They gave you some sugar, eggnog, to revive you, but then you were sort of exhausted for the rest of the day anyway. In the evenings we'd play cards. I was in a daze most of the time. Before they let you go or before they let you think you're well, you have to know that you've been sick. And I *had* been sick.

PHYLLIS: How could they decide you were sick if no one talked to you very much?

LAURA: Well, I was getting accustomed to dealing with these people. I did feel different really, like my youth had gone, disappeared in the interim. Not only that, but the shock is quite potent. You can't go through the shock and still have the same thoughts. It sort of interrupts your thoughts. You get new thoughts. My parents had been divorced for many years. The hospital was willing to let me out if someone would look after me.

PHYLLIS: Did you ever think of staying with your father?

LAURA: I can't. My father wouldn't have me. He doesn't want any children around.

PHYLLIS: What about friends? Lovers?

LAURA: Well, no one had visited me. They all had their own lives. Truthfully they weren't that concerned with me. I don't think my experiences were so unusual in that respect. They'd come over and sleep with you for a while and then they'd go back to their own lives but I got a teaching job in another state and that's where I met my husband. *For some reason or other he wanted to marry me—you know I can't analyze everybody's reasons.* So after a year I married him. He was the first man that really ever wanted to marry me. *Love? Well, I don't know what that is: you may think I'm a very strange person.* Before he married me *he asked me if I would support him while he got his doctorate. Like an idiot, I said yes.* So I worked, teaching, and he went to school and after about a year and a half of marriage I started imagining again.

PHYLLIS: Imagining what?

LAURA: This time I imagined he was having an affair and I imagined people were against me. I started that again. He *was* spending most of his time away and when he was home he wanted a meal and sleep. We hardly ever made love.

PHYLLIS: *Did you have any lovers?*

LAURA: *Oh no.* I started imagining and then I had *these temper fits* where I would start breaking things and screaming at him. A couple of times he went off to sleep in a hotel. I suggested that we see a marriage counselor because I was afraid the marriage was splitting up. He went to a therapist and this time my husband put me in a hospital.

PHYLLIS: On his say-so alone?

LAURA: Yes. He came in with these muscle men and they tied me up with something and they hung up the phone—I was on the phone with my mother. I got hysterical but they wouldn't let me talk to anybody, not even my therapist. My husband was just standing there. He knew I was scared to death of shock treatment and hospitals. I'd told him about the first time, but he thought in a private hospital they'd treat you differently. Last year I looked up my diagnosis in a medical textbook and it said I was incurable. I got very upset and took a cab up to see my therapist. I wanted to know if there was no hope for me.

PHYLLIS: Why do you think you have schizophrenia?

LAURA: Well, that's always been the diagnosis and the prognosis is supposed to be incredibly poor. My therapist was very reassuring. He's sometimes surprised that I'm not envious of married women, he expected me to be jealous of them all.

I think that age, as well as "unfeminine" behavior, i.e., troublesome, needy behavior, contributes to the incidence of female psychiatric hospitalization. Both Barbara and Carole attempted suicide, Barbara when she was thirteen and Carole when she was forty-five. Both were in hospitals because their families couldn't or wouldn't keep them, or because they didn't have families. Both had "fighting spirit": a trait not nurtured in families or in asylums. I am also taking the liberty of italicizing the very typically "feminine" and "masculine" behaviors that exist, side by side, very actively, in these two women.

Carole is sixty-five years old. She lives alone in a New York City welfare hotel, behind a locked door in a small room that houses a trunk filled with legal briefs and news clippings, a forbidden double burner, and an eternity of traffic noise. She has spent ten years in New York mental asylums. Her smile is dazzling, her energy mysteriously sourced. By profession, she is an actress. And, though properly brought up, and even more properly heterosexual, she never did marry.

CAROLE: From my childhood I wanted to be an actress. And the family, from the time I was sixteen, kept getting me engaged. I gave back eight rings, beautiful, big rings. *I didn't want to get just married*, y'know what I mean, go in for bridge and mahjong, it wasn't for me. They did everything they could to block me and they started this engagement business. I can't remember how many wealthy boys they "arranged" for me, but the rings always went back after two or three months. My family was very strict with me, and very disappointed in me. They wouldn't allow me to spend a night at a girl friend's house if she had a brother. What if someone had raped their precious piece of junk? Once when I came home a little late the whole house was lit up—what a scene! You're young, such scenes must have gone out before your time.

PHYLLIS: No, I had them too.

CAROLE: Well, they sent me to a friend who was a psychiatrist. Psychiatry isn't learned out of textbooks. When a psychiatrist treats somebody he uses his common sense and his heart to get to the trouble. I liked him. Not all psychiatrists are like the rats in Bellevue. He had more books than I'd ever seen in one house. Finally he called my parents in and said, "I don't want her to go to Hollywood. She's not up to that rat race out there. They'll take her like Grant took Richmond. I'll tell you what I want to do. I want her to go to medical school." My mother started laughing. She said, "You want *her* to be a doctor? *She couldn't even stand to see a baby diapered.*" Well, by the time I was twenty-five they were tearing their hair out. "You're an old maid, you've got a bad reputation, what's gonna become of you?" *So I had to cut myself off completely*: Hollywood, here I come.

PHYLLIS: How did you get into a mental asylum?

CAROLE: Well, Hollywood didn't "take" me completely. It was rough but I was able to save some money but everyone told me, "Go to New York, get yourself even a small part on the stage and they'll, y'know, they'll grab you back." So I came to New York. *Then I met him at an audition—a pudgy guy with sort of a good father's face.* He said he wanted to manage me. I was a "valuable piece of property." I admit I was leery of it, I mean, there was always sex strings attached out in Hollywood with anything. As it turned out he was leading up to the sex thing. He became my business manager, got me parts. I turned checks over to him and he said, "I'll give you just what you need." Then suddenly he's through! "Well, give me back the money you've been holding—" Nothing! Finally, I was so desperate I went over to his office. He grabbed my shoulder and beat me with his great big burly fist on my head and yelled, "Throw her out! Throw her out! Call the cops."*I was so ashamed.*

PHYLLIS: Did you ever sleep with him?

CAROLE: About four or five times. I was so ashamed that I was standing there calling "All right, call the cops, let everyone know." He ran around like a maniac. "I wasn't a whore when I came in here looking for a job and its non-existent pay," I yelled back at him. *I was reading scripts for him too, for nothing.* "But you are one, you are one," he yelled, with his fist up in the air. "Yes, it took a dirty, filthy, slimy thing like you to make one out of me." I ran out. I just lay crying at home for days. Some friends wanted to go over and beat him up. *I said no—I was too ashamed.* I was behind in my rent, I was physically run down, I just couldn't handle things. I went to the Diplomat Hotel and paid for two days in advance. I told them, "I'm very tired, I don't want to receive any telephone calls," and I hung up the "Don't Disturb" sign on the door and took phenobarbital and seconal. It was five-twenty-five when I last saw the clock and went off to sleep. I woke up five days later in Bellevue at night. They were hurling questions at me. "Why did you do it? Do you know where you are?" I hurt so badly. I couldn't walk, my vision was blurred.

Carole was medically injured and medically neglected. At her commitment hearing—she had insisted upon one—the judge asked whether "there was anyone to take care" of her.

CAROLE: I said no. I didn't want my aunts or my mother to know anything like this. And he says, "Well, you'll need some more treatment." And this bastard [a psychiatrist] gets up and says, "Well, in any state hospital she can get medical treatment."They'd hung this label of involutional psychosis and schizoid personality on me. I could barely walk *but was I aggressive, was I uncooperative!* That's the big one, if you're uncooperative, you're crazy. I knew I wouldn't get medical treatment in a state looney bin so *I asked the judge to have me killed if he wouldn't free me.* Well, that did it. I begged the judge, "Don't do this," but he sent me to the state asylum.

Barbara is nineteen and by conventional standards, very beautiful. She dresses in high-hippie fashion: a slender, human mobile of leather, suede, brass, and silver. She is newly a mother and couldn't talk for very long the first time we met: her husband wanted her back home as soon as possible. She chain-smoked and drank coffee and blew jokes at me like soap bubbles. Then she got very serious.

PHYLLIS: Why were you put into the hospital?

BARBARA: Because *I tried to kill myself.* There was too much pressure on me [she was thirteen at the time]. My father deserted us and I think my mother loved us but she had too many problems. She couldn't function. She put me in foster homes and my father would come to visit and tell me she didn't love me and I'd end up crying. I had foster fathers and all these weird foster parents that wouldn't feed you. I couldn't believe what was actually happening to me. When I got older and went to Catholic school, I was weird by that time. I wasn't a normal happy child and I used to get beat up by this nun who heard that my mother was spreading bad stories about her and I didn't have any friends and I was alone. My mother drank and tried to kill herself every once in a while. I gave my mother a very hard time. *I stayed out till four or five in the morning* when I was thirteen. I finally got shipped to Creedmoor to the children's ward.

PHYLLIS : How long were you there?

BARBARA: About five or six months, and then there was a head nurse, who, if the girls gave her too much of a hard time, would see that something was done about it. Some of her privileges would be taken away or she would be beat up. I had personal experience—to have the head nurse disapprove is a very bad thing in these hospitals. I had gotten beat up a few times myself. One girl had taken my mascara and she said she lost it so the head nurse said, "Are you going to let her get away with it?" We played a punch game where one girl got punched on the arm. We had to hold her and punch her on the arm—really sick things. The attendants were more messed up than the patients were.

I escaped from Creedmoor twice. A detective found me. I was staying with some people I knew from the hospital and her *(my girl friend's) uncle tried to rape me and I broke his finger. Then I called up the head nurse at Creedmoor and asked to come back*. This time I didn't have any trouble with the doctor or the head nurse or the social worker. I got along fine. I didn't mess up the ward.

PHYLLIS: Did you go to school while you were there?

BARBARA: From ten to twelve in the morning. It was called junior scholastic—it was real bad. They told me not to make things rough—to cooperate, etc., or else I'd have a hard time. I was standing in line getting toothbrushes or something and they gave me a big cup of liquid thorazine to drink plus some other thing and I passed out. I didn't know what it was at the time. I found out later that you could have momentary blackouts from too much thorazine. I woke up in bed and went to the nurse to ask her for something to make me feel better and she said, "You better get back to bed or I'm going to stick a needle up your ass."

These chronically ill women—they used to lock them up in the bathroom. They'd never get their clothes changed. They used to urinate all over them. When the visitors came they would give them a bath and tell them that "she's doing just fine." I went down and *told the supervisor that they were giving me more medication than they should* and she told me that if I open my mouth one more time she would shut it for good. It was just horrible. We cleaned the wards for two weeks before an official inspection.

They'd put the patients in seclusion without a bedpan or anything and then *they wanted us to clean it up and I wasn't going to do it.* They wanted me to put the diarrhea in a coffee can. If you are not really flipped out, it's very hard to stay and some had to stay for very long periods of time as no one really wants them.

I got involved with a girl there—sexually involved—when I was seventeen and there was nothing they could do about it. There was no kind of counseling, which I needed, and which this girl needed. They took this girl and asked if I ever had an orgasm with her and she said yes, which I did. It was a very sick relationship and not normal and when I was seventeen I couldn't figure out whether or not I was still gay. There was nobody I could talk to about it.

When I told my English teacher all the things that happened at Creedmoor, she didn't believe it. She thought I was lying when I told her about being beaten up and giving me all those drugs to put me into a state of helplessness. People are afraid of any people who are different from them. I didn't need to be at Creedmoor if there was someplace else for me to go to.

CHAPTER SEVEN

LESBIANS

Not counting my mother, my first lesbian experience took place when I was eight years old. After school, Ann would come over to my house and weave magic tales of what some boys had done to her the previous night. I asked many questions and so Ann would show me, kiss by kiss, caress by caress, what had actually happened. Of course, we both "graduated" to boys and had to put away our "childhood games."

Two years ago I met Ann, working as a bank teller. She was very pregnant and quickly told me all about her husband, her husband's job, her husband's down payment on a ranch house, and her husband's plans for a summer vacation. "Hey, Annie," I wanted to say, "do you remember those great kisses?" But I didn't. I remained silent.

I dedicate this chapter to the breaking of that silence between women.

The love of women for their own sex was equivalent to . . . orphic [homosexuality]. Here again the sole purpose was to transcend the lower sensuality, to make physical beauty into a purified psychic beauty. [In] Sappho's strivings to elevate her sex . . . she was concerned not with one alone; Eros drove her to them all. . . . Wherever she found physical beauty, Eros impelled her to create spiritual beauty as well. . . . In the presence of this idea she came to look with indifference on everything she had valued as a young girl, wealth, jewels, the ornaments of outward sweet existence.

J. H. Bachofen[1]

When a couple is new to swinging and the woman has never been exposed to another woman, she usually says that she would find this

repulsive and cannot imagine it. After the first two or three parties
where she sees women obviously enjoying each other, she is likely to
modify her stand and say, "I do enjoy having a woman work on me,
but I could never be active with another woman." Then, when she
has been in swinging for several months and attended many parties,
she may well say, "I enjoy everything and anything with a woman,
either way she wants to go." . . . At large open parties we observed
that almost all the women were engaged in homosexual activity with
obvious satisfaction, especially if a younger group was involved.

Gilbert D. Bartell[2]

MOST PSYCHOANALYTIC THEORISTS either sincerely misunderstood or
severely condemned lesbianism. Some did both. The "condition," they
said, was biologically and/or hormonally based. No, said others, it was
really an environmental phenomenon. In any event, all agreed, it was
maladaptive, regressive, and infantile: even if it wasn't, it led to undeniable
suffering, and was *therefore* maladaptive, regressive, etc.

More moderate voices suggested that lesbianism was not infantile, just
limited. We are all bisexual by nature, they said, and conditioning (society,
the patriarchal family) cripples and restricts both women and men to
heterosexuality. Bolder voices disagreed. Women are *naturally* more bisexual as well as more sensual than men. From a physiological point of view,
women are better sexual and emotional love partners for each other than
patriarchal men can be to them. Still bolder voices rejected the supposedly
"advanced" view of our bisexuality: no, they said, *in our culture*, bisexuality
for women is limited, is a compromise, a blatant and cowardly "cop-out."
Dr. Charlotte Wolff, in her book, *Love Between Women*, inadvertently and
only partially explains this last view in the following way:

The lesbian's yearning for her mother's love is always put in jeopardy
through the existence of a male . . . one wonders why [lesbians] are so
much resented by men and women. Because of the pride and vanity of the
male, only few men would consider lesbians to be serious rivals. Men's
dislike of them goes back to a fundamental psychological cause: the need

for the mother in a woman. The male wants to be "fed" by the female. He
needs ego support throughout his life. A lesbian who "feeds" (loves)
another woman puts him and his world into chaos; she is a rival because
she takes away maternal support which should be HIS not HERS.[3]

Women who "feed" both men and women cannot successfully "feed" the
long-starving (and often swollen-bellied) women in patriarchal society.
From a psychological point of view, it is only women who can "make up"
to each other for their lack of mothering. At this moment in history, only
women can (if they will) support the entry or re-entry of women into the
human race. In order for most women to overthrow their "feminine"
conditioning, women must receive the kind of emotional, sexual, economic, and intellectual support from others—both older and younger
than themselves—that men do. However, I am not suggesting that either
the means or goals of feminism will necessarily be accomplished by
women "becoming" lesbians or by women following the lifestyles or
values of pre-feminist lesbians.

Many researcher-clinicians have confused, or equated, lesbianism
with male homosexuality. Many researchers have also studied and "sympathized" more with the latter than with the former group of "patients."
Most have not "sympathized" at all. Merle Miller "came out" in the New
York *Times*; some of the letters he received from psychiatrists had the
following advice: "While I sympathize with Mr. Miller's failure to be cured
of the disease . . . [and feel] that homosexuals have the same civil rights
as anyone else, they also have the right to try and get treatment for their
'illness.'" Another psychiatrist offered to "counsel" Miller "free of charge
because it is clear from your tone that you are in desperate, even frantic
need of help."

Of course, since *whatever* men do is considered more important than
anything that women do, male homosexuality has certainly been more
overtly punished, socially, legally, and economically, than lesbianism has.
Probably the fear of male physical force, coupled with male sexual aggressiveness, is an important factor here. Male homosexuals are perceived as
potentially combining these two forms of force—and using them against

other, perhaps weaker or younger *men*. This threat is an intolerable one to men, who psychologically must retain the initiative of force or action, in order to be "men." This same threat is, however, a daily fact of life for most women. Heterosexual men threaten all women, especially young girls, with a combination of greater physical and "sexual" force—but they are neither feared nor punished by our culture for this. The very same behavior has a totally different meaning as a function of whether it is performed by men or women, and as a function of who the recipient of that action is.

Male homosexuality is often perceived as having a more "glorious" tradition and a more legitimate or valued meaning than lesbianism. Historically, for example, many male homosexuals have waged "heroic" wars together, have headed governments, churches, and industries, and created artistic and intellectual masterpieces. Some people think that male homosexuals are the keepers of Western culture: in a sense, they are quite right—but my feeling about what this *means* is probably different from theirs. It means, among other things, that our culture is anti-female, wildly egotistical, and pro-war.

Male homosexuals are sometimes seen as embodying a culturally *valued* concern for beauty, love, violence, and death. Like Thomas Mann's hero in *Death in Venice*, male homosexuals are seen as martyrs to a cause that is both more spiritual and sexual than is the cause of biological reproduction. The love of men for men has been seen as more real and more elevating than those sorry domestic events that involve women and one's own children. Platonic "spiritualism," and everything it implies (from sex without "love" and love without sex—to modern science), is a basic value of Western culture.

Lesbians do not have a gloriously extensive ancestry. Their mothers and grandmothers, like those of heterosexual women, lived with men and did not control the means of production. Lesbians are women: as such, most are traditionally more domestic, conventional, and sexually monogamous than male homosexuals are—traits to which women are condemned, but for which they are not really valued. Gender is, I believe, a more basic predictor of behavior than is race, class, or sexual *preference*.

Lesbianism has not been as legally punished as homosexuality. However, it has been "punished" by *being completely legislated out of the realm of possibility for most women*. There are probably more male homosexuals than there are lesbians.[4] Women are repressed, both sexually and economically, and are therefore more sexually timid (with either women or men), as well as more economically powerless than are either homosexual or heterosexual men. In one sense, it is more difficult for women to become and survive as lesbians than it is for men to survive as homosexuals. For example, men either don't need or don't *think* they need women for economic survival. Most women both *need* and *think* they need men in order to survive economically, as well as "psychologically." (Many married fathers are active homosexuals.) Women have no institutionalized sisterhood that both men and women really respect. Female sisterhoods are based on female self-sacrifice and service to a husband, child, or male God. Even women in certain religious orders are "brides" to a male Christ—and housekeepers to the local governing male prelate.

In 1969, The *New York Times* published and article which stated:

There is no law against the placement of a child with lesbians but, in divorce cases there are generalities about the moral atmosphere in the "home." "Most judges would not place a child in a house shared by lesbians," according to Carl Zuckerman, lawyer for the Community Service Society, "but if there were no better alternative, the child would be placed with a homosexual parent."

In 1973, the American Psychiatric Association proclaimed that homosexuality was no longer a psychiatric disease. A gay liberation movement had begun in the late 1960s. The tragic spread of AIDS (and continued sexual promiscuity) crushed the momentum of the male branch of this movement. At first, lesbian liberationists mainly challenged homophobia among heterosexual feminists; soon enough, their focus turned to lesbian employment, and discrimination issues, and to the problem of lesbian-on-lesbian battering and child custody losses.

Most lesbians and lesbian communities resisted acknowledging that lesbians could also batter their partners, and that, like heterosexual men and women, lesbians had also internalized sexist values. In addition, because lesbianism was punished and ostracized within the family, and within schools, offices, and the military, lesbians also suffered from many shame and stigma issues. Often, alcoholism and drug addiction remained an unacknowledged part of lesbian life.

By the late 1980s, gay liberationists were also actively organizing around issues of gays in the military, gay marriage, gay adoption, gay second-parent adoption, and gay custody.

Over the years, I have been consulted about and have testified in a number of lesbian and homosexual custody cases as well as on behalf of women whose gender or "careers" as psychiatric or psychotherapy patients rendered them vulnerable to a custodial challenge.

In my first book about custody, *Mothers on Trial. The Battle for Children and Custody,* which was published in 1986, most lesbian mothers who had been challenged for custody—and whom I had interviewed—lost it. In my opinion, they were all "good enough" mothers. It was clear that throughout the 1960s, 1970s, and the first half of the 1980s, that many mental health professionals, lawyers, and judges still viewed lesbianism as a psychiatric illness.

Actually, lesbian mothers had one psychological advantage: they knew to expect trouble. The heterosexual mothers were completely surprised when they were custodially challenged and were devastated when they lost custody.

Although many people believe in some civil rights for homosexuals and lesbians—many do not. The battle for civil rights for gays has not yet been won.

Most women are more conditioned to want and need motherhood than most men are conditioned to want or need fatherhood. Traditionally, a "bachelor" life is not viewed as tragically as motherless "spinsterhood" is—and often isn't as tragic in terms of mobility, alternatives, etc., within a given class or race.

In a sense, it is theoretically easier for women to love women than it is for men to love men. (The so-called "masculinization" of women is more accepted than the "feminization" of men. All things female are despised. It is easier for women to wear pants and work at jobs outside the home than it is for men to wear dresses and high heels and to stay at home in the kitchen. Yet I wonder: why would anyone willingly offer up their feet for binding? And if they do, isn't it to better attract, support, and worship men?)

Interestingly, I have been told that many male-to-female transsexuals identify as lesbians and look for lesbian partners.)

Our mothers were women and, Michelangelo aside, most object-models of sexual or aesthetic beauty in our culture are female. Also, most women know how to be *tender* (not that they always are) with other people. Traditionally, many men, whether they are homosexual or heterosexual, know more about seduction, rape, and pillage—in bed and on the battlefield.

The God-of-War ideal of masculinity is so overpowering that few men dare take off their helmets and armor—*especially with other men.* They probably do so more readily with women, because it is "safe." This fact no doubt is as painful to male homosexuals as the fact of heterosexual women psychologically "feeding" men and starving women, is to lesbians.[5] I suppose that twentieth-century lesbians and homosexuals "suffer" from a similar dream, imprinted by at least three centuries of patriarchal family life: namely, the dream of bourgeois domesticity, approved public coupling, a homecoming—a dream whose reality is denied to both lesbians and homosexuals.

Two studies have compared lesbians with male homosexuals, and lesbians with heterosexual women.[6] They found that both lesbians and heterosexual women sought psychotherapy with equal frequency (a female institution); and that both groups of women were as frequently depressed (a female "disorder"). However, they discovered that the lesbians attempted suicide, drank alcohol, and dropped out of college more often than did the heterosexual women.

The lesbians sought psychotherapy more often than did the male homosexuals, and were seen as having a "significantly higher prevalence of 'psychiatric disorders.'" Their female conditioning was still being viewed, by themselves and by professionals, according to a male standard of mental health. Lesbians also attempted suicide and used drugs more often than did male homosexuals.

Only some lesbians are sexually "aggressive," non-monogamous, anti-romantic, or verbally or actually involved in large-scale sexual orgies of the Roman steam bath school. This is understandable since such psychological stances and practices characterize both *male* homosexuality and *male* heterosexuality. With all due respect for the importance of sexual freedom for all people, and with a respect doubly necessary because I am not a male homosexual, I must suggest that male homosexuality, *in patriarchal society*, is a basic and extreme expression of phallus worship, misogyny, and the colonization of certain female and/or "feminine" functions.

Male homosexuals, like male heterosexuals (and like heterosexual women), prefer men to women. I think that more lesbians have experienced (or have wanted to experience) sexual relationships with men, often pleasurably, and often within a legal marriage, than male homosexuals have experienced or wanted to experience sexual relationships with women. It is as simple as that. In a sense, most male homosexuals are "kinder" and more honest with women than are male heterosexuals (a fact for which they are duly punished). Unlike heterosexuals, most male homosexuals do not seduce, make promises to, or marry those whom they fear, dislike, are jealous of, or have contempt for—i.e., women. Of course, the greater capacity for real friendship and respect that some male homosexuals have for some women is a valuable and often unique experience for the women. However, it is still purchased at the expense of female sexuality, or rather, the possibility of sexual intimacy with a friend. Women are only accepted by men—be they homosexual men or heterosexual men—as *either* "brains" or "cunt," as *either* "heart" or "cunt," as *either* "mother" or "cunt." Women are rarely accepted as emotional, intellectual, and sexual beings. Small wonder that women find it hard to develop all three capacities; with whom would they share them? Lesbians, particularly feminist lesbians who are trying to subdue their self-contempt, sexual timidity, and heterosexually modeled role-playing, feel that at this point in history only women can be a midwife, mother, sister, daughter, and lover to the woman as a *human being*.

The only theory I have read about lesbianism by a psychiatrist that begins to make sense to me (or, to be honest, that agrees with some of what I already thought and wrote) is Charlotte Wolff's presentation in *Love Between Women*. Dr. Wolff proposes "emotional incest with the mother" as the essence of lesbianism. She locates certain aspects of lesbian psychology in history and mythology:

> The similarity between [the lesbian's] virility and freedom from the fetters of being an object of the male makes the homosexual woman resemble the image of women in matriarchal times. . . . The wide range of activities, the undoubted capacity to manage her life without dependence on men, is the ideal of the homosexual woman. Female homosexuality is inseparable from the very qualities which were the prerogative of women in early history. It is of no consequence to these conclusions whether the matriarchate existed as a definite period of history, which I believe it did, or in mythology only. Mythology is history, transcending concrete data and revealing their true meaning.

Dr. Wolff suggests that "love" flourishes within a context of "sameness and harmony" and is impossible in an "alien" context:

> The alien object may arouse admiration, excitement, and even adoration, but it cannot inspire love. The girl who succeeds in getting the better of her father (and the male in general), without recourse to feminine tricks, may be full of satisfaction and triumph, but she will have learned little about the realities of love in the process.

Thus, Wolff is very sensitive to the "feminine" heterosexual woman's isolation and nurturance-deprivation:

> The love a man can give her is found to fall short in essentials, which

only a mother can provide. It is she herself who has to supply these. She has to become what she could not possess—the mother—in her relationship with the male.

Wolff views the "unhappiness" of lesbians in terms of specific social ostracism, general female oppression, and lesbian ambitiousness. Lesbians are more emotionally demanding of each other than heterosexual women are of men.

Women are conditioned to put up with a lot more from a man, and they will, because he is the provider and the father of the children. Women demand from each other love, kindness, tolerance, understanding, sex—the lot. And if they don't think they are getting it, it's easy enough to get out.

I have no more basic a theory to offer.

THE INTERVIEWS

I interviewed nine white lesbians and two black lesbians. Two women (one black, the other white) had no experience with therapy or psychiatric hospitalization. Six of the women had been hospitalized when they were approximately twenty-one years old, for approximately three hundred and twenty days. ("Approximately" means a "total average" for the entire group.) Nine of the women had been in private therapy for approximately forty-four months—thirty-nine months with male therapists and twenty-one months with female therapists.

Their ages ranged from seventeen to forty-four; the ages at which they "became" lesbians, psychologically and/or sexually, ranged from nine to twenty-four. One woman never finished high school, four had some college experience, five completed college, and one had completed some graduate school. Some of these women were sexually "frigid" with women: most were not. At least half had sexual relationships with men.

While the majority of the women did not seem to be involved in heterosexually based role-playing, and were neither very "feminine" nor very "masculine" in dress, body carriage, or mannerisms, most were as "romantic" and monogamous as heterosexual women. Only two women, one aged seventeen, the other aged thirty-seven, were emphatically and ecstatically, non-monogamous (at least in their verbal presentations of self). The seventeen-year-old came trooping into my house with four women from her "living-collective." Their laughter was infectious; they wore headbands and grease paint, carried frisbees and yo-yos, and told me, laughingly, that they all "made it" with one another.

Five of the six lesbians who were hospitalized had in varying ways, and at varying times, become feminists. By 1971, when these interviews took place, eight of the eleven lesbians had become feminists.

Without exception, every lesbian in private therapy was treated as "sick." One woman told her mother about lesbian play with a girl friend, when they were both ten years old. Her mother took her to a psychiatrist who administered shock therapy as a form of treatment.

LOIS: One female therapist got scared when I became "gay." "I can't treat homosexuals. There's nothing you can do with them." She made it sound like terminal cancer. One male therapist kept insisting I wasn't gay, but he told me it's something I'll outgrow. He told me I'd end up alone and bitter in the gay scene, and that didn't appeal to me. It still doesn't. Another woman therapist said, "But men are so marvelous to sleep with! Lesbianism isn't necessary, it's absurd!"

In a sense, being psychiatrically hospitalized helped me. I'd hit bottom. Now I could be a lesbian, that's not as bad as a crazy.

MARSHA: I've been trying to kill myself since I've been twelve—gas, pills. I was walking around with a load of anger that I had no place to put. I wound up in Bellevue and was sent to a private hospital where I saw a psychiatrist who was shocked by my homosexuality. After I left Bellevue I saw him for a couple of months, privately. He called my mother in for an interview (he said he thought he would get a better understanding of me if he met her). In the course of that interview, he told my mother that I was a lesbian and suggested that I be weaned away from this woman (my lover). My mother blew her stack. She called this woman's parents and family, and said how *their* daughter was destroying *her* daughter. The upshot of that was that I had been staying at my mother's house for a few weeks after getting out of the hospital. I moved out and I didn't speak to my mother for two years.

CAROLE: I became infatuated with my first therapist, who was a woman. She told me that lesbianism is a sickness. She also told me that I wasn't a lesbian. I stopped eating and I was down to ninety pounds. I looked like a little boy with long hair. The therapist there, a man, also kept insisting I wasn't a lesbian, that everyone had these feelings, and I should push them out of the way.

PHYLLIS: Did you ever ask, "Well, what would be wrong if I were?"

CAROLE: No, I only knew that from the general feeling on the ward, that it was wrong and that I'm not a lesbian. The therapist felt that the feelings I had for women were basically anti-male feelings instead of pro-woman feelings.

MARSHA: Then I saw a woman psychiatrist for a year. She kept encouraging me to relate to men. I couldn't handle things any more and I admitted myself to Hillside [a private hospital]. I was there for a year and the anxiety built up tremendously. I was falling in love with women at the hospital and this was considered "sick." When they have these dances Saturday night, which you are supposed to go to, you are not supposed to dance with another woman, you are supposed to dance with a man. They encourage you to have dates and to go to the movies. They have movies on whatever night it is. Saturday night. You are encouraged to have activities jointly with the men's wards or cottages.

Although supposedly "sick," these women were also discouraged from thinking of themselves as lesbians—and encouraged to date or have sexual relations with men. One well-meaning, very motherly therapist actually arranged several "heterosexual" dates for her painfully shy patient.

FRANCES: I fell in love with a girl for the first time when I was twenty-four. I'd been in therapy at a hospital clinic [Bellevue] and told my therapist about it when he came back from his vacation.

PHYLLIS: What was his reaction?

FRANCES: He freaked out. He started yelling at me. "You're doing this because you think I'm your father and you want to hurt your father. You're a spoiled child. The minute I go away you do this, you go and do something that can be so dangerous" and he just freaked me out! Y'know. Because, since I'd been in therapy, I was truly happy. I did what I wanted to do, 'n' she was really lovely, and I was very happy. But he freaked me out, y'know. Basically he just said that my behavior was arrested at a homosexual level. He sort of made me understand that it was a very unfortunate thing that I was doing and that it would result in heartache. Which I understand, I mean, I do. It's certainly much better to live within the system. Although this system is for shit. You know, my girl friend was also coming to Bellevue for treatment. So one angle he took was that she wasn't too cool, because look, she was coming to Bellevue for treatment and I said, "Oh, God, I'm here. What are you talking about?" Then he said, "How could you stand it—don't women smell awful?" and I said, "Wow, y'know, if you wash" and he said, "Oh, please, no matter how clean a woman is, no matter how clean, she still smells." And I said, "I don't know, it just doesn't bother me." He said, "Did you ever see the statue of David? A man's body is so much more beautiful than a woman's body!" "You're crazy," I said. "I'm not saying my values are the values, but you better dig it, Doctor, and check out your own set of eyes, you've got some thinking to do."

PHYLLIS: Did he encourage you to go out with men?

FRANCES: Yes, he did, and I said to him, "Do you want me to go out with these pigs, just because they have penises? They're stupid, they have nothing to say to me, I have nothing to discuss with them. The only thing they could possibly do is fuck me, and possibly take me out of this blissful existence with women. And you don't care what they are, they could be the worst, filthy, perverted bastards, as long as they're men, y'know, it's okay. Is that what you're telling me?" He says, "Well, I'm saying that you could find something to talk about." I said, "Look, I've tried, there's nothing that I could talk about with them."

He [the therapist] acknowledged that some of the men might have been pigs. "Y'know," he said, "well, maybe you went out with a few bad men, but, uh, not every one is bad. And you gotta keep looking, and you gotta find a man, and you gotta go with a man. Anyway, a woman can be just as rough, just as dangerous as a man."

He said, "Let a man touch you. You're too sensitive to a male touch,"—because I had been. I was getting very uptight, y'know, at being touched by men. A lot of men come up to you in a very familiar way, touch you like you're a piece of equipment, or, I don't know, like you don't belong to yourself. Y'know, they come and touch you as if you owe them this kind of thing, to be soft for them, and to be responsive to them. And it got me really uptight. And I told him about this, and he said, "Force yourself. Touch someone's hand. Force yourself to be touched by men. What are they going to do, kill you? They're not gonna kill you!" And I said, "Well, I'm really afraid of men. Y'know, I was abused by men, there were some incidents in my life that were very painful," and he said, "They're not gonna kill you, they're not gonna kill you." And that's what he tried to tell me. You know, the way I'm talking about him sounds really awful. I mean, I loved him at the time. I mean, I'm not committed to women only. 'Cause I think that's not good. I think that women should—y'gotta be committed to people, and to finding good people.

JOAN: I went into therapy because I was depressed about the way I look. I grew to about five feet ten inches, my present height, when I was twelve. I'd never dated. I was passionate about literature and music and I was totally isolated. I was isolating myself in such a way that I'd have to pay a price for it. When I was eighteen I became enamored of my girl friend. We would listen to operas together and go to libraries. We'd hold hands and that was very beautiful, it had a tremendous amount of meaning. But I did not want to be a homosexual and go over the brink. I had started masturbating after years of being a good Catholic. I guess I didn't believe in God any more.

Dr. B. was about forty-five and very charismatic, very demonic. He told me to masturbate and didn't believe that I did. He wanted me to show him, right there in the office. He said if I didn't get laid by the third date the guy was a fag. So I started fucking men. Dr. B. said I was very frigid, that I had a mask-like face.

PHYLLIS: You were about twenty?

JOAN: Yes.

PHYLLIS: Did you love this first man?

JOAN: No. I despised him. He always had to have new cars, like Cadillacs, but he couldn't say Beethoven's name properly. He was about ten years older than me and very materialistic. I started sleeping with a guy down the hall also. He sleeps with about five to ten different women each week. I had fifteen credits in college and a twenty-hour-a-week job and I was carrying on two affairs at once and I got very upset and very depressed. But I pulled myself together and did my schoolwork.

PHYLLIS: What did you feel?

JOAN: I was worried that I was somehow losing myself. I was abusing myself, not because I was losing my virginity, but because I was losing energy, and concentration, and control of myself.

Dr. B. didn't allow me to keep a journal because I was too introverted, too "fixed upon myself"—something I'd always been hearing. Fucking was very highly valued no matter how exhausted or hurt you got or how you picked up this disease or that disease. . . . He said I'm not a homosexual, I don't come on like one. I said, "What is a homosexual, because I never met one." But he would just assure me that I didn't look like one and that was strange because I was obviously at the beginning of becoming one.

I said I did not want children. I wanted my achievements rather than children. He really did not go into that. He thought that the whole society was so screwed up that there was no point in having children. He did not seem to value marriage much.

I attended group also. The group was ripping me apart. They ripped everyone apart. They didn't like the way I looked, I didn't wear make-up, I didn't take dating seriously.

PHYLLIS: Did the other women in this group yell at you for this too?

JOAN: Yes.

PHYLLIS: Were there any lesbians in the group?

JOAN: No.

PHYLLIS: Were there any male homosexuals?

JOAN: Yes.

PHYLLIS: How were they treated?

JOAN: With more consideration. They had a right but I didn't have a right to be where I was. The group's technique was to tear everyone's defenses down.

These two interviews make painfully apparent the extent to which lesbians (or lesbians who seek therapy) are as naive, fearful, and "suggestible" as heterosexual women: perhaps even more so. Their sexual experience remains a private, "personal" reality, one that they can't share with their mothers, employers, classmates, children—or even with their therapists. Their sense of reality, their *knowledge of pleasure*, is treated as either non-existent, second best, or dangerous. (I have certainly never heard of a therapist actively questioning his patient's heterosexual realities, or of subtly or overtly "prescribing" lesbian experiences.)

I would like to close this chapter by, in Charlotte Wolff's words, "letting life itself comment." The following interview was done with a black lesbian who had never been in therapy. She is not included statistically in either Lesbians in Therapy or Third World Women in Therapy. The interviewer was a black woman.

DORIS: Weren't you married?

MARY: Married, me? You must be thinking about my girl friend. Honey, I wouldn't get married to save my life. And I can truthfully say that most women who get married are sick! They're really sick!

DORIS: What you're saying is that all housewives are mentally sick? This is what it appears that you're saying, that they're crazy.

MARY: Wait a minute, do you realize that most housewives have a ninety-eight- or ninety-nine-hour work week slaving their fuckin' ass off for some bastard?

DORIS: You've got to work sometime.

MARY: Well, honey, it's a bullshit system and anyone who gets in it is crazy. But, all right, let's dig this. You come home, right?

DORIS: All right, all right.

MARY: And I come home and I have to cook, and then I have to clean, and then I have to wash dishes and I have to wash his little dirty shorts, right, and heaven help me if my husband won't bat the kids right around, right? Then he comes home from his little. . . .

DORIS: Isn't this what you were put here for?

MARY: Well, just wait a minute, honey. Just let me finish. When he comes home from his office job sitting behind his desk, right, and he eats.

DORIS: That's there with the job, honey.

MARY: Well, freak that. I have to wash his dishes, and then he wants to screw, on top of all this. And I just can't dig it! And, you know, ask me, I'm a lesbian, right? And I don't have to love 'em, I don't have to fuck 'em and I damn sure don't have to depend on 'em, and that is freedom, honey, because no matter how heavy my load, honey, I'm gonna make it 'cause I'm free. I feel that I am free!

DORIS: It appears that you are a man-hating woman.

MARY: No, I don't hate them. I don't hate them. I just don't dig them.

DORIS: What about child raising? Aren't you denied that rewarding experience of giving birth to a child someday?

MARY: Surely you jest, honey. Who in the hell ever told you that having a kid was such a wonderful experience? If you think that a woman walking around with a swollen stomach for nine months is a pretty sight, you better go scratch your ass, I mean right now, 'cause then you a liar. If you think that labor pain is such a wonderful experience. . . .

DORIS: This isn't the rewarding experience I'm talking about. I'm talking about—

MARY: Wait a minute—

DORIS:—this baby. Having someone to take—it's yours. Something of your own. I'm not talking about the labor pains. Of course, what's so rewarding about that? I agree with you. Have you ever been through it?

MARY: Wait a minute. Let me talk, let me talk. You think that laying on a metal table with your legs all cocked up and some old white bastard shoving some cold clamps up your thing. . . .

DORIS: There are black ones too.

MARY: Well, that's his business. You don't know many black ones, do you? While your fucking husband is probably out somewhere screwing everything in sight. Well, honey, I can't stand it and I can't dig it and anybody who goes through it is crazy. A man will feel you, fry you, fight you, fuck you, and then forget you, honey.

DORIS: You can always get a midwife.

MARY: He'll turn around and tell you, "You've come a long way, baby." Ain't that much coming in the world.

DORIS: How long have you been homosexually oriented?

MARY: Homosexually oriented, baby: why don't you just say "in the light"? That's what it breaks down to. Well, I'd say actively about six years. About six years.

DORIS: Phew, you ain't kidding, are you?

MARY: Well, no, are we. Actively about six years.

DORIS: What do you mean by actively? Actively, actively, what do you mean, you just keep going from one to the other?

MARY: No, well, when I say actively—I've probably been in the light all of my life because I can't remember having any meaningful experience with a man. You know, I can take them or leave them and, baby, I left them most of the time because they never interested me in any way. And, you know, in the books and everything—I must have slept through that period in my life when I was supposed to make that big transition from girl friend to boy friend, but I never made it. But what I'm saying is that I didn't have my first homosexual experience until I was about twenty-two.

DORIS: Why was it twenty-two? I'm sure you could have had some opportunities to engage, you know, at an earlier stage of life, or did you not?

MARY: Well, number one. . . .

DORIS: Were you sheltered?

MARY: No! Come on, girl. Well, number one, I was very confused and very frightened about where I was coming from, actually.

DORIS: What do you mean by "coming from"?

MARY: Well, I thought I was one of the sickest persons in this world. You know, I dreaded even thinking about the term "lesbian" and I used to cope with the situation by telling myself that I was normal, you understand? And the only thing that would take my normality away would be for me to have an actual gay experience. And I also used to tell myself that you're not gay if you never do it. So I didn't, 'cause I didn't want nothing to tread on my sanity. So I pretended to like boys and dresses and parties and all that bullshit.

DORIS: So you were just fooling yourself?

MARY: No, no, I wasn't fooling myself, I was trying to live with myself, and I went out with fellas and I let them fuck me. . . .

DORIS: Well, if you didn't want to be a girl why—

MARY: That's what I'm saying. The more they did it, the worse I got, and the more I pretended to act normal, the crazier I got. And I mean I was going out of my mind. When my mother died I just stopped pretending to be something that I wasn't because it ain't done much straightness in the world and it put my mind at ease, you better believe it, and I regained my sanity which was slowly seeping away from me, from trying to be ungay and I am definitely gay. And I realize that I am not the sick one. It's all those poor simple fools out there, those little housewives that sign their life away when they say, "I do." You know, they sign their death warrant. And like I said before, I am free. I am definitely free.

DORIS: Tell me a little about your family background. You know, your relationship with your parents. Something as far back as you can remember, you know. How things were.

MARY: Relationship with my parents—

DORIS: Ummmmm.

MARY: Well, that's a story in itself, honey, 'cause my father was a pure fuck.

DORIS: Oh, that's nice to hear.

MARY: My mother was a fool 'cause she lived with this fuck until she went foolish.

DORIS: What do you mean by fuck?

MARY: Well, he used to beat the shit out of her really. He used to beat the shit out of this woman every Friday, 'cause you know on Friday that's when the eagle flies. And it used to fly him straight to the liquor store; and he'd come home all sloppy drunk and stone broke and this went on until my mother died.

DORIS: What did your mother die of, honey?

MARY: Well, she died, the doctor said she had a heart attack. Well, that's what the doctor said, but I, me, I personally believe that she just gave up living 'cause her living was hell, baby, and she worked in a white woman's kitchen for twelve years and that's just where she died.

DORIS: What do you mean by "she just gave up"? She said, "Well, oh, I think I'll die" and just went on? What do you mean by "she just gave up life"? What do you mean by that?

MARY: Well, when—I mean when you ain't got nothing more to live for, man, you just give up. If your life ain't worth shit, you ain't worth shit, baby.

DORIS: Wait a minute, do you think she committed suicide or some-thing?

MARY: No! You don't understand what I'm saying.

DORIS: I don't really.

MARY: When you give up, you just give up. You can't take all this bullshit from everybody, especially from somebody who's supposed to be your husband and all this kind of crap, and you just can't, you can't dig on it. That's all. You know, about two or three weeks before she died my mother told me that she would be free soon. You know, she knew she was going to die and that's why she said it. It was a term she always used—that she would be free soon. And for me to settle down and get married to someone who I loved and depend on—

DORIS: Did she mean male or female?

MARY: Well, she meant male because my mother was a strict, you know, gospel woman and—

DORIS: Did she know of your experiences?

MARY: Are you kidding? Of course not.

DORIS: Are you sure?

MARY: I'm positive. And you know she was trying to tell me don't be a slave so I can live a better life than hers but what she was really saying was don't be a slave but be a free slave. Don't marry a fuck like she did.

DORIS: Don't be a slave but be a free slave. That sounds kinda off the wall. What do you mean?

MARY: Well, marry a nice fuck. Don't marry a fuck like she did. Well, my mother was pitiful. The only way she got her freedom was through death and I, when she died, I say this ain't going to be me 'cause I realized that the only way—

DORIS: What do you mean? How do you know that your mother didn't enjoy herself? She stayed with this man for such a long time.

MARY: That's right, she stayed there 'cause she had children to support and the only way that I'm gonna get my freedom, you know, to obtain my freedom, was through living the life that I want to, so I stopped pretending to be something that I—

DORIS: This is what I said. You don't want to go through the same thing that your mother went through so you chose something else. . . . Okay, I just want to ask you one more question. With the way the majority of most women are going, do you think there is an alternative to the present lifestyle?

MARY: You mean the women's present lifestyle?

DORIS: Right, yes.

MARY: Well how can you have a solution for something that's been going on for centuries? And the only possible alternative would be for somebody to be Lord and Saviour Christ for a day, and let's say if I was King Jesus, you know I would place a curse on every man alive and this curse would be a little thing they call a twelve-month pregnancy and each man would produce about seven girls.

DORIS: Why seven? Seven! My God!

MARY: Oh one for each day of the week, right. No woman would be without a lover or somebody to talk to, you know, affection.

CHAPTER EIGHT

THIRD WORLD WOMEN

When I was six years old in Brooklyn, Shirley was my best friend. She was black, and her mother had died in a fire in a country called Africa. She lived in a basement with her father, the janitor, who was always laughing. Shirley and I ran away from home together every afternoon. We also planned to co-captain the best punch-ball team ever. Our plans were ended by a supper invitation.

"What," my parents screamed at me, "you want to go down into the basement at night—with her father there, with men, cards, numbers, liquor, God knows what?"

"Her father lives there," I explained. "He's the janitor. But I promise we won't bother him. . . ."

Well, I never got to taste any African food in my sixth year (if that's what we would have eaten). And for years, whenever I went to the ocean, I saw black men laughing dangerously at me in every roaring wave. (The bands of embittered black youths who rove New York City, grabbing "tits 'n' ass" in a white rage, haven't helped me any with that one.)

And sometimes I wonder what adult uniform they gave Shirley: "welfare mother," suburban citizen, black militant, Dead on Arrival?

Shirley, I dedicate this chapter to everything that was between us—and to whatever revolution changes what couldn't be into an unremarkable occurrence.

Dr. Hill acknowledged, in an interview today, that [black] families headed by women were considerably more vulnerable to economic and social ills. An important reason is that women heads of family are likely to earn much less than men. . . . The report says that "national earnings data do not support the popular conception that wives' earnings in most low-income black families are often greater than husbands'. It is said that in eighty-five percent of the black families with incomes of $3,000 or less, the husband's income surpassed the wife's."

New York *Times*, July 27 and 28, 1971

In the first national comparative study of its kind, the Census Bureau has found that persons of origin in Spanish-speaking countries earn significantly greater incomes than blacks, even though they have poorer educations. . . .

Further, statisticians say, while the incomes of both groups still fall far behind those of whites, there is some evidence to suggest that the Spanish group is gaining somewhat faster than blacks are.

New York *Times*, October 18, 1971

Is women's liberation irrelevant to black women? Of course, as has been pointed out, half of blacks are women; the question might be asked whether the black movement has been relevant to them. The black movement is conceived as primarily directed toward the black man, and programs to meet its demands have reflected this. The Job Corp, with many blacks, was practically all male until a 1966 Act of Congress required at least one-third participation by females; of the 125,000 trainees under the Manpower Development and Training Act in 1968, only thirty-two percent were women; in 1968, in the Job Opportunities in the business sector program, only twenty-four percent of those hired were female; the training program of the National Alliance of Businessmen is restricted to black males.

Nancy Henley[1]

What do black women feel about Women's Lib? Distrust. It is white, therefore suspect. . . . They look at white women and see them as the enemy for they know that racism is not confined to white men, and that there are more white women than men in this country and that fifty-three percent of the population sustained an eloquent silence during times of greatest stress. . . . The problem of most black women is not getting into the labor force but in being upgraded in it, not in getting into medical school but in getting adult education, not in how to exercise freedom from the "head of the house" but in how to *be* the head of the household. . . .

For years in this country there was no one for black men to vent their rage on except black women. And for years black women accepted that rage—even regarded that acceptance as their unpleasant duty. But in doing so, they frequently kicked back, and they seem never to have become the "slave" that white women see in their own history. True, the black woman did the housework, the drudgery; true, she reared the children, often alone, but she did all of that while occupying a place on the job market, a place her mate could not get or which his pride would not let him accept. And she had nothing to fall back on: not maleness, not whiteness, not ladyhood, not anything. And out of the profound desolation of her reality she may very well have invented herself. . . .

. . . Black women have always considered themselves superior to white women. . . . Black women have been able to envy white women (their looks, their easy life, the attention they seem to get from their men;) they could fear them (for the economic control they have had over black women's lives) and even love them (as mammies and domestic workers can;) but black women have found it impossible to respect white women. I mean they never had what black men have had for white men: a feeling of awe at their accomplishments.

Toni Morrison[2]

Unfortunately, there seems to be some confusion in the Movement today as to who has been oppressing whom. Since the advent of black power, the black male has exerted a more prominent leadership role in our struggle for justice in this country. He sees the system for what it really is for the most part, but where he rejects its values and mores on many issues, when it comes to women he seems to take his guidelines from the pages of the *Ladies' Home Journal*. Certain black men are maintaining that they have been castrated by society but that Black women somehow escaped the persecution and even contributed to this emasculation. Let me state here and now that black women in America can justly be described as a "slave of a slave." . . .

Those who are exerting their "manhood" by telling Black women to step back into a domestic, submissive role are assuming a counter-

revolutionary position. Black women likewise have been abused by
the system and we must begin talking about the elimination of all
kinds of oppression. If we are talking about building a strong nation,
capable of throwing off the yoke of capitalist oppression, then we are
talking about the total involvement of every man, woman, and child,
each with a highly developed political consciousness. We need our
whole army out there dealing with the enemy and not half an army.

Frances Beale[3]

Black ladies, the last thing we have to worry about is genocide. In fact,
we could use a little. Look at what's happened to us in the last hundred
years; we've been bravely propagating and all we've gotten are a lot of
lumps and a bad name. On the other hand, there are people like Glazer
and Moynihan carrying on about our matriarchy and inferring that
we've botched up the job long enough and that if we insist on doing
something, confine ourselves to standing behind the man of the family
and bringing him up to par. . . . Anyway, there's the brother nattering
away about how we've been lopping off balls long enough, it's time to
stand aside. So you stand there looking as pink and white and helpless
as is possible under the circumstances. . . .

Joanna Clark[4]

Though it appears that both men and women live together within the
institutions of society, men really define and control the institutions
while women live under their rule. The government, army, religion,
economy, and family are institutions of the male culture's colonial
rule of the female. . . . A female culture exists. It is a culture that is
subordinated and under male culture's colonial, imperialist rule all
over the world. Underneath the surface of every national, ethnic, or
racial culture is the split between the two primary cultures of the
world—the female culture and the male culture.

National cultures vary greatly according to the degree of the
suppression of the female culture. The veil and seclusion of women
and their almost total segregation in Arab culture makes for differences between them and, for example, Sweden. A Swedish woman
may not be able to tolerate the suppressed life of Arab women but she
also, if she is sensitive, may not be able to tolerate her suppression as
a female in Sweden. Crossing national boundaries often awakens a

woman's understanding of her position in society. We cannot, like
James Baldwin, even temporarily escape to Paris or another country
from our caste role. It is everywhere—there is no place to escape.

Fourth World Manifesto,[5] January 13, 1971

THESE ARE ALL AMAZING VOICES AND POINTS OF VIEW. Since I quoted
them here, African American literary women such as Toni Cade Bambara,
bell hooks, Alice Walker, and Michelle Wallace went on to develop a
concept of "womanism," as another version of feminism, while the
glorious Toni Morrison went on to win the Nobel Prize in Literature.

African-, Hispanic-, and Asian American mental health researchers
and clinicians such as Drs. Teresa Bernardez, Jean Shinoda Bolen, Lillian
Comas-Diaz, Oliva Espin, Clarissa Pinkola Estes, Beverly Greene, Leslie
Jackson, and Gwendolyn Keita, to name only a few, went on to study and
teach feminist psychologies from a woman-of-color and multicultural
point of view.

Although not a mental health professional, bell hooks recognized that
feminist liberation movements had "radicalized the notion of mental
health." Given the ravages of racism, sexism, and poverty, she believes
that African American women must "purge" themselves of the "poison
and lies that assault the ego and threaten the heart." She calls for "self-
healing" and "soul healing." She sees African American women as
"wounded," isolated, opposed to therapy. hooks writes that "any liberation struggle to end domination is fundamentally about a revolution in
mental health."

Both Shinoda Bolen and Pinkola Estes write about psychological and
"goddess" archetypes in all women and envision women's spiritual
development as crucial for mental health. If God is conceived of as a white
man, then all women are in psychological trouble, women of color even
more so.

Interestingly, we have learned a great deal about Asian American and
Hispanic American female realities from literary works by Maxine Hong
Kingston (*The Woman Warrior*), Amy Tan (*The Joy Luck Club*), and Laura

Esquivel (*Like Water for Chocolate*). Anthologies edited by Sonia Shah (*Dragon Ladies: Asian American Feminists Breathe Fire*) and by Shamita Das Dasgupta (*A Patchwork Shawl: Chronicles of South Asian Women in America*) are also very useful. The National Research Center on Asian American Mental Health at the University of California at Davis provides an important bibliography of research in this area from about 1990 to 2004.

In the last thirty-forty years, feminist theorists and clinicians of color have researched and treated women and men of color. They have explored every conceivable issue, ranging from depression, suicide, and eating disorders, to domestic violence and the need for spiritual and religious approaches for women of color.

For example, we now know that most Native American women suffer all the indignities of entrenched poverty, racism, and sexism—which means they suffer from intense domestic violence, preventable diseases, alcoholism, and so on. They also have access to tribal and spiritual approaches to healing.

We now also know that many African American women are often the victims of intense family violence, including incest, battering, verbal abuse, and homicide. They suffer from poverty, untreated diseases, low-wage, and dead-end employment. Homicide is one of the leading causes of death for African American women ages 15- to 34. According to one controversial estimate, African American women are battered at a rate of 113/1,000 as compared to 30/1,000 among Americans of European origin. This is only the tip of the iceberg, since many African American women are reluctant to report domestic violence given that the police and criminal justice systems are racially biased.

Reva L. Heron and Diana P. Jacobs present a detailed discussion of the "coping skills" available to low-income battered and suicidal African American women and recommend programs that teach new coping and problem-solving skills, group therapy, partner conjoint therapy, vocational training, and a host of support services.

Diane J. Harris and Sue A. Kuba view eating disorders among women of color as an expression of "internalized oppression" and a response to "conflicting cultural demands for beauty and acceptance." They find that the highest incidence of eating disorders occurs among African American women between the ages of 45 and 54.

Hispanic American theorists and clinicians such as Drs. Teresa Bernardez, Lillian Comas-Diaz, and Oliva Espin, among others, have defined both the strengths and the dangers of ethnic, Catholic communities.

An increasing number of Muslim women currently live in the West. I write about Muslim female psychology in *The Death of Feminism: What's Next in the Struggle for Women's Freedom*. Psychoanalyst and Arabist Dr. Nancy Kobrin, has also written very important work in this area. In addition to issues of immigration, poverty, and racism, the sexism they face, both within their families and in the larger world, are quite formidable. While many exceptions exist, many Muslim women have not been allowed to develop a sense of "self" or individuality. They often suffer from pathologically low self-esteem; are increasingly expected to veil themselves; are usually forced into arranged marriages; and are, traditionally, the victims of honor killings.

To the best of my knowledge, as yet no feminist clinical practice has addressed the desperate needs of this particular population.

I still have no single theory to offer of Third World female psychology in America. No single theory will do descriptive justice to women of African, Latin-American, Middle Eastern, Asian, and native American descent. Furthermore, as a psychologist and feminist, I'm really more interested in exploring the laws of *female* psychology than in exploring their various exceptions and variations.

The experience and effects of sexism are different for Third World and white women in America. For example, more Third World women have worked outside the home and within the context of a female "kinship" system than have many middle-class white women. More white women have had more education put to less use, and more fathers and husbands economically supporting them in isolated family units than have most Third World women. However, the employed Third World woman really has no more mobility, psychologically or economically, than her white non-employed counterpart. The ghetto "kinship" system is as much a structure of bitter necessity as is female isolation within the middle-class family. The feminist desire to overcome dependence on men cannot be shared by those Third World women who, because of racism and class warfare, have never been allowed a similar dependence. (Although they may indeed have longed for such dependence and for the privileges and safety it represents.)

From my point of view, women have never fared as well as men in traditional Africa, Asia, the Middle East, or South America. The maternal death rate and infant death rate are very high on both continents. While most women in Africa have traditionally always worked strenuously in childbearing and rearing, in agriculture and/or commerce, they have not been political, military, or religious leaders as men have, nor has polyandry existed as often as polygamy. There have, of course, been many African queens and militarists, and many matriarchal cultures in "pre-historical" Asia, Africa, South America, and Europe. Once European intervention occurred, the African women's position was even further downgraded in comparison to her male counterpart: African men were forced and/or encouraged to participate in education, modern farming, land ownership, factory work, etc. Female warriors ceased to exist almost entirely. To date, most African revolutionary or traditional nationalist leaders, militarists, judges, and priests are men, not women.

This is one of the many reasons that those Third World women who can afford to be politically active in any sense are not feminists. An alliance of women either representing or fighting for women's rights belongs more to the future than to the past. For example, men have always been seen as more physically and intellectually powerful than women. To strictly heterosexual women, they are also the only possible sexual partners. For these reasons alone, Third World women, like most white women, will "stick" by their men sooner than they will "become" their own men, i.e., sooner than they will incorporate "male" or all human characteristics. The real gender revolution is harder and more threatening to people of both sexes, and of all classes and races, than are even other extremely difficult revolutions.

I understand what an African-, Hispanic-, or Asian American working woman feels and means when she says: "I want to *stop* working. I want to be *able* to stay home with my children. I want to be *able* to have a man care for me." She is talking about having *one* full-time job instead of two. But she doesn't necessarily feel, any more than white women do, that being a mother and "housewife" is an invaluable form of labor without which her husband (or the government) could not survive. Women of all classes and races are not socialized to regard the family as a public institution, or as particularly oppressive to women.

My hypothetical Third World woman is also talking about the many privileges of having white skin in America, especially if it belongs to a middle-income wallet. She is talking about racial differences in housing, schooling, and employment. (Lower income white women suffer these tragedies, also). She is talking about feeling safe on the streets or in her home—something that, whether realistic or not, most white women, even in cities, have always felt. [More *reports* of rape exist for Third World than for white women]. She is also talking about the privilege of psychological dependence and material security: even if these are temporary privileges, and purchased at the expense of human dignity and freedom, the pleasure of such female privileges is real and has kept many of us alive. From a psychological point of view, as long as a particular group is still "profiting" from the misery of the less fortunate, it is as cruel as it is foolish to expect the less fortunate to be self-sacrificial, noble, etc. Let all men (all white people) give up all their powers and privileges *first*—their wives, secretaries, prostitutes, their material comforts, their information, their *privileged childhoods*—then, and only then, will women or people of color begin to consider the redemptive features of "goodness" or "equality." Until then, women and people of color will want all the free drinks, the handshakes, the trophies, the inside tips—the "killings." Oppressed groups do not internalize the values of power any less than other groups.

The fact is, it is probably better to be the slave of a rich man than the slave of a poor man; better to be at the mercy of power than at the mercy of powerlessness. Strength can often afford mercy; weakness, rarely. It is even better to be the slave of one man whom you know—a husband—than the slave of many strange men—such as the men in the state legislature or in industry.

Many male theoreticians of color, and more recently, female theoreticians of color, have written about the "Third World" woman in America. and in the Third World proper. Frantz Fanon, an eloquent and brilliant black male psychiatrist, was, unfortunately, embarrassingly, painfully a sexist in his writing about Algerian women. I read Fanon in 1969 on a long bus ride on my way to a meeting. Furiously, I underlined nearly all of his *A Dying Colonialism*, as impressed as I was angry and disappointed by it.[6] A group of feminists must have been on a bus ride too, because their conclusions are similar to some of my own.[7] They say:

> Fanon is correct in saying that the French tried to destroy Algerian [male] culture and that this is a typical colonial tactic of one male culture vs. another colonized male culture. But Fanon shows a typical male inability to see the brutal colonization of females by males. In his use of the veil, as a symbol of Algerian culture that the French were trying to destroy, he oversimplifies in order to avoid a recognition of his own male guilt and the Algerian males' culpability towards the Algerian females' repressed and demeaned culture.
>
> If Fanon were more honest he would recognize that the French, as a male culture, had no more interest in the Algerian woman's freedom than had the Algerian male. But Fanon, who has such angry passion against the French colonizers, does not extend his vision to demand justice for the Algerian female. In fact, he pooh-poohs the idea that Algerian women are oppressed at all. Nowhere, except in things which he does not realize that he is revealing, does he admit the fact of female oppression by the male in Algeria. . . .
>
> Through the imposition of a servant status on women the female culture has elaborated a whole servile ethic of "self-sacrifice." Self-sacrifice—as the major ethic of the female culture—has been one of the most effective psychological blocks to women's open rebellion and demand for self-determination. It has also been a major tool of male

manipulation of females.

Kardiner[8] and Moynihan,[9] less eloquent than Fanon, are white male professionals. Their writing about black women and black "matriarchs" in America is racist and sexist, as well as uninspired. Grier and Cobbs, two black male psychiatrists, are, at best, mediocre in their ascribing a second-class humanity to black women. Let me quote from their chapters entitled "Achieving Womanhood" and "Marriage and Love" in *Black Rage*[10]:

> So it may be that after a brief struggle a black woman feels that femininity, as it is defined in these times, is something she cannot achieve. Rather than having her heart broken every day, she relinquishes the struggle and diverts her interest elsewhere. She has derived none of the intensely personal satisfaction she might have received as an honored and desirable sexual object. The full flowering of a woman's sexual function and her capacity to enjoy it are based on her evaluation of herself. If she considers herself an especially worthwhile person, she can joyfully submit to her lover, knowing that he will likewise prize and value her. Her enjoyment of the sexual function will not be impaired by the feeling of being degraded by the man. There is a natural inclination for a woman to yield herself to a powerful lover, gaining additional narcissistic supplies in her possession of him. Her own high evaluation of herself, in turn, evokes in the man a similar high evaluation of her. If her narcissism is impaired, the sexual act is a degrading submission to a man who does not value her, and she arises from it feeling a loss of self-esteem rather than a personal enhancement.
>
> With youthful narcissism crushed and sexual life perverted, [black women] drew back from these modes as a primary means of life expression. Letting youth go, and sex go, they narrowed their vision to the most essential feminine function—mothering, nurturing, and protecting their children. In such a role the black woman has been the salvation of many a family. To call such a family matriarchal, as many have done, is to obscure the essential maternal function and to suggest

an authoritarian for authority's sake. We suggest that the black woman has been beset by cruelty on all sides and as a result, centered her concern on the most essential quality of womanhood.

It is difficult to *document* racist practices in the selection and treatment of the "mentally ill." First, the statistics, like those on child molestation or rape, are not easily available. Second, most Third World people are simply too poor to be able to afford private therapeutic treatment: they are socially controlled and condemned in more direct, physical ways. (Henley points out that women, like blacks, are steered into heavy drug use, but into drugs that tend to pacify rather than eliminate them, perhaps illustrating that women are less expendable from the point of view of the dominant culture than are blacks.)[11] Third, racism, in psychiatric diagnosis and treatment, is usually further confused by class and gender biases. Nevertheless, it is undeniable that women and men of color are often discriminated against and misunderstood when they make contact with the psychiatric world. It is also undeniable that employees of the psychiatric establishment, such as attendants, orderlies, and nurses, particularly in low-paying jobs in state and county asylums, are brutal to inmates of all races. People internalize the oppressive values; they also do what they think they're expected to do—and what they can get away with.[12]

When an African-, Hispanic-, Asian-, or immigrant woman is hospitalized, her "treatment" is probably very similar to that of a white woman. It consists of domestic and "maternal" tasks—or of psychological preparation for domestic, maternal, and heterosexual tasks. Psychiatrically hospitalized black men are mistreated but not in this way. Despite differences between black, Puerto Rican and white women, and differences in how they are perceived by male professionals, the fact that they are *women* makes them all equally vulnerable to the predominantly masculine standard of mental health. Also, despite differences, crucial (and devalued) aspects of the female role are probably shared by women of all races and classes. For example, a study has suggested that significantly more women than men, both among the black and white populations, have *reported* nervous breakdowns, impending nervous breakdowns, psychological inertia, and dizziness. Both African- and white American women also report higher rates than men for the following symptoms: nervousness, insomnia, trembling hands, nightmares, fainting, and headaches.[13]

THE INTERVIEWS

I spoke with nine Third World women, six of African descent and three of Latin American descent. Their ages ranged from twenty-seven to forty-eight. Two women had some high school experience, four had some college experience, two had completed college, and one woman had some graduate school experience. Five women were legally single, one was legally married, two were divorced, and one was widowed. With one exception, a schoolteacher, none of the women earned more than five thousand dollars yearly, if that, and usually in a secretarial or clerical capacity. Three of the women were unemployed or living on welfare. Two of the women, both black Americans, were feminists.

Three of the women had been psychiatrically hospitalized: one woman briefly, for attempting suicide, another several times for "paranoid schizophrenia," and a third woman many times for a total of more than five years for "involutional schizophrenia." None were hospitalized in private institutions.

Seven of the women had been in private therapy with approximately three therapists apiece, for approximately twenty-five months: seventeen months with male therapists and twenty-four months with female therapists. ("Approximately" means a total average for the group of seven.) The women saw a total number of ten male therapists and eight female therapists. With the exception of two black male psychiatrists and one Puerto Rican female social worker, the therapists were all white.

I spoke to five of the women with another Third World woman present. Two of the interviews were conducted without me by a Third World woman. I spoke to one woman with a white friend and former therapist present, and to one woman alone, at her request.

Why did these women seek, accept, or feel comfortable with male therapists? Naiveté? Race hatred? Same-sex hatred? An opportunity to finally be with a white man who couldn't seduce or buy them? Or who would, but "nicely?" In general, most of the women were as "hooked" on heterosexuality, "love," and marriage as their white counterparts.

WILMA: I couldn't stand being without a man. Every time a guy left me I would do three things: be afraid I'd kill myself, run to a therapist, and find another boy friend as soon as possible.

CAROLINE: Dr. B. is a very handsome black man. Very attractive. Great personality. Good doctor. And he tried everything. He almost stood on his head. I just did not talk to him about what was really bothering me. He never got to me. I didn't relate to him. It was so terrible. I sat there for six months before we even talked a little bit about what I was feeling. You see he has this thing if I didn't talk he very rarely said anything. And I don't talk sometimes about things that are that close to me very well. So we sat through about twenty-five minutes in the session looking at each other and I sat there being miserable, and that's kinda what happened. I suppose I was resisting. I don't know what it was. He just couldn't seem to open me up. It was a long waste.

PHYLLIS: You don't blame him, though?

CAROLINE: No, I liked him. He was very nice, like a nice vase. You put it on the shelf to be admired and I wouldn't run in there and say anything intimate or earth-shaking to break the vase. I actually used to replace the flowers in his outer office (he neglected them terribly) and I really liked him but I just couldn't talk to him. [After my suicide attempt] I started seeing Dr. L., a white man, who I also liked a lot. He's really helped me. But you know, no matter what I say, he brings it back to me. If I got bubonic plague it would still be my fault. No, I can't talk to him about orgasms, I'm too embarrassed.

EVELYN: I started therapy primarily because of a guy I'd had a brief relationship with and he rejected me. And I had actually made a humiliating telephone call. The first time I'd ever done anything like that in my life—to just simply confront him verbally and this was after I'd drunk about three quarters of a bottle of vodka. I was absolutely smashed out of my skull in order to work myself up to this chance to call him and say, "Why did you put me down?" And he told me that there had been someone else in his life who had returned or some such jazz and I was just out of my skull with depression. My whole view of therapy had always been that it was only sick people that did it. It was an admission that you were weak and I was not weak. I was a strong, strong person and I don't need anybody and I don't need nothing. I don't even know how I got up the stuff to go the first time, but I did. I think I was attracted to him. He was white, male, and over twenty-one and I guess I viewed him as available and single. Whether or not he was I never did know, anyways. Then I remembered early fantasies about having sex with him and that kind of thing. And then I went through the thing where I'm sure I was trying to seduce him and he didn't turn on to it although he was very friendly and so forth. And I remember my being angry about his not turning on to it.

The problems of being both a woman of color in a racist and sexist society are staggering, the permutations of violence, self-destructiveness, and paranoia endless. I worked out one traditional permutation with an African American woman: for most of her life, it was clear to her that black men don't like black women, prefer white women, can't earn money, beat you up, run around, and aren't really as "acceptable" as white men; white women—they're bitchy, childish, rich, and racist: even the poor ones are rich, and anyway Lady Jane just isn't important, she can't love, she isn't strong, my God! why do the men want her? Black women— they're made of stronger stuff, but they're also bitchy, poor, racist, and would cut your throat to get a white man or a "good" black man. Ask me, I know, I'm a black woman; white men—don't ask, just don't ask.

How nice, white, verbal therapy can really help with these seemingly bottomless tragedies is quite beyond me.

Most of the women I talked to had childhood and marriage experiences of physical brutality, double-standard puritanism, and sexual dissatisfaction. I do not mean to imply that Third World men are less sexually giving than white men; however, twentieth-century poverty, racism, and doctrines of machismo or "primitive" pride aren't *helpful* to the sexual and sensual liberation of Third World women—who are already sexually repressed as a function of white patriarchal culture.

WILMA: I was never attracted to white men. I only went to bed with brothers. I really bought that myth of black male superiority in bed and kept going to bed with them—but it's not true! Practically none of them could screw; I mean they were incompetent. No, I really mean they didn't care about me, and they figured they were just such hot shit *naturally* that a *natural* screw ought to be good enough for any woman so, with three exceptions, they were pretty cold and clumsy—and they didn't *want* to learn. Eventually I would explain what I wanted—in words of one syllable—and that didn't work either. . . . They're just incompetent. Men are sexually incompetent.

PHYLLIS: Now don't go around spreading myths of sexual inferiority based on gender or race (laughter).

WILMA: Yeah, but white men didn't do anything for me either. The men all made me feel that it was my fault, that I was guilty, like I had to pretend. Are they [black men] any different with white women? Are white men?

LAVERNE: I went to bed with him when I was fifteen. The only thing he wanted to do was screw. He would never talk to me. He went out with other girls but told me not to worry, that he was going to marry me. I felt that the other women were whores and promiscuous. Sometimes I'd even pick one out for him—someone stupid and superficial. It took me about two years to really enjoy the sex with him.

CAROLINE: I was twenty-five when I had intercourse with a man for the first time. He was black, married, and five years older than me. It was very cold but I was very grateful that finally someone took me to bed. I blamed myself for not having orgasms. In my mind, it was going to be an affair but in my emotions I guess the first affair women think, no matter what, it's just not going to be like that at all.

RITA: I guess I had a very strict upbringing. I really thought if I'm not a virgin at my wedding that the church lights would go out. I was taught that it's all right for men not to be virgins and even to have girl friends after marriage, as long as he takes care of you and the children. I have to tell my husband everywhere I go before I go. Once I went to a dance with my girl friend but I was scared. He said he would kill me but he didn't. I never went out like that again—no courage, I guess.

These women, far from occupying a specially reserved place of reverence in the African- or Hispanic- male (or female) community, described being the taken-for-granted "natural" prey of black or Hispanic men. A study by Menachim Amir documented that in seventy-seven percent of the sample cases studies, in Philadelphia, both the rape victim and offender were black. In eighteen percent of the cases, both were white. Of course, black offenders are always more pursued than white offenders. We just do not know how many white men rape black or white women.[14] These women were in no way exempted from white male "preying." However, depending on their level of black or feminist consciousness, white male socio-sexual advances sometimes angered or frightened them less because of its socially more "acceptable" and (potentially) economically more rewarding nature—a sore but sexist point with many black men. As men, they would like to "own" women as white men can—or as certain African men can. We cannot overlook how brutally and literally most white men *buy* black (and white) women. Black and poor men in America are reduced to stealing and/or despising what wealthier men can buy. Rape will always exist in patriarchal-class society. Many of my interviewees were told to marry "up" (or "white") only to live in fear that they would be abandoned for a white woman. Many of the women described hostile relations with their mothers based on skin-color (they weren't "white" enough), and on issues of marriage, social status, and sexual behavior.

EVELYN: I'm curious to know from white women whether they get this same kind of attitude from black men. Like I'm their property automatically. It's like we're altogether surrounded by this enemy so therefore whoever of my people comes into this thing, we're together and we're buddies and you're mine. When I first started on this job [as a secretary], it was like absolute indignation that I wouldn't respond to their [black male] advances. I would walk along corridors and I would get these little sounds, you know, or I would get a comment and I wouldn't respond. Absolute indignation! It was like they weren't going to accept this. I had to confront them again and again, to tell them that I in no way wanted any kind of intercourse with them, socially or otherwise. That I was going to call the shots about who I was going to socialize with whether they liked it or not. It took three months for me finally to make them understand that I have a right to not want to be bothered. They would call out to me, "If I was a white man you wouldn't do that." It was fantastic. This happened to me about a half dozen times— "You'd talk to me if I was a white man." They didn't know me at all, but this was like their paranoia. I found about three different things. The white men, they would make advances, but when I would rebuff them, that would be the end of it. And I think what they probably felt was, well, she digs her own black men. Like they could only see me, I'm sure, in relation to my being an appendage to some other man. It's got to be some other man.

PHYLLIS: Did white men make as many advances?

EVELYN: No, although I find on the whole, taking the whole span of things, like from the beginning of the day to the end of the day, there's far more white men who make advances to me in the street: there are more white men in the population.

PHYLLIS: Did white men on the job make the same kinds of advances?

EVELYN: No. Not the same kinds. What they do is run a path back and forth in front of my door. They will only make a verbal thing if they think they can get away with it, and not be seen. I remember once, one white guy was going into a doorway, so he just called something because he was disappearing, right. But with white men too, the indignation is there. You can't set up the rules as to whom you socialize with. "If we extend ourselves to you and show you that we want to be friendly, O piece of black ass, you therefore should be ungrateful for this?"

CAROLINE: I'm twenty-seven years old now and my grandmother and her sisters, they look at me kind of queer. Like, what's the matter with her? Because my cousins are all married and have children. Growing up, I did have a lot of contempt for black men. You are always steered toward the one that's going to achieve a certain social position, that's going to raise your social status. I couldn't think of a common, everyday nine-to-five man that didn't have a career. He had to be a college graduate with a certain sort of social position. This is the kind of thing that my family is geared to. My mother married in that way but in order [for such a black man] to continue [his] upward climb he would get a white woman. Several of my mother's stepbrothers have married white women. There is always the feeling that if you get a black man on the rise that he might ditch you for a white woman if he gets a little bit higher. I think that part of the terrible isolation [that led to a suicide attempt] was that I didn't relate to men. I couldn't or wouldn't bring home to my family the socially acceptable ones and this led partly to the isolation. Also, the fact that I'm growing older and haven't gotten married and still hadn't embarked on a career and was stagnant and hadn't really done much of anything [led to the suicide attempt]. I feel I have to stand behind the black men because they've suffered.

PHYLLIS: Haven't black women suffered too?

CAROLINE: Well, yes, but the way out of that suffering is to help our men win the revolution. I've sometimes wondered, though, how could I help fight if I'm busy taking care of babies?

Two of the Third World women who were psychiatrically hospitalized had genuine "madness" or "schizophrenic" experiences. Like many white women in Western culture, they relived (the meaning of) the crucifixion and/ or the Immaculate Conception. During these experiences they were very ambivalent about or hostile to "woman's work," such as domestic servitude or sexual passivity. I don't know whether their "psychiatric careers" are very different from those of white women. I leave that for you to decide.

I spent my internship as a psychologist in a New York City hospital that "serviced" Spanish Harlem. It was there that I first saw but didn't meet Carmen. She was a dark-haired, heavyset woman in her mid-forties and was causing a "commotion" on the psychiatric ward. She had thrown a banana peel on the floor and, despite threats and pleas, refused to pick it up. "This is the crazy ward, isn't it?" she demanded in excellent English. "I can do what I like here—or I shouldn't be here." I laughed—one of the few laughs I had on that particular police job, and walked on. Now, three years later, I was sitting in Carmen's living room, a neatly kept project apartment, filled with plastic crucifixes, plastic flowers, plastic couch covers, plastic doilies, and real police sirens. Judith, a friend of mine, who had been one of the therapists on the psychiatric ward, had befriended Carmen and been befriended by her. They had kept in touch.

Because Judith asked, Carmen agreed to speak with me. Several times that afternoon, when Carmen cried, Judith held her, squeezed her hand and mine, and made cups of coffee for us all.

PHYLLIS: Why did you go to a mental asylum?

CARMEN: Well, the first time was after my daughter was born. I was thirty years old and had a very bad delivery with her. I never had no trouble before—I was seventeen when I had my first son. This time I was very nervous coming home. I came home and I started to get sick.

PHYLLIS: Sick in what way?

CARMEN: Well, I stopped eating, first of all. Stopped sleeping. I just didn't eat and sleep. My friends came to see me and I wouldn't talk to them. I just looked up at the ceiling. I lay down and looked at the ceiling and then I stopped eating. For two weeks I was like that, and everybody was coming here trying to find out what was wrong with me. My baby needed food and I just lay in bed and smoked. I just didn't feel like doing it. I couldn't make the corner straight on the bed sheet.

PHYLLIS: Was anyone helping you take care of the baby?

CARMEN: No. They just didn't know what was wrong. Finally, someone called a doctor and he said, "She's having a terrible nervous breakdown!" So they took me to Bellevue—it got so bad that I didn't recognize anybody—and I got very religious. I blessed everybody.

PHYLLIS: What happened at Bellevue?

CARMEN: It was terrible. They used to tie you up all the time—put you in seclusion. Once I wanted to take a shower. I didn't want to get into a tub because they line you up, naked in front of everybody, you strip down, get in line, and you get into a tub. There were only two tubs and I didn't want to get in because I was recently operated, you know, I had the Caesarian and I didn't want any dirt to get on me so I had a big argument with one of the attendants. Also I got scared of the shock treatments. It's a very scary feeling, especially when you feel like the metal things of the electricity goes through you—it's like a hammer hitting your head. I was afraid of the third one.

PHYLLIS: Did you say you didn't want it?

CARMEN: Oh, I fought against it. But they gave it to me by force.

PHYLLIS: Who signed for it?

CARMEN: My husband did. He said the doctor said, "She's not doing any good so let's try shock treatments."

PHYLLIS: How often did the doctor talk to you before deciding you weren't doing any good?

CARMEN: Well, I don't remember talking to a doctor. After three weeks I was doing wonderful. I was back to normal. I brought up my daughter and everything. I didn't expect I would ever get sick again. Then I started to get tumors and I was hemorrhaging, so I told the doctor, "I don't want no more children, so I'd like a hysterectomy before it turns into anything else." In the hospital I began to get religious again, after the hysterectomy. One of the doctors, he was a psychiatrist, he came to me. I remember him coming to my bed and he gave me an injection and then he asked me what was wrong with me. The only thing I answered was that I don't want to go to Bellevue, that's all. And then they said to my husband, "If you can get her home you can keep her home if you want to!" So my husband brought me my clothes and he brought me a black dress. I put it on but the next minute I took it off and said, "Nobody is dead in the family, I don't have to wear black." So I stripped.

JUDITH: Maybe you felt bad about the hysterectomy.

CARMEN: No. I had nine abortions. Them I was guilty about. An abortion is a direct sin against God. But an abortion is better than a hungry child, isn't it?

PHYLLIS: What happened after you kept refusing to put on the black dress?

CARMEN: I went to Bellevue. And Bellevue sent me to Rockland State.

When I found out I was in a mental hospital you don't know how I cried. I got gray overnight. When I got there I saw the gate and said, "Gee, this sort of looks like a prison." I said to this other patient, "What kind of a hospital is this?" And she said, "Don't you know you're in a mental hospital, honey?" "No," I said, "this is a nut house?" "Yeah," she said, "that's where you are." So they all started to laugh because I didn't know. Oh, I felt terrible after that. I don't know how I managed not to get sick again there.

You stay there till you get well. Most women when they're sick don't take care of themselves. I comb my hair right away. That shows you're advancing. That you're not so sick.

PHYLLIS: What happened at Rockland State?

CARMEN: Happened? What could happen? They keep you locked up all day. I used to go out to work just to get out.

PHYLLIS: What kind of work?

CARMEN: Oh, you mop floors, you make beds, you wash windows, you wash floors.

PHYLLIS: Did they ever pay you for that?

CARMEN: No, the only place they pay you is the commissary. Ten dollars a month for food. I worked there also. I was a private maid to one of the psychiatrists, a woman doctor. She knew that I spoke English and Spanish. She said, "I'd like you to work for me because my son wants to learn Spanish. In school he is learning Spanish and with you around you'll talk to him in Spanish and he'll pick up more."

PHYLLIS: Did she pay for that?

CARMEN: They're supposed to pay you three dollars a week but being my husband used to leave me five dollars a week she never paid me. I had to dust, pass the vacuum, had to change the sheets, pick up her clothes after her. I used to wash her panties. Now how low can you get, her panties I had to wash!

PHYLLIS: Why didn't you tell her?

CARMEN: I should have, but it was such a pleasure being out of the ward. Also, other places were worse. They had a laundry there and, let me tell you, you work hard there.

PHYLLIS: Who worked in the laundry?

CARMEN: A lot of girls. You see them marching like prisoners in the morning.

PHYLLIS: Did they get paid?

CARMEN: No, the only place that pays you is the commissary. I went back to Rockland a lot of times. I got religious a lot. I could bless people and make them well.

PHYLLIS: Maybe you could.

CARMEN: So now, my husband wouldn't wait long. If I didn't sleep one night he would find me in the kitchen sitting by the window. Then he'd take me right away. He wouldn't wait to see how bad off I was. He'd take me right away.

PHYLLIS: When you were sitting by the window, were you thinking?

CARMEN: Yes, thinking. Important things. I never stayed longer at Rockland than two or three months. Until my husband got a mistress. He was always a good husband. He'd bring home all his salary, and even with being with that mistress he had, he never let me be without anything. My rent was paid. I had money for my food and he even used to give me gifts, just as if there was nothing going on between him and another woman. But that last time I was there [at Rockland] it seemed like the two of them were trying to get rid of me. He left me in there ten months, close to a year. That mistress hurt me quite a lot, especially when I first knew about it. I thought my world would come to an end because I love my husband very much—he was a very good man.

PHYLLIS: How did you find out?

CARMEN: I started to get anonymous calls—letters—from her. She's crazy. He claimed that she was jealous and all that—it was true. That didn't make me sick, it was the funniest thing. I can't understand why I get sick because, like I say, my husband was very good to me, very good—all the time I got sick except for the last ten months. No, he didn't come to see me at all—I got mad at him. The only way I could get even with him was to make him believe that I had a man that wants to marry me—and that's when he jumped.

PHYLLIS: When you found out about your husband having a mistress did you get very upset in the hospital? Did somebody take notice of that fact?

CARMEN: No. It hurt me, though, because my daughter knew about it and she never told me.

PHYLLIS: She probably didn't want to upset you.

CARMEN: Probably. She was too young. Well, I resigned myself to the fact that she's the mistress, staying in the house—let her clean and cook, while I rest, in the hospital. Every time I'd come home for a week all I would do would be clean and cook and clean and wash and clean so I went back to the hospital. True you don't like to be locked up but I consoled myself, oh, somebody else is cleaning the house, doing the cooking.

PHYLLIS: Kind of like a maid.

CARMEN: Yeah, she's sorta Negro anyway—what I couldn't understand was the fact that she would actually fix food for my husband to take to see me so I don't know what kind of combination they had between the both of them or the convenience or the plans they had.

JUDITH: The convenience for your husband was great.

CARMEN: Oh, yeah, that's why he enjoyed it—that didn't make me sick but it got me mad because he was going to leave me there [in Rockland].

You see, the legal procedure is the husband signs you in. I tell you it's true because my father tried to get me out, my two sons tried to take me out, and the doctor would not let me go home. My father said, "I'd even take her with me to my house," and the doctor wouldn't agree to it either. I don't know what he wanted—so finally the only way I could get out was that my father and mother was supposed to live here with me.

PHYLLIS: How did you finally get out?

CARMEN: Like I told you, my two sons came to me. I said, "You gotta do something to get me out of here. He don't want to sign me out." And my two sons, one sat on each side of me and said, "This is enough, my mother has been here ten months—she is well—you're not going to keep her here any longer—so you're gonna sign her out whether you like it or not." My other son is a big bruiser so he said, "You don't want to get a little beat up, do you?" So finally my sons made him do it.

PHYLLIS: What happened then?

CARMEN: He [my husband] brought me home—we lived there like two companions, no sex, no talking of any kind. When he came from work I'd leave the food on the stove and I'd take my plate and go look at the television. There was no conversation between us or anything. The only one who got annoyed was his mistress. You know, he never loved her completely. In fact, I used to warn her. I told her, "Look, I throw him out every day and he don't want to leave—it's not my fault." She got red as a sheet. I said, "I don't want him," and I never gave the understanding that I was hurt what they were doing to me—because I told her, "I have a man of thirty-eight years who is willing to marry me so if you can take my husband off my hands I'd really appreciate it." Oh, I was ripping but I didn't let her know it. She said, "He's taking advantage of me." I said, "That's your problem, not mine." So she said to me, "Well, I can't blame you because we did it to you first." I said, "You don't bother me at all. I'm even tired of my husband for years already. In fact, I've been going out with this man for three years and he don't know about it."

She thought she was gonna come here and mess me up—'cause she wanted me to get sick.

Only once I had a fight with him. He called the cops and they thought it was just a family argument. Then my husband called them on the side and told them I had been a mental case and all that. Bellevue again.

He [my husband] thought I wouldn't let him leave me but he found out different when I changed the lock on the door. My current boy friend lives across the street. He's a very happy-go-lucky man. He'll say all of a sudden, "Let's go to a movie, you don't have to cook." I'd say, "Gee, that's nice, let's go!"

LaVerne is in her mid-twenties. She is a part-time college student and secretary. She talks as fast as I do, and sometimes exceeds me in manic gusto. She is very intelligent and twice as explosive. She has been in and out of private therapy for about six years and has been hospitalized three times.

PHYLLIS: Why did you go to a mental asylum?

LAVERNE: The first time, it was after a party. I came home very upset and, honey, I had a hallucination you wouldn't believe. I was not the Virgin Mary, but *another* Virgin Mary. I had three climaxes in a row and gave birth to another Jesus—the black Christ. It was a virgin birth. It was a virgin birth because I wasn't having sex with anybody. But he wasn't around. The child was gone. Now, the mother got to get herself together. If he is gone, I've done something wrong. I felt I better do something if I am a mother of Christ so I took a bath.

Then I made a lot of phone calls. I called Rockefeller because I wanted some things done about black-white relations. I wanted black people to love themselves. I knew, but they didn't. There was so much promiscuity around—and I *mean* that. By the time I called Rockefeller I calmed down. I was going to sleep. But my mother started calling neighbors because she was afraid of me. She was always afraid of me. She's half white and thinks she's better than me. She's a fucking whore— yes! She's had boy friends who've felt me up—and she just sits there and denies it. But now she called the neighbors in to sit with her all night.

Then I started hallucinating again. I thought people were trying to get through the walls at me—oh, shit.

Then I wanted to be like an American Indian—instincts, instincts is where it's at. So I turned up the record player and started dancing around the house. And I pulled up the shades—I wanted everyone to see me. My mother, she *locks* doors. I took a hammer very calmly and broke the locks on my bedroom, my mother's, my brother's, and the guest room. I was dancing around—people were looking in. "Hi, kids, how'rya doing?" I told them.

Then the cops came in. They were obviously afraid of me. "What are you afraid of?" I said, "You want some Kool-Aid?" One cop said, "Oh, God," and I said, "What are you saying, that's my Father because I gave birth to another Christ child." But I'm not going to tell them about the Christ because they'll think I'm nuts, and I'm not too sure about that scene myself so I'm going to be real cool.

They [the cops] asked who was responsible for me. "My mother," I said. But she was already at work. So they got the next-door neighbor. I held on to her. I was afraid, I was scared, and I asked her, "Please don't

leave me, they're gonna hurt me." But she pulled away from me. Oh, I
didn't want to go to a hospital. I know what they do to you there.

PHYLLIS: What happened at the hospital?

LAVERNE: They stuck me with needles. They feed you—force feeding,
or you won't get out. They put me in a strait jacket. They wouldn't let
me talk to a psychiatrist. Then when I did, I told him about getting too
much medication, and I cried, so they gave me more medicine because
I was upset.

PHYLLIS: What kind of medicine did you get?

LAVERNE: Thorazine, but that made me break out so they gave me
something else, but I have a sinus condition so they gave me stellazine,
which was the nicest thing but it wasn't strong enough, so they gave me
thorazine again.

PHYLLIS: Did they give you shock therapy?

LAVERNE: Oh no. I said if they ever did I would have intercourse with
the doctors, spit out my food. Shock therapy is a dangerous thing. I saw
what happens—you start forgetting things—I've spoken to patients.
And you get depressed again anyway.

   After ninety days they can't keep you. Anyway, I quieted down and
never yelled and never said anything. The patients said, "You want to get
out—this is what you do," and so I did it. I helped the nurses and told
them how cute they were. I washed the floors. I never washed a floor in
my life before.

PHYLLIS: How did you get into the hospital the second time?

LAVERNE: I got married, right! and I was working to send him through
school. He'd come home at night and tell me about the pretty girls he'd

seen. "You're so ugly without make-up, God, are you ugly," he'd tell me. "Your breasts are too small." But he wouldn't talk to me—oh no! He'd just wanna screw, turn over, and go to sleep.

Then we're at a party and I heard him talking to another guy. He said I was cute but stupid. "So whadya want her for, man—pussy?" "Yeah," he answers. Oh, shit! Since I'm thirteen years old—and he still just wants pussy! I wanted to get a gun and kill him, but I couldn't get a gun so easy. My brother talked me into taking a job instead, working with children. Well, I left him [my husband] and went back to live with my mother—and we don't get along, right? So we had a fight—ahh, she doesn't love me. She told me I was too stupid to go to college.

She let me just rot in the hospital that first time, she's a fuckin' whore, that's what I told her, that always gets to her. So she put me in the hospital again. She called her boy friend over and he beat me up because I had disrespect for my mother. "You son of a bitch, you try to put me in the hospital, I'll kill you." I tried to call my therapist but he punched me to the floor each time. They tied me down and put me in a strait jacket.

At the hospital—questions! "What's the matter?" the psychiatrist wants to know. "Wars stink. Prostitution stinks. You stink." "I think we're gonna have to keep you," he says. "No foolin'!" This time I had a beautiful woman doctor from Central America, and she really helped me get out.

They gave me a lot of psychological tests and, you know, I came out masculine. What does that mean? Like on one test they ask: do you want to be married and happy or rich and single? "Oh, shit! Rich and single," I said.

CHAPTER NINE

FEMINISTS

Why didn't our mothers and grandmothers and great-grandmothers tell us what battle it was we lost, or never fought, so that we would understand how total was our defeat, and that religion and madness and frigidity were how we mourned it?

Why were our mothers so silent about rape and incest and prostitution and their own lack of pleasure? Why, when they had so many words, did they not name our heroines for us, tell us about feminists and suffragists and Amazons and great-mothers?

I wish woman to live *first* for God's sake. Then she will not make an imperfect man her god, and thus sink to idolatry. Then she will not take what is not fit for her from a sense of weakness and poverty. Then if she finds what she needs in Man embodied, she will know how to live and be worthy of being loved. . . .

Woman, self-centered, would never be absorbed by any relation; it would be only an experience to her as to man. It is a vulgar error that love—*a* love—to woman is her whole existence; she also is born for Truth and Love in their universal energy. Would she but assume her inheritance, Mary would not be the only virgin mother. . . .

Margaret Fuller[1]

But early I perceived that men never in any extreme of despair wished to be women. On the contrary, they were ever ready to taunt one another at any sign of weakness with,

"Art thou not like the women, who—" The passage ends various ways, according to the occasion and rhetoric of the speaker. When they admired any woman, they were inclined to speak of her as "above her sex." Silently I observed this, and feared it argued a rooted skepticism which for ages had been fastening on the heart and which only an age of miracles could eradicate. Ever I have been treated with great sincerity; and I look upon it as a signal instance of this, that an intimate friend of the other sex said in a fervent moment that I "deserved in some star to be a man." He was much surprised when I disclosed my faith that the feminine side, the side of love, of beauty, of holiness, was now to have its full chance, and that if either were better, it was better now to be a woman; for even the slightest achievement of good was furthering an especial work of our time. He smiled incredulously. "She makes the best she can of it," thought he. "Let Jews believe the pride of Jewry, but I am of the better sort, and know better."

Margaret Fuller[2]

Nowhere is woman treated according to the merit of her work, but rather as a sex. It is therefore almost inevitable that she should pay for her right to exist, to keep a position in whatever line, with sex favors. Thus it is merely a question of degree whether she sell herself to one man, in or out of marriage, or to many men. Whether our reformers admit it or not, the economic and social inferiority of woman is responsible for prostitution. . . . It is conceded that woman is being reared as a sex commodity, and yet she is kept in absolute ignorance of the meaning and importance of sex. . . . "The wife who married for money, compared with the prostitute," says Havelock Ellis, "is the true scab. She is paid less, gives much more in return in labor and care, and is absolutely bound to her master. The prostitute never signs away the right over her own person, she retains her freedom and personal rights, nor is she always compelled to submit to man's embrace."

Emma Goldman[3]

I see neither physical, psychological, nor mental reasons why woman should not have the equal right to vote with man. But that cannot blind me to the absurd notion that woman will accomplish that wherein man has failed. If she would not make things worse, she certainly could not make them better. To assume, therefore, that she would succeed in purifying something which is not susceptible of purification, is to credit her with supernatural powers. Since woman's greatest misfortune has been that she was looked upon as either angel or devil, her true salvation lies in being placed on earth; namely in being considered human, and therefore subject to all human follies and mistakes. Are we, then, to believe that two errors will make a right? Are we to assume that the poison already inherent in politics will be decreased, if women were to enter the political arena? The most ardent suffragists would hardly maintain such a folly.

Emma Goldman[4]

The binding force in this collective is feminism . . . we act as mutual role-models for each other—that is, role-models as feminist professionals—something which we all find hard to come by in our everyday work settings. We are able to identify with each other's successes: "If good things can happen to this woman in the male-dominated world . . . then perhaps there's hope for me." . . . The collective acts as a supportive system during individual crises and uncertainties . . . we provide for each other those vital, informal channels of communication which are used so regularly by male professionals, and from which they so systematically exclude their female colleagues. Men will meet and exchange valuable information over dinner or coffee—but when a woman colleague is "lucky" enough to be included (this once happened to one of our members) they're apt to say "Pardon us for talking shop" and immediately start talking non-professional trivialities . . . the collective has provided for all of us a place where we feel comfortable to be ourselves—by this I mean a place where we are not castigated as being "aggressive," for taking over, being articulate, disagreeing, confronting. We really value each other's competence. . . .

The Chicago Women in Psychology Collective

WHY DID FEMINISM RESURFACE IN AMERICA? Why did so dangerous an idea as female humanity, or equality, or supremacy, or rights, surface as a potentially *mass* movement? Is modern feminism essentially a byproduct of certain changes in material reality such as birth control technology and planetary overpopulation? Is modern feminism one of many survival-responses to the changing nature and/or diminishing availability of agricultural and industrial work, at a time when, barring warfare, starvation, and ecological disasters, more people are living longer? This might explain why women are being encouraged or even forced to talk about "sharing" their spheres of domesticity and emotionality with men: the work for which men have been made into "men" and women into "women" is disappearing.

To the extent to which feminism is conceived of as a collective rather than an individualist ideology; to the extent to which it is tribal and pleasure-oriented, rather than unique and heroically oriented—it is feared as "barbaric," or "fascistic," by women as well as men. Certainly I fear it, if the "rituals" are anything less than bold and true, if the rituals impose mediocrity and conformity, rather than unique and diverse deeds and works of the imagination.

Is the American feminist movement a "return of the repressed": is it an old religion, an old polity, whose time has mysteriously come round again? Or is it a genuinely new mythology, technologically rendered, whose consequences are unforeseen? Will the structures of human psychology remain unchanged if women should "win" the sex war—should directly control the means of production and reproduction? Or if men should become social and biological mothers? Or if women ceased being the psycho-biological representations of birth—and, consequently, of death? Or if women became biological mothers and social fathers? Or if gender ceased to exist as a significant, identifying dimension?

Can women "win" the sex war, or banish such a war entirely, *without* becoming the dominant sex? If women were to dominate, would biological men then be as oppressed as biological women have been—and if so, would this matter to women? There must be some good or at least some overwhelming reasons why the injustice of female oppression has never mattered enough to men for them to banish it.

Is the sex war at the root of other major evils such as race and class slavery, capitalism, puritanism, imperialism, and warfare? And if so, can such evils be exiled from the mass human condition forever by any but a non-violent and feminist method? (What is a feminist method?) Given our conditioning as women, can we ever become feminist revolutionaries (or human beings), without becoming lesbians? As women, can we wage *any* sort of revolution if we are psychosexually bound to men or marriage or full-time child care? Many men can scarcely be revolutionaries under such conditions, even though their relationship to women, marriage, and child care is a far less committed one. But why even wage a struggle, if its goals are simply revenge or power? What if we "won" and became as removed from emotion and sexuality as so many men are?

With great intensity, women in groups are asking these and many other questions. It was in "consciousness-raising" groups that women began to break the twentieth-century silence between mothers and daughters. The small group provided a way and a place for women to name their common plight. It also served as a model of cooperative society, and extended family, especially for women whose experience with extended families or female kinship and living arrangements (or with genuine cooperativeness) was minimal.

Relatively privileged white middle-class women discovered that privilege was not freedom; that love was a foreign country with few survivors; and that the female body was as colonized as any ghetto or Third World country. They also discovered that neither men nor women liked women, especially strong or happy women. A discontented, complaining, "weak" woman, although disliked, is far more acceptable than a contented and/or powerful woman—who is experienced as dangerous, and is ostracized and "killed" far more quickly and inevitably than her male counterpart especially if she is in any way sexually knowledgeable, independent, or "aggressive."

Women in small feminist groups also talked, often endlessly, about sexual orgasms. Their tones were informative, comic, relieved, angry, and joyful—as they began to reclaim their bodies. Women's acceptance and enjoyment of their bodies is an absolute prerequisite for their self-development: and I am not talking about an American mechanistic "sexual sell," or about any type of male-originated or fantasied group or "free" sex. I suppose that women will only be able to experience their sexuality fully when their *mothers* have controlled the means of production and reproduction.

This "talking about orgasms," which was initially derided as bourgeois self-indulgence and "racist," actually constitutes a valid example of "giving" women what they "need" before, or as a way of talking "politics." (It goes without saying that neither female sexual orgasms nor ghetto breakfast programs alone, in themselves, are anything more than first but necessary steps in the right direction.) But I think that it was this "talking about orgasms," together with the expression of anger in an atmosphere of female approval, that led to whatever changes occurred in women.

And the changes occurred quickly, in an exhilarating and suspiciously instant, prefabricated way. For a while, it seemed as if some apocalypse was about to happen, as if all wrongs would be righted, and the gates of paradise forced open by reason and sorority. It took awhile before American women were directly introduced, politically, to the twentieth century; awhile before we realized the extent to which publicity, like all advertising, is a substitute for change, a compromise offering, instead of something of value; awhile before we understood how truly divided we were, how deep our female conditioning was, and how difficult it would be to change it. Until then—the events were dizzying, contradictory, and absolutely uncorrupted.

Almost overnight, women organized demonstrations, legal actions, bail funds, abortion services, wage strikes, national and international meetings, caucases, magazines, pamphlets, communes, disputes, rock bands, theater groups, women's studies programs, self-defense programs, all-female dances, and lesbian and women's centers in every major American city. For those women involved, the women's movement, to a greater or lesser extent, began to vie with, supplant, or shore up the institutions of marriage, love, and psychotherapy. Up to a point, women's liberation was more "therapeutic" than either marriage or psychotherapy:

it made women happier, angrier, more confident, more adventurous, more moral—and it produced a range of behavioral changes.

Some women quit their jobs and refused to be involved in alienated and/or oppressive labor, others began job training, college or graduate school, and planned careers seriously, for the first time. It is important to note that only those who could afford to do so—both financially and pychologically—did this. Most women, especially those over thirty with children, cannot just quit their jobs as mothers, housekeepers, factory worker, and secretaries: they can only demand wages, wage increases, and better working conditions.

Some women started living together; some began living alone for the first time. Some women insisted that their husbands share child care and housework equally; others organized all-female cooperatives for this purpose. Some women had abortions; others refused them, where they might not have done so before. Some women left their husbands; others began to live with a man, feeling somehow at less of a psychological disadvantage than before. Some women refused "alimony"; others insisted on it as back pay and as reparations. Some women withdrew from drugs; others turned to them—out of curiosity and despair. Many women stopped walking down city streets with their eyes averted, stopped not "hearing," stopped not "responding," or stopped responding in female ways to male verbal abuse. Some women found that, the stronger they grew and the more they understood, the more they "needed" a man or a monogamous "partner," either because they felt they could begin to hold their own in such a relationship or because they feared what they knew, and needed the blind comfort of traditional role-playing—just one more time. Their natures and conditioning were too strong and the woman's movement still too weak to help them grow beyond a certain point.

Many women started reading political and scientific books as passionately as they read novels: somehow, the glaze of "stupidity" that films over understanding—when understanding understands that, even if it understood, it could never inherit the castle and the kingdom—tentatively began to lift. The common female (and black) attitude of boredom and failure in white male-dominated and sexually integrated classrooms began to shift to curiosity and success. Within a small group, or at a woman's conference, women stopped giggling, "losing," and competing with each other for male attention and approval. There were no sexual distractions either: most women weren't "attracted" to each other. Many women found they could think, found that it gave them pleasure, realized that their thinking ability was needed by others.

Some women stopped going to beauty parlors, stopped wearing make-up, stopped shopping (or shopping frequently) for "sexy" or "fashionable" clothes. Women began to value their time: they needed fewer adornments to "make up" for being female. As a woman, I do not like puritanism—in thought or dress. However, as a woman, I cannot put my heart into the elite frivolity of expensive or frequently changed costumes—when such costumes are *not* only not available to all people but, more important, seem to signify a growing passivity and dependence in men as well as women. The fact that American men are being advertised into an involvement with cosmetics and fashions is not as much a sign of sexual equality as it is of capitalist market-seeking and greed. Perhaps the frantic costume changes from one historical period to another signify some collective desire to find the "path not taken." It is, however, politically naive to think that poverty, racism, sexism or pollution in America will be "solved" if women will only stop conspicuously consuming. The military-industrial and political complex in Washington and Detroit are far more crucial to such solutions than are the clothing, cosmetics, and detergent industries. Further, it is far easier for women who can't afford to "buy," to rationalize "not buying" into a form of power. But this is a cultural and moral gesture—not an economic boycott. Fighting for the right to buy, or stealing if employment is denied, are far more commonly pursued paths of action for powerless groups.

Some women affirmed, discovered, or began to explore their bisexuality or lesbianism. Some women remained celibate for long periods without any noticeable anxiety or suffering. Others felt that it was important to them to have both warmth and sexual intimacy on a frequent basis: either casually or non-casually, with other women, or with men. Some women masturbated to orgasm for the first time, or for the first time without guilt. Some women decided to have a child, or another child; others decided firmly against ever doing so.

What have contemporary American psychologists and psychiatrists thought and felt about feminism? How have they behaved toward feminism—as an ideology, as a movement, and as something that has been influencing their female patients? Publicly, they have behaved like any other group: they have engaged in nervous laughter, purposeful misunderstanding, hairsplitting, malicious cruelty, misguided sympathy, boredom, hostility, condescension, and commercial and academic capitalism. [*]

Some clinicians have been genuinely curious, sympathetic, and supportive. A minority have joined the women's movement. Several professional journals have devoted "special issues" to women—as a newly discovered but exotic minority-majority group. *The Radial Therapist*, a collective "underground" journal, has published articles about women and sexism in each of its issues. Groups of women psychologists, therapists, and patients or clients have organized referral lists to feminist therapists. As yet, no one has presented a new theory of human personality based on feminist ideologies—nor has anyone psychoanalyzed feminism.

Many male psychologists who are verbally "sympathetic" to feminism still call their middle-aged female patients "girls"; still describe them in terms of how "attractive" they are; and, of course, still relate to wives or girl friends in non-reciprocally dependent ways. Many are sympathetic to feminism because they are sexually "attracted" to feminists, whom they see as more "interesting" than their wives.

Most psychiatrists publicly deny the existence of sex-typed slave labor in state and county hospitals; minimize the effect of medical and

---

[*]   In 1969, a group of us formed the Association for Women in Psychology. In 1970, I addressed a crowded convention meeting of the American Psychological Association. I demanded token reparations for female mental patients (for legal fees, education, housing, etc.). The amount of money demanded was equal to the money that women psychologists had paid in membership dues over a five-year period—money which was never used to serve job security or advancement opportunity for these relatively privileged women professionals. The demand was met by very loud and hostile laughter and was followed by the hostile diplomacy of bureaucratic "procedurism." Needless to say, no money was ever received for this purpose—but most of the women involved in the demand found themselves invited speakers to the 1971 convention.

psychological "experiments" on their patients; tell "dirty jokes" at their staff meetings; and deride feminist grievances. They are more willing to pity women than to respect them; more comfortable with unhappy women than with angry women.

Most male and female clinicians are emotionally and financially bound by the romance of the bourgeois family. Few middle-aged clinicians of either sex have any class consciousness. At a recent professional meeting, one female clinician, in a nostalgic description of pre-World War II Vienna, recalled how "really liberated" all the Viennese women were. I asked her whether poor and uneducated women in Vienna were also "liberated." (I personally would not define Freud's wealthy Dutiful Daughters as "liberated" but as "privileged.") She answered that she really hadn't thought of it "in those terms." Clinicians seem to dislike and pity the paranoia and anger of feminists: slyly, confidently, they want to know why are they so "nervous" about being found sexually attractive by "poor" Tom, Dick, or Harry? Why are they so angry at verbal abuse in the streets? (The lower classes have always been rowdy, excitingly so, come to think of it—but the police will always be able to handle the poor if they get too out of control.) Don't these suddenly complaining women "unconsciously" invite harassment or rape, and don't they "unconsciously" enjoy it? Furthermore, isn't the point of women's liberation the liberation of men too, and not, heaven forbid, female power? Isn't capitalism the *real* enemy and feminism divisive and/or the "pouting" of spoiled white middle-class women? My feelings about this question are: first, that it is usually asked without information, seriousness, or respect; second, that sexism preceded capitalism and colonialism and may indeed have led to it; and, third, that ridicule and misunderstanding are forms of violence that must be avoided as much as possible—especially by our healers and secular priests.

Most contemporary clinicians are as confused about and hostile to feminism as most people are—and I am talking only about those clinicians who are *interested* enough to attend panels about female psychology and feminism or to publish on the subject. For years in the early 1970s, most women clinicians delivered impassioned speeches about the necessity and desirability of combining motherhood and professional careers—and they did so even if another topic was specifically being explored. Their male colleagues usually remained safely silent during this genteel Saturday night brawl. The women professionals first insisted they have no political ax to grind—and then quickly offered their political credentials: the existence of their own two or three children. Such offerings would be acceptable to me if we lived in a female-dominated culture, or in a culture that did not, rather dubiously "reward" women for breeding—more than for other activities.

After defending the motherhood faith, the convention clinicians usually took a breath and launched into a tirade against the "terrible and damaging mothers" their patients have had—those very same "mothers" whom feminists are apparently trying to sneak off the hook of maternal responsibility! They usually concluded their speeches with a description of their *male* patients in Pieta-like tones—to the approval of their male colleagues, who, in turn, were now not expected to fire them from their jobs or exclude them from their communication networks. No need to: such women are maternal and feminine, and not angry man-haters like "the others."

Female clinicians are generally as ambivalent about women as all other women are. The specifically painful price they've had to pay for even limited "success" outside the home will not allow them to quickly envision radical definitions of self. One successful woman academic told me, *sotto voce,* "Phyllis, of course it's conditioning, but conditioning *works*—and after such terrible conditioning, most women are in terrible condition. Would *you* want to work with them? More power to you for trying, but I just can't."

Some clinicians at professional panels have yelled at feminist participants, often rather hysterically and brutally. They have called them everything from neurotic and criminal to selfish. Often, they want the feminists present to talk more about how sexism has hurt men than about how it has hurt women. I asked a black male psychologist at one of these meetings whether he thought a meeting about black power, equality, and self-determination should dwell overlong, and with great clucking sympathy, on how racism has hurt white racists. He laughed.

What I am saying is that even the most sympathetic male professionals behave like patriarchal men.

THE INTERVIEWS

What did it mean to be a Second Wave feminist in America? Why did we
seek therapy and why were we psychiatrically hospitalized? What were
our lives like before we became feminists or therapy patients, and how
have they changed since?

I spoke to twenty-six feminists, including myself, "officially." Their
ages ranged from seventeen to fifty-eight: sixty-eight percent of the
women were between twenty and thirty years old; sixty-one percent were
either only or oldest children; ninety percent were white Americans. One
woman had some high school experience, seven women had some college
experience, twelve women had B. A. degrees, and six women had attended
or completed graduate school. Four of the women were unemployed and
living on welfare, four of the women were unsalaried students, four of the
women were salaried within the woman's movement at minimum wage
levels, two of the women were clerical workers, and twelve of the women
were employed in professional capacities, for example, as teachers,
journalists, or social workers.

Twenty-one of the women considered themselves feminists of about
two years' duration. Five women had a more recent commitment. Three
women were heterosexually married, six women were divorced, thirteen
women were legally single and living alone, three women were living in a
woman's collective, and one woman was living with a man. Seven of the
women were lesbians.

Twenty-five of the women had been (or still were) involved in private
therapy, for a total group average of forty-one months (see Table 3).
Feminists remained in treatment with male therapists for about thirty-one
months and with female therapists for about nineteen months. Seven of
the feminists, five of whom were also lesbians, had been psychiatrically
incarcerated. Their average length of hospital stay was 158 days.

With few exceptions, all the feminists grew up in families where sex roles, however they were defined, were rigidly defined; in families where most mothers stayed at home for child care and domestic purposes—at least during their daughter's first five years of life; in families where menstruation was somehow shameful and virginity was not; in families where, no matter what else was allowed or encouraged, love, marriage, and motherhood were touted as *the* most important goals of female life. Most of the women had "troubled" relationships with their mothers, and of course, with developing traits such as confidence, a sense of self, tenaciousness, initiative, sexuality, a wide range of interests, a deep and preferred enjoyment of other women and "younger" men, and an ability to say no to what they didn't initiate or choose. Most of the women had "trouble" with work—with the getting and keeping of "jobs." Such "trouble" often increased after they became feminists—whether their jobs were as housewives and mothers, students, feminists, or bourgeois professionals. Awareness doesn't lead to instant or easy happiness. It may lead to the ability to make choices, which is one aspect of wisdom.

ALICE: You won't believe this, well, maybe you will—but when I went to my first department meeting, I was the only woman there. And the men assumed, they just *assumed*, that I'd take the "minutes." I walked out— and told them I wouldn't be bringing back any coffee for them either. After that, I developed a reputation for being "difficult" and "paranoid." The secretaries, of course, preferred working for men. They were resigned to it, used to it—they might get flirted with or married. They didn't like working for a woman—and if my male colleagues saw me dictating a letter they'd say, "Oh ho! Caught you in the act, oppressing a sister, are you now?" But *they* didn't stop dictating letters, and I was responsible for as much on the job as they were—and of course, I was getting paid less money and couldn't really "fraternize" to make up for it. I could have had an affair with one man—and would have been somewhat protected by him—as his property. I could have flirted more to find out things, or acted as if it didn't matter in order to find out things; I could have played the usual game of token woman who doesn't like other women. I did none of these things—and everything was an uphill fight, just everything. And I had no wife to go home to at night to comfort me. I only had a boy friend, who really *needed* and *thought* he needed comforting—and didn't know how to comfort in return without feeling "castrated" and my first CR group thought I was too successful and therefore a "male-identified" woman and wouldn't comfort or support me either. You get real cooled out if you're an "achievement"-oriented woman. No matter how high a price you pay, you're alone when you get anywhere—in a way that no man ever has to be.

DEIRDRE: I had a really good woman analyst. I thought I had become stronger and more sure of myself. I felt I didn't have to play any games with men—and I didn't believe I was picking the sadists any more. So, I got pregnant—a woman's thing to do—no? And my boy friend began having temper-tantrums, affairs, and withdrawing from me. Now we had talked it all out before—about our having a child—and here he was behaving just like a trapped animal. And I had too much of a sense of self to do the usual crap—cry, beg, promise, lie. So I left him. I was very bitter. I felt that no matter how hard women and men tried to have a relationship, no matter how unique and exceptional they were, at some crucial pressure point, societal training of dominance-submission will rise to the surface. And men will be absolutely unyielding unless the woman plays her submissive role. I became so frightened of what would happen to me—a bitter woman alone, totally responsible for a baby, so frightened when I realized how universal this situation is for women— whether men are legally or economically there or not—that I frightened the child to death—I miscarried. I think it was then that I became a feminist.

Most of the feminists described certain middle-class and existential problems that neither individual therapists nor isolated consciousness-raising groups had any control over—in terms of causing or "curing." The groups, however, were generally more aware that the problems were real, external, and could not be solved by the individual woman alone.

MARILYN: In a lot of ways, he [my therapist] has reassured me about getting pleasure from sex just for the sake of it. He felt outraged on my behalf when I was with a guy who wouldn't sleep with me because he thought I treated him like a sex object. In a sense, he was right, I didn't love him or want to marry him, but I did want to sleep with him. . . . When he turned me down I had this incredible experience of wow, what's happening! I felt guilty about treating him like an object, and I was hurt too. But dig it: this guy stopped in the middle of making love. He didn't let me get away with anything.

DONNA: So I left my husband and gave up my "establishment" career. And was I grateful for [my boy friend's] struggling with his sexism. Gee: he's actually *trying*, I owe him even more than I owe a man who doesn't try. Eternally grateful, that's me, Polyanna Pure, Earth Mother—and I can't help it, I love it, I love feeling good vibes. . . .

So then he tells me I should get into pottery and tie-dyeing and drugs; fuck the career, it sucks—*and it does*—but he doesn't drop out. He puts his shoulder to the capitalist wheel so that I can potter around— and while I'm at it, I can cook and clean and be what I love most—Earth Mother.

Well, it's not a bad life, and he's more sensitive than other men, but somehow, psychologically, nothing's changed.

KATHRYN: How can a therapist or a love relationship or a single group "help" me with the accumulated and ongoing and constant damage of being a woman in this culture? I'm not supposed to *exist*—and I'm supposed to be happy about my non-existence. For example, the old, pre-feminist me is not supposed to notice or respond to male insults on the street—but secretly, I'm supposed to like them. I should lay back like a pale ghost and not move too much while I'm being raped, but I'm supposed to like it—see? It's like I'm not there, like I don't really exist— and I guess I didn't. Another example: in restaurants, my date or husband orders my meal for me. I don't speak to the waiters directly. And such public invisibility or non-existence is supposed to make me feel safe and loved and protected. It's Leda and the swan all over again: I'm supposed to get my rocks off by being raped. And I suppose *I did*: I went to beauty parlors and wore high heels and short skirts and make-up. Now that seems very sad and very frightening to me. I know how deep such conditioning goes and how hard it is to shake it.

Now take the new feminist me. I always pay for myself in restaurants. Often, when I'm with a poorer or younger companion, male or female, I'll pay for them too. Well, if it's a *male* companion, *he* gets the change and the waiter's thanks. Even with money, I still don't exist. Another thing, if I ask directions about how to get somewhere, or how to fix something, and if I have a male companion within *hearing* distance, *he'll* get the instructions. Last week I asked a male clerk in a country supermarket where the nearest liquor store was. A man standing nearby, whom I didn't even *know*, got the directions. And, oh yes, if men think you really want to be treated as if you exist, they *do it* coldly, and with a vengeance. "So you wanna be a man? Okay, take that on the chin." And you really get hit doubly hard with stiff upper lip, grin and bear it, brutality. They're saying to you: "It's nothing but punches to be a 'man,' especially if you happen to be a woman, so stay put—or watch out."

Most feminists are as concerned with heterosexual relationships and orgasms as other women are. Most feminists are as frightened of being without men, or without monogamous relationships, as other women are.

MARIA: Well, I thought feminism meant better relations between the sexes, certainly better sexual relations. I mean, the sexual relations couldn't get any *worse* but they could, they could. I guess it's true, and yet I don't like to think so. Men don't really like you to be there sexually. If they're not in control, if they're not "safe" emotionally—which usually means emotionally distanced, they won't lay down with you in a loving way. Or they won't pretend to be "loving"—that's more like it. If you're lucky they'll come and run—literally and figuratively. And if they come too fast, or if they're impotent, or if they don't really like oral sex or if they don't want to see you again—they make you feel guilty—or, to be absolutely fair, they don't resist the fact that we're not unwilling to play our guilty parts. And they're really scared. They're scared if you seem to be happy. They're scared if they think you want to trap them. They're scared if you *don't* want to trap them. Because if you don't—that would be a whole new game, or not a game at all. And they wouldn't know the roles, they'd have no "edge," they'd tumble into an abyss of vulnerability. So they're frightened, and they turn their fear into some kind of cruelty, and familiar scene, we're still left holding the bag of understanding and compassion. They don't "understand" us if we're *not* "confused" and "unhappy." If a woman knows what she wants and thinks clearly—forget it!

ALICE: I always went with men who were older than me. I was a Daddy's girl like everyone else. Life or feminism or having more money changed that a little. I became more open to having relationships with younger men. If a young girl takes up with an older man, sure, he pays for her, but she supports his ego, she's *there* for him sexually, emotionally, domestically. And up to a point she's probably happy about it. It's accepted. They can go places together. It all fits. If a young boy takes up with an older woman she may very well *pay* for him too—but *his* ego is still the one that needs supporting—especially if he's kidded or punished by other men or by uncomfortable social situations. Since he's been conditioned to be a "man," he really doesn't know how to support a woman sexually, emotionally, or domestically. The idea of doing so is usually very frightening to him. Even "feminine," counterculture, type young men can't handle a woman being "up," in any sense of the word. It's too devastating. A woman *may* get some more support from a group if she's careful not to engage in any individual acts of success. If you submerge your ego or self into a group process, or even into a private love relationship, and especially if you're troubled and unhappy and failing—*then* you might get sympathy from other women or from a man. In other words, if you remain more "female" than "male"—it's still easier to survive.

Feminists sought therapy just as other women did: often, for long periods of time, and with men rather than with women. They were "treated" with the same double standard of mental health with which all women are treated.

DONNA: "Why don't you fix yourself up?" he always said. "You look like a hobo—I'd almost think you were afraid of men!" Not a word about how right we are to be afraid. Not a word about athletics, lesbianism, politics, or my eternal soul. Just "Dress up for Daddy" as proof of mental health.

VICTORIA: I was eighteen when I started therapy for the second time. I went to a woman for two years, twice a week. She was constantly trying to get me to admit that what I really wanted was to get married and have babies and lead a "secure" life; she was very preoccupied with how I dressed, and, just like my mother, would scold me if my clothes were not clean, or if I wore my hair down; told me that it would be a really good sign if I started to wear make-up and get my hair done in a beauty parlor (like her, dyed blonde and sprayed); when I told her that I liked to wear pants she told me that I had a confusion of sex roles. I originally went to her when my friends started to experiment with sex, and I felt that I couldn't make it, and that my women friends with whom I had been close had rejected me for a good lay.

DEIRDRE: I interviewed six male analysts. Every one of them intimidated me with questions such as, Was I married? Did I want children? Why hadn't I any children? Why was I divorced? And they never looked up from their notebooks. And I never went back after the first time.

SUSAN: I've had many, many therapists. You might say I've been lonely and unhappy for a long time. My first therapist was a woman. She gave me an MMPI which she showed me, and it said I had very high ego strength which she said was a bad thing. I knew it's bad in the sense that if it's very high it's supposed to mean rigidity, but for a woman trying to do well in school, ego strength is very important. I suppose I was using therapy as a substitute for friendship.

My second therapist, a man, told me that I was the coldest woman he had ever had the misfortune to meet—that I was castrating. His professional judgment was that I would never get into any kind of long relationship. He pitied any man that ever got involved with me. My therapy with him was the worst experience of his life—he said. He went on in that vein for about ten minutes at which point I walked out on him. So then I decided I really didn't need to be in therapy. About a month later a fellow broke into my apartment—not to steal anything but to have some kind of sexual relations with me, and I finally scared him off. The police obviously didn't believe my story, and they said I was inviting him because I had long hair and sandals and red curtains in my bedroom and then they had a plan where I was to lie nude in bed with the curtain open. The whole scene got very frightening. I told my boy friend and he suggested I see his psychiatrist, a man. So I did. He kept saying that I should wear my hair long instead of pulled back because it was more feminine. But it got tangled in fifteen minutes and I couldn't stand it. And he told me to put no pressure on my boy friend, he told me to just be "giving" for a change. At the time, I was very afraid that the things he was saying were true—even though I would fight with him. There must be something wrong with a woman being assertive, intelligent, and capable: I was, and no one was loving me very much, and I was very unhappy.

You know, I met him [this therapist] a year later by accident, socially. I had been goaded into making a very passionate defense of women's liberation. [My old therapists's] wife kept saying, "Right on," and then when he tried to protest, and said, "Don't I help out?" she said, "What do you do around the house—you don't do this and you don't do that"—it was absolutely a bizarre evening.

Some feminists attribute major changes in themselves to the women's movement and to their consciousness-raising groups. Others feel that psychotherapy has accounted for major personal changes—including their conversion to feminism. Some feel that both experiences, occurring simultaneously, were essential for change. Some women are keenly aware of the limitations and dangers, as well as the advantages, of both feminist groups and psychotherapeutic experiences.

MARILYN: Feminism has helped me feel close to my mother for the first time in my life. My father was always perfect to me and I loved and enjoyed him in a way I never did my mother. Now I begin to see that one of the things that's gone on is that my father has really forbidden me to be close to my mother. He's really kind of separated her from her kids in a very sad way. I now feel so sisterly with my mother, it's incredible. At dinner the other night, I saw that every time I would talk to her he (my father) would put her down, he would try to make her look foolish to me.

SYLVIA: Modern men get along better in groups than women do. They've had more experience at it, from sports on up. That's why I thought it was very important that women were willing to form groups. But some feminist group rules are really destructive. For example, not being able to criticize a woman who prefers to sit and bullshit rather than grow, or carry off an action. Her fear intimidates me, makes me grow quiet and kind of despairing. Well, once I brought up in a meeting that we should transfer some of the tenderness that we all have toward men to each other and nobody had thought about it! So I think that most feminists are still living their lives much as they would have done anyway or very close to it. We haven't talked about any kind of structures for our lives. We still have our little apartment and many women are in—or want to be in—a one-to-one relationship. In another group, I brought up the idea of monogamy and how that worked against the women and that it was a very male kind of idea and the women who had close relationships with men were very threatened by that.

Many very active feminists cannot leave their current therapist, male or female: where else, in this world of shifting political allegiances and violence, can they be assured of some familiar feedback and attention? Some feminists cannot bring themselves to be really angry at former male therapists' (or husbands') behavior—even when they understand that it has hurt them.

LYDIA: Listen, Phyllis, I'm going to tell you something funny but promise me you won't draw any conclusions from it, okay? And don't make a big thing of it—it's not a big thing. Well, remember my shrink—yeah, he's a man—but he really did help me. Well, after feminism broke like a wave of the future he got very interested in me, very interested, and one thing led to another and he started calling me late at night to talk things over. Now he'd been a very proper shrink and had never behaved like this before. Then he started visiting me at home and one thing led to another—no, there's a twist. He wanted me to go to bed with him *and his wife*—he thought it would be good for her. Well, we're all a little bit crazy but he really *was* helpful before all this started.

MARILYN: I'm still seeing a male psychiatrist, and I'm pretty active in the movement. He's very different: he believed in female oppression before I even knew about it. I need to keep seeing him, mainly because I sometimes get so paranoid, so angry, that I *must* be wrong. I get scared, and there's no women's group that can really deal with this—for me. Sometimes he thinks I fuck men over too much—and I do.

PHYLLIS: How do you fuck men over? Is stepping out of the inferior—or slave—role "fucking men over"—because *they* experience it that way?

MARILYN: (laughing) Okay, okay. Well, I think I raised his [the psychiatrist's] consciousness the other day.

PHYLLIS: Did he pay you?

MARILYN: Oh shut up! (Laughing.) Really. He [the psychiatrist] was saying that if a therapist really has respect for other people he doesn't need his consciousness raised, he just won't oppress women. I really disagree with that. I gave Dr. X as an example. He used to be a director at a [private psychiatric hospital] and he had a lot of respect for people, sees people as autonomous, as making choices, and he's very hesitant to hospitalize a person ever. But this kind of guy could say to my supervisor, "I don't know why Marilyn is in women's lib—she's pretty, smart, and feminine."

Some feminists who are aware of the limitations of psychotherapy still see no other viable institutional alternative—especially if they are no longer relying on marriage and motherhood as major psychological and emotional havens.

PHYLLIS: Given your own bad experiences with psychotherapists, would you say that women should stop seeing therapists?

SUSAN: I don't think so, not immediately. I think that a lot of people use it as a substitute for friendship. There are times in your life when you're under a lot of stress and strain and you don't know people you can go to because you're in a new place or all the people you know have left or all the people you know are part of the problem. You want someone else to go to and we don't have an extended family in which there are people naturally to go to. So, there are therapists, and we go to them.

PHYLLIS: I agree, but I think that if we're hurting and we get slightly comforted by therapy, that it then makes it harder to reach out to some other place or persons for comfort or advice.

SUSAN: That's true, but I don't think abolishing or avoiding therapy is going to help because there are too many needy people and we don't have anything to shift to. I suppose a CR group could help women leave bad therapists, give them strength to find better therapists.

PHYLLIS: When you feel depressed or anxious, and you want "help" with these feelings, can you count on a feminist group, especially a project-oriented group, to "help" you, to pay as much attention to you as a therapist would—if you paid her?

SYLVIA: No, unfortunately. It gets boring to listen to someone else always talking about their problems. There's another girl in the group who is even more depressed than I am and after she talked about her depression everyone got tired of hearing about it. But therapy with a man is absolutely out—and therapy with a woman who's not a feminist is too painful. I guess I have no fantasy image of a good mother or a wise goddess.

I would like to close this chapter with a description of what one of the feminists describes as a basically good relationship with a woman therapist.

ALICE: I was very attracted to this woman. She's European, verbal, maternal, humane. I always felt I could talk to her about whatever was important to me without being misunderstood. She's not a feminist, but I sensed an inner peacefulness or wisdom and, most important, a happiness about being a woman. But she's really unable to share my anger about sexism or about individual men. She alternates from chiding me or indulging me to being disappointed in me or pitying me. When a man—on the street or at work or in a private relationship—starts "coming on," she doesn't believe I get really frightened and angry or that I should. For example, I was at a business meeting in a professional capacity. One of the men immediately wanted to know how old I was. He told me how attractive I was and said how I must be something to "date." I got very angry but didn't show it. I left, for a therapy appointment, as it happens, and was feeling very anxious. My therapist then told me I was "obsessed" by "this question" of sex and power. "The obsession might be productive," she said, "but it was extreme and you know extremism is not very grown up or civilized."

I suppose on some deep level I'm experiencing with her what all daughters experience with their mothers. I feel she's abandoning me to the "grown-up" world of men. She's saying, "You're a heterosexual woman. Be thankful. Go and try to find that one exceptional man, that one special 'feminine' man. Till your private garden and look out for yourself. Don't tempt too many demons." Good, solid, philosophical advice, compassionate advice, and yet being thrown out of any Garden of Eden never feels good.

She's really telling me I can't stay in the world of women: with her, with my mother before her, with other women now. I must go out, alone, and bear a man's child. She feels that the highest level of object-relating is between the sexes. She believes—she said she believes—that even if we were all raised equally, given biological differences, that there would still be a major attraction between the sexes. I don't know about that. And even if it's true, I don't know if it's the "highest" level of humanity or civilizedness. It's a very conventional and dominant idea, a very seductive idea. One thing for sure: she's tempering my passion, my anger, my courage. I do wonder, though, what the world could be like if she (and my mother) agreed with such anger, or had some kind of feminist vision: what would it be like?

Since I wrote this, I have published many books and articles that have continued documenting second and third wave feminism and "feminisms." What's changed, what's remained intractably the same? Many feminists of my era are still out there making a difference. They have accomplished many milestones, too numerous to list here.

But even I could not have anticipated the extent to which the educated daughters of second-wave-feminist-era mothers would have embraced motherhood as a woman's "right" and taken abortion rights for granted. Heterosexual, lesbian, and bi-sexual younger women, both coupled and single, have increasingly been as interested in creating inter-generational families composed of biological or adoptive children as their mothers' generation were once interested in putting private family life behind them. Nor could I have anticipated this generation's fear, amounting to a phobia, about identifying themselves as feminists. However, many younger women are pursuing both careers and private lives in admirable and practical ways.

Today, feminists, including feminist therapists, identify themselves as "women of color feminists," "postmodern and global feminists," "queer and lesbian feminists," and as "Third Wave feminists." Academic feminists have become increasingly non- and anti-activist or have defined "activism" as primarily opposing America. (Please see my book *The Death of Feminism. What's Next in the Struggle for Women's Freedom* for a longer discussion about this.)

I have had some very good experiences with younger feminists, who are now in their twenties and early thirties; and some very hurtful experiences as well. For me, Sanda Balaban, who was my first reader for *Letters to a Young Feminist*, and who is now an important and innovative educator, stands out as an intellectual heir, as does playwright and author Courtney Martin, who did a Masters thesis concerning the themes of *Women and Madness* and who consulted with me about it.

Many younger feminists (aged 20-45) have described familiar sororicidal battles with each other and infanticidal- or matricidal-like difficulties with older women. They talk and write about being slandered and ostracized by other girls and women. In general, younger feminists have fewer illusions about other women than my generation once did. They take it for granted that women are competitive, cruel, and envious; indeed, some have written useful and practical books on the subject.

May they all continue to go from strength to strength.

CHAPTER TEN

FEMALE PSYCHOLOGY: PAST, PRESENT, AND FUTURE

FEMALE PSYCHOLOGY IN OUR CULTURE: WOMEN ALONE

The women say, shame on you. They say you are domesticated, forcibly fed, like geese in the yard of the farmer who fattens them. They say, you strut about, you have no other care than to enjoy the good things your masters hand out, solicitous for your well-being so long as they stand to gain. They say, there is no more distressing spectacle than that of slaves who take pleasure in their servile state. They say, you are far from possessing the pride of those wild birds who refuse to hatch their eggs when they have been imprisoned. They say, take an example from the wild birds who, even if they mate with the males to relieve their boredom, refuse to reproduce so long as they are not at liberty.

Monique Wittig[1]

The women say with an oath, it was by a trick that he expelled you from the earthly paradise, cringing he insinuated himself next to you, he robbed you of that passion for knowledge of which it is written that it has the wings of the eagle, the eyes of the owl, the feet of the dragon. He has enslaved you by trickery, you who were great strong valiant. He has stolen your wisdom from you, he has closed your memory to what you were, he has made you that which is not which does not speak which does not possess which does not write, he has made of you a vile and fallen creature, he has gagged abused betrayed you. By means of stratagems he has stultified your understanding, he has woven around you a long list of defects that he declares essential to your well being, to your nature. He has invented your history. But the time approaches when you shall crush the serpent under your heel, the time approaches when you can cry, erect, filled with ardour and courage. Paradise exists in the shadow of the sword.

Monique Wittig[2]

MODERN FEMALE PSYCHOLOGY reflects a relatively powerless and deprived condition. Many intrinsically valuable female traits, such as intuitiveness or compassion, have probably been developed through default or patriarchal imposed necessity, rather than through either biological predisposition or free choice. Female emotional "talents" must be viewed in terms of the overall price exacted by sexism. It is illogical and dangerous to romanticize traits that one purchases with one's freedom and dignity— even if they are "nice" traits; even if they make one's slavery more bearable; even if they charm and soothe the oppressor's rage and sorrow, staying his hand, or leave-taking, for one more day.

In Chapter One, I discussed the myth of Demeter, the Earth Mother, and her raped daughter Persephone, the Divine Maiden, whom she rescues and reincorporates into her own biological-maternal destiny.[3] Nearly every woman in our culture has relived this myth in her own life. Its meaning still constitutes a powerful guide to our understanding of the female condition.

Persephone, like her mother, is denied uniqueness, individuality, and cultural potency. Neither Demeter nor Persephone is allowed to become a "heroine": one represents the earth, the other represents a return to earth. Their single fate symbolizes the inevitable, endless breaking of each individual woman on the wheel of culturally devalued biological reproduction. Women who live in patriarchal settings are defined by certain traits, or by the absence of other traits. For example, like Persephone, most women today are not bold, forceful, knowledge-able, physically strong, active, or sexually potent. Like Persephone and Demeter, women are still naive, helpless, or *reactive* victims.[*] Their sexuality is defined for them by men, as an act of incest for procreative purposes. In the myth, Persephone is gathering flowers of forgetfulness (poppies) when she is abducted and raped. Most women "forget" their dreams of individuality when they marry. "Marriage" is the modern counterpart to rape in mythology.

Unfortunately, most women today do not have Demeters for mothers. Female biology and nature have increasingly been devalued by our culture—but women have not yet been freed from being defined in biological terms. Thus, the modern Persephone is no longer graceful, no longer divine, no longer "saved" by her mother. Demeter exists no more—and certainly not for a daughter. Whatever Earth Mother qualities women retain are lavished almost exclusively on sons and husbands. Persephone has become Cinderella, struck dumbly domestic by a Demeter turned stepmother. *This*, if anything, is the female version of exile from the earthly paradise. Fairy-tale princes cannot rescue women from their exile; and mothers have become stepmothers. For this reason daughters and (step)mothers today, unlike Persephone and Demeter, are characterized by self-hatred and mutual mistrust. (Step)mothers have not prepared their daughters for pilgrimages, conquests, or reflection. They have put brooms into their hands and romantic or escapist illusions into their heads. Daughters can have no heroic pride in their sex, which seems to survive and fatten on its domesticity.

We must remember that the original Demeter was free and did have real powers. Demeter was not a terrible Goddess of Death but one of great

---

[*]Men are often victims of nature but women *are* "nature." When women seek to be something other than "natural," they experience their limitations or victimization at human male hands, and usually not through earthly—or divine—circumstances.

earthly riches, of Life. We must note that it is Persephone, a frail, pale being who as Pluto's unwilling wife, is the Queen of the Dead in patriarchal mythology. Ancient mythology did not always grant women the truly terrible powers it knew and feared they had. Stepmothers and witches in modern fairy tales are usually defeated. They too are not allowed a true measure of their wrath or power.

Today, women grow up in households where adult members of their sex do not have Demeter's powers. Mothers often glorify their servitude, sublimate their sexuality and intellect, and punish their daughters when they rebel against such a role. These conditions lead to the development of certain psychological traits. For example, women are submissive and are not rescued by their mothers when this trait leads to their victimization. Daughters learn to survive as they have seen their mothers survive: through self-sacrifice and "nesty" materialism, and through public protestations of "happiness."

Persephone, the purest image of the Divine Maiden, has many mythological reflections. Psyche, the wife of Eros, whom I discussed in Chapter One, is an important variation of the myth and is relevant to modern women in certain ways that Persephone is not. We do not know too much about Persephone's feelings about or relation to her husband Pluto. What is known suggests a quietly implacable disinterest and sense of utter strangeness. Persephone is known to us through her identification with and love for her mother. Psyche, on the other hand, loves her husband Eros (Cupid), or loves the love of men. In the story, she is quite literally deserted by her mother and sisters and wedded in all darkness (ignorance).[4]

Unlike Persephone, Psyche is happily and eternally reunited with her husband, and becomes the mother of a daughter called Pleasure. Psyche, an early prefiguration of the Catholic Madonna, embodies certain traits possessed by many women today. I am talking about female romanticism, tenderness, compassion, and altruism. Studies and common sense suggest that "altruism" in our culture often stems from guilt, fear, and low self-esteem rather than from freedom or self-love. (Margaret Adams has discussed the crippling limitations and definite social function of what she calls "the Compassion Trap" in women.[5]) Such traits are not devalued by either men or women. However, men benefit from such traits, almost exclusively, and reward them rather poorly. A genuinely compassionate person would have a hard time participating in the spheres of public action. There is a ruthlessness that politics or science demands—but its devotees are never totally destroyed by this demand. The devotees are men, who expect to be revived each night by female compassion in the individual, private family unit. This revival doesn't always take place— and women are always blamed as nags and bitches, as ungrateful and manipulative albatrosses around their suffering husbands' necks. This may even be true. However, it is time to blame or examine the public sphere that has exiled compassion or decency into private isolated places—and the ruthlessness involved in enforcing full-time "compassion"-service upon women.

Apparently there is no place for altruism or compassion in political and military ventures. The kind of training women receive as "compassion"-givers effectively keeps them at home, psychologically. In the twentieth century, the wives of upper-class men organized charity benefits for the poor; the wives of middle-class men organized peace and ecology demonstrations and worked as social workers, nurses, teachers, and psychologists; the wives of lower-class men took care of their families and of other people's children and husbands, as secretaries, domestics, and prostitutes. And yet poverty does not disappear; neither war nor pollution nor racism is abolished; and the universal female tie to childbearing and rearing remains as constant as ever.

The composite psychological portrait of Persephone-Psyche is one of a naive and heterosexually romantic victim, an unindividuated, fearful, and conservative being, whose greatest pride lies in either childbearing and compassion or in a return to the ways of the Mother. The Maiden as Cinderella retains most of these traits, but with no glory, with no home, and no princely or maternal "rescue."

Cinderella-Persephone-Psyche also embodies certain other unmistakably feminine traits which many women still possess. I am thinking of traits that men—and therefore women—either devalue or consider unimportant. For example, a certain type of "mindlessness" or "superficiality" (as men see it) exists among many women—which is neither mindless nor superficial. Two women talking often seem to be reciting monologues at each other, neither really listening to (or judging) what the other is saying. Two personal confessions, two sets of feelings, seem to be paralleling one another, rather "mindlessly," and without "going any-where." In fact, what the women are doing—or where they are "going"— is toward some kind of emotional resolution and comfort. Each woman comments upon the other's feelings by reflecting them in a very sensitive matching process. The two women share their feelings by alternating the retelling of the entire experience in which their feelings are embedded and from which they cannot be "abstracted" or "summarized." Their theme, method, and goal are non-verbal and/or non-verbalized. Facial expres-sions, pauses, sighs, and seemingly unrelated (or "non-abstract") responses to statements are crucial to such dialogue. A very special prescience is at work here. On its most ordinary level, it affords women a measure of emotional reality and a kind of comfort that they cannot find with men, and that men do not have with each other. On its highest level, it constitutes the basic tools of art and psychic awareness.

Thus, the psychological portrait of the individual and powerless woman consists of naiveté, compulsive heterosexuality, procreative "pride," fearfulness, self-hatred, mistrust of other women—and of com-passion, passion, and idealism. Let us look at such women in groups to see what happens to these individual themes in a social context.

FEMALE PSYCHOLOGY IN OUR CULTURE: WOMEN IN GROUPS

Every effort for progress, for enlightenment, for science, for religious, political and economic liberty, emanates from the minority, and not from the mass. Today as ever, the few are misunderstood, hounded, imprisoned, tortured, and killed. . . . The majority, that compact, immobile, drowsy mass, the Russian peasant, after a century of struggle, of sacrifice, of untold misery, still believes that the rope which strangles "the man with the white hands" [the intellectual] brings luck. . . . Not that I do not feel with the oppressed, the disinherited of the earth; not because I do not know the shame, the horror, the indignity of the lives the people lead, do I repudiate the majority as a creative force for justice or equality. . . . I wish not to concede anything to them [the masses] but to drill, divide and break them up, and draw individuals out of them.

Emma Goldman[6]

The aim of political action and social thought of all kinds is to create a tolerable background and leave people alone. The only tolerable background is an austerely simple one. The important parts of life will always be the things we do in our own small groups and on our own. They are art and science and sex and God and compassion and romantic love. These should be rich and complex. There isn't one damned thing that society can do to help you with any of these. All society can do is to make sure that it doesn't prevent them.

Paul Goodman[7]

I learned three and one-half years ago that women had always been divided against one another, were self-destructive, and filled with impotent rage. I thought the movement would change all that. I never dreamed that I would see the day when this rage, masquerading as a pseudo-egalitarian radicalism under the "pro-woman" banner, would turn into a frighteningly vicious anti-intellectual fascism of the left, and used within the movement to strike down sisters. . . . I am referring, of course, to the personal attacks . . . to which women in the movement, who have painfully managed any degree of achievement, have been subjected. . . .

If you are in the first category (an achiever) you are immediately labelled a thrill-seeking opportunist, a ruthless mercenary, out to get her fame and fortune over the dead bodies of selfless sisters who have buried their abilities and sacrificed their ambitions for the greater glory of feminism. Productivity seems to be the major crime—but if you have the misfortune of being outspoken and articulate, you are accused of being power-mad, elitist, fascist, and finally, the worst epithet of all: A MALE IDENTIFIER, AARRGGG!!! . . .

To emerge unscathed from this kind of assault is impossible. The effects I have observed, to name just a few, are: gradual or immediate decrease in productivity; an upsurge of self-doubt; depletion of whatever ego-strength had been salvaged from our pasts or recovered during the early stages of the movement; an increase in impotence and passivity, coupled with a rampant paranoia (completely justified); a severe dropping off of self-confidence and faith in one's ability; a detailed and obsessive self-examination for real or imagined sins which is completely useless since the mind-fucking has destroyed objectivity. . . .

One last plea: If we women are ever to pull ourselves out of the morass of self-pity, self-destruction, and impotence which has been our heritage for so long as we can remember, then it is perhaps even more important that we be supportive of each other's achievements and successes and strengths, than it is for us to be compassionate and understanding of each other's failures and weaknesses.

Anselma dell'Olio[8]

American children are reared to be exceptionally competitive and aggressive but increasingly are expected to "get along" with or be "liked" by others *in order* to "get ahead." More and more, people of all generations tend to "look alike" and, despite a potentially destructive and superficial individualism, conform rather than commit individual acts. Individuals in America, as elsewhere, risk ostracism, loneliness, grave self-doubt, and perhaps incarceration.

Juliet Mitchell makes a brilliant point in her analysis of the ideological function of the family in capitalist society. She says that "the family is a stronghold of what capitalism needs to preserve but actually destroys: private property and individualism." I don't think, however, that individualism was exactly permitted, especially to women, in a pre-capitalist era.[9]

Women, although similar to each other in many ways, are more isolated from each other *in terms of groups* than men are. Women are not consolidated into public or powerful groups. Women as mothers are "grouped" with their children (who grow up and leave them), and only temporarily and superficially with other women: in parks, at women's auxiliary functions, and at heterosexual parties. Such women only keep each other company temporarily as they engage in "freely" chosen private lives rather than mandatory wage labor. There is no need to organize for better working conditions if you don't feel you're working, or if you feel the definition of work for women is and should be different from that of men. Women as secretaries, domestics, waitresses, prostitutes, and factory workers are not well unionized. These are mainly female jobs and as such are not easy to organize for many reasons: female fatigue because of holding another job at home; female lack of skills and encouragement and consequently of optimism; female fear of male opposition; and, in the case of prostitution, fear of legal as well as physical reprisal, *plus* the knowledge that it is difficult if not impossible to earn as much money in any other job.

Professional or middle-income career women are neither leaders nor "brothers" within the professional male organizations. For example, as a professional woman I cannot continue either an important or a casual conversation with a male colleague in the bathroom; I *can* with a female colleague and it makes a difference. As a business woman, I cannot "do business" with a male colleague or client at an athletic or faculty club, or at a whorehouse or stag party. I have too few female colleagues to similarly indulge and in any event, as women, we have not been socialized to enjoy such institutions—even or especially if they were geared to our advancement. As a career woman I am less likely than a man is to take a sports trip or vacation with a male colleague: what would our spouses say? Without a wife, how could I afford the time away from my children and home? How can I risk being approached as a mistress and losing a professional connection? And if I must worry and stumble over each of these things, how can I have access to support and information that my male colleagues naturally share? If my chances of achieving real power are so slender compared to those of my male counterparts, no wonder my colleagues have no burning desire to cultivate my friendship or encourage my growth. Of course, I can be cultivated—as an assistant, confidante, mistress, or wife. I will not be experienced as a rival or as a protegé. I will be a weapon to be used against other men (real rivals). I will gain a token position by helping some male colleague become stronger or maintain his position. (Professional marriages are a common way for women to survive outside the home.)

Since the women's liberation movement many American professional women (especially within the universities) began to organize as women. Now woman professionals, particularly in non-female professions, may have other women as colleagues, clients, or employers. Now, feminist women and men have formed organizations for intellectual, economic, emotional, political, and social purposes. In the past, consciousness-raising groups offered women female approval for their anger and for their desire for sexual and economic advancement and liberation. They do not exist today—although book clubs and eating disorders do.

In feminist groups, many women experienced temporary and isolated refuge from hostile or indifferent family, school, and wage-labor environments. The feminist group experience was an attempt to institutionalize a new ideology of sisterhood, one not based on powerlessness or on support for the patriarchal status-quo.

Because of the revolutionary nature and vision of feminism, and woman's basic naiveté, many women suffered their first defeats with surprise. They were not yet aware of the enormity of the task being undertaken. Juliet Mitchell noted that "just as, on the one hand, it is crucial that we are never guilty of underestimating the potential of women, so we must never neglect to be aware of the difficulties of our position. In a different context (that of military struggle), Mao called going it alone and underestimating the difficulties "Left Sectarianism" and underestimating one's potential and fearing to struggle "Right Opportunism" the conditions of our oppression *do* condition us. And we have to assess the weakness of women as a political force in order *not* to succumb to it.[10]

In American groups, women were very critical of the "female" rules of handling conflict, such as indirect communication, tears, and evasion. They were equally critical of the "male" rules of handling conflict, such as hierarchical decision-making, compromise (as opposed to consensus), or violence. When conflicts arose, the confrontations were raw and women purposefully resisted both "male" or "female" resolutions. Such purism often led to the same bitterness and paranoia that have characterized many male-dominated groups.

"Middle-class" liberal work-oriented groups suffered these events somewhat less. They had specific tasks and goals and were not averse to exercising "male" rules of organization or conflict resolution. Their work was—and remains invaluable for women: their visions are not puristically romantic, and they can function with some success within our present culture. Medical, legal, economic, and political reform for women is not to be lightly tossed off as "reformist" and, therefore, useless. Some reforms are crucial and, depending on the context in which they occur, can also be revolutionary.

Unfortunately, one's psychology is no easier to change or escape from than is one's national or biological history. Any attempt to "revolutionize" any of these phenomena usually involves some strict continuation or some modified reappearance of old myths, values, and structures. The blinding recognition of a common plight (oppression) does not immediately do away with that plight: it is only the first of many difficult steps.

Thus, the American feminist movement has conformed to as many intrinsically valueless conditioned female traits as it has recognized those feminist conditioned female traits which are valuable, and as it has explored new ways for women to "be" in the universe. For example, many feminists have not been able to avoid the female experience of disliking, competing with, and feeling betrayed by other women. And the reasons given are as varied as they are endless: economically and professionally successful women are aggressive elitists; heterosexually committed women are cowards and deserters; happy mothers and Marxist women are fools and fifth columnists; lesbians are sick; white women are racists; black women can't wait to walk behind their men; middle-aged women wear hats and gloves; young women carry spears and throw bombs. These perceptions were and still are somewhat valid. However, what is being psychologically satisfied is the female belief that she cannot be enhanced or protected by the success or power of any other woman. Psychologically, what is also at work here is an absolute terror of differences.

We may remember (from Chapter One) that Demeter, the Earth Mother, incorporates her daughter, Persephone, into her own image. The sacrifice of "differences," of uniqueness, is deeply tied to the female's endless cycle of biological reproduction and cultural impotence. This is the mythological stratum of the "policing" of women by women, both within families and within feminist groups. Mothers initiate daughters into the sacred sisterhood of discontent not only in order that daughters survive. Mothers are lonely and need nurturance—something they did not receive from their own mothers or husbands, something, like Demeter, they may hope to receive from their daughters. Thus, "rebellious" daughters are treated harshly by their mothers as the deserting lovers and companions they are meant to be. The female "policing" phenomena is rooted in an anguish of powerlessness.

Mythologically then, a mother's (or adult woman's) success or power has meant a loss of freedom or uniqueness for her daughter. Psychologically and politically in patriarchal society, one woman's token or temporary "success" is usually purchased at another woman's expense. The "successful" woman today cannot protect (or mentor or "incorporate") other women into a non-biologically based image of power or individuality. There are still too few "successful" women to accomplish this. Also, the extraordinary demands placed on the "successful" woman either keep her from being a biological mother or make her allegiance to individual men (as husbands, sons, employers, or colleagues) nearly as necessary as her isolation from other women.

It seems to me that this dynamic of either female incorporation into the mother or doomed desertion of her will remain true as long as women bear the sole burden of motherhood within a patriarchal family. Also, the complicated Mother-Daughter interaction is a hard and tenacious model to shatter. The feminist language of "sisterhood," rather than "motherhood" and "daughterhood" reflects both the painfulness of this relationship as well as an attempt to break down corrupt hierarchal barriers between women.

I may note that "differences" among men certainly exist and are both experienced and resolved, or not resolved, differently. For men, being incorporated or initiated into the male role (or god-figure, or Oedipal father) ideally demands the development of some kind of public strength, mobility, and perhaps even a touch of uniqueness. (It also means renouncing heterosexuality except under certain "safe" conditions.) Male conformity, as I have already noted, implies conformity to action, struggle, thought, mobility, and pleasure; female conformity implies conformity to inaction, resignation, emotionality, and unhappiness. Naturally, incorporation into the Oedipal father is purchased at great emotional expense. The male "policing" of other men is rooted in an anguish of power, and it is a more literal, physical, and public policing than female policing is. Men police both men and women. Adult women cannot police adult men in quite this way.

Women alone and in groups, including feminist groups, found it hard to abandon the virulent double standard of male-female behavior. They still do. Paradoxically, while women must not "succeed," when they *do* succeed at anything, they have still failed if they're not successful at *everything*. Women must be perfect (goddesses) or they're failures (whores). (The violent conditioning of "spotlessness," coupled with a deep sense of "dirtiness," in female children runs deep indeed.) If a woman accomplishes a valuable task she, unlike men (who after all, are mortal), *still* has failed if she has, for example, abandoned the daily care of her children or her looks in order to do so. A woman has failed if she succeeds at winning a legal or intellectual battle but has hurt another woman's (or man's) feelings in the process.

Men have wives and female secretaries both to mother them and to smooth the ruffled feelings of others for them, to serve dinners, buy gifts, and answer the phone for them when they are in bad or busy tempers. Women don't. Men are also somewhat protected by the universal expectation that they don't have to be so "nice."

Another example: mothers are praised for child rearing but severely condemned, by others, by psychiatrists, and by themselves for anything that goes "wrong" with either their children or their marriages. Ironically, mothers are often seen as failures—by their husbands, by career women, and by some feminists—because they haven't also achieved careers or independence from their families.*

Traditionally, women as well as men expect or demand another woman's help or sacrifice more quickly and easily than they demand a man's sacrifice or even his cooperation. Objectively, such an expectation is safer and is more realistic. Psychologically, it represents our culture's higher valuation of men, as well as the assigned female role of "policing" other women in the service of male supremacy. Even within the feminist movement, women do not demand or force certain support from men— either from men whom they know, or from public male sources such as philanthropic foundations, private industries, or government. Beyond a certain point, women are not able to force men to do anything. Fear of male reprisal in terms of physical and sexual violence or further economic abandonment is very great. Also, since women are conditioned to inhabit only the "private" and personal realms, they are genuinely confused about public action and the nature of power. Thus, in America, Betty Freidan's, Gloria Steinem's, or Kate Millett's "contributions" to a particular woman's cause were more actively expected and sought after than were the U.S. Army's, General Motors', or the Vatican's—all institutions which have far greater resources than those of any individual woman or any individual woman's group. (Mommy is still safer to milk, blame, and hate than Daddy is. Daddy is feared and addressed in "good girl" tones, or not addressed at all.) Another example: most traditional and feminist child care centers or cooperatives were staffed with women, not men. Babysitting was usually expected of grandmothers, not grand-fathers, by daughter-mothers. In the past, feminist groups did not succeed in having their employed husbands collectively assume respon-sibility for housekeeping, child rearing, and compassionate "listening"

---

* Husbands may want their wives to "get out" of the house after they have done twenty years of domestic service and are no longer "young" or "interesting." Feminists want both nurturance and comradeship from women whose relationship to the patriarchal family makes this exceed-ingly difficult.

within a marriage. (There were many reasons why both feminist and non-feminist women wouldn't want this to happen: loss of their own identity and source of employment plus a legitimate mistrust of male competence in these areas are the two most obvious reasons.) Today, to some extent, matters have improved—slightly.

Women, as well as men, are deeply threatened by a woman who does not smile often enough and, paradoxically, who is not very unhappy. Women mistrust and men destroy those women who are not interested in *sacrificing* at least something for someone for some reason. Rather than achieve at least half or all of Caesar's power, many women, including some feminists, would prefer to leave it in Caesar's hands altogether and, in a misguidely "noble" gesture, sacrifice their individual advancement for the sake of less fortunate women, Third World people, one's biological children, one's weary husband, etc. In other words, it is still difficult for most women to stop sacrificing themselves (or saying that they want to) for specific other people, or in personal and private acts.[*] It is still difficult for most women to consider political or technological power as a potentially valid means of alleviating at least *some* of the human misery and inequality, including their own, that surrounds them.

> The women say that, with the world full of noise they see themselves as already in possession of the industrial complexes. They are in the factories aerodromes radio stations. They have control of communications. They have taken possession of aeronautical electronic ballistic data-processing factories. They are in the foundries tall furnaces navy yards arsenals refineries distilleries. They have taken possession of pumps presses levers rolling-mills winches pullies cranes turbines pneumatic drills arcs blow-lamps. They say that they envisage themselves acting with strength and happiness.
>
> Monique Wittig[11]

For example, women who eschew leadership and/or power are probably doing so because their conditioning forces them to, rather than because they recognize the ruthless aspects of leadership in our culture. As we shall see, this is similar to women eschewing violence or self-defense on principle—when they can't perform such acts anyway. Such avoidance is not based on choice or morality but on necessity. Women are no more to be congratulated on their "pacifism" than men are to be congratulated for their "violence."

Women, even more than men, seem to be threatened by those personal traits *in a woman* which are original or "male"-like. (Men can afford to be less threatened because so few women manifest such traits and, when they do, can easily be checked or adopted into male service.) For example, women, including many feminists, respond more positively to those projects which *ease* the burdens of the female status quo rather than to those projects which attempt to redefine or abolish the status quo. Easing the burdens of motherhood and supporting abortion reform are essential tasks, yet they both imply a continuation of a powerless female responsibility for children and for birth control. Women in the public labor force, whether as factory workers or professionals, want better wages and better working conditions (for themselves or their husbands), and more public child care centers. Most women are not yet able to sever their ties to biological reproduction or to the family.

For example, most women experience the male's physical or emotional abandonment of his family or children as either cruel or cruelly necessary. He may be a "louse"—or a "victim" of harsh job realities. His behavior is human. However, the female's similar abandonment of her family—for any purpose—viewed as "unnatural" and "tragic." The female's social role is still a biological one: as such she is seen as transgressing against nature when she attempts to change her social role. It is important to note that men are allowed more leeway in social-role failure than are women. Although men are expected to achieve publicly or economically, when they fail or refuse to do so, they are not necessarily seen as "unnatural," but as either heroes or victims, deserving of our sympathy, understanding, and support.

Conformity, inflexibility, and a tendency to romanticize the emotional infantilism and unrealistic dependencies of the powerless woman (and to confuse it with a form of wisdom or power) still exist among many women and men, whether they are feminists or not. Women have had little collective experience of public problem-solving and no valuable female role-models. "Power" and "public action" are indeed male, and foreign to them. To the extent to which women in groups dwell more or only on personal feeling than on action, more on "process" than on "product," they remain victims of female biology *and* sex-role conditioning. As long as women remain more comfortable with decisions or analyses made by others, or by groups, than with an individually made decision, they are remaining comfortably "female." This does not mean that only leaders have legitimacy or authority; it does mean that, ideally, each person should feel "legitimate" and should only let someone else speak "for them" if the listener agrees with her through understanding and not out of ignorance or fear.

Woman as Persephone-Psyche-Cinderella cannot accomplish certain things. It is absurd to expect that women, qua women, can any more easily or quickly than men achieve goals such as international peace or universal personal happiness. On the contrary, women, as *powerless* human beings, may have an even harder time than men—especially since men, who are relatively more powerful as a caste, are opposed both to absorbing "feminine" traits into the public sphere and to encouraging women to develop "masculine" traits for participation in the public sphere. Certainly, women's first successful organized accomplishments did concern issues such as child care, abortion, and birth control—"female"-sphere issues. Women, as a group, as an interest group, or as individuals, are only now beginning to address the "larger" issues of the economy, religion, war and peace.

What would an ideal group be? As a feminist and anarchist, I can only answer for myself and, unfortunately, in somewhat vague generalities. To me, the only acceptable groups are those that, unlike the patriarchal family, can function as places and ways of supporting our deepest cravings for individual liberty, security, achievement, and love. Groups (ideologies, religions, programmatic "solutions") which in any way kill the individual spirit; which despise and crucify that which it longs for; which enforce conformity, mediocrity, and conservatism—*for any reason*; which seek to diminish each person to "manageable" and familiar levels rather than to enhance each person to "unmanageable" and unique levels which the group *supports*—such "groupings" are depressingly well known, and are doomed to spin out old patterns of martyrdom and oppression.

Men are martyred or sacrificed when they preach or practice peace and love; women (and powerless men) when they preach or practice war. Even the evil laws of martyrdom obey the laws of sex-role stereotyping.

Such groups cannot provide women with the strength to gain power and to redefine power, love, and work. I honestly don't know exactly how such ideal groups would solve the problems of inequality and injustice.

As a feminist and psychologist, I can discuss this question of ideal groups in quite another way. If women have been rendered culturally impotent because of their biology, it might be useful to discuss those societies in which women reigned culturally supreme *because* of their biology; that is Amazon societies.

AMAZON SOCIETIES: VISIONS AND POSSIBILITIES

Were there actually such things as the fabulous nations of maidens, the mounted demons, galloping from the edges of the world to make ice and golden sand splash to all sides? Was there ever a "man-hating army" with clanging tresses and awesome customs? . . . In time and reality the Amazon kingdoms not only comprise an extremist end of matriarchy but also are a beginning and a purpose in themselves. Roaming daughter realms . . . they markedly differ from the serenely tolerant mother clan as old as mankind, which pacifically exiled a young upstart manhood by exogamy. The Amazon does not mime the male principle but denies it in order to unite the two fundamental forms of life in paradisaical harmony which had been divided by the great mother. . . . In the mother clan, there was a constant progression of great mothers begetting more great mothers. Amazons however, reproduced the daughter type, which practically skips a generation and is something altogether different. They were conquerers, horse tamers, and huntresses who gave birth to children but did not nurse or rear them. They were an extreme, feminist wing of a young human race, whose other extreme wing consisted of the stringent patriarchies.

Helen Diner[12]

The whole idea of the Amazon is the cancellation of the first, partheno-genetic female action, the separation and formation of the active principle and its shaping into a male. Amazons concede no separate existence to the active principle, reabsorb it, and develop it themselves in androgynous fashion: female on the left, male on the right. Their dematernalization begins with the shrinking or the removal of the right breast as a symbolic action of bold style. . . . All varieties of Amazon society share the characteristic that they reared only the girls into fullfledged specimens of mankind. . . .

Helen Diner[13]

Amazon society, as mythology, history, and universal male nightmare, represents a culture in which women reign culturally supreme *because* of their gender. Amazon societies are also important because women were trained to be warriors—militarily and, presumably, in other ways as well. Amazons also owned their own land and lived on it together. This is very different from our only examples of women living together: in jails, in ghettos, in Islamic purdah, or in schools while still "growing up." Women live together only in states of shameful default or absolute necessity, (just as men have reigned culturally supreme because of *their* gender). Female sacrifice or self-sacrifice, as we know it, could not have existed in Amazon societies. For example, to be an Amazon mother does not imply *cultural* behavior in which constant interaction between a woman and her biologi-cal child is necessary. Despite many odes to child rearing, the fact remains that the child-rearing assignment (with whatever tediousness or immobility a particular class or technological level imposes) has traditionally been drawn by the relatively powerless sex.

In Amazon societies, women were mothers and their society's *only* warriors; mothers and their society's *only* hunters; mothers and their society's *only* political and religious leaders. No division of labor based on sex seems to have existed in such societies. Although Amazon leaders existed and queens were elected, the societies seem to have been classless ones, or at least ones in which any *woman* could aspire to and achieve full human expression.

In Amazon society, only *men*, when they were allowed to remain, were, in widely differing degrees, powerless and oppressed. Diner notes that "the tyranny of woman over man (in the sexual realm) is never as complete as the converse sometimes is: there are only a few instances of anything like male prostitution, if for no other reason than because the male organ limits this possibility, for women." According to Diner,

> The mildest form of Amazon aversion [to men] caused them to engage in a quick assignation with their male neighbors, totally indiscriminate as a matter of principle, every spring. Female offspring was retained, the male was sent to its distant fathers. The more radical kind of administration did not send any babies away but crippled the newly born boys and rendered them innocuous for life through the twisting of one hand and one hip out of their sockets. Despised slave cripples, never touched erotically by the Amazons, they were used by them for the rearing of children, the spinning of wool, and domestic service. In the most extreme anti-male society, the male offspring was always killed, and sometimes the fathers were too.
>
> Of all the African Amazons, only the Gorgons seem to have maintained a pure Amazon state; the others, though keeping the army purely feminine, maintained some men in their camps. The Libyan Amazons, who removed their right breasts, had compulsory military service for all girls for a number of years, during which they had to refrain from marriage. After that, they became a part of the reserves and were allowed to take a mate and reproduce their kind. The women monopolized government and other influential positions. In contrast to the later Thermodontines, however, they lived in a permanent relationship with their sex partners, even though the men led a retiring life, could not hold public office, and had no right to interfere in the

government of the state or society. Children, who were brought up on mare's milk, were given to the men to rear, just as among the Egyptians, Kamtchatkans, and some of the North American Indians.[14]

Amazon society was *probably* better for the development of women's bodies and emotions than any male-dominated patriarchal society has ever been. It may have been better for the development of women's intellect and art—although this remains a totally conjectural matter. Amazon society probably did not value modern or western types of competitive art and intellect, any more than did other early or "primitive" societies. (I really wonder what a group of Amazon women would make of my *writing* about them. And I wonder how much or how long I'd be able to accept a disinterested, indulgent, or negative response. However, Diner notes that the entire Ionian tradition refers to the Thermodon Amazons as the founders of cities and sanctuaries.

> Though bestial until victory, they later like the Romans, became conciliatory. Gentleness and foresight earned them the adoration of the vanquished . . . their tradition was maintained uninterruptedly by temples, graves, cities, and whole countries. A large number of important cities boasted an Amazon as founder and godmother; Smyrna, Sinope, Cyme, Gryne, Pitania, Magnesia, Clete, Mytilene, and Amastris.[15]

Earlier, the Libyan (Moroccan and African) Amazons rode through Egypt "peacefully," but conquered.

> Syria, Phrygia, and all the lands along the seacoast to the Caicus River. . . . The islands of Samos, Lesbos, Pathmos and Samothrace [were conquered and inhabited] by "Myrine," a Libyan Amazon Queen.[16]

If women take their bodies seriously—and ideally we should—then its *full* expression, in terms of pleasure, maternity, and physical strength, seems to fare better when *women* control the means of production and reproduction. From this point of view, it is simply not in women's interest to support patriarchy or even a fabled "equality" with men. That women do so is more a sign of powerlessness than of any biologically based "superior" wisdom.

Female sacrifice—either self-sacrifice, ritual virgin sacrifice, prostitution, or the sacrifice of self that women make in order to be mothers—is perhaps not unalterably rooted in our biological condition.

I am not saying that a female-dominated or Amazon society based on the oppression of men is any more "just" than is a male-dominated society based on the oppression of women. I am merely pointing out in what ways it is better for women.

Perhaps someday a choice between *forms* of injustice will not be necessary. Also, I don't know whether it is in women's interest to forgo the act of childbirth—simply because men have enforced such an unfair price on it. I don't know whether birth control technology in a male-dominated society is particularly good for women. Being freed from enforced maternity or pregnancy fears does not necessarily lead to the abolition of female sexual "frigidity," or to the abolition of female prostitution. Birth control technology, by itself, will not necessarily lead to the abolition of sexism, any more than it will usher in an era of non-alienated labor or alternative family forms. It may, in fact, lead to male-dominated totalitarian decisions regarding sexual activity and maternity—decisions over which the individual woman has as little to say as she did about her enforced maternity.

To the extent to which American, Western, or modern women desire a more harmonious, tribal, collective, spiritual, and ritual existence, and *are willing to forgo certain modern values and technologies to achieve it*, then Amazon societies are probably better psychological models for women than are male-initiated models of "primitive" societies. (We must not forget that many primitive cultures feared the female body and exercised strong taboos against menstruation, puberty, and defloration—and practiced female genital mutilation.[17])

> Dropping out is not the answer; . . . Most women are already dropped
> out; they were never in. . . . Dropping out, however, is an excellent

policy for men, and *SCUM* will enthusiastically encourage it. . . .

Valerie Solanas

I sat through three hours of the film 'Woodstock' alternating between feelings of enchantment and repulsion. . . . For one thing, with the exception of a pregnant Joan Baez who couldn't seem to stop talking about her husband, all the musicians were men. Sweaty, bearded men were busy building the stage, directing traffic, shooting the film, and running the festival. *Brotherhood* was repeatedly proclaimed, both on stage and off. . . . The clearest indication of how rock music views womankind is in its lyrics. Women certainly can't complain that the image presented there is one-dimensional. On the contrary, the put-downs are remarkably multifaceted, ranging from open contempt to sugar-coated condescension. Above all, however, women are always available sexual objects whose chief function is to happily accommodate any man that comes along.

Marion Meade

Hip-hop and rap-era music has not improved on the portrayal of girls and women.

Amazon societies compose an early and little-explored culture, one in which women dominated all areas of conceivable or necessary life—i.e., what was necessary included more than just the enforced bearing and rearing of a single man's children.[18] An image of women fully engaged in the task of humanity—at any technological level—is practically visionary. It produces fear and disbelief—together with an overwhelming sense of excitement.

Of course, it is unrealistic and perhaps dangerous to take visions too seriously. Perhaps we must respect them as difficult truths with which to inform our lives—in some way. Perhaps we cannot go backward too longingly in time. (We can, of course, realize how little or badly forward we've come.) Despite the importance of knowing about goddesses and Amazons, I certainly believe that mass female liberation lies more in the technological future than in the biological past. The earth's female population is no longer small nor is the habit of warfare a desirable one.

In general, hand-to-hand combat is anachronistic and militarily ineffective—for women as well as for men. Men in advanced countries possess the nuclear and chemical power to destroy the planet and/or redefine our ways of life. However, total nuclear power has not been used since Nagasaki. Weaponry and military skills will ultimately prevail over any biologically muscled battle just as science will ultimately lead to more revolutionary victories than will apocalyptic military heroism. And yet I don't think that physical prowess and discipline are totally anachronistic for women.

Women are raped because we cannot defend ourselves. Much of our submissive, conciliatory, compassionate, and seductive behaviors have been cultivated in order to avoid either the fact or the onus of rape. Rape existed long before modern industrial capitalism, yet it seems an appropriate metaphor for that behavior (or social system) in which one man's pleasure or profit occurs only when someone else directly experiences physical pain and psychological humiliation. I believe that the biological fact and significance of heterosexual rape and pregnancy were primary factors in the formation of the patriarchal family. Also, a primary factor was man's need for proof of his genetic immortality; this need was so great that men felt entitled to colonize a woman's body and savagely limit her freedom in order to ensure that her children were created by his sperm.

For women not to fear rape because we can successfully defend ourselves against it is not anachronistic but revolutionary. For women to be considered as potential warriors (in every sense of the word, *including* its physical representation) is not anachronistic but revolutionary. If realized, it might imply a radical change in modern life.

I may note that men are often allowed more "warriorship" than women, and *without* having to renounce the comforts of companionship, progeny, domesticity, and sexual affection. Still it is hard for men to develop selves or perform political service while they must economically support families. What would it mean for a woman to be a warrior today? How could modern women control the means of production and repro-duction?

THE PROBLEM OF SURVIVAL: POWER AND VIOLENCE

> A time came when some of the people allowed doubt to enter their minds, and they began to wonder whether it was really possible, quantitatively and qualitatively, to resist the occupant's offensives. Was freedom worth the consequences of penetrating into that enormous circuit of terrorism and counter-terrorism? Did this disproportion not express the impossibility of escaping oppression?
>
> Frantz Fanon
> *A Dying Colonialism*[19]

Miracles of consciousness aside, I see no way for women to defeat or transfer patriarchy without achieving power. Unlike male groups, women have little power with which to either avoid or commit violence. Women traditionally are physically weak and politically powerless in a culture that values physical strength and its extended representation in the form of weaponry and money. Women, like men, must be capable of violence or self-defense before their refusal to use violence constitutes a free and moral choice, rather than "making the best of a bad bargain."

Survival is the characteristic property of power. Idealism may or may not, but often does, exist as a luxury for the powerful and as a necessity for the (female) powerless. Powerless or relatively powerless men are not necessarily idealistic, nor are they physically helpless or pacifists. On the contrary. But they *are* forced to perform the male rites of violence against each other, against their will, or at least to their detriment, by more powerful men. They do not survive. Old, wealthy, white American men did not die in Vietnam, in the Gulf War, in Afghanistan, or in Iraq. They sent younger and poorer men to do the job. When *powerless* male groups begin to use violence to gain power, since they are still powerless, most do not *survive* the early battle stages.

However, their violence is often viewed as heroic and courageous by other men and, of course, by many women. Twentieth-century women have personally nurtured, approved of, and impersonally obeyed male nationalist and/or Communist leaders: the reverse has been minimally if ever true. Just as the Catholic Pope, the Islamic mullah, the Jewish rabbi, and the European dictator cannot be women, so it would seem neither can a woman achieve the power and success of a Lenin, Stalin, Ho Chi Minh, Fidel Castro, Mao Tse-tung, or Ahmed Ben Bella.

In Soviet Russia, women comprised less than one percent of the executive Communist leadership from 1958 to 1962. Specifically, of the 306 top Soviet party executives, all but two were women.[20] Krupskaya, Lenin's *wife*, was the Minister of Education, and the novelist Alexandra Kollantai was allowed no more than the ambassadorship to Sweden. Stalin's wife was allowed to kill herself. In China, it was *Mrs.* Mao and *Mrs.* Chou who occupied relatively powerful positions: Mrs. Chou, or Ting-Ying Chao, was the vice president of the All-China Democratic Women's Federation. Despite *Mrs.* Allende's talents, it was her husband who was elected President of Chile. I wonder what position Leila Khaled or Hanan Ashrawi will occupy *after* the successful Palestinians finally accept Israel's longstanding offer of a state? Will she and other women like her suffer the fate of the Algerian women revolutionaries?

In America, it is often said that poor and Third World women are physically and mentally "tougher" than middle-class white women. However, they have not assumed *political leadership* within the middle-class *or* liberation-oriented Third World communities. Neither have Third World women been able to successfully protect themselves or their daughters from the crimes committed against them by both Third World and white men.

While equality, justice, and peace are more ethical and desirable than their opposites, such concepts constitute male (or power) ideals, and not male (or power) practices. Men are generally more verbal about "justice" and "equality" when it applies to abstract or public, global issues (*their* reference sphere); they do not apply such concepts to their personal or family lives—woman's reference sphere. Only feminists have begun to look for "equality" in personal relationships. As a group, many feminists are still as removed from the public reference sphere as are non-feminist women.

Traditionally, the ideal woman avoids committing direct physical violence—and does not practice self-preservation. Psychologically, self-

preservation is precisely what patriarchal society forbids women. Traditionally, the ideal female is trained to "lose" and the ideal male is trained
to "win." And women are trained to mount the sacrificial altar willingly.
For example, most mother-women give up whatever ghost of a unique
and human self they may have when they marry and rear children. Most
children in contemporary American culture invade their mothers' privacy,
life space, sanity, and selves to such an extent that she must give up these
things in order not to commit violence. (Invasion of a boundary into
deserted territory is perhaps less painful than one into occupied and
functional territory. Of course, such invasion is practiced by mothers
against children. Fathers invade children too, but not as frequently. They
don't have to: they already own the entire territory and need only make
occasional forays to check on their holdings.)

> Dr. Christiaan Barnard, South African heart transplant pioneer says he's
> a swinger. Here on a honeymoon trip with his nineteen-year-old bride,
> the forty-seven-year-old Barnard described himself to reporters at
> Kennedy Airport last night as a "doctor who is more open, swinging, and
> can enjoy life, not that sad-looking professor type the public has been
> used to." . . . "I don't know what's going on," Mrs. Barnard told reporters
> when they questioned her.
>
> New York *Post*

> Once Lola Pierotti earned $24,000 a year and worked long hours as an
> administrative assistant on Capitol Hill. Now she works longer hours
> and has even more responsibility—but no pay. What happened? Was
> she demoted? No, she just married the boss. Her bridegroom, of four
> years this month, was the senior Republican Senator from Vermont—
> George D. Aiken. "All he expects of me is that I drive his car, cook his
> meals, do his laundry and run his office," she enumerated, with a grin.
>
> New York *Times*

Women have fewer and fewer sexual, "romantic," and incestuous
options as they grow older. Their "fathers" want younger and younger

women. They have never had access to direct political and economic power at any age. The older a woman is, the more at a "loss" she is. Our culture does not reward enslavement to others as well as it does enslavement to self and to action. Ideally, male enslavement produces male "winners," whose prize is survival as we define it: money, sex, and maternal-like nurturance. Ideally, female enslavement produces female "losers," whose prize of survival is a short-lived one, based on allowance money and some limited sex, received indirectly through a husband-man—from whom maternal-like nurturance is hardly ever received.

It is not that women need men more than men need women; however, perhaps they do. I once asked a group of black and white high school students what they wanted to do when they "grew up"; all females answered in terms of "marriage"; all males answered in terms of achieving some skill, trade, or adventure. I turned to the women and asked them who they had in mind when they thought of marriage—each other? On the contrary, men need women very much, but as relatively interchange-able servants. Of course, poor American men serve in factories and in armies. They directly serve other men and indirectly the female *property* of those men. When poor men fight for wage increases or class revolution, their demands rarely include a doubling of their salary and a new method of payment, one that would reflect the importance of their wives' housework and childrearing. When poor men fight for wage increases it is to equalize some more power among men, and to allow more men to protect and own "their" women and children in better ways.

Women are conditioned to need one man as "irreplaceable." We may recall Farberow's statistics about how many more widows than widowers commit suicide in America.[21] Women are so trained to need a man that even male "losers" can find some woman to take care of them, certainly far more easily than female "winners" can find men or women to care for them. (In this respect, they are really no better off than female "losers.") Women have learned to live without being nurtured for so long that when they experience it they are often guilty, uncomfortable, and frightened.

I suspect that wives are more willing to keep relatively non-violent "mentally ill" husbands at home with them, certainly more than husbands are willing to keep "mentally ill" wives. Wives can still serve and nurture a "lost" and unemployed husband; "lost" wives cannot or will not serve their husbands and, as such, are annoying, inconvenient, threatening, and expendable.

Ideally, men become bigger and better "winners" as they grow older. Their alternatives and choices widen—or are supposed to—as a function of the increase in wealth, wisdom, and power that male aging denotes. Male power, which is based on the oppression of some men and all women, belongs to older men in patriarchal culture. Faced with these circumstances, "good" women destroy themselves gracefully, i.e., they get depressed and stay at home, or go mad and stay in asylums. In either case, they remove themselves from the path of adult male mobility and renewal. "Bad" women aren't good losers; they destroy, or rather attempt to destroy, others. Ophelia in *Hamlet* is a "good" loser; Medea in *Medea* is a "bad" loser.

To those who think I am suggesting that we have a war between the sexes, I say: but we've always had one—and women have always lost it. Women hardly notice this fact because they take "losing" for granted just as men take "winning" for granted. When women question or change what they take for granted, the vision of the sex war we are *already* waging will become clearer. Similarly, it is not a "generation gap" that exists today, so much as a generation war, and one that has always existed. Parents sacrifice their own growth and pleasure for their children's sake: the parental casualties in terms of psychological and physical death are many. The children's casualties are also great: young men are sent by their parents to die in war, young women are sent to die in marriage and motherhood. Child abuse, child molestation, the stifling of creativity and individuality are all generation war statistics. Like the sex war, it is an ancient battle. What is new, however, is the desire to either end the war or turn the "losers" into "winners."

SOME PSYCHOLOGICAL PRESCRIPTIONS FOR THE FUTURE

The women say, truly is this not magnificent? The vessels are upright, the vessels have acquired legs. The sacred vessels are on the move. . . .

The women say, this is a sacrilege, a violation of all the rules . . . must they not hold violence in abhorrence? Is not their structure fragile and will they not shatter at the first onslaught if they are not already in pieces from collision with each other?. . . Stamping the earth, they speed their movements.

Monique Wittig[22]

How can women learn to survive—and learn to value survival? How can women banish self-sacrifice, guilt, naiveté, helplessness, madness, and uncomprehending, self-blaming sorrow from the female condition? How—or should—women sever their ties to childbearing and rearing? Should women *stop* being compassionate? Should or can there be a single standard of behavior for both sexes? Is there such a thing as a biologically rooted female culture that should remain separate from male culture, partly because it is different than or superior to male culture?

Women must convert their love for and reliance on strength and skill in others to a love for all manner of strength and skill in themselves. Women must be able to go as directly to the heart of physical, technological, and intellectual reality as they presumably do to the heart of emotional reality. This requires discipline, courage, confidence, anger, the ability to act, and an overwhelming sense of joy and urgency. Only resourceful women, women with resources, can either share them with other women or use them to accumulate more resources for both themselves and others. Other things being equal, a group composed of resourceful *individuals* who are also pledged, through self-interest, to various ideals or goals is a potentially more powerful group than one composed of less resourceful members with similar ideals. The centuries of female spiritual, political, and sexual sacrifice will be better redeemed by the female entry into humanity and public institutions than by rejecting them because they are not perfect—or because the efforts to integrate them are difficult and heartbreaking—or because they have traditionally been based on the oppression of women. For example, science, religion, language, and psychoanalysis have as often as not been used against women. This does not mean that these modes and institutions—and their "prizes"—must necessarily be sacrificed or discarded as hopelessly tainted. We do not know if women would discover a completely different and better sort of science or language. However, it is clear that women who are feminists must gradually and ultimately *dominate* public and social institutions—so as to ensure that they are not used against women. I say "dominate" because I don't think that "equality" or "individuality" will be possible for women who have never experienced supremacy in public institutions as men have. Feminists may be: communists, socialists, Marxists, anarchists, capitalists, Democrats, Republicans, artists, scientists, nationalists, separatists, integrationists, violently revolutionary, non-violently revolutionary, etc. The point is to have our entire social drama played out as fully by women as by men. And it *is* revolutionary by definition to have women "out of the biological home," both psychologically and actually. Whatever happens *after* that is then a matter for . . . everyone.

I am, of course, implying that child care is a public and crucial concern. I am not implying that any public state method in either capitalist or Communist countries has done very well by children; nor am I implying that specific individuals cannot, under certain conditions, be nurturant to specific children—or people.

But how to do it? What will be necessary psychologically in order for women to finally enter the mainstream of *human* action, to finally have *social* rather than, or other than, soley biological roles?

Woman's primary ego-identity is rooted in a concern for limited and specific others, and for what pleases a few men. Woman's ego-identity must somehow shift and be moored upon what is necessary for her own survival as a strong individual. Women must somehow free themselves to be concerned with many things and ideas, and with many people. Such a radical shift in ego-focus is extremely difficult and very frightening. It grates and screeches against the grain of all "feminine" nerves and feelings, and implies grave retribution. Some women go "mad" when they make such a shift in focus, or when it occurs within them.

Such a shift in the basic female ego (or in the interpretation of female gender identity) implies a frank passion for achieving the power necessary to define oneself—a power which is always predicated on the direct control of worldly realities. Such a passion would do away with such common female behaviors as apologizing for, or disguising to oneself and to others, the concern with one's own survival and growth. From a psychological point of view, as I have noted, it is somewhat irrelevant whether a woman achieves this ego-shift as a "communist" or as a "capitalist"; as a liberal reformer or as a guerrilla in training; as an "individualist" or as a "collectivist"; as a lesbian, a heterosexual, or a bisexual woman; as a biological or non-biological mother or not as a mother. Any woman who successfully becomes interested in and achieves various powers directly, and not through or for a man or a family, is, within the psychological kingdom of patriarchy, committing a radical act, i.e., an act that risks "winning."

Only such a radical psychological act will make it possible for women to tolerate and develop many individual differences, and to follow sexual models other than that of rape-incest-procreation.

Those women involved in such an ego-transformation would, by necessity, withdraw from all human interactions which are not extremely supportive of their survival and achievement of individual power. Other ways of saying this might be: the growth in women of a greater psychological investment in female rather than in male survival, power, and pleasure; women must withdraw from patriarchal hatred of women's bodies and from our addiction to a relationship at any price.

Women whose psychological identities are forged out of concern for their own survival and self-definition, and who withdraw from or avoid any interactions which do not support this formidable endeavor, need not give up their capacity for warmth, emotionality, and nurturance. They do not have to forsake the "wisdom of the heart" and become men. They need only transfer the primary force of their supportiveness to themselves and to each other—but never to the point of self-sacrifice. Women need not stop being tender, compassionate, or concerned with the feelings of others. They must *start* being tender and compassionate with themselves and with other women. Women must begin to "save" themselves and their daughters before they "save" their husbands and their sons; before they "save" the whole world. Women must try to convert the single-minded ruthlessness with which they yearn for, serve, and protect a mate or biological child into the "ruthlessness" of self-preservation and self-development. Perhaps one of the effects of this transfer of affections might be an increase in the male capacity to nurture: themselves, each other, children, and hopefully women. Another effect would be the creation of a secure and revolutionary source of emotional and domestic nurturance for women, without which the courage for survival might falter.

Women need not reject their (usually unsatisfied) need for emotional comfort and affection. They must, in fact, find ways of satisfying these needs without losing their freedom or dignity. The female desire for love should be satisfied in a number of new ways, and as a counterpoint to or respite from events other than those dictated by powerlessness. Affection and sexuality among women must mingle with and mark the events of action and victory, of thought and wisdom.

It is important to realize that the kinds of changes in the female ego I am talking about are *psychological* changes. I am not "prescribing" or predicting any one economic or social form, or any one form of sexual behavior, to ensure such psychological changes. Perhaps the majority of women will be able to effect such psychological changes only after crucial changes in their economic and reproductive lives have already occurred. Perhaps only some young women, perhaps only a minority of all women, will be able to effect such changes through consciousness alone, through the strength of understanding, which, if transformed into wisdom, always means the performance of necessary actions.

THIRTEEN QUESTIONS

What to say to young girls who listen raptly and confidently to the most extreme feminist visions—and laugh, so happily, about them? What odes to write them? What deeds to teach them? What to learn from them? How can the creative impulse be nurtured in women—we, who have forgotten our myths, who have no rituals from which to proceed?

Who will our goddesses and heroines be? In what language shall we address them? How shall we experience divinity as also residing in the female body? When shall we rejoice in the birth of divine daughters, when shall we respect and trust older women? How can we learn to celebrate— not just tolerate—our differences? When will all foolish lies cease between mothers and daughters? How shall we celebrate that day?

Must we choose between the way of the spirit and the way of the sword? Must body and soul remain divided? Are murder and childbirth necessary? How closely are they related? Do women need a women's army? Or do we need an army of wise women? Or both? How shall we, as feminists, practice patience and collective loyalty—precisely when we must practice action and individuality?

Would intense maternal and paternal mothering in childhood lead to wisdom and strength among women? Amazons were probably not "smother-mothered"—or sexually seduced by fathers—as much as they were collectively reared, in peer groups, by many powerful adult women to face human necessity with efficiency and honor.

Are the helplessness and prolonged dependence of human children the models for all *culturally* oppressive relations? Can new methods of childbearing and rearing banish the human tendency to arbitrarily interpret biological differences in oppressive ways?

How can we dismiss all men as "hopeless"—when some of the by-products of power are knowledge, generosity, and likableness? How can we come to terms with this fact? Is it possible for socialized women ever to experience sexual equality with socialized men? Isn't this a contradiction in terms—if public power is still unequally distributed between the sexes?

Must women sever their Maiden's marriage bonds with Eros—until all men have married with Her? Will lesbianism, bisexuality, and homosexuality occur more and more naturally among young people? What will this mean? Will men be able to become more heterosexual just as women are able to become *less* heterosexual? How much will adults already socialized into rigid sex roles be able to partake of such changes? What will happen to us if they can't?

How shall women learn to go beyond an incestuous and procreative model of sexuality?

What does it mean to use or to have one's body, time, and mind used solely for economic profit? How different in meaning is the Nazi use of the human body for industrial purposes, for "profit"—from most labor in capitalist and Communist societies? How does this Nazi practice as metaphor differ from female—or male—prostitution? How shall we redefine work and "human need" in industrial-technological times?

How can we rear male infants to bisexuality—to respect, trust, fear, and love women and men equally? How can we rear female infants to do the same?

When can we stop assigning any significance to biological differences? And if biological differences remain, despite true cultural neutrality, shall we, can we, use science to achieve a single standard of human behavior? Who shall decide what the standards shall be? Who shall teach them, enforce them? And for what purpose? And can a single standard of behavior ever constitute anything more than a background against which more unique or dramatic behaviors can occur?

How shall we come to terms with our bodies and with the natural universe? Many "natural" events—like early death, disease, hardship—are neither desirable nor necessary. (Many "unnatural" events like slavery, monogamy, and pollution are not desirable either.) If male violence and female domesticity are indeed natural, then is it in humanity's interest to channel or banish these predispositions? If not, how may we stop oppressing that which is natural?

How shall we rid ourselves of our ignorance and paranoia about scientific skills? How shall we create a climate in which neither Prometheus nor

Christ is punished for their gifts of knowledge—a climate in which many female givers of knowledge can flourish?

NOTES

CHAPTER ONE

1. Adrienne Rich, "Snapshots of a Daughter-in-law," *Snapshots of a Daughter-in-law: Poems 1954-1962* (New York: W. W. Norton, 1968).

2. Peter Weiss, *Marat/Sade: The Persecution and Assassination of Jean-Paul Marat As Performed by the Inmates of the Asylum of Charenton Under the Direction of the Marquis De Sade* (New York: Atheneum, 1965).

3. Anais Nin, *Cities of the Interior,* distributed by Phoenix Box Shop (New York, 1959).

4. C. Kerenyi, *Eleusis: Archetypal Images of Mother and Daughters,* translated from the German by Ralph Manheim; Bollingen Series LXV, Bollingen Foundation (New York: Pantheon Books, 1967).

5. Lara Jefferson, *These Are My Sisters* (Tulsa: Vickers Publishing Co., 1948).

6. Erich Neumann, *Amor and Psyche: The Psychic Development of the Feminine. A Commentary on the Tale by Apuleius,* translated from the German by Ralph Manheim; Bollingen Series LIV, Bollingen Foundation (New York: Pantheon Books, 1956).

7. Sylvia Plath, *The Bell Jar* (New York: Doubleday, 1971). (Originally published in 1963 by Faber and Faber.)

8. Ludwig Binswanger, "The Case of Ellen West," ed. by Rollo May, in *Existence* (New York: Basic Books, 1958).

9. Ibid.

10. Nancy Milford, *Zelda* (New York: Harper & Row, 1970).

11. Jessie Bernard, "The Paradox of the Happy Marriage" ed. by Vivian Gornick and Barbara K. Moran, in *Woman in Sexist Society: Studies in Power and Powerlessness* (New York: Basic Books, 1971).

12. Elizabeth P. Ware Packard, *Modern Persecution or Insane Asylums Unveiled* and *The Liabilities of the Married Woman* (New York: Pelletreau and Raynor, 1873). These two remarkable volumes were her only source of

income after her "escape" from the asylum and during her legal battle for the rights of mental patients and married women.

13. Charles W. Ferguson, *The Male Attitude* (Boston: Little, Brown, 1966).

14. A. Alvarez, "Sylvia Plath: A Memoir," *New American Review* No. 12 (New York: Simon & Schuster, Inc., 1971).

15. I. J. Singer, "The Dead Fiddler," *The Seance* (New York: Avon, 1964).

16. C. G. Jung and C. Kerenyi, *Essays on a Science of Mythology: The Myth of the Divine Child and the Mysteries of Eleusis,* translated from the German by R. F. C. Hull, 1949 (New York: Bollingen Foundation. Princeton, N.J.: Princeton University Press, 1969); C. Kerenyi, Eleusis: Archetypal Images of Mothers and Daughters, translated from the German by Ralph Manheim; Bollingen Series LXV, Bollingen Foundation (New York: Pantheon Books, 1967); Sir James G. Frazier, *The Golden Bough* (New York: Macmillan, 1958).

17. Simon Dinitz, Russel Dynez, and Alfred Clarke, "Preferences for Male or Female Children: Traditional or Affectional," *Marriage and Family Living,* Vol. 16, May 1954; Alfred Adler, *Understanding Human Nature,* translated by W. Beran Wolfe, 1927 (New York: Fawcett World Library, 1969); Joan D. Mandle, "Women's Liberation: Humanizing Rather than Polarizing," *Annals of the American Academy of Political and Social Science,* September 1971. The history of many royal family "tragedies" in Europe involves the hysterical need for a male rather than a female heir. The Tudor families of Henry VIII in England and the Romanov families of Nicholas in Russia are two well-known examples. I may note that Queen Hatshepsut of ancient Egypt wore male dress and a ceremonial false beard during her reign: royalty and/or divinity are somehow more associated with the male than the female sex. In non-Western and/or pre-Catholic cultures there are, of course, many goddesses. Many are treated by gods in depressingly familiar mortal ways: for example, Zeus's treatment of his wife Hera. Buddha, Shiva, Allah, and Jehovah are most often depicted or thought of as men. It is interesting that the Egyptian god Osiris is a Demeter-Persephone-like male god of earth, vegetation, and rebirth, and that the three most important Egyptian goddesses—Isis, Nephthys, and Hathor—are concerned with "female" provinces: the protection of children, the home, love, happiness, dance, and music.

18. Emma Goldman, "Marriage and Love," *Anarchism and Other Essays* (New York: Dover Publications, Inc., 1969).

19. Judith Bardwick, *The Psychology of Women: A Bio-cultural Conflict* (New

York: Harper & Row, 1971).

20.   Naomi Wesstein, "Psychology Constructs the Female," ed. by Gornick and Moran, in *Woman in Sexist Society: Studies in Power and Powerlessness*, (New York: Basic Books, 1971).

21.   Shulamith Firestone, *The Dialectic of Sex* (New York: William Morrow, 1971).

22.   Neumann, op. cit.

23.   These and other of the myths I've drawn upon are discussed in the following two books, as well as in the books referred to in footnote 16: Helen Diner, *Mothers and Amazons: The First Feminine History of Culture,* edited and translated by J. P. Lundin (New York: Julian Press, 1965). (First published in the 1930s under the pseudonym of "Sir Galahad"); Phillip E. Slater, *The Glory of Hera: Greek Mythology and the Greek Family* (Boston: Beacon Press, 1971).

24.   Slater, op. cit.

25.   Regine Pernoud, *Joan of Arc By Herself and Her Witnesses,* translated from the French by Edward Hyams (London: MacDonald, 1964).

26.   Ibid.

27.   Slater, op. cit.

28.   Jung and Kerenyi, *Essays on a Science of Mythology.*

29.   Ibid.

30.   Virginia Woolf, *A Room of One's Own* (New York: Harcourt, Brace & World, 1929).

CHAPTER TWO

1.   Michel Foucault, *Madness and Civilization: A History of Insanity in the Age of Reason* (1961), translated by Richard Howard (New York: Pantheon, 1965).

2.   Allan M. Dershowitz, "Preventive Detention and the Prediction of Dangerousness. Some Fictions about Predictions," *Journal of Legal Education,* Vol. 23, 1969.

3.   Foucault, op. cit. Thomas S. Szasz, *The Manufacture of Madness* (New York: Harper and Row, 1970); George Rosen, *Madness in Society: Chapters in the Historical Sociology of Mental Illness* (New York: Harper & Row, 1968).

4.   Szasz, op. cit.

5.   Foucault, op. cit.; Thomas S. Szasz, *The Myth of Mental Illness: Foundations of a Theory of Personal Conduct* (New York: Hoeber-Harper, 1961); Erving Goffman, Asylums (New York: Doubleday-Anchor, 1961); T. J. Scheff, Being Mentally Ill: A Sociological Theory (Chicago: Aldine Press, 1966).

6.   Arnold Ludwig, Arnold J. Marx, Phillip A. Hill, and Robert M. Browning, "The Control of Violent Behavior Through Faradic Shock: A Case Study," *Journal of Nervous and Mental Diseases,* Vol. 148, 1969.

7.   C. M. Wignall and C. E. Meredith, "Illegitimate Pregnancies in State Institutions," *Archives of General Psychiatry,* Vol. 18, 1968.

8.   Bruce Dohrenwend and Barbara Dohrenwend, *Social Status and Psychological Disorders* (New York: John Wiley, 1969). Olle Hagnell quotes another theory of conditioned female "patient" behavior made by H. Holter in *A Prospective Study of the Incidence of Mental Disorders: The Lundby Project* (Sweden: Svenska Bokforlaget, 1966).

9.   Jean MacFarlane et al., *A Developmental Study of the Behavior Problems of Normal Children Between Twenty-one Months and Thirteen Years* (Berkeley: University of California Press, 1954); L. Philips, "Cultural vs. Intra Psychic Factors in Childhood Behavior Problem Referrals," *Journal of Clinical Psychology,* Vol. 13, 1957; D. R. Peterson, "Behavior Problems of Middle Childhood," *Journal of Consulting Psychology,* Vol. 95, 1961; L. M. Terman and L. E. Tyler, "Psychological Sex Differences," ed. by L. Carmichael in *Manual of Child Psychology* (New York: John Wiley, 1954).

10.   Leslie Phillips, "A Social View of Psychopathology," ed. by Perry London and David Rosenhan, in *Abnormal Psychology* (New York: Holt, Rinehart and Winston, 1969).

11.   E. Zigler and L. Phillips, "Social Effectiveness and Symptomatic Behaviors," *Journal of Abnormal and Social Psychology,* Vol. 61, 1960.

12.   Szasz, *The Myth of Mental Illness.*

13.   Frederick Engels, *The Origins of the Family, Private Property and the State* (New York: International Publishers, 1942).

14.   Konrad Lorenz, a noted writer on animal behavior, has recently been quoted as saying, "There's only one kind of people at a social disadvantage nowadays—a whole class of people who are treated as slaves and exploited shamelessly—and that's the young wives. They are educated as well as men and the moment they give birth to a baby, they are slaves . . . they have a 22-hour workday, no holidays, and they can't even be ill." Interview, New York *Times,* July 5, 1970.

15.   National Institute of Mental Health Statistics 1965-1968, U. S. Depart-

ment of Health, Education and Welfare; Phyllis Chesler, "Patient and Patriarch: Women in Psychotherapeutic Relationship," ed. by Gornick and Moran, in *Woman in Sexist Society: Studies in Power and Powerlessness* (New York: Basic Books, 1971); Judy Klemesrud, "When the Diagnosis Is Depression" (The Depression Research Unit in New Haven referred to treats mainly women between the ages of 21-65), New York *Times*, May 5, 1971; Lee Burke, E. Renkin, S. Jacobson, S. Haley, "The Depressed Woman Returns," *Archives of General Psychiatry*, Vol. 16, May 1967; Margaret M. Dewar and Iain MacCammend, "Depressive Breakdown in Women of the West Highlands," *American Journal of Psychiatry*, Vol. 119, 1962; Theodore Reich and George Winston, "Postpartum Psychoses in Patients with Manic Depressive Disease," *Journal of Nervous and Mental Disease*, Vol. 151, No. 1, 1970; Pauline Bart, "Portnoy's Mother's Complaint," ed. by Gornick and Moran, in *Woman in Sexist Society*.

16.   Pauline Bart, op. cit.

17.   Earl Pollack, Richard Redick, and Carl Taube, "The Application of Census Socioeconomic and Familial Data to the Study of Morbidity from Mental Disorders," *American Journal of Public Health*, Vol. 58, No. 1, January 1968.

18.   Alfred L. Friedman, "Hostility Factors and Clinical Improvement in Depressed Patients," *Archives of General Psychiatry*, Vol. 23, 1970.

19.   Joan Didion, *Play It As It Lays* (New York: Farrar, Straus & Giroux, 1970).

20.   Alfred L. Kinsey, Wardell B. Pomeroy, Clyde E. Martin, and Paul H. Gebhard, *Sexual Behavior in the Human Female* (Philadelphia: Saunders, 1953); Sigmund Freud, *Female Sexuality* (1931) (New York: Basic Books, 1959); Wilhelm Stekel, *Frigidity in Woman in Relation to Her Love Life* (New York: Washington Square Press, 1954); Karen Horney, *The Neurotic Personality of Our Time* (New York: W. W. Norton, 1967); William Masters and Virginia Johnson, *Human Sexual Response* (Boston: Little, Brown, 1966) and *Human Sexual Inadequacy* (Boston: Little, Brown, 1970).

21.   Masters and Johnson, *Human Sexual Response and Human Sexual Inadequacy*; Jacob Sprenger and Heinrich Kramer, *Malleus Maleficarum*, cited by Thomas S. Szasz in *The Manufacture of Madness*; Mary Jane Sherfoy, "The Evolution and Nature of Female Sexuality in Relation to Psychoanalytic Theory," *Journal of the American Psychoanalytical Association*, 1966.

22.   Sylvia Plath, "Lady Lazarus," *Ariel* (New York: Harper & Row, 1965).

23.   Norman L. Farberow and Edwin F. Schneidman, "Statistical Comparisons Between Attempted and Committed Suicides," *The Cry for Help* (New York: McGraw-Hill, 1965).

24. Richard H. Sieden, *Suicide Among Youth*. Prepared for the Joint Commission on Mental Health of Children, 1970.

25. Shirley Angrist, Simon Dinitz, Mark Lefton, Benjamin Pasamanick, "Rehospitalization of Female Mental Patients," *Archives of American Psychiatry*, Vol. 4, 1961. Her patient sample was drawn from state and private hospitals, and included people released after 1957. Her original intention was to compare the parents of "schizophrenics" with those of "normals."

26. Shirley Angrist, Simon Dinitz, Mark Lefton, Benjamin Pasamanick, *Women After Treatment* (New York: Appleton-Century-Crofts, 1968).

27. Frances Cheek, "A Serendipitous Finding: Sex Role and Schizophrenia," *Journal of Abnormal and Social Psychology*, Vol. 69, No. 4, 1964.

28. M. Letailleur, J. Morin, and Y. Le Borgne, "Heautoscopie Hetersexuelle et Schizophrenie [The Self-Induced Heterosexual Image and Schizophrenia]," *Ann. Med. Psychology*, Vol. 2, 1958.

29. David C. McClelland and Norman F. Watt, "Sex Role Alienation in Schizophrenia," *Journal of Abnormal Psychology*, Vol. 73, No. 3, 1968. The sample was drawn from a Boston hospital, and involved people who were hospitalized from one to twenty years. All groups were matched for age, education, and class

30. Ibid.

31. M. Lorr and C. J. Klett, "Constancy of Psychotic Syndromes in Men and Women," *Journal of Consulting Psychology*, Vol. 29, No. 5, 1969.

32. M. Lorr, J. P. O'Connor, and J. W. Stafford, "The Psychotic Reaction Profile," *Journal of Clinical Psychology*, Vol. 16, 1960.

33. Jonas Rappoport, *The Clinical Evaluation of the Dangerousness of the Mentally Ill*, (Springfield, Illinois: Charles Thomas, 1968.)

34. Alan M. Kraft, Paul R. Binner, Brenda Dickey, "The Community Mental Health Program and the Longer-Stay Patient," *Archives of General Psychiatry*, Vol. 6, January 1967.

35. Carl A. Taube, "Admission Rates by Marital Status: Outpatient Psychiatric Services," *Statistical Note 35*, Survey and Reports Section, *National Institute of Mental Health*, December 1970.

36. Marcel Saghir, Bonnie Walbran, Eli Robins, Kathy Gentry, "Psychiatric Disorders and Disability in the Female Homosexual," *American Journal of Psychiatry*, Vol. 27, 1970; Charlotte Wolff, *Love Between Women* (U.K.: St. Martins Press, 1971).

CHAPTER THREE

1.   Ilse Ollendorff Reich, *Wilhelm Reich: A Personal Biography* (New York: St. Martins, 1969).

2.   Paul Roazan, *Brother Animal* (New York: Knopf, 1969).

3.   Shulamith Firestone, *The Dialectic of Sex, The Case for Feminist Revolution* (New York: William Morrow and Co., 1970).

4.   Juliet Mitchell, *Woman's Estate* (New York: Pantheon Books, 1971).

5.   Kate Millett, *Sexual Politics* (New York: Doubleday & Co., 1970).

6.   Evelyn P. Ivey, "Significance of the Sex of the Psychiatrist," *Archives of General Psychiatry*, Vol. 2, 1960; William Schofield, *Psychotherapy: The Purchase of Friendship* (Englewood Cliffs, N.J.: Prentice-Hall, 1963); Phyllis Chesler, unpublished study, 1971.

7.   Carl A. Taube, "Transitional Mental Health Facilities Staffing Patterns," *Statistical Note 28*, NIMH Survey and Reports Section, October 1970.

8.   Carl A. Taube, "Consultation and Education Services in Community Mental Health Centers—January 1970," *Statistical Note 3*, NIMH Survey and Reports Section, February 1971.

9.   Phyllis Chesler, "Patient and Patriarch: Women in the Psychotherapeutic Relationship," ed. by Vivian Gornick and Barbara K. Moran, *Woman in Sexist Society: Studies in Power and Powerlessness* (New York: Basic Books, 1971).

10. Schofield, op. cit.

11. Matina Homer, "Fail: Bright Women," *Psychology Today*, November 1969.

12. Maurice K Temerlin, "Suggestion Effects in Psychiatric Diagnosis," *Journal of Nervous and Mental Disease*, Vol. 47, 1968.

13. Inge K. Broverman, Donald M. Broverman, Frank E. Clarkson, Paul S. Rosenkrantz, Susan R. Vogel, "Sex Role Stereotypes and Clinical Judgements of Mental Health," *Journal of Consulting and Clinical Psychology*, Vol. 34, 1970.

14. W. R. Orr, Ruth Anderson, Margaret Martin Des. F. Philpot, "Factors Influencing Discharge of Female Patients from a State Mental Hospital," *American Journal of Psychiatry*, Vol. 3, 1954.

15. Nathan K. Rickel, "The Angry Woman Syndrome," *Archives of General Psychiatry*, Vol. 24, 1971.

16. Herbert C. Modlin, "Psychodynamics in the Management of Paranoid States in Women," *General Psychiatry*, 1963.

17. Judith Bardwick, *Psychology of Women: A Bio-cultural Conflict* (New York:

Harper & Row, 1971).

18.   Mary Jane Sherfey, "The Evolution and Nature of Female Sexuality in Relation to Psychoanalytic Theory," *Journal of the American Psychoanalytical Association,* 1966.

19.   Judith Bardwick, *Psychology of Women: A Bio-cultural Conflict* (New York: Harper & Row, 1971).

20.   Joseph Rheingold, *The Mother, Anxiety and Death* (Boston: Little, Brown, 1967).

21.   Carl P. Malmquist, Thomas J. Kiresuk, Robert M. Spano, "Personality Characteristics of Women with Repeated Illegitimacies: Descriptive Aspects," *American Journal of Orthopsychiatry,* Vol. 35, 1966; Oscar B. Markey, "A Study of Aggressive Set Misbehavior in Adolescents Brought to Juvenile Court," *Journal of Orthopsychiatry,* Vol. 20, 1950; Kathryn M. Nielson, Rocco L. Motto, "Some Observations on Family Constellations and Personality Patterns of Young Unmarried Mothers," *American Journal of Orthopsychiatry,* Vol. 33, 1963; Irving Kaufman, Elizabeth S. Makkay, Joan Zilbach, "The Impact of Adolescence of Girls with Delinquent Character Formation," *Journal of Orthopsychiatry,* Vol. 29, 1959; Paul A. Walters, Jr., "Promiscuity in Adolescence," *American Journal of Orthopsychiatry,* 1965; Ames Robey, Richard J. Rosenwald, John E. Snell, Rita E. Lee, "The Runaway Girl: A Reaction to Family Stress," *American Journal of Orthopsychiatry,* March 9, 1964.

22.   Captain Noel Lustig, MC, USA; Captain John Dresser, MCS, USA; Major Seth W. Spellman, MCS, USA; Major Thomas B. Murray, MC, USA; "Incest," *Archives of General Psychiatry,* Vol. 14, January 1966; Irving Kaufman, Alice L. Peck, Consuelo K. Tagiuri, "The Family Constellation and Overt Incestuous Relations Between Father and Daughter," *Journal of Orthopsychiatry,* Vol. 24, 1954; Sol Chaneles, "Sexual Abuse of Children," The American Humane Association, Children's Division, 1966; Vincent de Francis, "Protecting the Child Victim of Sex Crimes Committed by Adults," The American Humane Association, Children's Division, 1966; Lindy Burton, *Vulnerable Children* (New York: Schocken Books, 1968); Yvonne Tormes, "Child Victim of Incest" The American Humane Association, Children's Division, 1966; David Gil, *Violence Against Children* (Waltham: Harvard University Press, 1970); Florence Rush, "The Sexual Abuse of Children: A Feminist Point of View," New York Radical Feminists Conference on Rape, April 17, 1971; Harry Nelson, "Incest: 1 Family out of 10," New York *Post,* September 1971.

23. Charles William Wahl, "The Psychodynamics of Consummated Maternal Incest: A Report of Two Cases," *Archives of General Psychiatry*, Vol. 3, 1960.

24. Harold Greenwald, *The Elegant Prostitute* (New York: Ballantine Books, 1958).

25. Sigmund Freud, "Some Psychological Consequences of the Anatomical Distinction Between Sexes," *Collected Papers*, Vol. 5 (London: Hogarth Press, 1956).

26. Sigmund Freud, *New Introductory Lectures in Psychoanalysis* (New York: W. W. Norton, 1933).

27. Erik H. Erikson, "Inner and Outer Space: Reflections on Womanhood," *Daedalus*, Vol. 3, 1965.

28. Bruno Bettelheim, "The Commitment Required of a Woman Entering a Scientific Profession in Present Day American Society" in *Woman and the Scientific Professions*, M. I. T. Symposium on American Women in Science and Engineering, Cambridge, Mass., 1965.

29. Joseph Rheingold, *The Fear of Being a Woman* (New York: Grune and Stratton, 1964).

30. Carl G. Jung, *Contributions to Analytical Psychology* (New York: Harcourt, Brace, 1928).

31. M. Esther Harding, *The Way of All Women* (New York: Longmans, Green, 1933).

32. Sigmund Freud, *Case of Dora: An Analysis of a Case Hysteria* (New York: W. W. Norton, 1952).

33. Leonard Simon, "The Political Unconscious of Psychology: Clinical Psychology and Social Change," unpublished manuscript, 1970.

34. Felix Duetsch, "A Footnote to Freud's 'Fragment of an Analysis of a Case of Hysteria,'" *The Psychoanalytic Quarterly*, Vol. 25, 1957.

35. Thomas S. Szasz, *The Myth of Mental Illness: Foundations of a Theory of Personal Conduct* (New York: Hoeber-Harper, 1961).

36. Karen Horney, "The Flight from Womanhood," ed. by H. Kelman in *Feminine Psychology* (New York: W. W. Norton, 1967).

37. Sigmund Freud, "Female Sexuality" (1931) *Collected Papers*, Vol. 4 (New York: Basic Books, 1959).

38. Ilse Ollendorff Reich, *Wilhelm Reich: A Personal Biography* (New York: St. Martins, 1969).

39. Wilhelm Reich, *The Function of the Orgasm: The Discovery of the Orgone* (New York: Farrar, Straus & Giroux, 1942).

40. Ronald D. Laing and A. Esterson, *Sanity, Madness and the Family* (New York: Pelican Book, 1970).

41. David Cooper, *The Death of the Family* (New York: Pantheon Books, 1970).

42. Thomas S. Szasz, *The Manufacture of Madness* (New York: Harper & Row, 1970).

43. Jules Michelet, *Satanism and Witchcraft: A Study in Medieval Superstition* (Toronto: Citadel Press, 1939).

44. Una Stannard, "The Male Maternal Instinct," *Trans-action,* December 1970.

45. Sigmund Freud, "On the History of the Psychoanalytic Movement," *Collected Papers (1914) Vol. I* (New York: Basic Books, 1959).

46. Thomas S. Szasz, *The Myth of Mental Illness: Foundations of a Theory of Personal Conduct* (New York: Hoeber-Harper, 1961).

47. William Schofield, *Psychotherapy: The Purchase of Friendship* (Englewood Cliffs, N.J.: Prentice-Hall, 1963).

CHAPTER FOUR

1. Judith Bardwick, *The Psychology of Women: A Bio-cultural Conflict* (New York: Harper & Row, 1971).

2. "Selected Symptoms of Psychological Distress," U. S. Department of Health, Education and Welfare, Public Health Services and Mental Health Administration, 1970. This study is based on data collected in 1960-62 from a probability sample of 7,710 persons selected to represent the 111 million adults in the U. S. non-institutional population, aged eighteen to seventy-nine.

3. Gerald Gurin, J. Veroff, and S. Feld, *Americans View Their Mental Health* (New York: Basic Books, 1960).

4. Leo Srole, Thomas S. Langner, Stanley T. Michael, Mervin K. Opler, Thomas A. C. Rennie, *Mental Health in the Metropolis: Midtown Manhattan Study* (New York: McGraw-Hill, 1962).

5. Dorothy C. Leighton, John S. Harding, David B. Machlin, Allister M. Macmillan, Alexander H. Leighton, *The Character of Danger: The Stirling County Study of Psychiatric Disorder and Sociocultural Environment, Vol. III* (New York-London: Basic Books, 1963).

6. Olle Hagnell, *A Prospective Study of the Incidence of Mental Disorders: The Lundby Project* (Sweden: Svenska Bokforlaget, 1966).

7. Phyllis Chesler, "Patient and Patriarch: Women in the Psychotherapeutic Relationship," ed. by Vivian Gornick and Barbara K. Moran, in *Woman in Sexist Society: Studies in Power and Powerlessness* (New York: Basic Books, 1971); Hagnell, op. cit., Leighton, et al., op. cit.; Edwin Zolik, Edna Lantz, Richard Sommers, "Hospital Return Rates and Prerelease Referrals," *Archives of General Psychiatry,* Vol. 18, June 1968; "Chronic Illness in a Large City," *The Baltimore Study* (1957); Anita K. Bahn, Margaret Conwell, and Peter Hurley, "Survey of Psychiatric Practice: Report on a Field Test," *Archives of General Psychiatry,* Vol. 12, 1965; William Ryan, *Distress in the City: Essay on the Design and Administration of Mental Health Services* (Cleveland: The Press of Case Western Reserve University, 1969); Charles Thrall, "Presenting Problems of Psychiatric Out-Patients: Out-Patient Studies Section," Biometrics Branch, NIMH, 1963; Richard Redick, "Age-Sex Diagnostic Distribution of Additions to Community Mental Health Centers 1968," *Statistical Note 13,* NIMH Survey and Reports Section, January 1970; William Schofield, *Psychotherapy: The Purchase of Friendship* (Englewood Cliffs, N. J.: Prentice-Hall, 1963); Alan M. Kraft, Paul R. Binner, Brenda Dickey, "The Community Mental Health Program and the Longer-Stay Patient," *Archives of General Psychiatry,* Vol 16, January 1967; Gerald Landsberg, David Cole, Eleanor Sabbagh, Rachel Deutsch, "Characteristics of Enrolled Patients as of September 1969," Maimonides Medical Center, Community Mental Health Center, December 1969; Rachel Deutsch, Gerald Landsberg, David Cole, "Report of a Survey of Patients: January 17, 1970–June 16, 1970," Maimonides Medical Center, Community Mental Health Center, June 1970; Phyllis Chesler, Janice Lasecki, Lucy DiPaola, unpublished manuscript, 1971.

8. Kraft et al., op. cit.; Hagnell, op. cit.; Charles Thrall, "Presenting Problems of Psychiatric Out-Patients," Out-Patients Studies Section, Biometrics Branch, NIMH, 1963; Kurt Gurwitz, Anita Bahn, Gerald Klee, and Murray Solomon, "Release and Return Rates of Patients in State Mental Hospitals of Maryland," *Public Health Reports,* Vol. I, 1966.

9. Kraft et al., op. cit.; Provisional Data on Length of Stay of Admissions to State and County Mental Hospitals U. S., NIMH, 1971.

10. Charles Kadushin, *Why People Go to Psychiatrists* (New York: Atherton Press, 1969).

CHAPTER FIVE

1.   Fernando Enriquez, *Prostitution and Society: Primitive, Classical and Oriental* (New York: Grove Press, 1962); Emma Goldman, "The Traffic in Women," reprinted in *Anarchism and Other Essays* (New York: Dover, 1969); Harold Greenwald, *The Elegant Prostitute: A Social and Psychoanalytic Study* (New York: Ballantine Books, 1958); Steven Marcus, *The Other Victorians* (New York: Basic Books, 1964); Kate Millett, *Sexual Politics* (New York: Doubleday, 1971); W. W. Sanger, *The History of Prostitution* (New York: Eugenics Publishing, 1937); Charles Winick and Paul M. Kinsie, *The Lively Commerce* (Chicago: Quadrangle Books, 1971); Eric Pace, "Feminists Halt Session on Prostitution, Demanding To Be Heard," New York *Times,* September 15, 1971; Robert Prosser, "The Speedy Call Girls in Formosa," San Francisco *Chronicle,* December 23, 1970; "Russia's Bedroom Blackmail," San Francisco *Chronicle,* December 28, 1970; Jim Brewer, "San Francisco Child Prostitutes," San Francisco *Chronicle,* May 9, 1970; David Sanford, "A Brothel in Curacao," *Village Voice,* March 13, 1969; Ernest Lenn, "State Crackdown on B-Girls, Vice," San Francisco *Examiner* and *Chronicle,* July 13, 1969; "Aimed at Prostitutes, the Loitering Law Is Voided," New York *Post,* September 14, 1970; "Straw Judge Is Ordered Ousted Over His Arrest in a Vice Raid," New York *Times,* November 24, 1970; "Prostitutes—Some New Tricks for the Oldest Profession," New York *Times,* March 28, 1971.

2.   Uniform Crime Reports 1960-1970; Rosalyn Lacks, "The Politics of Rape—A Selective History," *Village Voice,* February 4, 1971; New York Radical Feminist Conference on Rape, April 17, 1971; *Female Liberation Newsletter #8,* April 16, 1971; "Women Who Are Tired of Being Harassed," New York *Times,* September 7, 1971; "The Civilized Rapist," *Village Voice,* September 9, 1971; "Cops Use TV to Trap Rape Suspect," New York *Daily News,* March 19, 1971; Gloria Emerson, "Vietnamese Voice Hostility to G. I.s," New York *Times,* May 2, 1971; "Bronx School Posts 2 Guards after Attacks on Teachers," New York *Post,* May 6, 1971.

3.   Captain Noel Lustig, MC, USA; Captain John Dresser, MCS, USA; Major Seth W. Spellman, MCS, USA; Major Thomas B. Murray, MC, USA; "Incest," *Archives of General Psychiatry,* Vol. 14, January 1966; Irving Kaufman, Alice L. Peck, Consuelo K. Tagiuri, "The Family Constellation and Overt Incestuous Relations Between Father and Daughter," *Journal of Orthopsychiatry,* Vol. 24, 1954; Sol Chaneles, "Sexual Abuse of Children,"

The American Humane Association, Children's Division, 1966; Vincent de Francis, "Protecting the Child Victim of Sex Crimes Committed by Adults," The American Humane Association, Children's Division, 1966; Lindy Burton, *Vulnerable Children* (New York: Schocken Books, 1968); Yvonne Tormes, "Child Victim of Incest," The American Humane Association, Children's Division, 1966; David Gil, *Violence Against Children* (Waltham: Harvard University Press, 1970); Florence Rush, "The Sexual Abuse of Children: A Feminist Point of View," New York Radical Feminist Conference on Rape, April 17, 1971; Harry Nelson, "Incest: 1 Family Out of 10," New York *Post,* September 1971; George Carpozi, Jr., "Seize Dad, Daughter in Nudie Case," New York *Post,* May 6, 1971.

4. Conrad Van Emde Boas in his article "The Doctor-Patient Relationship" (Journal of Sex Research, Vol. 2, No. 3, November 1966) says: "In my own practice—largely psycho-therapeutical and sexuological—I have noticed that the frequency of this kind of officially frowned upon relationship varies within the different branches of the medical profession. Gynecologists offer the most frequent targets. Second on the list are dentists and family doctors. But let me add immediately that psychotherapists, too, are not far behind, according to the 'statistics'—obviously limited and incomplete—which I have compiled from my own observations."

5. Boas, op. cit.; Charles C. Dahlberg, "Sexual Contact Between Patient and Therapist," *Contemporary Psychoanalysis,* Spring 1970; Judd Marmor, "The Seductive Therapist," *Psychiatry Digest,* October 1970; William Masters and Virginia Johnson, *Human Sexual Response* (Boston: Little, Brown, 1966); William Masters and Virginia Johnson, *Human Sexual Inadequacy* (Boston: Little, Brown, 1970); James L. McCartney, "Overt Transference," *Journal of Sexual Research,* Vol. 2, No. 3, November 1966; Leon J. Saul, "The Erotic Transference," *Psychoanalytic Quarterly,* Vol. 31, 1962; Martin Shepard, *The Love Treatment: Sexual Intimacy Between Patients and Psychotherapists* (New York: Peter H. Wyden, 1971); Arthur J. Snider, "One Analyst's Touching Tale," New York *Post,* November 17, 1969.

6. Louis Lewis, "Psychotherapeutic Malpractice," unpublished manuscript, 1971; William Greaves and Leo Standore, "Secretary Sues Analyst for Sexual Malpractice," New York *Post,* April 1971.

7. Paul Roazen, *Brother Animal* (New York: Knopf, 1969).

8. Marmor, op. cit.

9. McCartney, op. cit.

10. Marmor, op. cit.

11.   Saul, op. cit.

12.   Dahlberg, op. cit.; Marmor, op. cit.; McCartney, op. cit.

13.   Dahlberg, op. cit.; Frieda Fromm-Reichman, *Principles of Intensive Psycho-therapy* (Chicago: University of Chicago Press, 1950); Clara Thompson, "A Critical Incident in Psychotherapy," *Interpersonal Psychoanalysis* (London: Basic Books, 1964).

14.   Dahlberg, op. cit.

15.   McCartney, op. cit.

16.   Dahlberg, op. cit.

17.   Roazen, op. cit.

CHAPTER SIX

1.   Allan M. Dershowitz, "Preventive Detention and the Prediction of Dangerousness. Some Fictions About Predictions." *Journal of Legal Education,* Vol. 23, 1969.

2. $40,000 Damages Awarded Against Psychiatrist. *Stowers v. Wolodzko.* Supreme Court of Michigan, November 9, 1971. *The Mental Health Court Digest,* Vol. 15, No. 8, February 1972.

CHAPTER SEVEN

1.   J. J. Bachofen, *Myth, Religion and Mother Right,* translated by Ralph Manheim, 1926, Bollingen Series LXXXIV (Princeton, N.J.: Princeton University Press, 1967).

2.   Gilbert D. Bartell, *Group Sex* (New York: Peter H. Wyden, 1971).

3.   Charlotte Wolff, *Love Between Women* (New York: St. Martins, 1971).

4.   Alfred C. Kinsey, Wardell B. Pomeroy, Clyde E. Martin, Paul H. Gebhard, *Sexual Behavior in the Female* (New York: Pocket Books, 1953).

5.   Hubert Selby, Jr., "The Queen Is Dead," *Last Exit to Brooklyn* (New York: Grove Press, Inc., 1957).

6.   Marcel Saghir, Eli Robins, Bonnie Walbran, and Kathy Gentry, "Homosexuality IV: Psychiatric Disorders and Disability in the Female Homosexual," *American Journal of Psychiatry,* Vol. 27, 1970; Wolff, op. cit.

CHAPTER EIGHT

1. Nancy Henley, "On Sexism and Racism, A resource paper published as part of the Report of the Sub-Committee on Women of the Committee on Equal Opportunity in Psychology, February 1971.

2. Toni Morrison, "What the Black Women Think About Women's Lib." New York *Times Magazine*, August 22, 1971.

3. Frances Beale, "Double Jeopardy: To Be Black and Female," ed. by Toni Cade, in *The Black Woman: An Anthology* (New York: New American Library, 1970).

4. Joanna Clark, "Motherhood" in *The Black Woman: An Anthology*, op. cit.

5. Barbara Burris in agreement with Kathy Barry, Terry Moon, Joann DeLor, Joann Parenti, Cate Stadelman, *The Fourth World Manifesto: An Angry Response To An Imperialist Venture Against The Women's Liberation Movement* (New Haven: Advocate Press, January 13, 1971).

6. Frantz Fanon, *A Dying Colonialism*, translated from the French by Haakon Chevalier (New York: Grove Press, 1965). Originally published in France as L' An Cinq de la Revolution Algerienne, 1959, by François Maspero.

7. Barbara Burris et al., op. cit.

8. Abram Kardiner, M. D., and Lionel Ovesey, M. D., *The Mark of Oppression* (Cleveland: Meridian Books, The World Publishing Co., May 1967).

9. Daniel P. Moynihan, "Moynihan Report and the Politics of Controversy," a Trans-action Social Science and Public Policy Report (Cambridge, Mass.: M. I. T. Press, 1967).

10. William H. Grier and Price M. Cobbs, *Black Rage* (New York: Basic Books, 1968).

11. Nancy Henley, op. cit.

12. Herbert Gross, Myra Herbert, Genell Knatterud, Lawrence Donner, "The Effect of Race and Sex on the Variation of Diagnosis in a Psychiatric Emergency Room," *Journal of Nervous and Mental Disease,* Vol. 148, No. 6, 1969; Carl A. Taube, "Differential Utilization of Out-Patient Psychiatric Services by Whites and Nonwhites, 1969," *Statistical Note 36*, NIMH Survey and Reports Section, December 1970; Carl A. Taube, "Admission Rates to State and County Mental Hospitals by Age, Sex and Color, 1969," *Statistical Note 41*, NIMH Survey and Reports Section, February 1971; Earl S. Pollack, Richard Redick, Carl A. Taube, "The Application of Census Socioeconomic and Familial Data to the Study of Morbidity from

Mental Disorders," *American Journal of Public Health,* Vol. 58, No. I, 1968.

13. "Selected Symptoms of Psychological Distress," U. S. Department of Health, Education and Welfare, Public Health Services and Mental Health Administration, 1970.

14. Martha Weinman Lear, "Q: If You Rape a Woman and Steal Her TV, What Can They Get You for in NY? A: Stealing Her TV," New York *Times Magazine,* January 30, 1972.

CHAPTER NINE

1. Margaret Fuller, "The Great Lawsuit—Man versus Men; Woman versus Women," *The Dial,* July 1843. Reprinted in *Margaret Fuller: American Romantic. A Selection from Her Writings and Correspondence.* Edited by Perry Miller (Ithaca, N. Y.: Cornell University Press, 1963).

2. Ibid.

3. Emma Goldman, "The Traffic in Women," in *Anarchism and Other Essays.* Introduction by Richard Prinnon (New York: Dover Publications, 1970). Also reprinted in *Red Emma Speaks: Selected Writings and Speeches by Emma Goldman.* Compiled and edited (and beautifully introduced) by Alix Kates Shulman. (New York: Vintage Books, Random House, 1972).

4. Emma Goldman, "Woman Suffrage," in *Anarchism and Other Essays,* op. cit.

CHAPTER TEN

1. Monique Wittig, *Les Guerilleres,* translated from the French by David Le Vay (New York: The Viking Press, 1971).

2. Ibid.

3. C. G. Jung and C. Kerenyi, *Essays on a Science of Mythology: The Myth of the Divine Child and the Mysteries of Eleusis,* Bollingen Series XXII, translated from the German by R. F. C. Hull (Princeton, N. J.: Princeton University Press, 1949); Sir James Frazier, *The Golden Bough* (New York: Macmillan, 1958); C. Kerenyi, *Eleusis: Archetypal Image of Mother and Daughter,* translated from the German by Ralph Manheim, Bollingen Series LXV (New York: Pantheon Books, Random House, 1967).

4. Erich Neumann, *Amor and Psyche: The Psychic Development of the Feminine. A Commentary on the Tale by Apuleius,* translated from the German

by Ralph Manheim, Bollingen Series LIV (New York: Pantheon Books, 1956).

5. Margaret Adams, "The Compassion Trap," *Psychology Today,* Vol. 5, No. 6, November 1971.

6. Emma Goldman, "Minorities versus Majorities" reprinted in *Anarchism and Other Essays, introduction by Richard Drinnon* (New York: Dover Publications, Inc., 1970).

7. Paul Goodman, "On Society, the Young, and Sex," *Psychology Today,* Vol. 5, No. 6, November 1971.

8. Anselma dell'Olio, unpublished manuscript.

9. Juliet Mitchell, *Woman's Estate* (New York: Pantheon Books, Random House, 1971).

10. Ibid.

11. Wittig, op. cit.

12. Helen Diner, *Mothers and Amazons: The First Feminine History of Culture,* edited and translated by J. P. Lundin (New York: Julian Press, 1965). (First published in the 1930s under the pseudonym of "Sir Galahad.")

13. Ibid.

14. Ibid.

15. Ibid.

16. Ibid.

17. Frazier, op. cit., 1958; Sigmund Freud, "Contributions to the Psychology of Love: The Taboo of Virginity," *Collected Papers,* Vol. 4 (1918) (New York: Basic Books, 1959).

18. Robert Briffault, *The Mothers* (New York: Grosset and Dunlap, 1927); Bachofen, Das Mutteracht, cited by Diner, op. cit.; Frazier, op. cit.; J. F. Lafitau, *Moeurs de Sauvages Américains Compares aux Moeurs des Premiers Temps* (Paris: 1724); Matthew Paris, *Chronica Magna* (Chronicles and Memorials of Great Britain and Ireland), ed. by S. Henry Richards Luard, 7 Vols. (London: 1872-83); Nancy Reeves, *Womankind* (Chicago: Aldine, Atherton, 1971). Jesco von Puttkamer and Altair Sales have recently discovered caves in Brazil they believe were inhabited by Amazon warriors (*Time* magazine, December 27, 1971).

19. Frantz Fanon, *A Dying Colonialism,* translated by Haakon Chevalier (New York: Grove Press, Inc., 1965). Originally published in France as *L' An Cinq de la Révolution Algérienne,* 1959, by Francois Maspero.

20. George Fischer, *The Soviet System and Modern Society* (Chicago: Aldine-Atherton, 1968) .

21. Norman L. Farberow and Edwin F. Schneidman, *The Cry for Help* (New York: McGraw-Hill, 1965).

22. Wittig, op. cit.

BIBLIOGRAPHY

My generation knew nothing of the rich psychoanalytic and radical feminist literature that preceded *Women and Madness* by more than a century. Much of the feminist literature of my Second Wave generation was "lost" by the 1980s. I have included some of it here. As you read this, please remember that many of the classic feminist works with which you may be most familiar were all preceded by the most amazing and exciting speeches, pamphlets, journals, articles, and books, many of which have since been forgotten.

The works in this bibliography are alphabetized according to author within each seven-year period. Please note that certain lesser known books often precede a later, more visible work by anywhere from one to five years.

Dear Reader: You may consider using parts of this bibliography as a core curriculum. I have now added the most important, evolving work in terms of the many feminist approaches to female and male psychology and psychotherapy.

CLASSICAL GREEK

Aeschylus. *The Agamemnon*; *The Libation Bearers*; *The Eumenides*. (458 BCE). Trans. David Grene and Richmond Lattimore. Chicago and London: University of Chicago Press, 1953.

Euripides II. *Iphighenia in Taurus*; *Helen*. (414-412 BCE). Trans. Richmond Lattimore. Phoenix Books. Chicago and London: University of Chicago Press, 1952.

Euripides V. *Electra*. (414-410 BCE). Trans. Emily Townsend Vermeule. Ed. David Grene and Richmond Lattimore. Chicago: University of Chicago Press, 1957.

Sophocles II. *Electra and Philoctetes*. (420-410 BCE). Trans. David Grene. Ed. David Grene and Richmond Lattimore. Chicago and London: University of Chicago Press, 1957.

FIFTEENTH–MID-TWENTIETH CENTURY

Adler, Alfred. *Individual Psychology*. Paterson, NJ: Littlefield Adams & Co, 1963; originally published 1925.

———. *Understanding Human Nature*. New York: Fawcett Premier Publishing, 1927.

de Beauvoir, Simone. *The Second Sex*. New York: Vintage Books, 1989; originally published 1949.

Binswanger, Ludwig. "The Case of Ellen West." In *In Existence*. Trans. Werner M. Mendel and Joseph Lyone. Ed. Rollo May, Ernest Angel, and Henri F. Ellenberger. New York: Basic, 1958, pp. 237-364.

Briffault, Robert. *The Mothers: The Matriarchal Theory of Social Origins*. Ed. Gordon Rattray Taylor. 3 Vols. New York: H. Fertig, 1993; originally published 1931.

Diner, Helen. *Mothers and Amazons*. Ed. and trans. John Philip Lundin. New York: Julian Press, 1965; originally published in the 1930s under the pen name Sir Galahad.

Freud, Sigmund. *Civilization and Its Discontents*. New York: W. W. Norton & Company, 1962; originally published 1929.

———. *Collected Papers: Volumes I-V*. New York: Basic Books, 1959; originally published from 1888-1938.

———. *Moses and Monotheism*. New York: Vintage Books, 1939.

———. *The Basic Writings of Sigmund Freud*. Ed. and trans. Dr. A. A. Brill. New York: The Modern Library, 1938.

Gilman, Charlotte Perkins. *"The Yellow Wallpaper" and Other Stories*. Old Westbury, NY: The Feminist Press, 1973; originally published 1892.

———. *The Living of Charlotte Perkins Gilman. An Autobiography*. New York: Arno Press, 1972; originally published 1935.

Goldman, Emma. *Living My Life*. 2 vols. New York: Dover Publications, 1970; originally published 1931.

Horney, Karen. *Feminine Psychology*. New York: W. W. Norton & Co., 1967; originally published from 1922–1937.

Jung, C. G. *Modern Man In Search of a Soul*. London: Kegan Paul Trench Trubner (1955 ed. Harvest Books ISBN 0156612062; originally published 1933.

———. *The Archetypes and the Collective Unconscious*. Princeton, NJ: Bollingen, 1981; 2nd ed. Collected Works Vol. 9, Part 1. ISBN 0691018332; originally published from 1934–1954.

Jung, Carl G. *Two Essays on Analytical Psychology*. London: Routledge, 1966; revised 2nd ed. Collected Works Vol. 7; originally published 1917, 1928.

Klein, Melanie. *Contributions to Psychoanalysis*. London: Hogarth Press and The Institute of Psycho-Analysis, 1948; originally published from 1921–1945.

———. *Envy and Gratitude & Other Works*. New York: Dell Publishing Company, 1975; originally published 1946–1963.

Mill, John Stuart. *The Subjection of Women*. Mineola, New York: Dover Publications, 1997; originally published 1869.

de Pisan, Christine. *The Book of the City of Ladies*. Trans. Earl Jeffrey Richards. New York: Persea Books, 1983; originally published 1400.

Plath, Sylvia. *The Bell Jar*. New York: Harper & Row, 1971; originally published 1963.

Winnicott, Donald W. *Collected Papers: Through Paediatrics to Psychoanalysis*. London: Tavistock; New York: Basic Books, 1958; London: Hogarth Press and Institute of PSA, 1975; London: Institute of PSA and Karnac Books, 1992; Brunner/Mazel, 1992.

Wollstonecraft, Mary. *The Vindication of the Rights of Woman*. Harmondsworth, Middlesex, England: Penguin Books, 1982; originally published 1792.

Woolf, Virginia. *A Room of One's Own*. New York: Harcourt Brace & World, 1966; originally published 1938.

———. *Three Guineas*. New York: A Harbinger Book, 1938.

1963-1970

Amatniek, Kathy. "Funeral Oration for the Burial of Traditional Womanhood." In *Notes from the First Year*. New York: New York Radical Women, June 1968. See in addition: Shulamith Firestone, "The Women's Rights Movement in the U. S."; Anne Koedt, "The Myth of the Vaginal Orgasm."

Bart, Pauline B. "Portnoy's Mother's Complaint." *Trans-action*. November–December 1970.

Chesler, Phyllis. "Women and Psychotherapy." *The Radical Therapist*. September 1970. Reprinted in *The International Socialist Review*. November 1970; *The Radical Therapist Collective Anthology*. Ed. Jerome Agel. New York: Ballantine Books, 1971.

Densmore, Dana. *Chivalry—the Iron Hand in the Velvet Glove*. Pittsburgh: Know, Inc. Pamphlet, 1969.

———. "On Celibacy." *No More Fun and Games: A Journal of Female Liberation*. Somerville, Massachusetts: October 1968. See in addition: Roxanne Dunbar, "Slavery" and "Dirge for White America."

Firestone, Shulamith. *The Dialectics of Sex*. New York: William Morrow & Co., 1970.

Firestone, Shulamith, ed. and Anne Koedt, assoc. ed. *Notes from the Second Year: Major Writers of the Radical Feminists*. New York: Notes from the Second Year, Inc., 1970. See in addition: Ti-Grace Atkinson, "Radical Feminism" and "The Institution of Sexual Intercourse"; Lucinda Cisler, "On Abortion and Abortion Law"; Roxanne Dunbar, "Female Liberation as the Basis for Social Revolution"; Carol Hanisch, "The Personal is Political"; Joreen, "Bitch Manifesto"; Pat Mainairdi, "The Politics of Housework"; Anselma dell' Olio, "The Founding of the New Feminist Theatre"; Kathie Sarachild, "A Program for Feminist Consciousness Raising"; Meredith Tax, "Woman and Her Mind: The Story of Everyday Life"; Ellen Willis, "Women and the Left."

Flexner, Eleanor. *Century of Struggle: The Women's Rights Movement in the United States*. New York: Atheneum, 1968; originally published 1959.

Friedan, Betty. *The Feminine Mystique*. New York: Dell, 1963.

Greer, Germaine. *The Female Eunuch*. New York: McGraw-Hill, 1971; originally published in England, 1970.

Horney, Karen. *Feminine Psychology*. New York: W. W. Norton & Co., 1967; originally published 1922–1937.

McAfee, Kathy and Myrna Wood, eds. "Bread and Roses." *Leviathan*. Vol. 1, June 1969.

Millett, Kate. *Sexual Politics*. New York: Doubleday, 1970.

Morgan, Robin, ed. *Sisterhood Is Powerful: An Anthology of Writings from the Women's Liberation Movement*. New York: Random House, 1970.

Seaman, Barbara. *The Doctor's Case Against the Pill*. New York: Peter Wyden, 1969.

———. *Free and Female*. New York: Coward, McCann & Geoghegan, 1972.

Solanas, Valerie. *Scum Manifesto*. New York: Olympia Press, 1968.

Steinem, Gloria. "After Black Power, Women's Liberation?" *New York* magazine, 1969.

———. "A Bunny's Tale." *Show Magazine*, 1963.

Szasz, Thomas S. *The Manufacture of Madness: A Comparative Study of the Inquisition and the Mental Health Movement*. New York: Harper & Row, 1970.

Wages For Housework: Women Speak Out. Toronto: May Day Rally. Pamphlet, 1969.

Weisstein, Naomi. "Kinder, Kuche and Kirche: Psychology Constructs the Female." *Scientific Psychology and Social Relevance*. New York: Harper & Row, 1971; originally published by New England Free Press, 1968.

Wittig, Monique. *Les Guerilleres*. New York: Viking Press, 1971; originally published in France, 1969.

1971–1977

Atkinson, Ti-Grace. *Amazon Odyssey*. New York: Links Books, 1974.

Bardwick, Judith M. *Psychology of Women: A Study of Bio-Cultural Conflicts*. New York: Harper & Row, 1971.

Breggin, Peter. "Lobotomies: An Alert." *American Journal of Psychiatry*. Vol. 129, July 1972.

Brownmiller, Susan. *Against Our Will*. New York: Simon & Schuster, 1975.

By and For Women. *The Women's Gun Pamphlet*. Pamphlet, 1975.

Chesler, Phyllis. "Sex Role Stereotyping and Adjustment." In *Psychology of Adjustment*. Ed. James F. Adams. Holbrook Press, 1973.

———. *Women and Madness*. New York: Doubleday and Co., 1972.

———. "Women and Mental Illness." *Women: Resources for a Changing World*. The Radcliffe Institute, Radcliffe College, October 1972.

Chesler, Phyllis and Emily Jane Goodman. *Women, Money and Power*. New York: William Morrow & Co., 1976.

Connell, Noreen and Cassandra Wilson, eds. *Rape: The First Sourcebook For Women*. New York: Plume Books, New American Library, 1974.

Davis, Elizabeth Gould. *The First Sex*. New York: G. P. Putnam & Sons, 1971.

Deming, Barbara and Arthur Kinoy. *Women & Revolution: A Dialogue*. Pamphlet, 1975.

Dreifus, Claudia. *Women's Fate: Raps from a Feminist Consciousness-Raising Group*. New York: Bantam, 1973.

Dworkin, Andrea. *Woman Hating*. New York: E. P. Dutton, 1974.

Ehrenreich, Barbara and Deirdre English. *Witches, Midwives and Nurses: A History of Women Healers*. Pamphlet, 1972.

Frankfurt, Ellen. *Vaginal Politics*. New York: Quadrangle Books, 1972.

Gornick, Vivian and B. K. Moran. *Women in a Sexist Society: Studies in Power and Powerlessness*. New York: Basic Books, 1971. See in addition: Phyllis Chesler, "Patient and Patriarch: Women in the Psychotherapeutic Relationship"; Alta, "Pretty"; Una Stannard, "The Mask of Beauty"; Ruby R. Leavitt, "Women in Other Cultures"; Cynthia Ozick, "Women and Creativity: The Demise of the Dancing Dog"; Linda Nochlin, "Why Are There No Great Women Artists?"; Margaret Adams, "The Compassion Trap."

Gould, Robert. "Masculinity by the Size of the Paycheck." *Ms.* February 1973.

————. "Socio-Cultural Roles of Male and Female." *Comprehensive Textbook of Psychiatry*, 2nd ed. Eds. Freedman, Kaplan, and Sadock. Baltimore: Williams & Wilkins, 1975.

Henley, Nancy M. *Body Politics: Power, Sex, and Non-Verbal Communications*. Englewood Cliffs, New Jersey: Prentice-Hall, 1977.

Hite, Shere. *The Hite Report on Female Sexuality*. New York: Macmillan Publishing Co., 1976.

Johnston, Jill. *Lesbian Nation: The Feminist Solution*. New York: Simon & Schuster, 1973.

Jong, Erica. *Fear of Flying*. New York: Holt, Rinehart, and Winston, 1973.

Katz, Naomi and Nancy Milton, eds. *Fragment from a Lost Diary and Other Stories: Women of Asia, Africa, and Latin America*. New York: Pantheon Books, 1973.

Kingston, Maxine Hong. *The Woman Warrior: Memoirs of a Girlhood Among Ghosts*. New York: Knopf, 1976.

Koedt, Anne, ed. and Shulamith Firestone, assoc. ed. *Notes from the Third Year: Women's Liberation*. New York: Notes from the Second Year, Inc., 1971. See in addition: Susan Brownmiller, "Speaking Out on Prostitution"; Barbara Burris, "The Fourth World Manifesto"; Dana Densmore, "Independence from Sexual Revolution"; Claudia Dreifus, "The Selling of a Feminist"; Jo Freeman, "The Building of the Gilded Cage"; Judith Hole and Ellen Levine, "The First Feminists"; Pamela Kearon and Barbara Mehrhof, "Rape: An Act of Terror"; Judy Syfers, "Why I Want a Wife."

Laws, Judith Long. "The Psychology of Tokenism: An Analysis." *Sex Roles*. Vol. 1, 1975.

Martin, Del. *Battered Wives*. San Francisco: Glide Publications, 1976.

————. *Battered Wives*. New York: Pocket Books, 1977.

Medea, Andra and Kathleen Thompson. *Against Rape: A Survival Manual for Women: How to Avoid Entrapment and How to Cope with Rape Physically and Emotionally*. New York: Farrar, Straus, and Giroux, 1974.

Miller, Jean Baker. *Toward a New Psychology of Women*. Boston: Beacon Press, 1976.

Mitchell, Juliet. *Psychoanalysis and Feminism*. London: Allen Lane, 1974.

————. *Woman's Estate*. New York: Random House, 1971.

Oakley, Ann. *Women's Work: The Housewife, Past and Present*. New York: Pantheon, 1974.

Piercy, Marge. *Small Changes*. New York: Doubleday, 1973.

————. *Woman on the Edge of Time*. New York: Knopf, 1976.

Rich, Adrienne. *Of Woman Born: Motherhood as Experience and Institution*. New York:

W. W. Norton and Co., 1976.

Rowbotham, Sheila. *Women, Resistance, and Revolution*. London: Penguin, 1972.

Rubin, Lillian Breslow. *Worlds of Pain: Life in the Working-Class Family*. New York: Basic Books, 1976.

Russ, Joanna. *The Female Man*. New York: Bantam Press, 1975.

Russell, Diana E. H. and Nicole Van de Ven, eds. *The Proceeding of the International Tribunal on Crimes Against Women*. California: Les Femmes, 1976.

Schatzman, Morton. *Soul Murder: Persecution in the Family*. New York: Random House, 1973.

Shulman, Alix Kates. *Memoirs of an Ex-Prom Queen*. New York: Random House, 1972.

Snodgrass, Jon, ed. *A Book of Readings for Men Against Sexism*. New York: Times Change Press, 1977.

Stone, Merlin. *When God Was a Woman*. Great Britain: Virgo Limited, 1976.

Unger, Rhoda Kesler and Florence L. Denmark, eds. *Woman: Dependent or Independent Variable?* New York: Psychological Dimensions, Inc., 1975.

Williams, Juanita H. *Psychology of Women: Behavior in a Biosocial Context*. New York: W. W. Norton & Co., 1974.

1978–1984

Armstrong, Louise. *Kiss Daddy Goodnight: A Speak-Out on Incest*. New York: Hawthorn, 1978.

Barry, Kathleen. *Female Sexual Slavery*. Englewood Cliffs, New Jersey: Prentice-Hall, 1979.

Barry, Kathleen, Charlotte Bunch, and Shirley Castley, eds. *International Feminism: Networking Against Female Sexual Slavery*. New York: The International Women's Tribune Centre, Inc., 1984.

Bernikow, Louise. *Among Women*. New York: Harmony Books, 1980.

Bolen, Jean Shinoda. *Goddesses In Every Woman: Powerful Archetypes in Women's Lives*. New York: HarperCollins, 1984.

Brodsky, Annette M. and Rachel Hare-Mustin, eds. *Women and Psychotherapy: An Assessment of Research and Practice*. New York: The Guilford Press, 1980.

Bulkin, Elly, Minnie Bruce Pratt, and Barbara Smith. *Yours in Struggle: Three Feminist Perspectives on Anti-Semitism*. Brooklyn, New York: Long Haul Press, 1984.

Chernin, Kim. *The Obsession: Reflections on the Tyranny of Slenderness*. Harper & Row: New York, 1981.

Chesler, Phyllis. *About Men*. New York: Simon and Schuster, 1978.

———. *With Child: A Diary of Motherhood*. New York: Lippincott & Crowell, 1979.

Chodorow, Nancy. *The Reproduction of Mothering: Psychoanalysis and the Sociology of Gender*. Berkeley: University of California Press, 1978.

Clement, Catherine. *Opera: Or the Undoing of Women*. Minneapolis: The University of Minnesota Press, 1988; originally published as *Li opera ou la defaite des femmes*. France: Bernard Grasset, 1979.

Daly, Mary. *GYN/Ecology: The Metaethics of Radical Feminism*. Boston: Beacon Press, 1978.

————. *Pure Lust: Elemental Feminist Philosophy*. Boston: Beacon Press, 1984.

Degler, Carl N. *At Odds: Women and the Family in America From the Revolution to the Present*. Oxford: Oxford University Press, 1980.

Demos, John Putnam. *Entertaining Satan: Witchcraft and the Culture of Early New England*. New York: Oxford University Press, 1982.

DuBois, Ellen Carol, ed. *Elizabeth Cady Stanton, Susan B. Anthony: Correspondence, Writings, Speeches*. New York: Schocken Books, 1981.

Eisenstein, Hester. *Contemporary Feminist Thought*. Boston: G. K. Hall, 1983.

Eisenstein, Zillah R., ed. *Capitalist Patriarchy and the Case for Socialist Feminism*. New York: Monthly Review Press, 1979.

Farley, Lin. *Sexual Shakedown: The Sexual Harassment of Women on the Job*. New York: McGraw-Hill, 1978.

Fisher, Elizabeth. *Women's Creation: Sexual Evolution and the Shaping of Society*. Garden City, New York: Anchor/Doubleday, 1979.

Frank, K. Portland. *The Anti-Psychiatry Bibliography and Resource Guide*. Vancouver: Press Gang Publishers, 1979.

Fritz, Leah. *Dreamers & Dealers: An Intimate Appraisal of the Women's Movement*. Boston: Beacon Press, 1979.

Gilbert, Sandra M., and Susan Gubar. *The Madwoman in the Attic: The Woman-Writer and the Nineteenth-Century Literary Imagination*. New Haven: Yale University Press, 1979.

Gilligan, Carol. *In a Different Voice: Psychological Theory and Women's Development*. Cambridge: Harvard University Press, 1982.

Gould, Robert. "Men's Liberation." In *Modern Man and Woman in Transition*. Eds. Millman and Goldman. Dubuque: Kendall/Hunt, 1978.

Greenspan, Miriam. *A New Approach to Women & Therapy*. New York: McGraw-Hill, 1983.

Griffen, Susan. *Woman and Nature: The Roaring Inside Her*. New York: Harper & Row, 1978.

Herman, Judith Lewis. *Father-Daughter Incest*. Cambridge: Harvard University Press, 1981.

Hite, Shere. *The Hite Report on Male Sexuality*. New York: Ballantine Books, 1981.

Holroyd, J. C. "Erotic Contact as an Instance of Sex-Biased Therapy." In *Bias In Psychotherapy*. Eds. J. Murray and P. R. Abramson. New York: Praeger, 1981, pp. 285–308.

Holroyd, J. C. and Brodsky, J. M. "Does Touching Patients Lead to Sexual Intercourse?" *Professional Psychology* 11 (1980): 807–811.

hooks, bell. *Ain't I a Woman: Black Women and Feminism*. Boston: South End Press, 1981.

————. *Feminist Theory from Margin to Center*. Boston: South End Press, 1984.

Hull, Gloria T., Patricia Bell Scott, and Barbara Smith. *All the Women Are White, All the Blacks Are Men, But Some of Us Are Brave: Black Women's Studies*. Old Westbury, New York: The Feminist Press, 1982.

Johnson, Sonia. *From Housewife to Heretic: One Woman's Struggle For Equal Rights and Her Excommunication From the Mormon Church*. Garden City, New York:

Doubleday & Co., 1981.

Jones, Ann. *Women Who Kill*. New York: Holt, Rinehart, and Winston, 1980.

Joseph, Gloria. "Black Mothers and Daughters: Traditional and New Populations." *Sage*. Vol. 1, 1984.

Lorde, Audre. *Sister Outsider: Essays and Speeches*. Trumansburg, New York: The Crossing Press, 1984.

Malcolm, Janet. *In the Freud Archives*. New York: Random House, 1983.

Masson, Jeffery Moussaieff. *The Assault on Truth*. New York: Penguin Books, 1984.

McAllister, Pam, ed. *Reweaving the Web of Life: Feminism and Nonviolence*. Philadelphia: New Society Publishers, 1982.

Miller, Alice. *Prisoners of Childhood: How Narcissistic Parents Form and Deform the Emotional Lives of Their Gifted Children*. New York: Basic Books, 1981.

Moraga, Cherrie and Gloria Anzaldúa, eds. *This Bridge Called My Back: Writings By Radical Women of Color*. Watertown, Massachusetts: Persephone Press, 1981.

Orbach, Susie. *Fat Is A Feminist Issue*. New York: Berkley Publishing, 1979.

Pleck, Joseph H. and Robert Brannon, eds. "Male Roles and the Male Experience." *Journal of Social Issues*. Vol. 34, 1978.

Ruddick, Sara. "Maternal Thinking." In *Mothering: Essays in Feminist Theory*. Ed. Joyce Trebilcot. Totowa, New Jersey: Rowman and Allanheld, 1983.

Rush, Florence. *The Best Kept Secret: Sexual Abuse of Children*. New Jersey: Prentice-Hall, 1980.

Russ, Joanna. *How to Suppress Women's Writing*. Great Britain: The Women's Press, 1983.

Russell, Diana E. H. *Rape in Marriage*. New York: Macmillan Publishing Co., 1982.

Seidenberg, Robert. *Women Who Marry Houses*. New York: McGraw-Hill, 1983.

Sheehan, Susan. *Is There No Place on Earth for Me?* New York: Random House, 1982.

Smith, Barbara, ed. *Home Girls: A Black Feminist Anthology*. New York: Kitchen Table, Women of Color Press, Inc., 1983.

Snitow, Ann, Christine Stansell, and Sharon Thompson, eds. *Powers of Desire: The Politics of Sexuality*. New York: Monthly Review Press, 1983.

Spender, Dale. *Women of Ideas and What Men Have Done to Them from Aphra Behn to Adrienne Rich*. London: Routledge, Kegan and Paul Ltd., 1982.

Torton Beck, Evelyn, ed. *Nice Jewish Girls: A Lesbian Anthology*. Boston: Beacon Press, 1982.

Walker, Alice. *In Search of Our Mothers' Gardens*. New York: Harcourt Brace Jovanovich, 1983.

Walker, Lenore E. *The Battered Woman*. New York: Harper & Row, 1979.

Wallace, Michelle. *Black Macho and the Myth of the Black Super Woman*. New York: The Dial Press, 1978.

1985–1991

Alexander, Vicki, M. D. "Black Women and Health." *On the Issues*. Vol. 6, 1986.

Barry, Kathleen. *Susan B. Anthony: A Biography*. New York and London: New York University Press, 1988.

Baruch, Elaine Hoffman and Lucienne J. Serrano. *Women Analyze Women*. New York and London: New York University Press, 1988.

Bates, C. M. and Brodsky, A. M. *Sex In the Therapy Hour: A Case of Professional Incest*. New York: Guilford Press, 1989.

Benjamin, Jessica. *The Bonds of Love: Psychoanalysis, Feminism, and the Problem of Domination*. New York: Pantheon Books, 1988.

Bernay, Tony and Dorothy W. Cantor, eds. *The Psychology of Today's Woman: New Psychoanalytic Visions*. Cambridge, Massachusetts and London, England: Harvard University Press, 1989.

Braude, Marjorie, ed. *Women, Power and Therapy*. New York: Harrington Park Press, 1988.

Brody, Claire M., ed. *Women's Therapy Groups: Paradigms of Feminist Treatment*. New York: Springer Publishing Co., 1987.

Cantor, Dorothy W. *Women As Therapists: A Multitheoretical Casebook*. New York: Springer Publishing Co., 1990.

Caplan, Paula J. *The Myth of Women's Masochism*. New York: E. P. Dutton, 1985.

———. *Don't Blame Mother: Mending the Mother-Daughter Relationship*. New York: HarperCollins, 1989.

Caputi, Jane. *The Age of Sex Crime*. Bowling Green: Bowling Green State University Press, 1987.

Chernin, Kim. *The Hungry Self: Women, Eating, and Identity*. New York: Random House, 1985.

Chesler, Phyllis. "Anorexia Becomes Electra: Women, Eating and Identity." *New York Times* Book Review. July 21, 1985.

———. *Mothers On Trial: The Battle for Children and Custody*. New York: McGraw Hill Book Company, 1986.

———. "Mother-Hatred and Mother-Blaming: What Electra Did to Clytemnestra. Motherhood: A Feminist Perspective." *Journal of Women and Therapy*. Vol. 10, 1990.

———. "Mothers On the Run: Sweden 1990." *On the Issues*. Spring 1991.

———. "Mothers On Trial: The Custodial Vulnerability of Women." *Feminism and Psychology: An International Journal*. Vol. 1, 1991.

———. "Re-examining Freud." *Psychology Today*. September 1989.

———. *Sacred Bond: The Legacy of Baby M*. New York: Times Books/Random House, 1988.

Cole, Ellen and Esther D. Rothblum, eds. *Women and Sex Therapy: Closing the Circle of Sexual Knowledge*. New York: Harrington Park Press, 1988.

Dworkin, Andrea. *Mercy*. New York: Four Walls Eight Windows, 1991.

Fine, Michelle and Susan Merle Gordon. "Effacing the Center and the Margins: Life at the Intersection of Psychology and Feminism." *Feminism and Psychology*. Vol. 1, 1991.

Gartrell, N., Herman, J., Olarte, S., Feldstein, M., and Localio, R. "Reporting Practices of Psychiatrists Who Knew of Sexual Misconduct by Colleagues." *American Journal of Psychiatry* 143, 9 (1987): 1126–1131.

Gartrell, N., Herman, J., Olarte, S., Feldstein, M., and Localio, R. "Psychiatrist Patient

Sexual Contact: Results of a National Survey. II. Attitudes." *American Journal of Psychiatry* 144, 2 (1987): 164–169.

Gilligan, Carol, Jane Victoria Ward, Jill McLean Taylor, and Betty Bardige. *Mapping the Moral Domain: A Contribution of Women's Thinking to Psychological Theory and Education.* Cambridge: Harvard University Press, 1988.

Glaser, R.D. and Thorpe, J. S. "Unethical Intimacy: A Survey of Sexual Contact Advances Between Educators and Female Graduate Students." *American Psychologist* 41 (1986): 43–51.

Gotlib, Ian H., Valerie Whiffen, John H. Mount, Kenneth Milne, and Nikkie I. Cordy. "Prevalence Rates and Demographic Characteristics Associated with Depression in Pregnancy and the Postpartum." *Journal of Consulting and Clinical Psychology* Vol. 57, No. 2 (1989): 269–274. American Psychological Association.

Gotlib, Ian H., John H. Mount, Pamela M. Wallace, and Valerie E. Whiffen. "Prospective Investigation of Postpartum Depression: Factors Involved in Onset and Recovery." *Journal of Abnormal Psychology* 100, 2 (1991): 122-132.

Grahn, Judy. *Another Mother Tongue.* Boston: Beacon Press, 1990.

Howard, Doris, ed. *The Dynamics of Feminist Therapy.* New York: Haworth Press, 1986.

Jeffreys, Sheila. *The Spinster and Her Enemies: Feminism and Sexuality, 1880–1930.* London: Pandora, 1985.

Jones, Jacqueline. *Labor of Love, Labor of Sorrow: Black Women, Work, and the Family from Slavery to the Present.* New York: Basic Books, 1985.

Kaplan, Marcia J., Carolyn Winger, and Noel Free. "Psychiatrists' Beliefs about Gender-Appropriate Behavior." *American Journal of Psychiatry* 147, 7 (July 1990).

Karlsen, Carol F. *The Devil In the Shape of A Woman: Witchcraft in Colonial New England.* New York: W. W. Norton & Co., Inc., 1987.

Kaschak, Ellyn, ed. "Motherhood: A Feminist Perspective." *Women & Therapy: A Feminist Quarterly,* Special Issue. Vol. 10, Nos. 1/2. New York: The Haworth Press, 1990.

Kaye/Kantrowitz, Melanie and Irena Klepfisz, eds. *The Tribe of Dina: A Jewish Women's Anthology.* Montpelier, Vermont: Sinister Wisdom Books, 1986; originally published in *Sinister Wisdom,* 1986.

Kitzinger, Celia. *The Social Construction of Lesbianism.* California: Sage Publications, 1987.

Laidlaw, Tonni Ann et al. *Healing Voices: Feminist Approaches to Therapy with Women.* San Francisco: Jossey-Bass Inc., 1990.

Lobel, Kerry, ed. *Naming the Violence: Speaking Out About Lesbian Battering.* The National Coalition Against Domestic Violence Lesbian Task Force. Seattle: Seal Press, 1986.

Luepnitz, Deborah Anna. *The Family Interpreted.* New York: Basic Books, 1988.

MacKinnon, Catherine A. *Feminism Unmodified: Discourses on Life and Law.* Cambridge: Harvard University Press, 1987.

Menaker, Esther. *Appointment in Vienna: An American Psychoanalyst Recalls Her Student Days in Pre-War Austria.* New York: St. Martin Press, 1989.

Millett, Kate. *The Loony Bin Trip*. New York: Simon & Schuster, 1990.

Miner, Valerie and Helen Longino, eds. *Competition: A Feminist Taboo?* New York: The Feminist Press, 1987.

North, Carol. *Welcome, Silence: My Triumph Over Schizophrenia*. New York: Simon and Schuster, 1987.

Perkins, Rachel. "Therapy for Lesbians?: The Case Against." *Feminism and Psychology*. Vol. 1, 1991.

Pogrebin, Letty Cottin. *Deborah, Golda and Me*. New York: Crown, 1991.

Pope, Kenneth S. "Therapist-Patient Sexual Involvement: A Review of the Research." *Clinical Psychology Review* 10 (1990): 477–490.

Pope, Kenneth S., Keith-Spiegel, P., and Tabachnick, B. G. "Ethics of Practice: The Beliefs and Behaviors of Psychologists as Therapists." *American Psychologist* 42 (1987): 993–1006.

Raymond, Janice G. *A Passion for Friends: Toward a Philosophy of Female Affection*. Boston: Beacon Press, 1986.

Rosewater, Lynne Bravo and Lenore E. A. Walker, eds. *Handbook of Feminist Therapy: Women's Issues in Psychotherapy*. New York: Springer Publishing Co., 1985.

Siegel, Rachel Josefowitz, ed. *Seen but Not Heard: Jewish Women in Therapy*. New York: Harrington Park Press, 1991.

Spender, Dale. *For the Record: The Making and Meaning of Feminist Knowledge*. Great Britain: The Women's Press Limited, 1985.

Symonds, Alexandra, M.D. "A Re-Evaluation of Depression in Woman." *On the Issues*. Vol. 4, 1985.

Tan, Amy. *The Joy Luck Club*. New York: Putnam, 1989.

Ussher, Jane. *Women's Madness: Misogyny or Mental Illness?* Amherst, MA: University of Amherst Press, 1991.

Walker, Barbara G. *The Skeptical Feminist: Discovering the Virgin, Mother and Crone*. San Francisco: Harper & Row, 1987.

Walker, Lenore, E. *Terrifying Love: Why Battered Women Kill and How Society Responds*. New York: Harper & Row, 1989.

Walsh, Mary Roth, ed. *The Psychology of Women: Ongoing Debates*. New Haven and London: Yale University Press, 1987.

Walters, Marianne, Betty Carter, Peggy Papp, and Olga Silversmith. *The Invisible Web: Gender Patterns in Family Relationships*. New York: The Guilford Press, 1988.

Wittig, Monique. *Crossing the Acheron*. London: Peter Owen, 1987; first published in French, 1985.

1992–1999

Abe, J. S. and Zane, N. W. S. "Differential Responses to Trauma: Migration-Related Discriminants of Post-Traumatic Stress Disorder Among Southeast Asian Refugees." *Journal of Community Psychology* 22, 2 (1994): 121–135.

Adams, Eve M. and Nancy E. Betz. "Gender Differences in Counselors' Attitudes Toward and Attributions About Incest." *Journal of Counseling Psychology* 40, 2 (1993): 210–216.

Adleman Jeanne and Gloria Enguidanos, eds. *Racism in the Lives of Women: Testimony, Theory, and Guides to Antiracist Practice*. New York: The Haworth Press, 1995.

Allison, Dorothy. *Skin: Talking About Sex, Class & Literature*. Ithaca, New York: Firebrand Books, 1994.

Antonelli, Judith, S. "Beyond Nostalgia: Rethinking the Goddess." *On the Issues*. Vol. 6, 1997.

Appignanesi, Lisa and John Forrester. *Freud's Women*. New York: Basic Books, 1992.

Armstrong, Louise. "Who Stole Incest?" *On The Issues*. Fall 1994.

Ballou, Mary and Laura Brown, Eds. *Rethinking Mental Health and Disorder: Feminist Perspectives*. New York: Guilford Press, 2002.

Baker, Nancy Lynn. "Class as a Construct in a 'Classless' Society." *Women and Therapy*. Vol. 18, 1996.

Bolen, Jean Shinoda. *Crossing to Avalon*. New York: Harper Collins, 1994.

Borch-Jacobsen, Mikkel. "Sybil—The Making of a Disease: An Interview with Dr. Herbert Spiegel." *New York Review of Books* (April 24, 1997): 60–64.

Broden, Melodie S. and Albert A. Agresti. "Responding to Therapists' Sexual Abuse of Adult Incest Survivors: Ethical and Legal Considerations." *Psychotherapy* 35, 1 (1998).

Brown, Laura S. "Boundaries in Feminist Therapy: A Conceptual Formulation." *Women and Therapy*. Vol. 15, 1994.

———. *Subversive Dialogues: Theory in Feminist Therapy*. New York: Basic Books, 1994.

———. "Politics of Memory, Politics of Incest: Doing Therapy and Politics That Really Matter." *Women and Therapy*. Vol. 19, 1996.

Berns, Sara B., Eric Gortner, John M. Gottman, Neil S. Jacobson. "When Women Leave Violent Relationships: Dispelling Clinical Myths." *Psychotherapy* 34, 4 (1997): 343-351.

Caplan, Paula J. *Lifting a Ton of Feathers: A Woman's Guide to Surviving in the Academic World*. Toronto: University of Toronto Press, 1993.

———. *They Say You're Crazy: How the World's Most Powerful Psychiatrists Decide Who's Normal*. Philadelphia: Perseus Books, 1995.

———. "Try Diagnosing Men's Mind Games Instead of Pathologizing Women." *On The Issues*. Winter 1997.

Chesler, Phyllis, Esther Rothblum, Ellen Cole. *Feminist Foremothers in Women's Studies, Psychology, Mental Health*. New York: Harrington Park Press, 1995.

Chesler, Phyllis. *Letters to a Young Feminist*. New York: Four Walls Eight Windows, 1997.

Chesler, Phyllis. "A Reappraisal of Women and Madness." In *Feminism & Psychology*, Vol. 2, No. 4. London: SAGE, 1994. Articles by Dale Spender, Sue Wilkinson, Judi Chamberlin, Jane Ussher, and Helen Bolderston.

Chesler, Phyllis. "Custody Determinations: Gender Bias in the Courts." In *Encyclopedia of Childbearing: Critical Perspectives*. Ed. Barbara Katz Rothman. Phoenix: Oryx Press, 1992.

———. "A Double Standard for Murder?" *New York Times* OP-ED, January 9, 1992.

———. "The Shellshocked Woman." *New York Times* Book Review, August 23, 1992.

———. "When a 'Bad' Woman Kills: The Trials of Aileen Wuornos." *On the Issues.* Summer 1992.

———. "The Men's Auxiliary: Protecting the Rule of the Fathers." In *Women Respond to the Men's Movement.* Ed. Kay Leigh Hagan. San Francisco: Harper San Francisco, 1992.

———. "Sexual Violence Against Women and a Woman's Right to Self-Defense: The Case of Aileen Carol Wuornos." *St. John's University Law Review* (Fall–Winter 1993), and *Criminal Practice Law Report* Vol. 1 (October 1993).

———. "The Dead Man is Not on Trial." *On the Issues.* Winter 1994.

———. "Heroism is Our Only Alternative." A Response to a Retrospective on Women and Madness. *The Journal of Feminism and Psychology.* Vol. 4, May 1994.

———. *Patriarchy: Notes of an Expert Witness.* Monroe, Maine: Common Courage Press, 1994.

———. "When They Call You Crazy." *On the Issues.* Summer 1994.

———. "Rebel with a Cause." *On the Issues.* Fall 1995.

———. "What is Justice for a Rape Victim." *On the Issues.* Winter 1995.

Chew, Lin. "Global Trafficking in Women: Some Issues and Strategies." *Women's Studies Quarterly* 1 & 2 (1999): 11–18.

Comas-Diaz, L. "An Integrative Approach." In *Women of Color: Integrating Ethnic and Gender Identities in Psychotherapy* Eds. L. Comas-Diaz & B. Greene. New York: Guilford Press, 1994, pp. 287-318.

Comas-Diaz, Lillian and Frederick J. Jacobsen. "Psychopharmacology for Women of Color: An Empowering Approach." *Women and Therapy.* Vol. 16, 1995.

Chalifoux, Bonnie. "Speaking Up: White, Working-Class Women in Therapy." *Women and Therapy.* Vol. 18, 1996.

Copelon, Rhonda. "Surfacing Gender: Reconceptualizing Crimes Against Women in Time of War." In *Mass Rape: The War Against Women in Bosnia-Herzegovina.* Ed. Alexandra Stiglymyer. Lincoln and London: University of Nebraska Press, 1992.

Das Dasgupta, Shamita, ed. *A Patchwork Shawl: Chronicles of South Asian Women in America.* New Jersey: Rutgers University Press, 1998.

Denmark, Florence L. and Michele A. Paludi, eds. *Psychology of Women: A Handbook of Issues and Theories.* Westport, Connecticut: Greenwood Press, 1993.

Dorkenoo, Efua. "Combating Female Genital Mutilation: An Agenda for the Next Decade." *Women's Studies Quarterly* 1 & 2 (1999): 87–97.

Douglas, Claire. *Translate This Darkness: The Life of Christiana Morgan: The Veiled Woman in Jung's Circle.* New York: Simon & Schuster, 1993.

Dumquah, Meri Nana-Ama. *Willow Weep for Me, A Black Woman's Journey Through Depression: A Memoir.* New York: W. W. Norton & Co., 1998.

Dutton, Donald G. and Susan K. Golant. *The Batterer: A Psychological Profile.* New York: Basic Books, 1995.

Dworkin, Andrea. *Letters from a War Zone.* Chicago: Lawrence Hill Books, 1993.

Estes, Clarissa Pinkola. Women *Who Run with the Wolves: Myths and Stories of the Wild Woman Archetype.* New York: Ballantine Books, 1992.

Farley, M., I. Baral, M. Kiremire, and U. Sezgin. "Prostitution in Five Countries: Violence and Post-Traumatic Stress Disorder." *Feminism & Psychology* 8, 4 (1998): 405–426.

Feldmar, Andrew. *R. D. Laing: Creative Destroyer.* London: Cassell, 1997.

Firestone, Shulamith. *Airless Spaces.* New York: Semiotext(e), 1998.

Freyd, Jennifer J. *Betrayal Trauma.* Cambridge: Harvard University Press, 1995.

Geller, Jeffrey and Maxine Harris. *Women of the Asylum: Voices from Behind the Walls, 1940–1945.* New York: Anchor Books, 1994. Foreword by Phyllis Chesler.

Geller, Jeffrey L. and Maxine Harris. *Women of the Asylum: Voices from Behind the Walls 1840–1945.* New York: Bantam Doubleday Dell Publishing Group, 1994. Introduction by Phyllis Chesler.

Gelso, Charles J., Ruth E. Fassinger, Maria J. Gomez, and Maria G. Latts. "Countertransferences Reactions to Lesbian Clients: The Role of Homophobia, Counselor Gender, and Countertransference Management." *Journal of Counseling Psychology* 42, 3 (1995): 356–364.

Green, Dorsey. "When a Therapist Breaks the Rules." *Women and Therapy.* Vol. 18, 1996.

Greene, Beverly and Nancy Boyd-Franklin. "African-American Lesbian Couples: Ethnocultural Considerations in Psychotherapy." *Women and Therapy.* Vol. 19, 1996.

Grobe, Jeanine, ed. *Beyond Bedlam: Contemporary Women Psychiatric Survivors Speak Out.* Chicago: Third Side Press, 1995.

Hall, Marney, Celia Kitzinger, Joanne Loulan, and Rachel Perkins. "Lesbian Psychology, Lesbian Politics." *Feminism and Psychology.* Vol. 2, 1992.

Halnon, Karen Bettez. *Women's Agency in Hysteria and Its Treatment.* Michigan: UMI Company, 1995.

Hamilton, Jean A. and Margaret F. Jensvold. "Sex and Gender as Critical Variables in Feminist Psychopharmacology Research and Pharmacology." *Women and Therapy.* Vol. 16, 1995.

Hammer, Barbara U. "Anti-Semitism As Trauma: A Theory of Jewish Communal Trauma Response." In *Jewish Women Speak Out.* Eds. Kayla Weiner and Arinna Moon. 1995.

Harris, Diane J. and Sue A. Kuba. "Ethnocultural Identity and Eating Disorders in Women of Color." *Professional Psychology: Research and Practice* 28, 4 (1997): 341-347. American Psychological Association.

Healy, Shevy. "Confronting Ageism: A Must for Mental Health." *Women and Therapy.* Vol. 14, 1993.

Heller, Tom, Jim Reynolds, Roger Gomm, Rosemary Muston, and Stephen Pattison. *Mental Health Matters.* London: Macmillan Press Limited, 1996.

Herman, Judith Lewis. *Trauma and Recovery.* New York: Basic Books, 1992.

Heron, Reva L., Diana P. Jacobs, Nadine J. Kaslow, and Heather B. Twomey. "Culturally Competent Interventions for Abused and Suicidal African American Women." *Psychotherapy* 34, 4 (1997): 410–422.

Hill, Marcia. "We Can't Afford It: Confusions and Silences on the Topic of Class." *Women and Therapy.* Vol. 18, 1996.

Hite, Shere. "Write What You Want." *On the Issues*. Vol. 4. 1995.

Holtzman, Clare G. "Counseling Adult Women Rape Survivors: Issues of Race, Ethnicity, and Class." *Women and Therapy*. Vol. 19, 1996.

hooks, bell. *Sisters of the Yam: Black Women and Self-Recovery*. Cambridge, MA: South End Press, 1993.

Hughes, Donna M. "Defeating Woman-Haters." FrontPageMagazine.com, January17, 2005. http://www.frontpagemagazine.com/Articles/ReadArticle.asp?ID=16640, as accessed 4/14/2005.

——. "Iran's Sex Slaves," FrontPageMagazine.com. June 11, 2004.

——. "The Mullah's Killing Fields." FrontPageMagazine.com. December 14, 2004.

Jamison, Kay Redfield. *An Unquiet Mind: A Memoir of Moods and Madness*. New York: Knopf, 1995.

Kaschak, Ellyn. *Engendered Lives: A New Psychology of Women's Experience*. New York: Basic Books, 1992.

Kaschak, Ellyn and Marcia Hill. *Beyond the Rule Book: Moral Issues and Dilemmas in the Practice of Psychotherapy*. New York: The Haworth Press, 1999.

Kaysen, Sussanah. *Girl, Interrupted*. New York: Vintage, 1994.

Kerr, John. *A Most Dangerous Method: The Story of Jung, Freud, and Sabina Spielrein*. New York: Knopf, 1993.

Kitzinger, Celia (with Rachel Perkins). *Changing Our Minds: Lesbian Feminism and Psychology*. New York: New York University Press, 1993.

Kivel, Paul. "Raising Sons as Allies." *On the Issues*. Vol. 5, 1996.

Lalich, Janya. "Dominance and Submission: The Psychosexual Exploitation of Women in Cults." *Women and Therapy*. Vol. 19, 1996.

Lerman, Hannah. "The Practice of Ethics Within Feminist Therapy." *Women and Therapy*. Vol. 15, 1994.

Loulan, JoAnn. "Our Breasts, Ourselves." *Women and Therapy*. Vol. 19, 1996.

Mallinckrodt, Brent, Beverly A. McCreary, and Anne K. Robertson. "Co-Occurrence of Eating Disorders and Incest: The Role of Attachment, Family Environment, and Social Competencies." *Journal of Counseling Psychology* 42, 2 (1995): 178–186.

McGoey, Christine Schaack. "When Regular Guys Rape: The Trial of the Glen Ridge Four." *On the Issues*. Fall 1993.

McNair, Lily D. "African American Women in Therapy: An Afrocentric and Feminist Synthesis." *Women and Therapy*. Vol. 12, 1992.

McNair, Lily D. and Helen A. Neville. "African American Women Survivors of Sexual Assault: The Intersection of Race and Class." *Women and Therapy*. Vol. 18, 1996.

Miller, Jean Baker and Irene Stiver. *The Healing Connection: How Women Form Relationships in Therapy and in Life*. Boston: Beacon Press, 1997.

Paludi, Michele A. *The Psychology of Women*. Dubuque: WCB Brown & Benchmark, 1992.

Pipher, Mary. *Reviving Ophelia: Saving the Selves of Adolescent Girls*. New York: Putnam, 1994.

Pope, Kenneth S. "Scientific Research, Recovered Memory, and Context: Seven

Surprising Findings." *Women and Therapy.* Vol. 19, 1996.

Pope, Kenneth S. and Barbara G. Tabachnick. "The Therapist as a Person: Therapists' Anger, Hate, Fear, and Sexual Feelings: National Survey of Therapist Responses, Client Characteristics, Critical Events, Formal Complaints, and Training," 1993. http://kspope.com/therapistas/fear1.php, accessed 7/6/2005.

Pope, Kenneth S. and Melba J. T. Vasquez. *Ethics in Psychotherapy and Counseling: A Practical Guide,* 2nd ed. San Francisco: Jossey Bass, 1998.

Radford, Jill and Diana E. H. Russell, eds. *Femicide: The Politics of Woman Killing.* New York: Macmillan Publishing Co., 1992.

Raven, Arlene. "Judy Chicago: The Artist Critics Love to Hate." *On the Issues.* Vol. 3, 1994.

Renzetti, Claire M. *Violent Betrayal: Partner Abuse in Lesbian Relationships.* Newbury Park, California: Sage Publications, 1992.

Rohrlich, Ruby. "Biology and Destiny." *On the Issues.* Vol. 6, 1997.

Rollins, Joan H. *Women's Minds, Women's Bodies: The Psychology of Women in a Biosocial Context.* New Jersey: Prentice-Hall, 1996.

Rothblum, Esther D. "The Rich Get Social Services and the Poor Get Capitalism." *Women and Therapy.* Vol. 18, 1996.

Russ, Joanna. *What Are We Fighting for? Sex, Race, Class, and the Future of Feminism.* New York: St. Martin's Press, 1997.

Sapinsley, Barbara. *The Private War of Mrs. Packard.* New York: Kodansha, 1995. Introduction by Phyllis Chesler.

Sapinsley, Barbara. *The Private War of Mrs. Packard.* New York: Paragon House, 1991; with New Introduction by Phyllis Chesler, 1995.

Shah, Sonia. *Dragon Ladies: Asian American Feminists Breathe Fire.* Cambridge, MA: South End Press, 1997.

Shaka Zulu, Nzinga. "Sex, Race, and the Stained-Glass Window." *Women and Therapy.* Vol. 19, 1996.

Sharratt, Sara and Ellyn Kaschak. *Assault on the Soul: Women in the Former Yugoslavia.* New York: The Haworth Press, 1999.

Siegal, Rachel Josefowitz. "Between Midlife and Old Age: Never Too Old to Learn." *Women and Therapy.* Vol. 14, 1993.

Steinem, Gloria. "What If Freud Were Phyllis?" *Moving Beyond Words.* New York: Simon & Schuster, 1994.

Stiglymyer, Alexandra, ed. "The Rapes in Bosnia-Herzegovina." *Mass Rape: The War Against Women in Bosnia-Herzegovina.* Lincoln and London: University of Nebraska Press, 1992.

Strong, Marilee A. *Bright Red Scream: Self-Mutilation and the Language of Pain.* New York: Penguin, 1998.

Teifer, Lenore. "Towards a Feminist Sex Therapy." *Women and Therapy.* Vol. 19, 1996.

Vaz, Kim Marie. "Racial Aliteracy: White Appropriation of Black Presences." *Women and Therapy.* Vol. 16, 1995.

Walker, Lenore E. "Psychology and Domestic Violence Around the World." *American Psychologist* (1999). American Psychological Association.

Weiner, Kayla and Arinna Moon, eds. *Jewish Women Speak Out: Expanding the Boundaries Of Psychology.* Seattle: Canopy Press, 1995. Foreword by Phyllis Chesler. See in addition: Kayla Weiner, "Survivors Nonetheless: Trauma in Women Not Directly Involved with the Holocaust."

Weiner, Kayla and Arinna Moon. *Jewish Women Speak Out: Expanding the Boundaries of Psychology.* Foreword by Phyllis Chesler. Seattle, WA: Canopy Press, 1995.

Wolfe, Janet L. and Iris G. Fodor. "The Poverty of Privilege: Therapy with Women of the 'Upper' Classes." *Women and Therapy.* Vol. 18, 1996.

Wolper, Andrea. "Exporting Healing: American Rape Crisis Counselors in Bosnia." *On the Issues.* Spring 1994.

Wood, Mary Elene. *The Writing On the Wall: Women's Autobiography and the Asylum.* Chicago: University of Illinois Press, 1994.

Wood, Mary Elene. *The Writing on the Wall: Women's Autobiography and the Asylum.* Chicago: University of Illinois Press, 1994.

Wurtzel, Elizabeth. *Prozac Nation.* New York: Riverhead Books, 1994.

Young-Bruehl, Elisabeth. *The Anatomy of Prejudices.* Cambridge: Harvard University Press, 1996.

2000–2005

Caplan, Paula J. and Lisa Cosgrove, eds. *Bias in Psychiatric Diagnosis.* Maryland: Jason Aronson, 2004. See especially: Ali, Alisha, "The Intersection of Racism and Sexism in Psychiatric Diagnosis"; Bullock, Heather E., "Diagnosis of Low-Income Women," from *Bias in Psychiatric Diagnosis*; Caplan, Emily J., "Psychiatric Diagnosis in the Legal System"; Cosgrove, Lisa and Bethany Riddle, "Gender Bias and Sex Distribution of Mental Disorders in the DSM-IV-TR"; Fish, Vincent, "Some Gender Biases in Diagnosing Traumatized Women"; Javed, Nayyar, "Clinical Cases and the Intersection of Sexism and Racism"; Poland, Jeffrey, "Bias and Schizophrenia"; Poland, Jeffrey and Paula J. Caplan, "The Deep Structure of Bias in Psychiatric Diagnosis"; Profit, Wesley E., "Should Racism Be Classified As a Mental Illness?"; Rabinor, Judith R., "The 'Eating-Disordered' Patient"; Wiley, Autumn, "Abnormal Psychology Textbooks Exclude Feminist Criticisms of the DSM."

Chesler, Phyllis. *Woman's Inhumanity to Woman.* New York: Thunder's Mouth Press/ Nation Books, 2002; Plume, 2003.

———. *The New Anti-Semitism.* San Francisco: Jossey-Bass, 2003.

———. *The Death of Feminism: What's Next in the Struggle for Women's Freedom.* New York: Palgrave Macmillan, 2005.

———. "The Psychoanalytic Roots of Islamic Terrorism." FrontPageMagazine.com. May 3, 2004; www.phyllis-chesler.com.

———. "'Gender Cleansing' in the Sudan." FrontPage Magazine. July 26, 2004; www.phyllis-chesler.com

———. "Forced Female Suicide." FrontPage Magazine. January 22, 2004; www.phyllis-chesler.com

Chesler, Phyllis and Rivka Haut. *Women of the Wall: Claiming Sacred Ground at*

Judaism's Holy Site. Vermont: Jewish Lights Publishing, 2003.

Chesler, Phyllis and Donna M. Hughes. "Feminism in the 21st Century." *Washington Post*, February 22, 2004; www.phyllis-chesler.com.

Chesler, Phyllis and Nancy H. Kobrin. "Osama, Bush and a Little Girl." FrontPageMagazine.com. November 1, 2004; www.phyllis-chesler.com.

Clarke, Victoria. "Stereotype, Attack and Stigmatize Those Who Disagree: Employing Scientific Rhetoric in Debates About Lesbian and Gay Parenting." *Feminism and Psychology* 10, 1 (2000): 142–149. London: Sage.

Clarke, Victoria. "The Lesbian Personality: A Reappraisal of June Hopkins' Milestone Work." Special Issues, *Lesbian & Gay Psychology Review* 3, 2 (2000). The British Psychological Society.

Cottone, John G., Philip Drucker, and Rafael A. Javier. "Gender Differences in Psychotherapy Dyads: Changes in Psychological Symptoms and Responsiveness to Treatment During Three Months of Therapy." *Psychotherapy: Theory/ Research/Practice/Training* 39, 4 (2002): 297–308. Educational Publishing Foundation.

Enns, Carolyn Zerbe. *Feminist Theories and Feminist Psychotherapies: Origins, Themes, and Diversity*, 2nd ed. New York: The Haworth Press, 2004.

Farley, Melissa. *Prostitution, Trafficking, and Traumatic Stress*. New York: The Haworth Press, 2003.

Graham, Jennifer E., Marci Lobel, and Robyn Stein DeLuca. "Anger After Childbirth: An Overlooked Reaction to Postpartum Stressors." *Psychology of Women Quarterly* 26 (2002): 222-233. Division 35, American Psychological Association. Blackwell Publishing.

Gregory, Julie. *Sickened: The Memoir of a Munchausen by Proxy Childhood*. New York: Bantam, 2003.

Guttmann, Melinda Given. *The Enigma of Anna O.: A Biography of Bertha Pappenheim*. Rhode Island: Moyer Bell, 2001.

Hebald, Carol. *The Heart Too Long Suppressed: A Chronicle of Mental Illness*. Boston: Northeastern University Press, 2001.

Hubert, Susan. *Questions of Power: The Politics of Women's Madness Narratives*. Newark: University of Delaware Press, 2002.

Jackson, Helene, Leonard Diller, Ronald L. Nuttall, and Elizabeth Philip. "Traumatic Brain Injury: A Hidden Consequence for Battered Women." *Professional Psychology: Research and Practice* 33, 1 (2002): 39–45. American Psychological Association.

Jackson, Leslie and Beverly Greene, eds. *Psychotherapy with African American Women: Innovations in Psychodynamic Perspectives and Practice*. New York: Guilford Press, 2000.

Kettlewell, Carolyn. *Skin Game: A Memoir*. New York: St. Martin's Press, 2000.

Kline, Ruth. *It Coulda Been Worse: Surviving a Lifetime of Abuse and Mental Illness*. North Carolina: Pentland Press, Inc./Ivy House Publishing, 2003.

Klonoff, Elizabeth A., Hope Landrine, and Robin Campbell. "Sexist Discrimination May Account for Well-Known Gender Differences In Psychiatric Symptoms." *Psychology of Women Quarterly* 24 (2000): 93–99. Division 35,

American Psychological Association. USA: Cambridge University Press.

Knapp, Caroline. *Appetites: Why Women Want.* New York: Counterpoint, 2003.

Kobrin, Nancy. "Political Domestic Violence in Ibrahim's Family: A Psychoanalystic Perspective." In *Eroticisms: Love, Sex and Perversion,* vol. 5. Eds. J. Piven, C. Boyd, and H. Lawton. New York: iUniverse, Inc., 2003; also in *Terrorism, Jihad and Sacred Vengeance.* Giessen: Psychosoziel-Verlag, 2004.

Kobrin, Nancy and Yoram Schweitzer. "The Sheik's New Clothes: Islamic Suicide Terrorism and What It's Really All About." Introduction by Phyllis Chesler. Unpublished Manuscript.

Murphy, Julie A., Edna I. Rawlings, and Steven R. Howe. "A Survey of Clinical Psychologists on Treating Lesbian, Gay, and Bisexual Clients." *Professional Psychology: Research and Practice* 33, 2 (2002): 183–189. American Psychological Association.

National Institute of Mental Health. "The Numbers Count: Mental Disorders in America." http://www.nimh.nih.gov/publicat/numbers.cfm, accessed 7/11/2005.

National Research Center on Asian American Mental Health. http://psychology.ucdavis.edu/nrcaamh/Publications/, accessed 7/12/2005.

Pope, Kenneth S., James N. Butcher, and Joyce Seelen. *The MMPI, MMPI-2, and MMPI-A In Court: A Practical Guide for Expert Witnesses and Attorneys,* 2nd ed. American Psychological Association, 2000.

Pope, Kenneth S. and Melba J. T. Vasquez. *How To Survive and Thrive as a Therapist: Information, Ideas & Resources for Psychologists.* American Psychological Association, 2005.

Rabin, Claire Low. *Understanding Gender and Culture in the Helping Process: Practitioners' Narratives from Global Perspectives.* Foreword by Phyllis Chesler. California: Wadsworth, 2005.

Reiland, Rachel. *Get Me Out Of Here: My Recovery from Borderline Personality Disorder.* Minnesota: Hazelden Publishing and Educational Services, 2004.

Rickhi, Badri, Hude Quan, Sabine Moritz, Dipl Biol, Heather L. Stuart, and Julio Arboleda-Florez. "Original Research: Mental Disorders and Reasons for Using Complementary Therapy." 2003. http://www/cpa-apc.org/Publications/Archives/CJP/2003/august/rickhi.asp, accessed 7/11/2005. Canadian Psychiatric Association—Study.

Shannonhouse, Rebecca. *Out of Her Mind: Women Writing On Madness.* New York: The Modern Library, 2000.

World Health Organization. "Gender Disparities in Mental Health: The Facts." *Gender and Women's Mental Health.* http://www.who.int/mental_health/prevention/genderwomen/en/, accessed 7/11/2005.

Wurtzel, Elizabeth. *More, Now, Again: A Memoir of Addiction.* New York: Touchstone, 2001.

INDEX

PHOTO CREDITS

1, 11. The British Museum, London.

2. Galleria Borghese, Rome.

3. From *Joan of Arc* by Retine Pernoud, translated by Edward Hymans, MacDonald & Company Limited, London, 1965.

4. Galleria Palatine, Palazzo Pitti.

5. The Tate Gallery, London.

6. Andrew Mellon Collection, The National Gallery of Art, Washington, D. C.

7, 8. The Bettmann Archive.

9, 12, and 13. Authenticated News International.

10. Ny Carlsberg Glyptothek, Copenhagen.

14. Gilda Kuhlman, from *Up from Under.*

15. The Metropolitan Museum of Art, Rogers Fund, 1907.

16. The Metropolitan Museum of Art, Fletcher Fund, 1944.

17, 18. The Metropolitan Museum of Art, Gift of John D. Rockefeller, Jr., 1932.